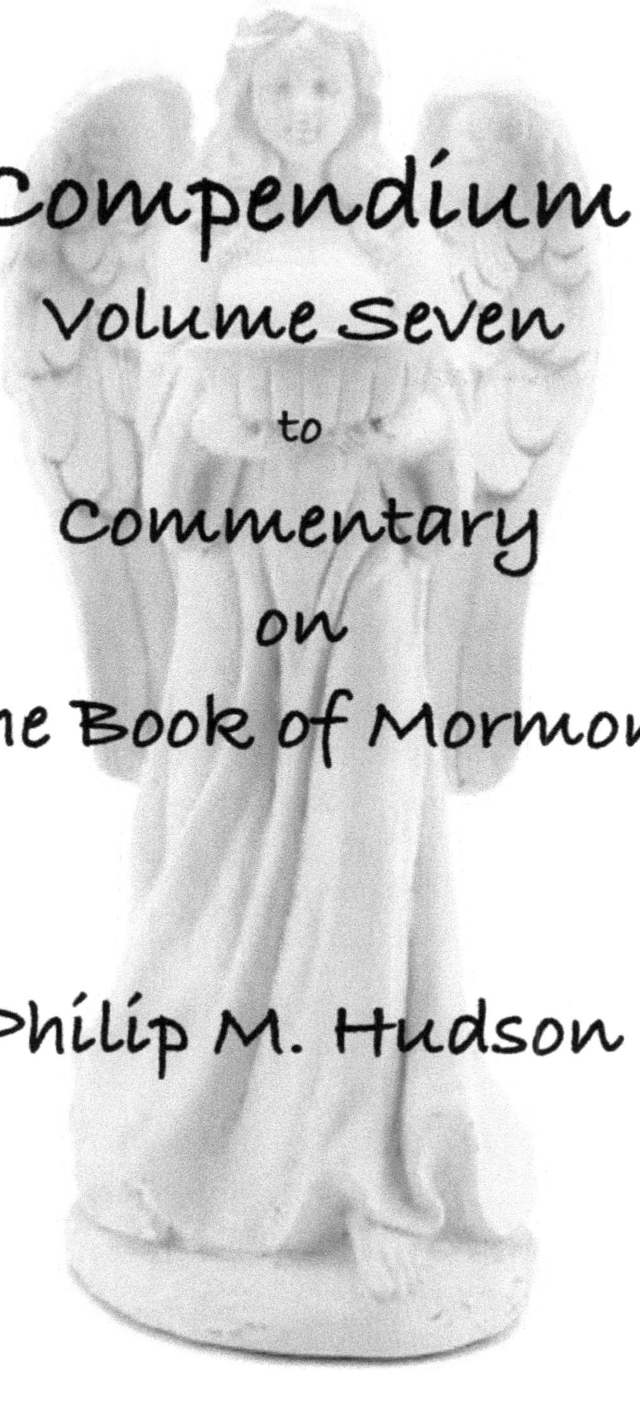

Compendium

Volume Seven

to

Commentary

on

The Book of Mormon

Philip M. Hudson

The Holy Ghost instills within each one of us a sound understanding as we study The Book of Mormon, that we might recognize the word of God. But this is not all; as we give ourselves to fasting and prayer, we enjoy the spirit of prophecy and the spirit of revelation, so that our investigation reveals to our view the glory, might, majesty, power, and dominion of God. (See Alma 5:50).

Copyright 2024 by Philip M. Hudson.
Published 2024.
Printed in the United States of America.
All rights reserved.

No portion of this book may be reproduced,
stored in a retrieval system, or transmitted
in any form or by any means, mechanical,
electronic, photocopy, recording, scanning,
or other, except for brief quotations in
critical reviews or articles, without
the prior written permission
of the author.

ISBN 978-1-957077-80-2
Illustrations - Google Images.

This book may be ordered from
online bookstores.

Publishing Services
by BookCrafters, Parker, Colorado.
www.bookcrafters.net

It is rumored
that there is a certain
Eastern European village
where there still survives a time-
honored tradition. On the first day of
school, the rabbi gives each child a slate
on which the first two letters of the Hebrew
alphabet are written in honey. The child is
then asked to lick up the letters with their
tongue, savor the taste, and to then to use
the slate to learn to read and write, while
remembering how sweet the experience
can be, as long as the endeavor has
been initiated with "a perfect heart
and with a willing mind."
(See 1 Chronicles
28:9).

Index to Compendia Volumes 3-7

The Nephites always paid a hefty price for
their lack of vision. Whenever their culture lost its
spiritual equilibrium, too often, it simply adjusted its
values in a realignment with worldly coordinates. We can
be sure that it justified its worship of gods of wood and stone
as multi-culturalism. It embraced perversion, and legitimized
it as an alternative lifestyle. The poor were exploited in the name
of government lotteries. When unborn children were killed, the
collective conscience was soothed by calling it pro-choice. Power
was abused and it was dismissed as "politics." If obscenities
polluted the media, it would have been characterized as the
freedom of expression. The target had been moved so
many times, that they thought they were scoring
repetitive bulls-eyes, when in reality, they
were far from the mark.

Volume 3 Essays

Abstinence in a Permissive World
Additional Scripture
Addressing Deity
Agency
Agency and Opposition
Agency and Youth
Age of Accountability
Alma's Discourse on Faith
And it Came to Pass
And Thus We See
Angels
Are Mormons Christian?
Are We Alone in The Universe?
(The) Atonement
Bah Humbug!
Baptism
Batteries are Not Included
Become as Little Children
Before a Wound Can Heal
Behold
Being Well Grounded
(The) Bible
(The) Biggest Loser
Blood, Covenant, and Land Israel
(The) Book of Mormon as History
Book of Mormon Strengths

(The) Book of Mormon was Preserved for our Day
Born Again Christians
Brevity)
Buddy Can You Spare a Dime?
Caesar
(A) Change of Heart
(The) Character of God
Choose the Harder Right
Choose ye This Day
Christians
(A) Christmas Miracle
Christ's Church is Restored
(The) Church
(The) Church of Jesus Christ in Former Times
Circle of Knowledge
Citizenship in The Church and Kingdom
Civil Liberties
(A) Coat of Many Colors
Cogito Ergo Sum
Cognates in The Book of Mormon
Combatting Evil
Commitment
Conditional Sentences in The Book of Mormon
Connections
Construction Zone: Proceed with Caution
Conversion

The Devil,
who has always
been a consummate con
man, a master deceiver, and
a liar from the beginning, even
now continues his efforts to foil the
distribution of The Book of Mormon and
the education of the children of God, by the
substitution of his own counterfeit proposal.
That it was an unworkable alternative to God's
Plan that would have required neither repentance
nor an Atonement by a Savior is undisputable.
Fortunately, at a Council in Heaven where both
plans were discussed, we were able to see thru
the deceptions of Lucifer. Today, members
of the Lord's church retain that eternal
perspective, and their actions reflect
their continuing determination
to be disciples of Christ and
heirs to the kingdom
of God.

Volume 4 Essays

Courage	Faith is a Principle of Power
Covenant Consciousness	(The) Fall
Covenants	Fasting
(The) Creation of The World	Fate
Dancing With the Stars	Father Forgive Them
(The) Desert Shall Rejoice	Finding Balance in Our Lives
Diversity	Friendship
Doctrine – The Meaning of	Focus
(The) Door Swings Both Ways	Follow the Prophet
Dry Humor in The Book of Mormon	Forgiveness
(The) Dust of The Earth	For Unto Us a Child is Born
(The) Duty of The Priest	(The Importance of) Friends
Education	Friendship
(The Best) Education	Gathering of Israel
Enduring to The End	General Conference
Entropy in The Physical and Eternal Worlds	(The) Germination of our Faith
Environmental Concerns: An Eternal Perspective	Gifts of The Spirit
Establishing the Word	God is NowHere
(Our) Eternal Nature	Godly Qualities
Eternal Progression in a Dynamic Universe	God's Tactical Flashlight
Everyone Wants to Go to Heaven	Gold – The Appearance of
Evidences of God	Grace
Faith and Knowledge	Gratitude
Faith Building	

It will not be easy for those who have put Moroni's challenge to the test, but have then turned their backs on the confirming witness of the Spirit, to be saved in the kingdom of heaven..

Volume 5 Essays

Happiness
Happiness and Sharing the Gospel
Happiness / Wickedness
Having Been Commissioned of Jesus Christ
Heaven Can Wait
Heavenly Father Knows Us
(The) Heavens Were Opened
Higher Dimensional Realities
(The) Holy Ghost
(The) Holy Grail of Religious Doctrine
Honesty
(The) Hourglass of Life
How Does God Get Things Done?
Huckleberries and Chokeberries
Humility
Hypocrisy
I am a Child of God
I Have Fought a Good Fight
I Have Overcome the World
Isaiah in The Book of Mormon
Is Heaven Hotter Than Hell?
It's Our Book
Joseph Smith: A Rough Stone Rolling
Joseph Smith History
Joseph Smith's World

Jumping Out of Our Skin
Just Get Back on The Bike
Justice
Justice and Mercy
Keep Smiling
Labels
Lamanites by The Waters of Sebus
(The) Last Judgment
Life is a Three Act Play
Life or Death?
Life's Greatest Questions
Life's Important Decisions
Light
Light and Darkness
Light and Truth
(The) Light of Christ
(The) Light of The World
Limiting Beliefs
Living Water
Look Who's Coming to Town
Lost Books of The Bible
(The) Lost Manuscript
(The) Lost Ten Tribes
Lucifer

If we have
faith in the atoning
power of Jesus Christ, and
if we furthermore possess the
resolve to do whatever we must to
activate the spiritual energy that is
lying dormant within us, we will
profit by the teachings of The
Book of Mormon.

Volume 6 Essays

- (A) Mailbox Marked With an "X"
- Management by The Spirit
- (The) Manifestation of Spirits
- May the 4th Be With You
- (The) Millennium
- (The) Mind of God
- Missing Scripture
- Missionary Work
- Moral Discipline
- Mothers
- Multi-tasking
- (The) Name of Christ in The Book of Mormon
- (The) Nature of God and Our Covenants
- (Our) Neighbors
- No Greater Call
- (The) Number of Disciples Was Multiplied
- Obedience
- One Lord, One Faith, One Baptism
- Persecution
- Personal Revelation
- (The) Plan of Salvation
- (The) Plan of Salvation 15 Names
- (A) Positive Mental Attitude
- Power: The Ultimate Test of Character
- Pragmatism in The Book of Mormon
- Premortal Life
- Preparation
- Pride
- (The) Priests of Baal in Our Lives
- (The) Prime Directive
- Professors
- Proper Prior Preparation
- (The) Prophet Joseph Smith
- Prophet, Seer, and
- (The) Q Continuum
- Quorum Sensing
- Receiving Revelation
- Recognizing the Church of Christ
- Removing the Barnacles of Life
- Restoration – The Early Days
- Revelation
- Reverence
- (The) Sabbath
- (The) Sacrament
- Sacramental Waters
- Satan
- (The) Scope of Our Decisions
- (The) Second Mile
- Service
- Set Apart
- Sharing the Gospel
- Sharper Than a Two-edged Sword
- (The) Sons of Mosiah
- Speak Kind Words to Each Other
- (The) Spirit of Revelation

The solicitation of the prophets of The Book of Mormon is to come unto Jesus, and develop our own sure witness of the truth. To that end, we need look no further than to the simple guidance given by His servants in the scriptures. One recommended that we "ask with a sincere heart, with real intent, having faith in Christ." (Moroni 10:4). The counsel of another, who was an apostle of Jesus Christ during His mortal ministry in the Holy Land, was that we "ask in faith, nothing wavering." (James 1:6).

Volume 7 Essays

- Spiritual Calisthenics
- Spiritual Gifts
- Spiritual Identity Theft
- (A) Standard of Excellence
- Strangers in The Land
- Strengths and Weaknesses
- Studying the Scriptures
- Success Strategies
- Symbols
- Talents
- Teaching in The Church
- Teaching Key Doctrine
- Technological Traps
- (A) Testimony of Christ
- (A) Thirty Day Spiritual Fitness Program
- Thou Hast Done Wonderful Things
- (The) Thrill of Victory / Agony of DeFeet
- Tithing
- Too Good to Be True
- (The) Tools of The Trade
- Touching His Garment
- Tough Questions
- Travel at The Speed of Thought
- (The) Twelve Tribes of Israel
- Types, Rites, Ceremonies, and Symbols (Alma Unity
- Updates are Ready
- Walk in The Light of The Lord
- (Our) Weaknesses
- Were There Two Cumorahs?
- What Think Ye of Christ?
- Wherefore and Therefore in The Book of Mormon
- (A) Whirlwind into Heaven
- Who is Packing Your Parachute?
- Why We Laugh
- Words of Mormon
- Work and Personal Responsibility
- Worship in Music
- Writing on Metal Plates Was a Pain
- Zion

Those who turn
their backs to The Book of
Mormon are left to grope about
in the dark and gasp for a breath
of celestial air. The faithful keep their
faces oriented toward the light of Christ
so they will always feel a gentle heavenly
breeze upon their cheeks. At the same time,
because the shadows are always behind
them, they might not even be aware
of the encroaching gloom. At the
very least, they will no longer
be afraid of the dark.

Compendium Volume 3-7 Scriptures

Introduction - Look Who's Coming to Town
1 Nephi 1:20 - Follow the Prophet
2 Nephi 1:30 - Friendship
1 Nephi 2:1-3 - Life's Important Decisions
1 Nephi 3:7 - Obedience
1 Nephi 3:15-16 - Just Get Back on The Bike
1 Nephi 8:2 - Cognates in The Book of Mormon
1 Nephi 8:20 - (The) Hourglass of Life
1 Nephi 8:24 & 11:25 - Being Well Grounded
1 Nephi 9:5-6 - (The) Lost Manuscript
1 Nephi 11:6 & 8 - Jumping Out of Our Skin
1 Nephi 11:25 - Living Water
1 Nephi 13:26 - (The) Lost Books of The Bible
1 Nephi 14:7 - Book of Mormon Strengths
1 Nephi 14:10 - (The) Church
1 Nephi 15:14 - Teaching Key Doctrine
1 Nephi 15:20 - Gathering of Israel
1 Nephi 15:30 - God's Tactical Flashlight
1 Nephi 17:22 - Speak Kind Words
1 Nephi 17:50-51 - Multi-tasking
1 Nephi 19:12 - Environmental Concerns
1 Nephi 20:6 - Circle of Knowledge
1 Nephi 21:25 - Combatting Evil
2 Nephi 1:30 - Friendship
2 Nephi 2:4 - (The) Fall
2 Nephi 2:11 - Entropy
2 Nephi 2:15-16) - Work & Responsibility
2 Nephi 2:16 & 27 - Agency
2 Nephi 2:2 &, Alma 42:8 - Why We Laugh
2 Nephi 2:27 - Fate
2 Nephi 2:28 - Cogito Ergo Sum
2 Nephi 3:7 - Joseph Smith: A Rough Stone
2 Nephi 3:7 & 15 - (The) Prophet Joseph Smith
2 Nephi 31:16 & 18, & Moroni 10:5 - Joseph Smith

2 Nephi 4:35 - Life's Greatest Questions
2 Nephi 9:13 - Plan of Salvation Names
2 Nephi 9:13 - Holy Grail of Religious Doctrine
2 Nephi 9:18 - (The) Church in Former Times
2 Nephi 9:29 - Agency and Opposition
2 Nephi 9:29 - Education
2 Nephi 11:7 - (The) Creation of The World
2 Nephi 12:5 - Walk in The Light
2 Nephi 15:20 - Light and Darkness
2 Nephi 21:6-9 - (The) Millennium
2 Nephi 21:22-23 - (The) Desert Shall Rejoice
2 Nephi 21:31 - Quorum Sensing
2 Nephi 21:31 - (The Meaning of) Doctrine
2 Nephi 24:1 - Strangers in The Land
2 Nephi 24:12 - Lucifer
2 Nephi 25:23 - Grace
2 Nephi 25:1 - Are Mormons Christian?
2 Nephi 26:14 - (The) Church in The Last Days
2 Nephi 26:16 - Book of Mormon Preserved
2 Nephi 26:16 - Establishing the Word
2 Nephi 26:29 - (The) Priests of Baal
2 Nephi 27:10-11 - Receiving Revelation
2 Nephi 27:26 - Wonderful Things
2 Nephi 28:3-4 - (The Best) Education
2 Nephi 28:12 - Pride
2 Nephi 28:20 - God is NowHere
2 Nephi 28:26 - Power: Ultimate Test of Character
2 Nephi 28:30 - Christ's Church is Restored
2 Nephi 28:30-32 - Updates are Ready
2 Nephi 29:3 - (The) Bible
2 Nephi 29:6 - For Unto Us a Child is Born
2 Nephi 29:7-8 - Additional Scripture
2 Nephi 30:2 & 2 Nephi 24:1-2 - Blood, Covenant, and Land Israel

Our love of the scriptures, and particularly of The Book of Mormon, has been nurtured within our spiritual kindergarten. It is heightened in our mortal classroom, and it will be established in eternity, when heaven will smile upon us and we will be clothed in the glory of God.

2 Nephi 31:16 & 18, & Moroni 10:5 - Joseph Smith History
2 Nephi 31:17-18 - Eternal Progression
2 Nephi 31:19-20 - (The) Prime Directive
2 Nephi 31:20 - Spiritual Calisthenics
2 Nephi 32:5-6 - Faith and Knowledge
2 Nephi 33:4 – (The) Second Mile
Jacob 1:6 - Revelation
Jacob 1:13-14 - (Our) Neighbors
Jacob 2:31 - Abstinence in a Permissive World
Jacob 4:6 – (The Spirit of) Revelation
Jacob 4:8 – (The) Mind of God
Jacob 4:11 - Faith Building
Jacob 4:13 - Too Good to Be True
Jacob 5:10 - Is Heaven Hotter Than Hell?
Enos 1:27 - Spiritual Identity Theft
Jarom 1:4 - Godly Qualities
Jarom 1:5 – (The) Sabbath
Jarom 1:20 - Plan of Salvation
Omni 1:26 - Fasting
Words of Mormon 1:3 - Words of Mormon
Words of Mormon 1:5 - Brevity
Mosiah 2:1 - General Conference
Mosiah 2:17 - Service
Mosiah 2:25 – (The) Dust of The Earth
Mosiah 3:12-13 - Proper Prior Preparation
Mosiah 3:15 - Symbols
Mosiah 3:19 – (The) Atonement
Mosiah 4:9 - Are We Alone in The Universe?
Mosiah 4:19 - Buddy Can You Spare a Dime?)
Mosiah 4:20-21 - Batteries are Not Included
Mosiah 4:27 - Finding Balance in Our Lives
Mosiah 5:7 - I am a Child of God
Mosiah 5:7 - Born Again Christians
Mosiah 5:7 - A Change of Heart
Mosiah 5:8-10 - Huckleberries and Chokeberries
Mosiah 8:13 & 16-17 – Heavens Were Opened
Mosiah 8:16 - Prophet, Seer, and
Mosiah 15:14-18 – (The) Thrill of Victory &
   The Agony of DeFeet
Mosiah 18:20 - Before a Wound Can Heal
Mosiah 18:21 – (A) Positive Mental Attitude
Mosiah 23:16-17 & 25:29 - Having Been
   Commissioned of Jesus Christ
Mosiah 25:19-20 - (The) Duty of The Priest

Mosiah 26:22 - Father Forgive Them
Mosiah 27:3 - Teaching in The Church
Mosiah 27:8-9 - Agency and Youth
Mosiah 27:11 - Angels
Mosiah 29:2 - Caesar
Mosiah 29:12-13 - Citizenship
Alma 5:7 - Set Apart
Alma 5:26 - Worship in Music
Alma 5:46 - Personal Revelation
Alma 7:20 - How Does God Get Things Done?
Alma 9:19-23 - Talents
Alma 11:43 - (The) Biggest Loser
Alma 12:27 - (The) Last Judgment
Alma 13:3 - Life is a Three Act Play
Alma 13:3 - Premortal Life
Alma 17:2-3 - (The) Sons of Mosiah
Alma 17:4 - Sharing the Gospel
Alma 17:34-36 - Lamanites by The Waters of Sebus
Alma 22:18 - Removing the Barnacles of Life
Alma 26:8 - Gratitude
Alma 27:27 - Honesty
Alma 26:23-24 - (The) Scope of Our Decisions
Alma 29:1 - Happiness and Sharing the Gospel
Alma 29:1-2 - No Greater Call
Alma 29:4 - Life or Death?
Alma 30:7-9 - Choose Ye This Day
Alma 30:13 - Everyone Wants to Go to Heaven
Alma 30:13 - Evidences of God
Alma 30:41 – (A) Testimony of Christ
Alma 30:44 - Dancing With the Stars
Alma 31:5 - Studying the Scriptures
Alma 31:5 - (Spiritual Fitness Program
Alma 32:5 - Limiting Beliefs
Alma 32:27 - Alma's Discourse on Faith
Alma 32:28 – (The) Germination of Our Faith
Alma 32:35 - Light
Alma 32:42-43 – (The) Tools of The Trade
Alma 34:32 - Preparation
Alma 36:12-14 - Bah Humbug!
Alma 36:19 - I Have Overcome the World
Alma 37:45 - Types, Rites, Ceremonies,
   and Symbols
Alma 40:20 - Construction Zone

In many ways, The Book of Mormon sounds like a Hebrew text. John A. Tvedtnes has pointed out that The Book of Mormon employs cognates more than one would expect if the original language of the book had been English. These cognates illustrate the book's Hebrew influence. One of the most widely recognized examples is the familiar "I have dreamed a dream" (1 Nephi 8:2). That is exactly the way the same idea is expressed in literal translation from Old Testament Hebrew. It looks like Joseph Smith has scored another bullseye! (See Genesis 37:5 & 41:11).

- Alma 40:23-24 – (Our) Eternal Nature
- Alma 41:10 – Happiness
- Alma 41:13 – Justice
- Alma 42:13-15 – Justice and Mercy
- Alma 42:26 – (The) Character of God
- Alma 46:12 – A Coat of Many Colors
- Alma 46:15 – Christians
- Alma 46:20 – May the 4th Be With You
- Alma 48:7 – Courage
- Alma 48:19 – Choose the Harder Right
- Alma 50:23 – Happiness / Wickedness
- Alma 51:5-6 – Civil Liberties
- Alma 56:47-48 – Mothers
- Alma 60:6-7 – Focus
- Helaman 3:25-28 – The Number of Disciples Was Multiplied
- Helaman 3:33 – Professors
- Helaman 3:35 – Touching His Garment
- Helaman 3:35 – Humility
- Helaman 5:12 – Covenant Consciousness
- Helaman 6:37 – Missionary Work
- Helaman 10:6 – Heavenly Father Knows Us
- Helaman 12:7-10 – Sharper Than a Two-edged Sword
- Helaman 16:23 – Satan
- Helaman 18:19-20 – Missing Scripture
- Helaman 13:38 – Heaven Can Wait
- 3 Nephi 1:12-13 – (A) Christmas Miracle
- 3 Nephi 9:33 – Conversion
- 3 Nephi 11:10-11 – (The) Light of the World
- 3 Nephi 12:2 – What Think Ye of Christ?
- 3 Nephi 12:10 – Persecution
- 3 Nephi 12:48 – Nature of God and Covenants
- 3 Nephi 13:9 – Addressing Deity
- 3 Nephi 13:14 – Forgiveness
- 3 Nephi 13:14-15 – Door Swings Both Ways
- 3 Nephi 13:22 – (The) Q Continuum
- 3 Nephi 14:5 – Hypocrisy
- 3 Nephi 14:11 – Spiritual Gifts
- 3 Nephi 14:22-23 – (A) Mailbox Marked With an "X"
- 3 Nephi 15:9 – Enduring to The End
- 3 Nephi 16:1-3 – (The) Twelve Tribes of Israel
- 3 Nephi 17:4 – (The) Lost Ten Tribes
- 3 Nephi 19:30 – Keep Smiling
- 3 Nephi 23:1 – Isaiah in The Book of Mormon
- 3 Nephi 24:8-10 – Tithing
- 3 Nephi 26:14 – Become as Little Children
- 3 Nephi 27:5 – (The) Name of Christ in The Book of Mormon
- 3 Nephi 27:8 – Recognizing the Church of Christ
- 3 Nephi 27:13-20 – Baptism
- 3 Nephi 27:22 – Restoration, The Early Days
- 3 Nephi 27:28-29 – Tough Questions
- 3 Nephi 28:6 – Travel at The Speed of Thought
- 3 Nephi 28:13-15 – Higher Dimensional Realities
- 3 Nephi 28:13-15 – (A) Whirlwind into Heaven
- 3 Nephi 29:3 – Covenants
- 4 Nephi 1:17 – Labels
- 4 Nephi 1:17-18 – Unity
- Mormon 1:3-4 – Book of Mormon as History
- Mormon 3:20-22 – It's Our Book
- Mormon 6:2 – Were There Two Cumorahs?
- Mormon 8:5 – (The Importance of) Friends
- Mormon 8:8 – Age of Accountability
- Mormon 8:35 – Connections
- Mormon 8:35 – Joseph Smith's World
- Mormon 8:38 – (Our) Neighbors
- Mormon 8:38 – Technological Traps
- Mormon 9:6 – Who is Packing Your Parachute?
- Mormon 9:32-33 – And it Came to Pass
- Ether 4:12 – Light and Truth
- Ether 12:24-25, Jacob 4:1 & Mormon 8:17 – Writing on Metal Plates Was a Pain
- Ether 12:26 – (Our) Weaknesses
- Ether 12:27 – Strengths and Weaknesses
- Ether 15:11 – Gold – The Appearance of
- Moroni 2:2 – (The) Holy Ghost
- Moroni 4:1 – (The) Sacrament
- Moroni 5:1-2 – Sacramental Waters
- Moroni 6:9 – Reverence
- Moroni 7:13 – Management by The Spirit
- Moroni 7:19 – (The) Light of Christ
- Moroni 7:24 – Diversity
- Moroni 7:33 – Moral Discipline
- Moroni 7:41 – Success Strategies
- Moroni 7:44 – Faith is a Principle of Power
- Moroni 8:8 – Commitment
- Moroni 8:25-26 – One Lord, One Faith, One Baptism

When Laman, Lemuel, Sam, and Nephi returned to Jerusalem to obtain the Plates of Brass from Laban, they first went back to their home on the outskirts of the city, and gathered up all the treasures they had left behind. These they took to the house of Laban, and offered them in exchange for what they really considered precious. But the Lord did not allow them to receive the spiritual gift of the scriptures in exchange for the profane baubles and ornaments of the world. Ultimately, at the hands of their unscrupulous cousin, they lost these telestial trinkets so that the Lord might thereafter prove to them that He was mightier than man, saw the end from the beginning, and was firmly in control of both their temporal and their spiritual destiny.

Moroni 10:8 - Gifts of The Spirit
Moroni 10:8 - (The) Manifestation of Spirits
Moroni 10:31 - Zion

Moroni 10:31 - (A) Standard of Excellence
Moroni 10:34 - I Have Fought a Good Fight

One thing we learn from excitedly reading about the contraries of
the Nephites and Lamanites in The Book of Mormon is that some people
are defined by their temporal trappings that distract them from the intangible
substance that can be found at the core of their existence, while others have woven
ecclesiastical embroidery into the coat of many colors that should be a foundation
garment of their heavenly wardrobe. These may consist of doctrinal decorations or
improvised accouterments that are designed to prop up their faltering faith. Self-
actualized members of the church, however, take their cues from the inside. The
source of their real power lies in dreams, ideals, values, and core operating
principles. These are not easily subject to change, and are not readily
affected by outside influences. Their healthy reliance upon the
tender mercies of Christ provides just the balance they need,
and gives them a vision of their potential to become self-
directed, self-managed, and self-motivated,
all within the context of God's Plan.

If you don't find what you are looking for in the Index of Volumes 3 – 7, check out this list of topics with related essay references.

Abstinence – Abstinence in a Permissive World
Accountability – Age of Accountability
Adaptivity – Updates are Ready
Apocrypha – Additional Scripture
Apocrypha – Lost Books of The Bible
Apocrypha – Missing Scripture
Apostolic Church – (The) Church of Jesus Christ in Former Times
Are We Alone in The Universe? – Dancing With the Stars
Attitude – Just Keep Smiling
Authority – Having Been Commissioned of Jesus Christ
Born Again – A Change of Heart
Ceremonies – Types, Rites, Ceremonies, and Symbols
Character – Our Eternal Nature
Charity – Buddy Can You Spare a Dime?
Charity – A Mailbox Marked With an X
Chastity – Abstinence in a Permissive World
Christians – Are Mormons Christians
Christ – What Think Ye of Christ?
Church – Recognizing The Church of Christ
Consequences – The Scope of Our Decisions
Corrections – Writing on Metal Plates Was a Pain
Covenants – Covenant Consciousness
Covenants – The Nature of God and Our Covenants
Cumorah – Were There Two Cumorahs?
Darkness – Light and Darkness
Death – Everyone Wants to Go to Heaven
Dependency – Who is Packing Your Parachute?
Devil – Lucifer
Discipline – Moral Discipline
Doctrine – Teaching Key Doctrine
Evangelicals – Born Again Christians
Evil – Combatting Evil
Excellence – A Standard of Excellence
Faith – Alma's Discourse on Faith
Faith – The Germination of our Faith
Faith – Alma's Discourse on Faith
Feet – The Thrill of Victory / The Agony of DeFeet

Forgiveness – The Door Swings Both Ways
Forgiveness – Father Forgive Them
Freedom of Choice – Agency
Free Will – Agency
Gathering of Israel – The Desert Shall Rejoice
Gifts of The Spirit – Spiritual Gifts
Government – Caesar
Government – Management by The Spirit
Great Apostasy – Apostasy
Heaven – Higher Dimensional Realities
Holy Ghost – Batteries are Not Included
Holy Ghost – God's Tactical Flashlight
Humility – The Dust of The Earth
I Am a Child of God – Spiritual Identity Theft
Immorality – Abstinence in a Permissive World
I Think, Therefore I Am – Cogito, Ergo Sum
Joseph's Technicolor Dream Coat – A Coat of Many Colors
Kindness – Speak Kind Words to Each Other
Knowledge – The Circle of Knowledge
Last Days – The Church in The Last Days
Laughter – Why We Laugh
Light – Walk in The Light
Mercy – Justice and Mercy
Missionary Work – Happiness and Sharing The Gospel
Missionary Work – No Greater Call
Missionary Work – The Number of Disciples Was Multiplied
Missionary Work – Sharing The Gospel
Missionary Work – The Sons of Mosiah
Missionary Work – Strangers in The Land
Music – Worship in Music
Non-members – Strangers in The Land
Omniscience – (The) Q Continuum
One Way – One Lord, One Faith, One Baptism
Opposition – Agency and Opposition
Opposition – Lamanites by The Waters of Sebus
Optimism – Huckleberries and Chokeberries

The tree of life represents the love of God. The fruit of this tree, as expected, represents eternal life, which is the greatest gift our Father could give His children. There are many who are actively, passionately, and desperately fighting their way through swirling mists of darkness toward the tree of life and its precious fruit. In Nephi's account, when they finally arrive at the tree, they'll fall down completely spent and exhausted for their efforts. New meaning is given to the apostle Paul's admonition that we ought to work out our own salvation with fear and trembling before the Lord. (See Philippians 2:12).

Peer Pressure – (The) Priests of Baal in Our Lives
Permissiveness – Abstinence in a Permissive World
Perseverance – Just Get Back on The Bike
Personal Responsibility – Work and Personal Responsibility
Plan of Salvation – (The) Hourglass of Life
Plan of Salvation – Life is a Three Act Play
Plates – Writing on Metal Plates Was a Pain
Power – May the 4th Be With You
Preaching the Gospel – Establishing the Word
Preparedness – Spiritual Calisthenics
Priest's Duty – (The) Duty of The Priest
Primitive Church – (The) Church of Jesus Christ in Former Times
Pseudepigrapha – Additional Scripture
Repentance – Before a Wound Can Heal
Repentance – Removing the Barnacles of Life
Responsibility – Work and Personal Responsibility
Restoration – Christ's Church is Restored
Revelation – The Heavens Were Opened
Revelation – Personal Revelation
Revelation – (The) Spirit of Revelation
Revelation – Receiving Revelation
Rites – Types, Rites, Ceremonies, and Symbols
Satan – Lucifer
Scripture Not in The Bible – Additional Scripture

Scriptures – Studying the Scriptures
Speed of Light / Thought – Travel at The Speed of Thought
Spirits – (The) Manifestation of Spirits
Spiritual Fitness – (A) Thirty Day Spiritual Fitness Program
Spiritual Gifts – Gifts of The Spirit
Symbols – Types, Rites, Ceremonies, and Symbols
Technology – Technological Traps
Telestial / Celestial – Jumping Out of Our Skin
Ten Tribes – (The) Lost Ten Tribes
Translation – (A) Whirlwind into Heaven
Truth – Light and Truth
Types – Types, Rites, Ceremonies, and Symbols
Unity – Quorum Sensing
Weakness – Strengths and Weaknesses
Why Things Fall Apart – Entropy in The Physical and Eternal Worlds
Wickedness – Happiness and Wickedness
Wishful Thinking – Too Good to Be True
Word of God – Sharper Than a Two-edged Sword
Work in Progress – Construction Zone: Proceed With Caution
Worship – Worship in Music
Youth – Agency and Youth

We are enveloped in light. (See Mosiah 16:9). When the Nephites were at their best, they did as Helen Keller suggested, when she said: "Keep your face to the sunshine, and you can't see the shadow." The shadow will still exist, but if we are oriented toward the light, it will always be behind us, out of sight, and out of mind. Light can be the catalyst that transforms timidity and temerity into powerful presence of mind, which then acts as a platform for assertive action. It is not bravado, but boldness. It is an intense and compellingly positive response to challenge. In the fight or flight scenario, it is the launching pad for the anticipated adrenalin rush that carries us beyond the threat. It is the foundation quality upon which our nobility rests.

Table of Contents

"Scripture consists not in what we read,
but in what we understand."
(St. Hilary).

The Book of Mormon softens our telestial tendencies and creates an impenetrable shield of faith. The Plan of Salvation of which it testifies, provides a sounding board against which we might discern between the polarized opposites that seek our attention. The Atonement lies at the doctrinal center of the book and strikes familiar chords within our heartstrings as it describes the differences between joy and its worldly counterfeits.

Author's Note

Author's Note..1

Introduction

Introduction...3

Essays

Essays...11

It will not take long
for you to see that the observations
that have been sprinkled throughout this
volume have been carefully crafted to represent a
variety of geometrical designs. It may be surprising to
learn that the construction of these patterns has helped me to
coherently organize my thoughts. In many cases, the outcome
almost seems to have been foreordained, as I moved words around
until, as if my magic, they dropped into their proper positions on the
page. Often, I had envisioned beforehand the particular framework that I
wanted to achieve, and when I had appropriately arranged the words, one
or two would stand out and grab my attention, because they still didn't
feel quite right. Frequently, it was not difficult to find an alternative
that would not only fit better physically, but also was etymologically
much better suited to the spiritual concept that I wished to convey.
As my work on the project continued, I was intrigued by the
natural evolution of the process. That made me consider
whether my success might have been stimulated
by unconventional thought processes that
are more commonly characterized as
inspiration or discernment.

Observations

Observations..229

Commentary, Compendia, & Observations Index

Commentary, Compendia, & Observations Index..365

We read in The Book of Mormon how some of the Nephites saw things as they were, and asked: "Why?" But the focused faithful dreamed of things that never were, and asked: "Why not?" They worked thru problems, instead of skirting around them, and their reliance upon the Atonement of Jesus Christ compelled them to be disciplined in their commitment, with sustained effort and an ongoing responsibility with accountability. Someone once said that the Lord gave us two ends: One to think with and the other to sit on. Which one we use will determine how well we do in life. In other words: Heads we win, and tails we lose.

Author's Note

These Compendia have taken on a life of their own, expanding into a collection of eight volumes of detailed information about The Book of Mormon that supplement my three volumes of Commentary. In essence, they are a distillation of my feelings that relate to The Book of Mormon. Their content is more visceral that that of the Commentary, and perhaps it more accurately reflects my personal feelings about the monumental themes that run throughout all of scripture. They summarize the more comprehensive body of work in my Commentary and showcase my feelings, in the hope that they might become living documents that not only reflect my present understanding of The Book of Mormon, but also the paradigms that expand with the utilization of new tools of discovery. It's a good bet that there is more to come. As the adage encourages, we need to "Think ourselves empty, read ourselves full, write ourselves clear, pray ourselves hot, and let ourselves go!"

Whenever the arm of the Lord is revealed (see 2 Nephi 8:9), we can be certain of His mighty power - our sure source of strength and support. The arm of flesh, conversely, is unstable, and is prone to uncontrollable spasm, atrophy, and paralysis, that are all symptoms of clumsy outbursts of behavior that is destructive and ineffectual.

Introduction

Grace
retains the
power to raise us
from physical death
by the resurrection, and
from spiritual death thru the
Atonement of Christ. We receive
the grace of God proportionately
as we conform to His standard of
personal righteousness that can
only be found in the teachings
of the gospel of Jesus Christ,
and particularly within
the pages of The Book
of Mormon.

Cicero wrote: "The first law for the historian is that he shall never dare utter an untruth. The second is that he shall suppress nothing that is true. Moreover, there shall be no suspicion of partiality or of malice in his writing." The accounts in The Book of Mormon written by the prophets Nephi, Jacob, Alma, Mormon, Moroni, and others, and abridged by the prophet-historian Mormon, were true to the mandate given by Cicero. Although, as Washington Irving brooded: "It is the rule that history fades into fable; fact becomes clouded with doubt and controversy; the inscription moulders, and columns, arches, and pyramids are but heaps of sand, and their epitaphs, nothing but characters written in the dust," yet The Book of Mormon stands as a shining example of the divine model.

It "is the witness that testifies to the passing of time. It illuminates reality, vitalizes memory, provides guidance in daily life, and brings us tidings of antiquity." It is the "evidence of time, the light of truth, the life of memory, the directress of life, committed to immortality." (Cicero, "De Oratore," ii, 36). In its pages, "the centuries roll back to the ancient age of gold." (Horace, "Odes," IV, ii, 39).

In one of the beautiful simplicities of the gospel, we are taught that the Plan allows all of us to enjoy the same access to the simplest, and yet most powerful, witness to the truth. In an inarticulate voice softer than the faintest whisper of sweet breath on the cheek, the Holy Ghost gently testifies, or bears witness, of truth. As Moroni 10:5 teaches (in a verse that is often overlooked, in favor of the previous verse): "By the power of the Holy Ghost ye may know the truth of all things."

The Holy Ghost has revealed all that is true, and has illuminated every eternal principle that has guided the minds of men and women since the dawn of history. We constantly benefit from that which He reveals. In the Last Days, when the Spirit is "poured out upon all flesh, and when "young men see visions, and old men dream dreams," (Joel 2:28), it will be the Holy Ghost Who provides the creative drive. The irony is that many will fail to recognize the source of their inspiration. Job did not. He wrote: "For God speaketh once, yea twice, yet man perceiveth it not. In a dream, in a vision of the night, when deep sleep falleth upon men, in slumberings upon the bed; then he openeth the ears of men, and sealeth their instruction." (Job 33:14-16). We cannot help but think of the experience of Joseph Smith in his bedchamber, when we read Job's description of how, at certain times, Heavenly Father chooses to communicate with His children.

All who desire to have a sure personal witnesses must carefully and prayerfully read The Book of Mormon, and then ask in faith if what they have studied is true. They will then receive the testimony of the Holy Ghost to motivate them to seek out the Priesthood and to enter into sacred covenants with God. It will be as it was on the Day of Pentecost, when Peter and others were preaching to a multitude whose hearts and minds were open and receptive to the truth. The words of the Apostles carried the weight of authority, and penetrated the hearts of their listeners to the end that they asked: "Men and brethren, what shall we do? Then Peter said unto them, Repent, and be baptized every one of you in the name of Jesus Christ for the remission of sins, and ye shall receive the gift of the Holy Ghost." (Acts 2:37-38). And on that day, there were about 3,000 souls added to the kingdom of God on earth. (See Commentary Reference to 3 Nephi 15:21-24).

A similar scenario exists today. Since the restoration of the gospel, there has been a Pentecostal outpouring of the Spirit, and those with a sincere desire to understand the will of God bring the same humble petition to the doorstep of the missionaries: "Now that we have heard your message, have put it to the test of prayerful inquiry, and have received a witness of the Spirit, what shall we do?" The response of the servants of the Lord is unequivocal: "You must exercise saving faith that leads to the waters of baptism and to continuing commitment, dedicated discipleship, selfless service, and sustained spirituality."

Shakespeare wrote: "The past is prologue." ("The Tempest," Act 2, Scene 1). The phrase was intended to imply that our

With our Book of Mormon study, the righteousness of our efforts will be revealed in spectacular plainness and simplicity. Any walls of opposition that have been thrown up to block our purposeful and sincere inquiry will crumble and fall away. During our efforts, the Lord will comfort and succor us with the Bread of Life. As we journey through the harsh and unforgiving environment of Babylon, seeking the Lord while He may be found, oases will spring up in the deserts for living water to slake our thirst.

past is merely a prologue, or an introduction, to the great adventure upon which we will embark if we follow through on our plans. This original interpretation teaches that what has come before on our journey through life doesn't matter in the grand scheme of things, because a new future lies before us, subject to the choices we will yet make. The human condition does not change much over time, which is one reason why the Lord has revealed The Book of Mormon in the Last Days, so that we might profit from the experiences of the Nephites who are distant from us in time and yet are so like us.

Hugh Nibley observed: "Men fool themselves, when they think for a moment that they can read scripture without ever adding something to the text or omitting something from it." Therein lies the power inherent in its study. We glean insight and understanding every time we investigate the word of God. I have learned to love the scriptures, and I often think of St. Hilary, who wrote: "Scripture consists not in what we read, but in what we understand." In these Compendia, I have consistently tried to anchor to the scriptures the ideas swirling around in my head.

Utilization of commentaries and compendia does not replace personal scripture study. The spiritual awakening that accompanies prayerful efforts to understand the mysteries of God through the study of His word cannot be achieved through another person's interpretation. Perhaps, though, my own perspectives on the eternal themes expressed within The Book of Mormon will be helpful to you as you read and seek your own guidance. It is my hope that you will use these compendia only to assist you in your own personal journey to Christ.

Our challenge is to enlist the aid of the Holy Ghost as we undertake that journey. Many years ago, Dalin Oaks wrote: "Latter-day Saints know that learned or authoritative commentaries (and compendia) can help us with scriptural interpretation, but we maintain that they must be used with caution. (They) are not substitutes for the scriptures any more than a good cookbook is a substitute for food. When I refer to "commentaries," I mean everything that interprets scripture, from the comprehensive book-length commentary to the brief interpretation embodied in a lesson or an article, such as this one."

"One trouble with commentaries," he continued, "is that their authors sometimes focus on only one meaning to the exclusion of others. As a result, commentaries, if not used with great care, may illuminate the author's chosen and correct meaning but close our eyes and restrict our horizons to other possible meanings. Sometimes, those other less obvious meanings can be the ones most valuable and useful to us as we seek to obtain answers to our own questions. This is why the teaching of the Holy Ghost is a better guide to scriptural interpretation than is even the best commentary." ("Ensign," 1/1985).

Harold B. Lee taught: "We are convinced that our members are hungry for the gospel undiluted, with its abundant truths and insights. There are those who have seemed to forget that the most powerful weapons the Lord has given us against all that is evil are His own declarations – the plain and simple doctrines of salvation as found in the scriptures." (Regional Representatives Seminar, 10/1/1970).

Bruce R. McConkie explained that "revelation is necessary because ... each pronouncement in the holy scriptures is so written as to reveal little or much, depending on the spiritual capacity of the student." ("A New Witness for The Articles of Faith," p. 71).

And so, as President Oaks continued, "the scriptures are not the ultimate source of knowledge, but what precedes the ultimate source. The ultimate source comes by revelation. We encourage everyone to make careful study of the scriptures and of prophetic teachings ... and to prayerfully seek personal revelation to know their meaning for themselves ... If we seek and accept revelation and inspiration to enlarge our understanding, we will have the mysteries of God unfolded to us by the power of the Holy Ghost."

Even as our ears are assaulted by sounding brass and tinkling cymbals, when we have tended our testimonies of The Book of Mormon, we'll find within ourselves the ability to sift thru the discordant cacophony of confusing voices to find rhythms of revealed truth and a harmonious balance between heaven and earth. Our craving to be clean will find an avenue for expression in celestial sparks that will ignite our desire to repent.

Elder McConkie also said: "I sometimes think that one of the best kept secrets of the kingdom is that the scriptures open the door to the receipt of revelation." ("Doctrines of The Restoration," p. 243). And President Oaks reaffirmed: "We do not overstate the point when we say that the scriptures can be a Urim and Thummim to assist each of us to receive personal revelation."

President Oaks enlarged upon the perspective of the young prophet: "Joseph was, by his own admission, no writer. He felt imprisoned by what he called the 'total darkness of paper, pen, and ink." (Joseph Smith to William W. Phelps, 11/27/1832, B.Y.U. Press, 2002, p. 287). He thus considered it 'an awful responsibility to write in the name of the Lord'. (Joseph Smith Papers, 1:367).

He did not suppose that he could receive the revelations perfectly, nor did the Lord ever set that standard. Joseph and his appointed brethren edited the revelations (see D&C 70:1-4) based on (that) same premise ... namely, that he represented the voice of God as he spoke in what he characterized as his own 'crooked, broken, scattered, and imperfect language'. (Joseph Smith to William W. Phelps, 11/27/1832, quoted in "Making Sense of the Doctrine & Covenants, a Guided Tour Through Modern Revelation," Steven Harper. "Personal Writings of Joseph Smith," p. 186-187).

President Oaks concluded his own epistle by stating a simple truth: "Latter-day Saints know that true doctrine comes by revelation from God, and not by worldly wisdom." (See Moses 5:58). He was in good company, for the Apostle Paul wrote that we are not capable of thinking any thing of ourselves; but we look to God for our wisdom. (See 1 Corinthians 3:5).

I could not agree more heartily with these wise words of counsel. As a matter of fact, every time I proofed my compendium (and I did this many times) I found myself scribbling additional notes in the margins and thinking to myself, "Why didn't I see that before?." That is precisely what I hope will be the experience of everyone who takes the time to read my compendia. I trust the process will motivate you to search the scriptures more carefully and to be instructed by the Spirit, as you do so, that you might be led in directions that will prove to be personally illuminating.

I would expect that my older grandchildren who read this compendium will be impacted in ways that are different from my adult children or my contemporaries. I hope that my observations will touch you differently each time you read them. When I am long-gone, perhaps the considerable thought that went into its production will generate a palpable bond that will span the years separating us. Maybe, the gulf that then divides us will not be as great, and our shared energies will pave the way to an eventual joyous reunion.

If we ever hope to
be able to successfully
deal with the inequalities of
life and escape the quicksand
of self-pity, we must personalize
the lessons of The Book of Mormon.
That is best accomplished during the
hour of prayer that is found within
Sacrament meeting. Pondering the
Savior's forgiveness of our sins, we
visualize Him standing before the
golden gate of heaven, patiently
waiting for us to acknowledge
the transcendent beauty of
His power to transform
our lives.

Essays

At first,
it may be the easier
wrong that appears to be
more convenient, but that is
only because it harmonizes with
the values of Babylon. Worldliness
is all around us. If we cannot find the
stabilizing influence provided by faith in
Christ as we study The Book of Mormon, our
moral equivocation can quickly turn into a
path of least resistance, until it become the
pattern of our conduct. Faith invites us to
trust in the divine design of our Father
in Heaven that is grounded upon the
Atonement of His Son. It nurtures
our belief that it is only in Him
that our lives can become as
fairy tales waiting to be
written by the hand
of God.

Spiritual Calisthenics

"Press forward with a
steadfastness in Christ, having
a perfect brightness of hope, and
a love of God and of all men."
(2 Nephi 31:20).

The Lord showed Abraham "the intelligences that were organized before the world was; and among all these there were many of the noble and great ones" who had high ideals, excellent moral character, and proven performance capabilities and potential. (Abraham 3:22). These may have been the stand-out superstars in the Lord's Pre-mortal Spiritual Calisthenics Fitness Program.

Perhaps in pre-earth life, the best of the best rolled out of bed very early every morning to do mind-bending stretching exercises leading to intellectual flexibility, interpersonal pliability, and spiritual capability. Even before breakfast, they may have climbed the stadium steps of discipline before running several laps around the scriptures and engaging in refreshingly repetitive rehearsals for life's educational experiences. Each wind-sprint through The Book of Mormon would have brought familiarity and clarity, paving the way for later religious recognition.

After thus awakening and arousing their faculties, perhaps they were then served a satisfying meal of restraint, fortified with the nutritional supplement of principle. This would have prepared them to renew their strength, mount up as on the wings of eagles, and run and not be weary, and walk, and not faint. (See Isaiah 40:31). Their thirst would have been quenched, not by supposed energy drinks laced with sweeteners and stimulants, but by water springing from a living fountain. Their hunger would have been satisfied by the performance potential found in the bread of life.

Such a bountiful boot camp experience would have provided balanced stimulation designed to ward off the rigidity, inflexibility, and fanaticism of spiritual sclerosis. It would instead have promoted the concept of aerobic fitness to a group already determined to "press forward with a steadfastness in Christ, having a perfect brightness of hope, and a love of God and of all men." (2 Nephi 31:20). It would have renewed their resolve to persevere in a world where, due to neglect, many would suffer from the atrophy of their spiritual muscles leading to an emaciation of the spirit.

Forewarned and forearmed, they would have worked extra hard to trim the fat of indolence, mediocrity, laziness, and inattention, by obeying the principles of good spiritual and emotional nutrition. They would have realized that by observing a steady diet of discipleship, ultimately "all things (would) be restored to their proper order, every thing to its natural frame—mortality raised to immortality, corruption to incorruption." (Alma 41-4).

They would have recognized that only organically grown spiritual food is wholesome, delicious, and high in moral fiber content, and they would have been able to easily distinguish it from the empty calories of carnality, sensuality, and devilishness, and from the malnourishment that is caused by the mold of misinformation. They would have learned to identify the noxious weeds of worldliness that would lie in their path, and to listen for the poisonous pandering that is so characteristic of the uncommitted and unconverted. They would have resolved to avoid the excesses of those who would be slothful, and who would fail to regularly exercise their faith and diligence. (See Alma 37:41).

They would have learned the art of self-defense, for they knew the time would come when the fiery darts of the adversary would fill a darkening sky. They would already have been engaged in the building of a fortress of security to guard against the day when his assault would surely come.

They would have learned to identify the spiritual equivalents of high fructose corn syrup, trans-fats, bleached flour, and white rice. Even before receiving a body of flesh and blood, they would have developed the capacity to get naturally high on endorphins and the discipline to avoid performance-enhancing or mind-altering drugs. With the memory of the ideological War in Heaven still fresh in their minds, they would have renewed their resolve to keep their minds clear and focused as they valiantly and pointedly promoted the cause of Zion.

They would have recognized the value of nourishment from the good word of Christ, while avoiding the fleeting rush of artificial sweeteners, the empty calories of convenience, and the hypoglycemia of hypocrisy. They would have developed the discipline to refrain from boarding the Excess Express in a vain search for a shortcut to perfection. In their mind's eye they could already see those whose "spiritual bodies were one sorry sight!. No more than skeletons, covered with skin. They would get up to heaven, but never get in. 'Another soul's mine!' they could hear Satan scream. 'Give man something nice, and he'll take the extreme!' OK, I'll admit it; I'll outright confess. For the fast way to hell, take the Excess Express." (Anonymous).

In our own pre-mortal life, we must have recognized that strenuous spiritual exercise would give us vigorous vitality and leave us stronger, and so we surely learned to use our recovery time wisely. We must have developed the capacity to carefully monitor our bodies' vital signs; to feel the spiritual equivalents of oxygen-debt and lactic acid buildup; to monitor the efforts of our minds to keep pace with our spiritual development. We experienced brief bursts of energy resulting in spectacular achievement, but more importantly we found that sustained effort would carry us further along the road leading to eternal life. In that setting, we must have learned the value of developing endurance, so that when the time would come to go the second mile or turn the other cheek, it would be easier simply because of the force of habit.

We must have taken our Coach at His word when He assured us that resistance training would one day pay big dividends. When He urged us to do 10 push-ups through The Book of Mormon, we probably voluntarily tacked on another 13 through the Articles of Faith. Instead of bench-pressing only the Aaronic Priesthood, we added on the additional weight of The Oath and Covenant of The Melchizedek Priesthood, because we knew we'd need that additional muscle fiber and strength down the road. When he asked us to get our heart rate up to a steady 75 verses a day to facilitate our comprehension of gospel principles, we instead pushed our limits to whole chapters and even books of scripture. The elliptical trainer of consecration, the stationary bike of service, and the treadmill of sacrifice put us through the whole range of motion to develop and strengthen our inner core, and our reward was the increased capacity of our hearts to pump life-giving blood throughout our bodies. We knew that one day these same hearts would enlarge to encompass empathy for our fellow men, and that our bowels would be filled with compassion as we witnessed their struggles.

When we had free time, we didn't watch the equivalent of television reality shows, but we understood the concept of "The Biggest Loser." We learned that shedding pounds would be less important than giving up our sins to know the Savior, and we knew we would be better for our efforts to keep that burdensome weight off. We also learned the principles of search and rescue and recovery to be used on behalf of those who would falter in their own fitness programs.

Even then, His counsel must have rung true, that we should "cease to be idle; cease to be unclean; cease to find fault one with another; cease to sleep longer than is needful; retire to thy bed early, that ye may not be weary; arise early, that your bodies and your minds may be invigorated." (D&C 88:124). We received our own witness that there is a direct correlation between physical and spiritual energy and vitality. Our quickening prepared us for our experiences in the womb, when our first stirrings of life would send a tangible message of hope from our heavenly home into the mortal world.

When He asked us to awake and arouse our faculties, we took that to mean we should plant the word in our hearts, so that it might swell by faith. We tried to wrap out minds around the alien concept that our spirits would one day be inseparably joined to physical bodies, and that individually our soul would "be restored to the body, and the body to the soul; yea, and every limb and joint…to its body." (Alma 40:23).

When we were tempted to ease up on our training schedule, surely the counsel of one of our squad leaders rang in our ears: "Be not slothful, but followers of them who through faith and patience inherit the promises." (Hebrews 6:12). On another occasion, he encouraged us: "Bodily exercise profiteth little: but godliness is profitable unto all things." (1 Timothy 4:8). In other words, it would matter little if our mortal frame turned out to be large or small, fat or thin, or if we could run faster or jump higher or father than another. What would ultimately determine our intrinsic self-worth would be our capacity to incorporate into our being the divine nature, the ability to say, at the end of the contest: "I have fought a good fight, I have finished my course, I have kept the faith." (2 Timothy 4:7).

Then would our mortal frames be renewed in unimaginable ways. By magnifying our callings, we would be sanctified by the Spirit unto the renewing of our bodies." (D&C 84:33). Therein, we would find, lies the fitness secret of the ages. It was his mastery of this very principle that allowed Adam to stand up "in the midst of the congregation … notwithstanding he was bowed down with age, being full of the Holy Ghost,." (D&C 107:56).

We knew while clothed in mortality we would be wrought upon and cleansed by the power of the Holy Ghost. Then we would be numbered among the people of the church of Christ; and our names would be taken, that we might be remembered and nourished by the good word of God, to keep us in the right way, to keep us continually watchful unto prayer, relying alone upon the merits of Christ, who even while we were in Spiritual Boot Camp was already the author and finisher of our faith. (See Moroni 6:4).

In the deep recesses of memory, as I think about what it must have been like for us, I can still hear the Voice gently urging me: "O.K. Buttercup. One more lap around the scriptures!" Today, when my obedience seems inconvenient, I try to remember that long ago I learned that perspiration always precedes inspiration and that the dictionary is the only place where success comes before work. When my faith seems fragile, I try to remember that it is darkest just before the dawn, but that the new day always holds the promise of rebirth, recommitment, renewal, and redemption.

Some of the starlight we now see shining down from above may have been hurtling thru space for around 2,025 years (traveling over 12 million billion miles during that time), ever since it left its host star. At least some of the light we see today, then, may have burst forth from its home system at a time when the drama was unfolding in the Land of Zarahemla at the same time as the Savior's birth. (See Helaman Chapter 14). If that's the case, we might even now be participating in the spectacular light show of the Nativity. We remember that it was the Savior who asked Job: "Where wast thou when I laid the foundations of the earth? ... When the morning stars sang together, and all the sons of God shouted for joy?" (Job 38:4&7). We might have been 12 million billion miles away from the events that were unfolding in Bethlehem.

Spiritual Gifts

"If ye then ... know how to give
good gifts unto your children, how
much more shall your Father who
is in heaven give good things
to them that ask him?"
(3 Nephi 14:11).

"Now there are diversities of gifts, but the same Spirit ... But the manifestation of the Spirit is given to every man to profit withal. For to one is given by the Spirit the word of wisdom; to another, the word of knowledge by the same Spirit; to another, faith by the same Spirit; to another, the gifts of healing by the same Spirit; to another, the working of miracles; to another, prophecy; to another, discerning of spirits; to another, divers kinds of tongues; to another, the interpretation of tongues." (1 Corinthians 12:4 & 7-10).

"All things must be done in the name of Christ, whatsoever you do in the Spirit." (D&C 46:31). The baptism of water qualifies us for membership in the church but doesn't guarantee the total spiritual transformation necessary to regain the presence of God. This comes through the baptism of fire and the Holy Ghost, which is the receipt of the Spirit unto sanctification: "For by the water ye keep the commandment; by the Spirit ye are justified, and by the blood ye are sanctified." (Moses 6:60).

Alma asked his brethren: "Have ye spiritually been born of God?" (Alma 5:14). He wanted to know if these baptized members of the church had experienced the pure and unconditional love of Christ, and if they had charity for all men. He already knew they had been converted to the church; what he really wanted to find out was if they had also been converted to the gospel. Mahatma Gandhi once said" "If a single man achieves the highest kind of love, it will be enough to neutralize the hatred of millions." Alma knew that the pure love of Christ in the hearts of his people would be a dynamic influence for good. With this kind of dedication, they would perform mighty miracles in His name, through the workings of the Spirit.

The Spirit is ready to guide us unerringly, that we may know the truthfulness of all things. (See Moroni 10:5). Even more importantly, it molds and shapes us into new creatures in Christ. As Joseph Smith said: "By the power of the Spirit our eyes were opened and our understandings were enlightened, so as to see and understand the things of God." (D&C 76:10).

As our powers expand, we experience the glittering facets of the life of the Spirit, and we are cast off into a stream of revelation that brings us into direct experience with God. "To use the careful preparation and training we receive as a springboard, to be capable of disciplined, controlled procedure and to be receptive to flashes of insight, is what a solid Latter-day Saint should have going for him in his inner life. The gospel sets us free to be creative, and sets us creative to become more free," as we learn to respond to the guidance of the Spirit and enjoy spiritual gifts. It is the perfect law of liberty." ("My Religion & Me," Lesson #9).

Every member of the Church "is given a gift by the Spirit of God." (D&C 46:11). These gifts can be positive, motivational, and uplifting, by allowing us to vividly pre-play, role-play, and re-play our life's experiences. They provide us with a safety net circumscribing the healthy expression of our agency.

When we have the image of God engraved upon our countenances, we will recognize our spiritual gifts, and give thanks to Him Who has bestowed them. "Who shall ascend into the hill of the Lord," asked the Psalmist, "or who shall stand in his holy place" to partake of the Divine Nature? "He that hath clean hands and a pure heart; who hath not lifted up his soul unto vanity, nor sworn deceitfully." (Psalms 24:4-5).

"To some is given one, and to some is given another, that all may be profited thereby." (D&C 46:12). Sometimes, it is necessary to fast and pray to gain a witness of the Spirit and receive a strong, independent testimony of the gospel. Only when we have paid the price, can we comprehend the language of the Spirit. Otherwise, it is foreign to us. If we have never made the journey to Christ, if we have not traveled the path leading to the tree of life, if we have not partaken of the delicious fruit of that tree, if we disregard the essentials, we are tongue-tied, and cannot receive "the things of the Spirit of God, for they are foolishness unto (us), neither can (we) know them, because they are spiritually discerned." (1 Corinthians 2:14-15). Faith precedes the miracle of the receipt of spiritual gifts.

Regarding our comprehension of the different manifestations of the Spirit, Marion G. Romney taught: "Having a testimony and being converted are not necessarily the same thing. A testimony comes when the Holy Ghost gives the earnest seeker a witness of the truth. A moving testimony vitalizes faith, that is, it induces repentance and obedience to the commandments. Conversion, on the other hand, is the fruit or the reward for repentance and obedience." (C.R., 10/1963). Spiritual gifts follow conversion that is built on the foundation of testimony.

The Gifts of the Spirit are given to the members of the church in priesthood ordinances. Our Heavenly Father is anxious to bless us with these gifts. Without interfering with our agency, they are sufficient to guide us in the direction of behavioral lifestyle choices that are in harmony with celestial principles. God wants each of us to succeed, to pass our individual tests of mortality, and then to move on toward our celestial home, having satisfied the entrance requirements for admittance to His kingdom. With what greater gifts could our Heavenly Father bless us than those that help us to reach this goal?

"And it shall come to pass that he that asketh in Spirit shall receive in Spirit." (D&C 46:28). It is appropriate to ask for spiritual gifts, that we might grow in the grace of God. As we do so, we become more and more like Him, developing His divine attributes, and growing in spiritual stature. We follow the path of His Only Begotten Son, Who commanded: "I would that ye should be perfect, even as I, or your Father who is in heaven is perfect." (3 Nephi 12:48, See Matthew 5:48). God glories in the possibility that we might become like Him, as we endure to the end in righteousness.

"It is a serious thing to live in a society of possible Gods and Goddesses," wrote C.S. Lewis, "to remember that the dullest and most uninteresting person you talk to may one day be a creature which, if you saw it now, you would be strongly tempted to worship. It is in the light of these overwhelming possibilities, it is with the awe and the circumspection proper to them, that we should conduct all our dealings with one another ... all friendships, all loves, all play, all politics. There are no ordinary people. You have never talked to a mere mortal. It is immortals with whom we joke, work, marry, snub and exploit. Our charity must be a real and costly love. Next to the blessed sacrament itself, your neighbor is the holiest object presented to your senses. If he is your Christian neighbor, he is holy in almost the same way, for in him also Christ is truly hidden and glorified." ("The Weight of Glory," p. 14-15).

"If ye by the grace of God are perfect in Christ, and deny not his power, then are ye sanctified in Christ by the grace of God, through the shedding of the blood of Christ, which is in the covenant of the Father unto the remission of your sins, that ye become holy, without spot." (Moroni 10:33). It would be difficult to put more succinctly, or to state more powerfully, the essence of the gospel of Jesus Christ, than in this verse. If we open our hearts, we can become holy, without spot. "Holy," Peter taught, is one of the name-titles of God Himself. As Paul described Him, He was as a lamb without spot or blemish. (See 1 Peter 1:19, & Hebrews 9:14).

Spiritual gifts cannot be purchased with the treasures of the earth. Perhaps this is why in their efforts to obtain the sacred records, Lehi's sons were stripped of all their gold, silver, and precious things. The task was to be accomplished in the Lord's way, by the power of His mighty arm that is great in the sight of the faithful, but that has a terrible effect upon the wicked. As Alma asked: "Can ye dispute the power of God?" (Mosiah 27:16). Certainly not, for the arm of flesh is weak in comparison to the power of the Spirit.

The gift of faith is a gift of power that motivates us to action. The miracles from the scriptures with which we are familiar were only made possible by the exercise of a faith that may be active, or may lie dormant, within each of us. When we read in the sacred records of these experiences, a way is prepared that we, too, might be "partakers of the heavenly gift." (Ether 12:8). It becomes possible for us to share the intensity of feeling experienced by the two disciples on the Road to Emmaus, who, after communing with the resurrected Lord, declared: "Did not our heart burn within us, while he talked with us by the way, and while he opened to us the scriptures?" (Luke 24:32).

The gift of discernment stands in sharp contrast to the cold, harsh rationality of those in the world, who, as long as they have visible proof, grudgingly acknowledge the hand of the Lord in their affairs. These individuals can discern neither good nor evil; their only reality is that which may be defined by their five physical senses.

Heavenly Father, on the other hand, has provided a way to discern truth through the operation of the Spirit. For example, He does not offer up holy writ to be scrutinized, analyzed, criticized, and rationalized by pompous doctors and professors of religion clothed in the robes of the false priesthood and cloistered in the ivory towers of academia. "You cannot prove the genuineness of any document to one who has decided not to accept it," declared Hugh Nibley. "When a man asks for proof we can be pretty sure that proof is the last thing in the world he really wants. His request is thrown out as a challenge, and the chances are that he has no intention of being shown up. After all these years, the Bible itself is still not proven to those who do not choose to accept it. So, The Book of Mormon as an 'unproven' book finds itself in good company." ("An Approach to The Book of Mormon," p. 2).

Nor will the Lord indulge the prurient interest of men who only want theological titillation to satisfy their adulterous curiosity. Again, The Book of Mormon provides a classic example. Critics of that book "often remark sarcastically that it is a great pity that the golden plates have disappeared, since they would conveniently prove Joseph Smith's story. They would do nothing of the sort. The presence of the plates would only prove that there were plates, no more. It would not prove that Nephites wrote them, or that an angel brought them, or that they had been translated by the gift and power of God, and we can be sure that scholars would quarrel about the writing on them for generations without coming to any agreement, exactly as they have done about parts of the Bible. The possession of the plates would have a very disruptive effect and it would prove nothing.

On the other hand, a far more impressive claim is put forth when the whole work is given to the world in what is claimed to be a divinely inspired translation. In such a text, any cause or pretext for disagreement and speculation is reduced to an absolute minimum. It is a text which all the world can read and understand, and it is a far more miraculous object than any gold plates would be." (High Nibley, "An Approach to The Book of Mormon," p. 17-18). The only thing that a spiritual witness does not do is pander to the base instinct of the world's fallen and depraved nature.

The gift of wisdom is given to those who press forward with complete dedication, feasting upon the words of Christ, receiving physical and spiritual strength and nourishment, and enduring to the end with continuing responsibility and accountability. These are they who have been promised the spiritual gift of hidden treasures of knowledge.

Moroni wrote: "To one is given by the Spirit of God, that he may teach the word of wisdom." (Moroni 10:9). The Lord instructed Joseph Smith to "teach one another the doctrine of the kingdom," to the end that all might be edified in Christ. (D&C 88:77). Perhaps the most dramatic spiritual manifestation that was the result of one seeking wisdom from God, was that received by Joseph Smith in The Sacred Grove. He had read in James 1:5-6: "If any of you lack wisdom, let him ask God, that giveth to all men liberally, and upbraideth not; and it shall be given him. But let him ask in faith, nothing wavering." This promise was powerfully fulfilled, when he learned that wisdom leading to salvation comes from God by personal revelation.

The Lord said that we should not seek not for riches, but for wisdom. To understand spiritual things, we must have discernment or guidance from the Holy Ghost. For example, those who are sincerely investigating the church are taught by the Spirit, and receive its witness. When they are confirmed as members of the church they are endowed by ordinance with the special gift of the companionship of the Holy Ghost. One of His purposes is to guide the faithful from the covenant waters of baptism, along the strait and narrow path leading to the other covenants of the priesthood that are necessary for us to obtain eternal life. This is one reason why members of the church are given the Holy Ghost in an initial priesthood ordinance beside the waters of baptism, or shortly thereafter.

The mysteries of God are those truths that can only be known by revelation from the Holy Ghost. When we "hunger and thirst after righteousness," the doctrine of the priesthood, or words of wisdom, will distill upon our souls as the dews from heaven, and the Holy Ghost will be our constant companion. (See D&C 121:45-46). Then, to him that will not harden his heart "is given the greater portion of the word (of wisdom), until it is given unto him to know the mysteries of God until he know them in full." (Alma 12:10). We gain access to the spiritual gift of knowledge of the mysteries of God, that are the saving principles of the gospel of Jesus Christ.

To those who harden their hearts to the truth, however, "is given the lesser portion of the word until they know nothing concerning his mysteries, and then they are taken captive by the devil, and led by his will down to destruction. Now this is what is meant by the chains of hell." (Alma 12:11). The terrible thing about hardening our hearts is that our understanding of the word is withheld, leaving us vulnerable to the devil's influence. The scriptures identify the consequences of sin in very plain language. Its effect on those who sin after having been taught the principles of the gospel in plainness is that the guidance of the Spirit is withdrawn, and they are left alone to grope in darkness. Guilt causes them to shrink from church activity, and in the absence of the Spirit, they have no claim on the blessings of prosperity or preservation. Having eyes, they see not, and having ears, they hear not.

Tragically, these individuals, feeling uncomfortable in proximity to spiritual experiences, withdraw to lifestyles that are devoid of such associations. Thus begins a downward spiral that can only gain momentum as sinful practices, more easily committed, become entrenched. Even worse, "the man that doeth this, the same cometh out in open rebellion against God." (Mosiah 2:37). "Thus saith the Lord concerning all those who know my power, and have been made partakers thereof, and suffered themselves through the power of the devil to be overcome, and to deny the truth and defy my power. They are they who are the sons of perdition." (D&C 76:31-32). They suffer a spiritual death that is devoid of light and truth.

When the word and the will of the Lord came to the Saints through Brigham Young, it was: "Let him that is ignorant learn wisdom by humbling himself and calling upon the Lord his God, that his eyes may be opened that he may see, and his ears opened that he may hear. For my Spirit is sent forth into the world to enlighten the humble and contrite." (D&C 136:32-33).

The gift of knowledge is given to those who seek "line upon line, precept upon precept." (D&C 98:12). Personal revelation is the ultimate source of our understanding of God's will. "These currents and many more are part of the flowing fountain of the church. If we do not drink, if we die of thirst while only inches from the fountain, the fault comes down to us. For the free, full, flowing, living water is there." (Truman Madsen, "Christ & The Inner Life," p. 31).

Mormon wrote of Alma's teaching style: "And now, as the preaching of the word had a great tendency to lead the people to do that which was just - yea, it had had more powerful effect upon the minds of the people than the sword, or anything else, which had happened unto them - therefore, Alma thought it was expedient that they should try the virtue of the word of God." (Alma 31:5).

Joseph Smith similarly taught: "A person can get nearer to God by reading The Book of Mormon than by reading any other book." (H.C., 4:461). There is great motivating and sanctifying power in the words of The Book of Mormon, precisely because as a companion to the Bible it is Another Testament of Jesus Christ.

"Young men," counseled Ezra Taft Benson, "The Book of Mormon will change your life. It will fortify you against the evils of our day. It will bring spirituality into your life that no other book will. It will be the most important book you will read in preparation for a mission and for life. A young man who knows and loves The Book of Mormon, who has read it several times, who has an abiding testimony of its truthfulness, and who applies its teachings, will be able to stand against the wiles of the devil and will be a mighty tool in the hands of the Lord.

Oh, my brethren," he continued, "let us not treat lightly the great things we have received from the hand of the Lord. His word is one of the most valuable gifts He has given us. I urge you to recommit yourselves to a study of the scriptures. Read them in your families, and teach your children to love and treasure them. Then, prayerfully and in counsel with others, seek every way possible to encourage the members of the church to follow your example." (C.R., 4/1986).

Moroni wrote: "To another (it is given) that he may teach the word of knowledge." (Moroni 10:10). Joseph Smith taught: "It is impossible for a man to be saved in ignorance" of the saving principles of the gospel." (D&C 131:6). We must have knowledge of them, and of our Heavenly Father, for as Jesus taught: "This is life eternal, that they might know thee the only true God, and Jesus Christ, whom thou hast sent." (John 17:3). Our knowledge of Them is a gift of the Spirit.

The gift of administration is given to those who correctly discern the services and agencies through which the Lord operates His church. "These ordinances are not empty, passive rituals; rather, they bind individuals to receive the promises and blessings of the gospel by means of a covenant of action between themselves and the Lord." ("Doctrinal Commentary on The Book of Mormon," 4:319). These ordinances bridge the gulf between earth and heaven, attest to the nature of God, confirm that His church is founded on unchanging principles, and illustrate that the requirements for obtaining salvation are the same for all.

Churches that operate on borrowed light are sometimes quite popular with people who seek the form without the substance, the sizzle without the steak, and who enjoy the relative ease of putting forth minimal effort in an organization that makes no demands for personal sacrifice. But the church of Christ is powered by the Spirit, and there is a performance requirement associated with every blessing received.

When we think of the gift of speaking in tongues, the missionaries who serve throughout the world come to mind. We also remember the Nephite children whom Jesus blessed. These received an endowment of spiritual power, for the Savior "did loose their tongues, and they did speak unto their fathers great and marvelous things, even greater than he had revealed unto the people." (3 Nephi 26:14). The multitude "both saw and heard these children; yea, even babes did open their mouths and utter marvelous things; and the things which they did utter were forbidden that there should not any man write them." (3 Nephi 26:16).

The gift of the interpretation of tongues may include the ability to comprehend the words of the scriptures. As the Lord told Joseph Smith: "These words are not of men nor of man, but of me; wherefore, you shall testify they are of me and not of man. For it is my voice which speaketh them unto you; for they are given by my Spirit unto you, and by my power you can read them one to another; and save it were by my power you could not have them." (D&C 18:34-35).

The gift of faith to be healed was illustrated most dramatically during the Savior's post-mortal ministry among the Nephites. He manifested His power, and His disciples exhibited their faith, when He "healed all their sick, and their lame, and opened the eyes of their blind and unstopped the ears of the deaf." (3 Nephi 26:15). Certainly, His efforts to bless the people were enhanced by their great faith in Him. The Savior does not want lukewarm converts; He desires those whose commitment is profound. Then, He can truly bless their lives. After entering the fold, such devoted disciples may see and hear "unspeakable things, which are not lawful to be written." (3 Nephi 26:18). They will remember the counsel of the Master, Who said: "Ye know the things that ye must do in my church; for the works which ye have seen me do that shall ye also do." (3 Nephi 27:21). Without realizing it, the children of Christ are transformed into a Zion society, "for this is Zion – the pure in heart." (D&C 97:21). Collectively, they are the church of Christ.

Malachi was speaking of the gift of faith to heal when he declared in the name of the Lord: "Unto you that fear my name shall the Sun of righteousness arise with healing in his wings." (Malachi 4:2). There is also another dimension of faith to heal. Only six generations after Adam, "Enoch looked upon the earth; and he heard a voice from the bowels thereof, saying: Wo, wo is me, the mother of men; I am pained, I am weary, because of the wickedness of my children. When shall I rest, and be cleansed from the filthiness which is gone forth out of me? When will my Creator sanctify me, that I may rest, and righteousness for a season abide upon my face?" (Moses 7:48). When one comprehends the significance of the terrible pollutions on the face of the earth, and the physical and spiritual cleansing that will be required of it before the Kingdom of God can return, the concept of "healing" moves to a more comprehensive, all-encompassing, level.

At the millennial day, all shall lift up their voice and sing, declaring that "the earth hath travailed and brought forth her strength," as a mother who has borne a new child, "and the heavens have smiled upon her," for she is pure and delightsome. "And she is clothed with the glory of her God," adorned in the strength of His priesthood. "For he stands in the midst of his people (with) glory, and honor, and power, and might. For he is full of mercy, justice, grace and truth, and peace." (D&C 84:101-102). Peter indicated that true Saints "have obtained like precious faith with us through the righteousness of God and our Saviour Jesus Christ. According as his divine power hath given unto us all things that pertain unto life and godliness, through the knowledge of him that hath called us to glory and virtue; whereby are given unto us exceeding great and precious promises: That by these ye might be partakers of the divine nature." (2 Peter 1:1, 3 & 4). These are they who know the power of God, understand His nature, and experience the whisperings of the Spirit.

The gift of prophesy is "the testimony of Jesus." (Revelation 19:10). It follows that those who have received this spiritual gift are prophets, since a testimony can only be received by revelation from the Holy Ghost, and since prophecy consists of the words we speak when we are moved upon by the Spirit.

"Wo unto him that shall deny the revelations of the Lord, and that shall say the Lord no longer worketh by revelation, or by prophecy, or by gifts, or by tongues, or by healings, or by the power of the Holy Ghost!" (3 Nephi 29:6). In contrast, the church testifies "to the world that revelation continues, and that the vaults and files of the church contain these revelations which come month to month, and day to day." (Spencer W. Kimball, C.R., 4/1977).

The gift of the working of miracles is a manifestation of the power of God that is incomprehensible to the world. For "the natural man receiveth not the things of the Spirit of God: for they are foolishness unto him: neither can he know them, because they are spiritually discerned." (1 Corinthians 2:14).

"Wo unto him," in the Last Days, "that shall say that there can be no miracle wrought by Jesus Christ; for he that doeth this shall become like unto the son of perdition, for whom there was no mercy, according to the word of Christ!" (3 Nephi 29:7). Those who deny the divinity of Christ cannot be saved on His merits, because they have not generated saving faith in his power. They are like the hypothermic individual whose core temperature cannot be raised without an external source of warmth unless they experience a profound attitude adjustment that allows the Holy Ghost to quicken their own spirits with vitality, their progression will come to a grinding halt, and they will be damned.

Those who enjoy the gift of a testimony of Jesus Christ unflinchingly testify that He was "the Son, the Only Begotten of the Father, full of grace, and mercy, and truth." (Alma 5:48). "Either this man was, and is, the Son of God, or else a madman or something worse," declared C.S. Lewis. "But don't let us come with any patronizing nonsense about His (only) being a great human teacher" as the secular apologists would have us believe. ("Mere Christianity," p. 55).

The gift to believe the testimony of others may be enjoyed by investigators, little children, and church members in general, who listen to the Authorities of the church bear testimony. "And by doing so, the Lord God prepareth the way that the residue of men may have faith in Christ, that the Holy Ghost may have place in their hearts." (Moroni 7:32).

Alma said that preaching the gospel with power and authority is the responsibility of those who bear the priesthood of God. "This is the order after which I am called," he said, "yea, to preach unto my beloved brethren, yea, and every one that dwelleth in the land." (Alma 5:49). The objects of his attention were members and non-members alike. He felt that it was his duty to bring the gift of the gospel to all, and his message was the same, that all must repent and be born again.

Some have all the spiritual gifts. "Unto some it may be given to have all those gifts, that there may be a head, in order that every member may be profited thereby." (D&C 46:29). When members of the church have faith in the atoning power of Christ, and if they furthermore possess the resolve to do whatever is necessary to activate that energy in their own lives, they will profit by the administration of the gifts of the Spirit. Those who have faith in the power of Christ to save them from their sins will have a profound motivation to live in accordance with His will. They will see with an eye of faith, or with an eternal perspective. They will not only believe in Christ, but they will believe Christ, when He says that they are celestial raw material. The manifestation of spiritual gifts will dramatically validate their continuing efforts to be transformed. On the other hand, those who are not valiant in the testimony of Jesus, who do not stand for something, will fall for anything. If they don't know where they are going, they will end up somewhere else, and probably won't even care if they made the trip.

Beginning in 1830, an unbroken line of prophets has led the restored church. Since 1847, these have administered its affairs "from Salt Lake City, Utah. They have dedicated themselves to their appointed mission of helping the people of the world prepare for eternal life, and for the second coming of Jesus Christ. They have provided leadership for the international missionary program of the Church and for the building of temples. The living prophet continues to receive revelations, select and ordain leaders by the spirit of prophecy, and serve as the principal teacher of the church, instructing its members in doctrine and in righteous living." (L.D.S. Infobase). The prophet is supported in these efforts by all of the gifts of the Spirit.

Spiritual gifts were created "for the benefit of the children of God." (D&C 46:26). It will be difficult for those who have lived a telestial existence to justify their actions before God, in light of the many signs and wonders He has provided as both warnings and blessings. "Any man who hath seen any or the least of these hath seen God moving in his majesty and power." (D&C 88:47). "Earth is crammed with heaven, and every common bush with fire of God. But only those who see take off their shoes. The rest stand around picking blackberries." (Elizabeth Barrett Browning, "Aurora Leigh," Book Seven, 1856).

Ours is the Age of Inspiration and of the gifts of the Spirit, when the Holy Ghost is being poured out in rich abundance. With prophetic foresight, Joseph Smith promised: "God shall give unto you knowledge by His Holy Spirit, yea, by the unspeakable gift of the Holy Ghost, that has not been revealed since the world was until now." This is a time when "nothing shall be withheld. All thrones and dominions, principalities and powers, shall be revealed. And also, if there be bounds set to the heavens or to the seas, or to the dry land, or to the sun, moon, or stars," all this "shall be revealed in the days of the dispensation of the fulness of times." (D&C 121:26-31).

Those to whom the gospel has been dispensed "receive the gifts of sensory delight, of fragrance, sound, and form and color." Theirs "is the realm of human associations, of gratitude, loyalty, and appreciation, of selflessness, helpfulness and forgiveness, of friendship, love, and compassion. It is the realm of human growth and transcendence and of truth discovered and accepted, of beauty created and enjoyed, of goodness deepened and made manifest in life.

None of us are strangers to these realms of spirit. We have sensed the world about us, smelled its fragrance, heard its sounds, and glimpsed its form and colors. We have warmed our souls in the glow of human associations; have had our moments of selflessness and gratitude, love and forgiveness. We have felt an upward reach within us when made suddenly aware of a truth, a beauty, a goodness above and beyond our own attainment." (P.A. Christensen, "A Land Unpromised and Unearned," B.Y.U. Studies, Autumn, 1975).

These whisperings confirm to our hearts that there is more to the gospel than outward observances, obedience, and covenants. Spiritual enlightenment is the key to the discovery of undreamed-of vistas of otherwise inaccessible experience.

The Apostle Paul testified that "eye hath not seen, nor ear heard, neither have entered into the heart of man, the things which God hath prepared for them that love him." (1 Corinthians 2:9). Nephi declared: "No tongue can speak, neither can there be written by any man, neither can the hearts of men conceive so great and marvelous things as we both saw and heard Jesus speak." (3 Nephi 17:7). Joseph Fielding Smith, Jr., described the spiritual "impressions on the soul that come from the Holy Ghost (as) far more significant than a vision. It is where spirit speaks to spirit, and the imprint upon the soul is far more difficult to erase." ("Seek Ye Earnestly," p. 213-14).

The scriptures allude to the thin line between the material world and the world of spiritual matters: "And when the servant of the man of God was risen early, and gone forth, behold, an host compassed the city both with horses and chariots. And his servant said unto him, Alas, my master, how shall we do? And he answered, Fear not: for they that be with us are more than they that be with them. And Elisha prayed, and said, Lord, I pray thee, open his eyes, that he may see. And the Lord opened the eyes of the young man; and he saw: and, behold, the mountain was full of horses and chariots of fire round about Elisha." (2 Kings 6:15-17).

"When you lay down this tabernacle, where are you going?" asked Brigham Young. "Into the spirit world." he replied. "Where is the spirit world? It is right here. Do the spirits go beyond the boundaries of this organized earth? No, they do not. They can see us, but we cannot see them, unless our eyes were opened." ("The Vision," p. 55-56).

A reminiscence by a friend and associate of Joseph Smith reflects the gossamer fabric of the veil separating the world we know from the world of spirits. "I am getting tired and would like to go to my rest, said Joseph. His words and tone (both) thrilled and shocked me, like an arrow, pierced my hopes that he would long remain with us, and I said, as with a heart full of tears: Oh Joseph, what could we, as a people, do without you and what would become of the great Latter-day work, if you should leave us? He saw and was touched by my emotions, and in reply he said. Benjamin, I would not be far away from you, and if on the other side of the veil, I would still be working with you, and with a power greatly increased, to roll on this kingdom." ("The Vision," p. 140-141).

It is the challenge of every member of the church to learn to understand the language of the Spirit with perfect fluency, because twenty-first century "Americans (especially), tend to fill space, as if what we have, what we are, is not enough. Being affluent, we strangle ourselves with what we can buy, things whose opacity obstructs our ability to see what is (really) there." (Gretel Erlich, "The Atlantic Magazine"). The bestowal of spiritual gifts is the antidote for poisonous telestial tendencies that choke the expression of celestial sureties.

"And ye must give thanks unto God in the Spirit for whatsoever blessing ye are blessed with. And ye must practice virtue and holiness before me continually." (D&C 46:32-33). The gifts of the Spirit cause our breasts to swell with joy. Spirituality, the kind of life where we may enjoy these gifts, "is the consciousness of victory over self, and of communion with the infinite." (David O. McKay). The gifts of the Spirit help us to be richer today than we were yesterday, to laugh often, to give something, to forgive even more, to make new friends, to change stumbling blocks into stepping-stones, to think more in terms of "thyself" than "ourselves," to be cheerful even when we are weary, and to bless the lives of others. The gifts of the Spirit help us to receive the image of Christ in our countenances, and to experience a mighty change in our hearts. "This changed feeling is indescribable, but it is real. Happy is the person who has truly sensed the uplifting, transforming power that comes from this nearness to the Savior, this kinship to the Living Christ." (David O. McKay, C.R., 4/1944).

We must "always remember and always retain in (our) minds what those gifts are, that are given unto the church." (D&C 46:10). For "whatsoever is good cometh from God." (Alma 5:40). The gifts of the Spirit are given so that we may have the fortifying influence necessary to combat evil in the world. "We have no excuse to err in our knowledge and understanding of right and wrong. By inquiring of the Lord and listening to the voice of His Spirit, and having a willingness to be guided thereby, we will always find ourselves on the Lord's side of every issue, and be strengthened to hold fast to that which is good." (Delbert Stapeley, C.R., 4/1965).

As we do this, the windows of heaven will be opened unto us, and the blessings of the Lord will be poured out upon our heads, to the end "that (we) may not be seduced by evil spirits, or doctrines of devils, or the commandments of men." D&C 46:7). The mission statement of all who have ever labored in our behalf is summarized in the last verses of The Book of Mormon. It is to "come unto Christ, and lay hold upon every good gift, and touch not the evil gift, nor the unclean thing." It is to "come unto Christ, and be perfected in him, and deny (ourselves) of all ungodliness." (Moroni 10:30 & 32).

That we may not be deceived we must seek "earnestly the best gifts, always remembering for what they are given." (D&C 46:8). God will continue the ministry and work miracles among the children of men as "long as time shall last, or the earth shall stand, or there shall be one man upon the face thereof to be saved." But "if these things have ceased, wo be unto the children of men, for it is because of unbelief, and all is vain." (Words of Mormon 1:36-37). The Last Days reflect the final days of the Nephites, when "there were sorceries, and witchcrafts, and magics, and the power of the evil one was wrought upon all the face of the land" because of the lack of faith of the people. (Mormon 1:19).

When the gifts of the Spirit are absent, we must declare, as did Mormon, that "faith (has) ceased also; and awful is the state of man, for they are as though there had been no redemption made." (Words of Mormon 1:38). Alma warned: "For behold, if ye have procrastinated the day of your repentance even until death," or if you have waited to develop saving faith until you were spiritually dead to the Light of Christ, "behold, ye have become subjected to the spirit of the devil, and he doth seal you his," because you can no longer make the vital distinction between good and evil, or light and darkness. "Therefore, the Spirit of the Lord hath withdrawn from you, and hath no place in you, and the devil hath all power over you," for you have voluntarily surrendered your agency to act independently, "and this is the final state of the wicked," for there is no recovery, and it will be as if there had been no redemption made for such individuals who refuse to repent. (Alma 34:35).

Mormon exhorted his brethren to rise to the occasion. He said: "I judge better things of you, for I judge that ye have faith in Christ because of your meekness; for if ye have not faith in him then ye are not fit to be numbered among the people of his church." (Moroni 7:39). He was like wise old Tevya, in "The Fiddler on The Roof," who told his daughters: "In Anatevka, God knows who you are, and what you may become."

Those who ask "for a sign that they may consume it upon their lusts," only want theological titillation. (D&C 46:9). Those whose spiritual sensitivities are dulled, desire only the thrill of the moment. While signs and wonders, and gifts of the spirit, may be exhilarating and spine-tingling, they are completely misunderstood and wasted on such individuals.

But the wicked may still receive spiritual manifestations for a variety of reasons. Sometimes they demand and receive signs as proof of the authority of servants of the Lord. (See John 2:18 & 6:30). Those who have adulterous hearts seek signs to satisfy their carnal desires that require greater and greater intensities of validation for the same level of gratification. (See Matthew 12:39). Signs are sometimes given for no reason other than to vindicate the prophets. (See Mosiah 20:21). Signs thus given leave the wicked with responsibility for what happens. Because consequence follows action, signs establish accountability. (See D&C 63:7 & 11).

Mormon recorded that the people who lived in Zarahemla just before the birth of the Savior attributed the signs that had been given them to "the power of the devil, to lead away and deceive the hearts of the people." (3 Nephi 2:2) In reality, it was the devil himself who was the source of their rationalizations: "And thus did Satan get possession of the hearts of the people again, insomuch that he did blind their eyes, and lead them away to believe that the doctrine of Christ was a foolish and a vain thing." (3 Nephi 2:2).

When Mormon observed that "the people began to wax strong in wickedness and abominations," he might have been drawing particular attention to those who had made covenants with God, and who should have known better when they consciously chose to conspicuously compromise their conduct. (3 Nephi 2:3). It is one thing for an ignorant people to live in opposition to the laws of God, but it is quite another for those who have had the light, and who have enjoyed spiritual gifts, to turn from them, willfully rebel, and intentionally seek out darkness. That circumstance is an abomination because it represents unfaithfulness to God. It is not easy for those who refuse to accept the gifts of God to obtain forgiveness. Those who have not allowed Christ into their lives "die in their sins, and they cannot be saved in the kingdom of God." (Moroni 10:26).

Professors of religion have made a business of teaching "for doctrines the commandments of men. Having a form of godliness...they deny the power thereof." (J.S.H. 1:19). Creeds are an abomination in the sight of God and are corrupt when they lead people away from the truth. Insult is added to injury when hypocrisy further perverts and transforms doctrine into humanized, spiritually impotent dogma; when it is only a caricature of its former self; when people do not really believe, but are only "professors" of religion.

The Saints are entitled to the unspeakable gifts of the Spirit. Melvin J. Ballard related an experience that might be shared by all those who have received the covenants and hope to enjoy the witness of the Second Comforter. He said: "I found myself one evening in the dreams of the night in the sacred building, the temple. After a season of prayer and rejoicing, I was informed that I should have the privilege of entering into one of those rooms, to meet a glorious Personage, and, as I entered the door, I saw, seated on a raised platform, the most glorious Being my eyes have ever beheld or that I ever conceived existed in all the eternal worlds. As I approached to be introduced, he arose and stepped towards me with extended arms, and he smiled as he softly spoke my name. If I shall live to be a million years old, I shall never forget that smile. He took me in his arms and kissed me, pressed me to his bosom and blessed me, until the marrow of my bones seemed to melt. When he had finished, I fell at his feet, and as I bathed them with my tears and kisses, I saw the prints of the nails in the feet of the Redeemer of the world. The feeling that I had in the presence of Him who hath all things in his hands, to have his love, his affection and his blessing was such that if I ever can receive that of which I had but a foretaste, I would give all I am, all that I ever hope to be, to feel what I then felt." ("Sermons and Missionary Experiences of Melvin Joseph Ballard," p. 156).

The Book of Mormon has given the pure love of Christ a chance to prove to the world that it really does reflect our true nature. Charity endures forever, "and whoso is found possessed of it at the last day, it shall be well with him." (Moroni 7:47). As a bellwether of Christian service, it prepares us to be like God. It is a gift that is bestowed upon the faithful by His grace, to prepare us to be comfortable with the inauguration of a day that will be celebrated by His all-encompassing love.

Spiritual Identity Theft

"Who steals my purse steals trash; 'tis something, nothing; 'twas mine, 'tis his, and has been slave to thousands. But he that filches from me my good name robs me of that which not enriches him and makes me poor indeed."
(Shakespeare, "Othello," Act 3, Scene 3).

"I soon go to the place of my rest, which is with' my Redeemer ... And I rejoice in the day when my mortal shall put on immortality, and shall stand before him; then, shall I see his face with pleasure."
(Enos 1:27).

The scriptures testify unequivocally that we are children of God.

Of this truth, there is no question, for "the Spirit itself beareth witness with our spirit, that we are the children of God." (Romans 8:16). We know this intuitively. How sweet it is to hear Primary age children as young as three sing the songs that reinforce what the Spirit whispers to each soul: "I am a child of God, and he has sent me here, has given me an earthly home with parents kind and dear. I am a child of God, and so my needs are great. Help me to understand his words before it grows too late. I am a child of God. Rich blessings are in store. If I but learn to do his will, I'll live with him once more. Lead me, guide me, walk beside me, help me find the way. Teach me all that I must do to live with him someday." (Naomi Randall).

The Lord knows each of us because we are His literal children.

On one occasion, He spoke to Joseph Smith and said: "be still and know that I am God." (D&C 101:16). On another, he simply stated: "Thou art Joseph." (D&C 3:9). He said to a great Book of Mormon prophet: "Thou art Nephi." (Helaman 10:6), and He told Moses: "Thou art my son." (Moses 1:4). He explained: "Thou art one in me, a son of God; and thus, may all become my sons." (Moses 6:68). Thus was Moses inspired to exclaim: "Thou hast said, I know thee by name." (Exodus 33:12).

In fact, He knows each of us by name. To Jeremiah, He said: "Before I formed thee in the belly I knew thee," (Jeremiah 1:5), and although from our perspective we are forever in His debt, He sees our potential to become like Him. As Paul explained: "Wherefore thou art no more a servant, but a son, and if a son, then an heir of God through Christ."

(Galatians 4:7). Through Him, we may receive the greatest of gifts, to have eternal life, or a familiar relationship with both God the Father and His literal Son Jesus Christ. (See John 17:3).

We must zealously guard our identity and protect our good name.

We must be as Captain Moroni who "was a strong and a mighty man; he was a man of a perfect understanding ... a man whose soul did joy in the liberty and the freedom of his country." In fact, "if all men had been, and were, and ever would be, like unto Moroni, behold the very powers of hell would have been shaken forever;' yea, the devil would never have power over the hearts of the children of men." (Alma 48:11 & 17).

We must be as Enos, who on his deathbed wrote: "I soon go to the place of my rest, which is with my Redeemer ... And I rejoice in the day when my mortal shall put on immortality, and shall stand before him; then shall I see his face with pleasure." (Enos 1:27).

Moroni wrote a special personal invitation to all those who would read The Book of Mormon: "I soon go to rest in the paradise of God, until my spirit and body shall again reunite, and I am brought forth triumphant through the air, to meet you before the pleasing bar of the great Jehovah." (Moroni 10:34).

We must be aware that Satan exists to steal from us our spiritual identity.

Satan wears many hats. He is an honorary member of the Screen Actor's Guild, and has been enthusiastically awarded its Life Achievement Award. He is a much sought-after image consultant. He methodically cruises the Internet, and is a permanent resident of chatrooms. He is the great deceiver who bombards us with spam emails. He is a prize-winning author of books and periodicals. He is a talented composer, lyricist, and scriptwriter. He is the creative influence behind television programs, video games and other diversions too numerous to mention. He is a fashion designer, travel agent, vintner and beer distributor, an actor, newscaster, politician, scientist, and power broker. He may even be a teacher or wear clerical robes.

He uses truth whenever and however it serves his evil purposes. As the serpent said unto the woman, "Ye shall not surely die. For God doth know that in the day ye eat thereof, then your eyes shall be opened, and ye shall be as gods, knowing good and evil." (Genesis 3:4-5).

Our free will allows us to resist his destruction of our spiritual identity: "If it seem evil unto you to serve the Lord," said Joshua, "choose you this day whom ye will serve ... but as for me and my house, we will serve the Lord." (Joshua 24:15). Our resistance allows us to be as "Shadrach, Meshach, and Abed-nego who, it was reported to Darius the King: "serve(d) not thy gods, nor worship(ped) the golden image which (he had) set up." (Daniel 3:12).

Sometimes, the exercise of our free will has consequences that may seem, at least superficially, to be profoundly negative. As Joan of Arc was carried to the stake, she was given the opportunity to obtain her freedom by denying her beliefs. Instead, she made this statement: "I know this now. Every man gives his life for what he believes. Every woman gives her life for what she believes. Sometimes, people believe in little or nothing, and so they give their lives for little or nothing. One life is all we have, and we live it as we believe in living it, and then it is gone. But to surrender what you are, and to live without belief, is more terrible than dying, even more terrible than dying young."

How bold is Satan?

He tried to steal the Savior's own identity on the Mount of Temptations. He brazenly demanded that Jesus renounce

His citizenship in exchange for pride, the honors of men, and the admiration of the world. "If thou be the Son of God," he cried, "command that these stones be made bread." (Matthew 4:3). "If thou be the Son of God," he urged, "cast thyself down." (Matthew 4:6). "All these things will I give thee," he promised, "if thou wilt fall down and worship me." (Matthew 4:10).

When other means fail, Satan employs strong-arm tactics by directly assaulting us, beating us up until we are down and out, and then trying to rob us of that which we would, under normal circumstances, hold near and dear.

The scriptures call a spade a spade: "He that entereth not by the door into the sheepfold, but climbeth up some other way, the same is a thief and a robber." (John 10:1).

That the thief and robber from the unseen world is actively seeking our destruction is certain, evidenced by the fact that because of his influence we are often "in perils of waters, in perils of robbers, in perils by (our) own countrymen, in perils by the heathen, in perils in the city, in perils in the wilderness, in perils in the sea, in perils among false brethren, in weariness and painfulness, in watchings often, in hunger and thirst, in fastings often, in cold and nakedness." (2 Corinthians 11:26-27).

He attempts to influence us by deceit.

Those who are deceitful falsely represent themselves. They write checks they cannot cash. Their tank is running on empty and there is no reserve. They need to be deceitful because they are spiritually and morally bankrupt. "Who shall ascend into the hill of the Lord," asked the Psalmist, "or who shall stand in his holy place?. He that hath clean hands, and a pure heart, who hath not lifted up his soul unto vanity, nor sworn deceitfully." (Psalms 24:3-4).

Paul hoped that, in the Last Days, we would "henceforth be no more children, tossed to and fro, and carried about with every wind of doctrine, by the sleight of men, and cunning craftiness, whereby they lie in wait to deceive." (Ephesians 4:14) Elsewhere, he cautioned, "beware lest any man spoil you through philosophy and vain deceit, after the tradition of men, after the rudiments of the world." (Colossians 2:8). We must be on our guard, "for many deceivers are entered into the world." (2 John 1:7). "For there shall arise false Christs, and false prophets, and shall shew great signs and wonders, insomuch that, if it were possible, they shall deceive the very elect." (Matthew 24:24).

We can learn to deal with the deceit of Satan by studying the scriptures. Amalickiah and Moroni, for example, provide stark contrasts in style: "While Amalickiah had thus been obtaining power by fraud and deceit, Moroni, on the other hand, had been preparing the minds of the people to be faithful unto the Lord their God." (Alma 48:7)

God's Plan is under the spiritual equivalent of "cyber-attack" billions of times a day.

Satan has a PhD (Philosophy of the Devil) in computer science, and is preoccupied with hacking into and compromising the integrity of our most basic systems. The Pentagon's computer systems, by comparison, are under cyber-attack over 2 million times a day. Shawn Henry, assistant director of the FBI's cyber division, told a conference in New York:. "Other than a nuclear device or some other type of destructive weapon, the threat to our infrastructure, the threat to our intelligence, the threat to our computer network is the most critical threat we face." (January 7, 2009). The righteous face equivalent challenges.

The devil can rob us of our spiritual individuality.

If he can succeed in reducing our distinctive personality signatures to the lowest common denominator, he will destroy us. If we surrender the traits that make us unique, we will fade into a shadow of what we might have otherwise been.

The inevitable happens when Satan does manage to steal our spiritual identity.

When we lose our sense of direction, our purpose, or "when we undertake to cover our sins, or to gratify our pride, our vain ambition, or to exercise control or dominion or compulsion upon the souls of the children of men, in any degree of unrighteousness, behold, the heavens withdraw themselves; the Spirit of the Lord is grieved; and when it is withdrawn, Amen to the priesthood or the authority of that man." (D&C 121:37).

When that happens, we are as Alma the Younger, who was "racked with eternal torment, for (his) soul was harrowed up to the greatest degree and racked with all (his) sins." He "remember(ed) all (his) sins and iniquities, for which (he) was tormented with the pains of hell ... The very thought of coming into the presence of ... God did rack (his) soul with inexpressible horror" to the point that he was "racked, even with the pains of a damned soul." (Alma 36:12-16).

When Satan has breached the firewalls of our spiritual security system, has neutralized our body's defense mechanisms, and his infectious virus has spread uncontrollably, the effect of the resulting contamination is compromise, conflict, and chaos.

When our hearts are set upon temporal things only, our spirituality is weakened until the things of God are no longer a part of our daily life. Worse, "ere he is aware, (man) is left unto himself, to kick against the pricks, to persecute the saints, and to fight against God." (D&C 121:38). Satan's mission statement is to hold us captive, to bring us down to hell, and to reign over us in his own kingdom. (See 2 Nephi 2:29). Brigham Young said: "The spirit is pure, and under the special control and influence of the Lord, but the body is of the earth, and is subject to the power of the devil, and is under the mighty influence of that fallen nature that is of the earth. If the spirit yields to the body, the devil then has power to overcome the body and spirit of that man, and he loses both."

We have all witnessed "that after a people have been once enlightened by the Spirit of God, and have had great knowledge of things pertaining to righteousness, and then have fallen away into sin and transgression, they become more hardened, and thus their state becomes worse than though they had never known these things." (Alma 24:30).

Joseph Fielding Smith, Jr. taught: "Before you joined the church you sat on neutral ground. When the gospel was preached, good and evil were set before you. You could choose either or neither. There were two opposite masters inviting you to serve them. You left the neutral ground, and you can never get back on to it. Should you forsake the Master you enlisted to serve, it will be by the instigation of the evil one, and you will follow his dictation and be his servant." (C.E.S. Manual, p. 258).

Benjamin said: "After ye have known and have been taught all these things, if you should transgress and go contrary to that which has been spoken, that ye do withdraw yourselves from the Spirit of the Lord, that it may have no place in you to guide you in wisdom's paths that ye may be blessed, prospered, and preserved ... I say unto you, that the man that doeth this, the same cometh out in open rebellion against God; therefore, he listeth to obey the evil spirit, and becometh an enemy to all righteousness." (Mosiah 2:36-27). Joseph Fielding Smith, Jr. said: "When the Spirit is withdrawn, darkness supersedes the light, and apostasy will follow. This is one of the greatest evidences of the divinity of the latter-day work. In other organizations, men may commit all manner of sin and still retain their membership, because they have no companionship with the Holy Ghost to lose, but in the church when a man sins and continues without repentance, the Spirit is withdrawn, and when he is left to himself the adversary takes possession of his mind and he denies the faith." ("Doctrines of Salvation," V. 3, p. 309).

Thus did Mormon report of Nephite dissenters: "It is strange to relate, not long after their dissensions they became more hardened and impenitent, and more wild, wicked and ferocious than the Lamanites – drinking in with the traditions of the Lamanites; giving way to indolence, and all manner of lasciviousness; yea, entirely forgetting the Lord their God." (Alma 47:36).

When we pay price to regain our spiritual identity, we will feel liberated, enjoy the Light of Christ, and express ourselves through our love of God and our fellowmen.

We will exclaim, as did those in Zarahemla so long ago: "The Spirit of the Lord Omnipotent…has wrought a mighty change in us, or in our hearts, that we have no more disposition to do evil, but to do good continually. And we, ourselves, also, through the infinite goodness of God, and the manifestations of his Spirit, have great views of that which is to come; and were it expedient, we could prophesy of all things. And it is (our) faith … that has brought us to this great knowledge, whereby we do rejoice with such exceedingly great joy." (Mosiah 5:2-4).

Those who safeguard their spiritual identity understand their relationship with the Lord. As Benjamin instructed the Saints in Zarahemla: "Now, because of the covenant which ye have made ye shall be called the children of Christ, his sons, and his daughters; for behold, this day he hath spiritually begotten you; for ye say that your hearts are changed through faith on his name; therefore, ye are born of him and have become his sons and his daughters. And under this head ye are made free." (Mosiah 5:7-8). As a grateful father said of his Prodigal Son: "This thy brother was dead, and is alive again; and was lost, and is found." (Luke 15:32).

We do not need to suffer the consequences of spiritual identity theft. In 2008, 8.4 million people in the United States had their identities stolen at a total cost of $49.3 billion. How many more have had their spiritual identities stolen, and at what a cost? It is better to act preventively rather than redemptively. The poor example of the world emphasizes the need for conscious efforts to resist Satan.

The following are adapted from the Twelve Steps of Addiction Recovery (L.D.S. Social Services). We must acknowledge to ourselves that we are at risk of the constant and unrelenting assaults of Satan upon our spiritual identities. We must come to believe that only the power of God can restore us to complete spiritual health. We must turn our lives over to the care and keeping of God. We must constantly re-evaluate the stability and integrity of our moral shields. We must acknowledge the power of the priesthood as a key ally in our fight against, and resistance, to Satan's onslaughts. We must be ready to allow the power of God, and not our own, to defeat Satan. We must ask Jesus Christ to come to our defense, and in particular to help us to heal the damage done in consequence of the weaknesses in our armor. We must be true to our friends, family, and acquaintances; to be true to our word, and to honor our commitments and covenants, in order to draw upon the power of God through ordinances and covenants. We must be absolutely honest in our dealings with our fellow warriors, and right whatever wrongs for which we are responsible. We must constantly monitor our defensive network of systems designed to resist Satan, recognize when they fail, accept responsibility for the outcomes that are a consequence of the failure, and take steps to restore the integrity of the network. We must do everything within our ability to maintain open lines of communication with the powers of heaven. We must not only believe in Christ, but also believe Him when He says that He can heal us through the power of His Atonement. We must then use the Atonement as our secret weapon in the defense of our spiritual identity.

Every time those who embark upon the marvelous adventure of the study of The Book of Mormon with the intention of finding out for themselves if it speaks the truth, the Holy Ghost will energize their capabilities with a vitality that they would not otherwise enjoy. (See Moroni 10:4). As Bagheera, the powerfully built black panther confided to Mowgli the man-cub: "I had never seen the jungle. They fed me behind bars from an iron pan until one night I felt that I was Bagheera the Panther, and no man's plaything, and I broke the lock with one blow of my paw, and came away." (Rudyard Kipling, "The Jungle Book," p. 26).

(A) Standard of Excellence

*"Genius is one percent inspiration
and ninety-nine percent perspiration."
(Thomas Edison).*

*"Awake, and arise from the dust,
O Jerusalem; yea, and put on thy beautiful
garments, O daughters of Zion; and strengthen
thy stakes and enlarge thy borders forever, that thou
mayest no more be confounded, that the covenants
of the Eternal Father which he hath made unto
thee, O house of Israel, may be fulfilled."
(Moroni 10:31).*

When Alma met the Sons of Mosiah on the road leading from the land of Gideon, fourteen years after they had bid each other farewell at the commencement of their missions, it must have seemed altogether remarkable that his highest and best hopes for the welfare of his brethren had been confirmed. As he learned the details of their experiences during those eventful years, he surely recognized and appreciated the unchangeable formula for success that had guided them so unerringly. Ammon, Aaron, Omner, and Himni "had waxed strong in the knowledge of the truth; for they were men of a sound understanding and they had searched the scriptures diligently, that they might know the word of God." (Alma 17:2).

"Who shall ascend into the hill of the Lord?" David had asked. "Or who shall stand in his holy place? He that hath clean hands, and a pure heart; who hath not lifted up his soul unto vanity, nor sworn deceitfully. He shall receive the blessing from the Lord, and righteousness from the God of his salvation." (Psalm 24:3-5). The Sons of Mosiah precisely fit this description.

The scriptures had become their message and were the tools of their trade. Their confidence, we shall see, was directly related to their knowledge of holy writ. "But," Mormon explained, "this is not all. They had given themselves to much prayer, and fasting; therefore, they had the spirit of prophecy, and the spirit of revelation, and when they taught, they taught with the power and authority of God." (Alma 17:3). They were missionaries who had endured and overcome every obstacle that had been thrown in the path of their progress. "God help all honest men," said Marion G. Romney, "to be born again, to be of sound understanding, to know the word of God, and to maintain the spirit thereof by study, fasting, prayer, and work." (C.R., 10/1941).

The challenges we face are part of life, and the example of the Sons of Mosiah gives us courage to push on with less concern about winning or losing. What is important is to carry the struggle further. In our pursuit of excellence, we know that we will face our share of trials, all tailored by a wise Father to meet our individual needs for growth. We view these not as stumbling blocks to our progression, but as stepping-stones to greater heights of achievement. We carry the struggle as far as need be, relying on His strength to sustain us when we feel we can go no further by ourselves.

We have spiritual challenges, but recognize chastisement from the Lord as an invitation to repent. Throughout the week, we prepare ourselves to receive the Sacrament each Sunday. We strengthen our testimonies through fasting and prayer. To reinforce our understanding of gospel principles, we undertake a consistent program of scripture study. We make the sweet spirit within the temple a regular part of our experience. We resist temptations by recognizing and avoiding the trigger points of compromising situations. We learn to act upon spiritual promptings and exercise our agency wisely.

We have intellectual challenges, and deal with them by reading uplifting literature and by exercising our minds with stimulating thoughts and meaningful conversation with others. We speak with purpose. We maintain a working knowledge of the current events that shape the world around us, but ignore the media when it focuses attention on trivial matters. We constantly push ourselves to develop new interests in creative fields and are mentors to those who show interest in developing expertise in those areas in which we excel.

We face emotional challenges head-on. When we have time on our hands, we remember to ponder and pray rather than wander and play. When things do not seem to go our way, we fall back on our eternal perspective. We use a cosmic yardstick to measure our progress. Our only recreational drug of choice is endorphins. We make extraordinary efforts to positively influence those situations over which we retain some control. We learn to accept that which we cannot change, but at the same time we create reservoirs of positive energy upon which we may draw in time of need.

We make every effort to avoid the pitfalls of the poor soul who "worked out for years to reduce all his fat; whose muscles were firm and whose stomach was flat; who jogged day and night to keep himself trim, and still found time to play tennis and swim. He drank protein drinks, and ate health food galore, then lifted, stair-climbed, and lifted some more. He told family and friends that it gave him a 'high.' They encouraged him on as he waved them good-bye. 'If things work out,' he yelled back from afar, 'I'll be a great athlete; I'll be a big star!' But how could he miss the big truck up ahead? One thud and his beautiful body lay dead. And then, he saw something that filled him with fright. His spiritual body was one sorry sight! No more than a skeleton, covered with skin. He got up to heaven, but didn't get in! 'Another soul's mine!' Satan started to scream. 'Give man something nice, and he'll take the extreme!' OK, I'll admit it; I'll outright confess. For the fast way to hell, take the excess express." (Peter G. Czerny).

We will have physical challenges as the years pass. In anticipation of these, we establish fitness programs tailored to our individual needs and designed to help us sustain higher levels of health. We view physical limitations positively as opportunities to develop patience and perspective. We regularly re-evaluate our adherence to the spirit of the Word of Wisdom and commit ourselves to goals of improvement based upon greater adherence to its principles.

There will be service challenges, because our time is always at a premium and there will always be competition between selfish and selfless endeavors. We consistently discipline ourselves to make time to be of service to our own families, to individuals outside our families, and to the church. We trust in the Lord's protection when we consciously and deliberately put ourselves at risk as we venture out into the world to reclaim lost sheep. We commit to regular and sustained efforts to contribute in positive ways to the welfare of our communities, region, nation, and the world.

We may face character challenges along the way. To guard against compromise, we learn to appreciate experiences that teach us humility, and we look forward with anticipation to those that challenge our paradigm. We attempt to so live our lives that we would be happy to give our parrot to the town gossip. We try to be the kinds of persons our dogs believe us to be. We commit the 13 Articles of Faith to life as well as to memory, and make them the tangible particles of our faith. We are honest, true, chaste, benevolent, virtuous, and do good to others. As our faith increases, so does our capacity to see God's influence over all aspects of our lives. We learn to recognize and accept the suffering that is a part of life, and strive to see adversity as a necessary and beneficial aspect of our experience. In times of trial, we remember the Savior, Who descended beneath all things, and Who is our Exemplar. We shun the shadows and are drawn to His light. As we are immersed in the Spirit as a tangible element, we exult in His glorious influence. It becomes part of our nature to relate comfortably with all that is virtuous, lovely, of good report and praiseworthy. We seek after that which creates an atmosphere conducive to improvement.

Our challenges stimulate within us our innate capacity for extraordinary responses. As Joseph Smith exhorted the church, so we say: "Brethren, shall we not go on in so great a cause? Go forward and not backward. Courage, brethren, and on, on to the victory! Let your hearts rejoice and be exceedingly glad. Let the earth break forth into singing ... and let all the sons of God shout for joy!." (D&C 128:22-23).

We visualize our reunion with our Father, imagine stepping on shore, and finding it heaven. We sense ourselves taking hold of a hand, and finding it God's hand. We envision breathing deeply, and discovering it is celestial air that fills our lungs. We picture in our minds eye feelings of invigoration, and finding it immortality. We create the atmosphere of passing from storm and tempest to an unbroken calm. In our dreams we pre-play the self-fulfilling prophecy of awakening, and finding it Home.

A successful evangelical minister offered a recipe for success: "Read yourself full, think yourself straight, pray yourself hot, and let yourself go!" (J. Douglas Gibb). The first three admonitions involve preparation and set the stage for purposeful action, when we can really "let ourselves go."

Strangers in The Land

"For the Lord will
have mercy on Jacob, and
will yet choose Israel, and set them
in their own land; and the strangers
shall be joined with them, and they shall
cleave to the house of Jacob."
(2 Nephi 24:1).

In one of his prophecies, when Isaiah was reassuring Israel that she would return to her own land in the last days, he said something quite striking: "And the strangers shall be joined with them, and they shall cleave to the house of Jacob." (Isaiah 14:1). Just who are these "strangers," and what claim could they possibly have on the blessings of Israel through the Covenant?

The Prophet Ezekiel was one of the captives of Judah carried away by Nebuchadnezzar into Babylonia. He began to prophesy in Israel around 498 B.C., just 11 years before Jerusalem and the Kingdom of Judah fell. He wrote: "And it shall come to pass that ye shall divide (the land) by lot for an inheritance unto you, and to the strangers that sojourn among you, which shall beget children among you; and they shall be unto you as born in the country among the children of Israel; they shall have inheritance with you among the tribes of Israel." (Ezekiel 47:22).

Nephi understood this broad concept of "strangers" living among the children of the covenant. He made the bold declaration that righteousness before the Lord is more important than lineage, when he wrote: "As many of the Gentiles as will repent are the covenant people of the Lord; and as many of the Jews as will not repent shall be cast off; for the Lord covenanteth with none save it be with them that repent and believe in his Son, who is the Holy One of Israel." (2 Nephi 30:2). Nephi wanted his people to know that the converted Gentiles who were not of the House of Israel would be numbered among the Covenant People of the Lord. This may have been as difficult for Nephi to teach his people as it was for Paul to teach the Jewish Christians of his day. Sometimes, it even seems difficult for members of the L.D.S. Church to understand that the gospel of Jesus Christ is to be shared with the world, and that sinners are welcome in the congregations of the Saints.

One of the greatest treasures in The Book of Mormon describes in language plain and simple the universality of God's love for all of His children: "He inviteth them all to come unto him and partake of his goodness; and he denieth none that come unto him, black and white, bond and free, male and female; and he remembereth the heathen; and all are alike unto God, both Jew and Gentile." (2 Nephi 26:33).

In the Last Days, then, Israel must be viewed from three perspectives: Blood Israel, or the ancient covenant people of the Lord; Covenant Israel, or those who accept Christ and His covenants and who are by adoption members of the house of Israel, and who thus have rights to the blessings of Abraham; and Land Israel, or those whose ancestors have inhabited the Land of Promise since ancient times.

Isaiah 14:2 tells us that unnamed foreigners will assist latter-day Blood & Covenant Israel in gathering to their lands of promise. "And the people shall take them and bring them to their place: yea, from far unto the ends of the earth; and they shall return to their lands of promise." Note the plural form of the noun: "lands." Israel shall govern these lands, and she shall preside over those who were her former taskmasters. "And the house of Israel shall possess them, and the land of the Lord shall be for servants and handmaids; and they shall take them captives unto whom they were captives; and they shall rule over their oppressors." In that day, Israel shall rest from millennia of sorrow, fear, and bondage. And it shall come to pass in that day that the Lord shall give thee rest, from thy sorrow, and from thy fear, and from the hard bondage wherein thou wast made to serve." (Isaiah 14:3).

The Covenant that is of significance to Blood Israel and Covenant Israel did not originate with Father Abraham. He received the Covenant of Salvation, or baptism, and then the Higher Priesthood and the Covenant of Exaltation, or Celestial Marriage, as had Adam and his righteous posterity. As Abraham wrote: "And, finding there was greater happiness and peace and rest for me, I sought for the blessings of the fathers, and the right whereunto I should be ordained to administer the same; having been myself a follower of righteousness, desiring also to be one who possessed great knowledge, and to be a greater follower of righteousness, and to possess a greater knowledge, and to be a father of many nations, a prince of peace, and desiring to receive instructions, and to keep the commandments of God, I became a rightful heir, and High Priest, holding the right belonging to the fathers. It was conferred upon me from the fathers; it came down from the fathers, from the beginning of time, yea, even from the beginning, or before the foundation of the earth, down to the present time." (Abraham 1:1-2).

Abraham was given the unique promise that through his seed, all the nations of the earth should be blessed. Thereby, Heavenly Father was able to bless others through "Blood Israel" or those of the lineage of Abraham, by offering them the priesthood ordinances of salvation, that they might also become "Covenant Israel," or those who, by adoption, enjoy the blessings promised to Abraham.

However, Land Israel, identified by both Isaiah and Ezekiel, will be among those who will receive the blessings associated with habitation of the Promised Land. Today, there are over 60 million Arabs living in the Middle East who are also children of Abraham through Ishmael; many live in Israel and in its annexed territories. It will be interesting to see just how the Lord chooses to remember these of His children.

(Our) Strengths & Weaknesses

"I give unto men weakness that they may be humble; and my grace is sufficient for all men that humble themselves before me; for if they humble themselves before me, and have faith in me, then will I make weak things become strong unto them."
(Ether 12:27).

"We generally think of Satan attacking us at our weakest spot. But weakness is not our only vulnerability. Satan can also attack us where we think we are strong, in the very areas where we are proud of our strengths. He will approach us through the greatest talents and spiritual gifts we possess. If we are not wary, Satan can cause our spiritual downfall by corrupting us through our strengths, as well as by exploiting our weaknesses." (Dallin Oaks, "Ensign," 10/1994).

Just before King David died, Zadok the priest and Nathan the prophet anointed Solomon as the new king of Israel. Solomon, who was a son of David and Bathsheba, received the following counsel from his father: "Be thou strong… and shew thyself a man; and keep the charge of the Lord thy God, to walk in his ways, to keep his statutes, and his commandments, and his judgments, and his testimonies … that thou mayest prosper in all that thou doest" (1 Kings 2:2-3).

Soon after Solomon became king, the Lord appeared to him in a dream and said: "Ask what I shall give thee." (1 Kings 3:5). Solomon replied: "Give, therefore, thy servant an understanding heart to judge thy people, that I may discern between good and bad." (1 Kings 3:9). The Lord granted his request, "and all Israel heard of the judgment which the king had judged; and they feared the king: for they saw that the wisdom of God was in him, to do judgment." (1 Kings 3:28). "And God gave Solomon wisdom and understanding exceeding much." (1 Kings 4:29).

Solomon must have felt he had a special need for that blessing, because the scriptures record his heartfelt prayer: "And now, O Lord my God, thou hast made thy servant king instead of David my father: and I am but a little child: I know not how to go out or come in." (1 Kings 3:7-8). The Lord was pleased with Solomon's request for an understanding heart, and "said unto him, because thou hast asked this thing, and hast not asked for thyself long life; neither hast asked riches for thyself, nor hast asked the life of thine enemies; but hast asked for thyself understanding to discern judgment; Behold, I have done according to thy words: lo, I have given thee a wise and an understanding heart; so that there was none like thee before thee, neither after thee shall any arise like unto thee." (1 Kings 3:11-12).

Today, the Lord grants similar spiritual gifts to His unselfish servants. "To some it is given by the Holy Ghost to know that Jesus Christ is the Son of God, and that he was crucified for the sins of the world. To others it is given to believe on their words, that they also might have eternal life if they continue faithful. And again, to some it is given by the Holy Ghost to know the differences of administration, as it will be pleasing unto the same Lord, according as the Lord will, suiting his mercies according to the conditions of the children of men. And again, it is given by the Holy Ghost to some to know the diversities of operations, whether they be of God, that the manifestations of the Spirit may be given to every man to profit withal. And again, verily I say unto you, to some is given, by the Spirit of God, the word of wisdom. To another is given the word of knowledge, that all may be taught to be wise and to have knowledge. And again, to some it is given to have faith to be healed; And to others it is given to have faith to heal. And again, to some is given the working of miracles; And to others it is given to prophesy; And to others the discerning of spirits. And again, it is given to some to speak with tongues; And to another is given the interpretation of tongues. And all these gifts come from God, for the benefit of the children of God." (D&C 46:13-26).

The Lord told Solomon He would grant him these gifts of the Spirit, with conditions: "If thou wilt walk in my ways, to keep my statutes and my commandments, as thy father David did walk, then I will lengthen thy days." (1 Kings 3:14).

The first situation requiring King Solomon's judgment concerned a child custody dispute. "And the king said, Bring me a sword. And they brought a sword before the king. And the king said, divide the living child in two, and give half to the one, and half to the other. Then spake the woman whose the living child was unto the king, for her bowels yearned upon her son, and she said, O my lord, give her the living child, and in no wise slay it. But the other said, Let it be neither mine nor thine, but divide it. Then the king answered and said, Give her the living child, and in no wise slay it: she is the mother thereof." (1 Kings 3:24-27).

During his reign, King Solomon oversaw the construction of a temple. He said: "I purpose to build an house unto the name of the Lord my God, as the Lord spake unto David my father, saying, Thy son, whom I will set upon thy throne in thy room, he shall build an house unto my name." (1 Kings 5:5). Regarding the temple, the Lord promised Solomon: "Concerning this house which thou art in building, if thou wilt walk in my statutes, and execute my judgments, and keep all my commandments to walk in them; then will I perform my word with thee, which I spake unto David thy father: And I will dwell among the children of Israel, and will not forsake my people Israel." (1 Kings 6:11-13).

Today, the Lord has similarly promised: "And inasmuch as my people build a house unto me in the name of the Lord, and do not suffer any unclean thing to come into it, that it be not defiled, my glory shall rest upon it; Yea, and my presence shall be there, for I will come into it, and all the pure in heart that shall come into it shall see God. But if it be defiled I will not come into it, and my glory shall not be there; for I will not come into unholy temples." (D&C 97:15-17).

Following seven years of construction, in the temple dedicatory prayer, Solomon asked for answers to prayers, forgiveness, rain, help during famine and sickness, and help in battle. (1 Kings 8). Ezra Taft Benson said of the latter-day house of the Lord: "In the peace of these lovely temples, sometimes we find solutions to the serious problems of life. Under the influence of the Spirit, sometimes pure knowledge flows to us there. Temples are places of personal revelation. When I have been weighed down by a problem or a difficulty, I have gone to the House of the Lord with a prayer in my heart for answers. These answers have come in clear and unmistakable ways." ("Liahona," 6/1992).

Solomon prayed that the temple would help lead unbelievers to the Lord. (1 Kings 8:41-43). "Moreover concerning a stranger that is not of thy people Israel, but cometh out of a far country for thy name's sake; (For they shall hear of thy great name, and of thy strong hand, and of thy stretched out arm;) when he shall come and pray toward this house; Hear thou in heaven thy dwelling place, and do according to all that the stranger calleth to thee for: that all people of the earth may know thy name, to fear thee, as do thy people Israel; and that they may know that this house, which I have builded, is called by thy name." (1 Kings 8:41-43).

After he offered the dedicatory prayer, Solomon counseled his people: "Let your heart…be perfect with the Lord our God." (1 Kings 8:61). He directed that "two and twenty thousand oxen, and an hundred and twenty thousand sheep" be sacrificed as an offering to the Lord during the dedication. (1 Kings 8:63). Then, "on the eighth day he sent the people away: and they blessed the king, and went unto their tents joyful and glad of heart for all the goodness that the Lord had done for David his servant, and for Israel his people." (1 Kings 8:66).

Following the dedication of the temple, the Lord cautioned Solomon, saying: "I have heard thy prayer and thy supplication, that thou hast made before me: I have hallowed this house, which thou hast built, to put my name there for ever; and mine eyes and mine heart shall be there perpetually. And if thou wilt walk before me, as David thy father walked, in integrity of heart, and in uprightness, to do according to all that I have commanded thee, and wilt keep my statutes and my judgments: Then I will establish the throne of thy kingdom upon Israel for ever, as I promised to David thy father, saying, There shall not fail thee a man upon the throne of Israel. But if ye shall at all turn from following me, ye or your children, and will not keep my commandments and my statutes which I have set before you, but go and serve other gods, and worship them. Then will I cut off Israel out of the land which I have given them; and this house, which I have hallowed for my name, will I cast out of my sight; and Israel shall be a proverb and a byword among all people: And at this house, which is high, every one that passeth by it shall be astonished, and shall hiss; and they shall say, Why hath the Lord done thus unto this land, and to this house? And they shall answer, Because they forsook the Lord their God, who brought forth their fathers out of the land of Egypt, and have taken hold upon other gods, and have worshipped them, and served them: therefore, hath the Lord brought upon them all this evil." (1 Kings 9:3-9).

As time passed, Solomon became obnoxiously wealthy and married non-Israelite women out of the covenant, who persuaded him to worship idols. He "exceeded all the kings of the earth for riches and for wisdom." (1 Kings 10:23). But he "loved many strange women, together with the daughter of Pharaoh, women of the Moabites, Ammonites, Edomites, Zidonians, and Hittites; Of the nations concerning which the Lord said unto the children of Israel, Ye shall not go in to them, neither shall they come in unto you: for surely they will turn away your heart after their gods: Solomon clave unto these in love." (1 Kings 11:1-2).

"And he had seven hundred wives, princesses, and three hundred concubines: and his wives turned away his heart… after other gods: and his heart was not perfect with the Lord his God." (1 Kings 11:3-4). Note that J.S.T. 1 Kings 11:4 adds the following: "and it became as the heart of David his father." Then the order of expressions in verse 6 is significantly changed in the J.S.T. from: "And Solomon did evil in the sight of the Lord, and went not fully after the Lord, as did David his father," to read: "And Solomon did evil in the sight of the Lord, as David his father, and went not fully after the Lord."

To forewarn Solomon, and to guard against the possibility that his strengths might result in his downfall, the Lord had counseled Solomon: "Let your heart, therefore, be perfect with the Lord our God, to walk in his statutes, and to keep his commandments, as at this day." (1 Kings 8:61). Nevertheless, Solomon's blessings of wisdom, riches, and honor ultimately contributed to his downfall, and he lost his kingdom. "And the time that Solomon reigned in Jerusalem over all Israel was forty years. And Solomon slept with his fathers, and was buried in the city of David his father: and Rehoboam his son reigned in his stead." (1 Kings 11:42-43).

The Lord has similarly warned Latter-day Israel to be true and faithful to her covenants, promising: "If your eye be single to my glory, your whole bodies shall be filled with light, and there shall be no darkness in you; and that body which is filled with light comprehendeth all things." (D&C 88:67).

To prevent our strengths from becoming our downfall, humility can be the catalyst for all learning, and the greatest antidote against pride. Through the prophet Moroni, the Lord gave us insight into the role of humility: "I give unto men weakness that they may be humble; and my grace is sufficient for all men that humble themselves before me; for if they humble themselves before me, and have faith in me, then will I make weak things become strong unto them." (Ether 12:27).

We can prevent the adversary from exploiting our spiritual gifts if we are humble and teachable, and listen to the promptings of the Spirit. We can rely on the Lord's direction and promise: "Be thou humble; and the Lord thy God shall lead thee by the hand, and give thee answer to thy prayers." (D&C 112:10).

Studying the Scriptures

"The word (of God)
had a great tendency to lead
people to do that which is just. Yea, it
had had more powerful effect upon the
minds of the people, than the sword, or
anything else which had happened to
them. Therefore, Alma thought it
was expedient that they should
try the virtue of the word."
(Alma 31:5).

If your house were on fire, as you made your way to safety, you would grab only that which was most valuable. When Lehi and his family fled persecution in Jerusalem, they initially took only that which was really important to them, namely the provisions necessary to sustain them as they journeyed through the wilderness to the Land of Promise.

However, it was not long before Lehi's sons returned to Jerusalem at the Lord's command, in order to rescue from Laban's treasury something of even greater value, namely, The Plates of Brass. First, Laman, Lemuel, and Nephi stopped by their former home, where they gathered up all the temporal wealth they had left behind. They took this to Laban, where it was offered in exchange for their precious scriptures.

But in order to prove to them that He is mightier than man, the Lord did not allow Lehi's sons to so easily receive His spiritual gifts in exchange for profane baubles and worldly ornaments. Their hopes seemed dashed when, without receiving the desired records, they lost all their telestial trinkets to the unscrupulous Laban. When Laman and Lemuel immediately thereafter complained that their fortune had slipped through their fingers, Nephi countered that whenever the Lord gives a commandment, He provides a way for us to fulfil our obligation. In their case, it would be through the Lord's divine intervention that they would learn that sacrifice consists of giving up one thing for something else that is even better.

Was it worth the effort? We can decide for ourselves, as we study the chapters in The Book of Mormon that are direct quotations from The Plates of Brass, as well as by reading many other chapters that are commentaries on these scriptures, such as 1 Nephi 20 & 21, 2 Nephi 7 & 8, 12 - 24, 27, Jacob 5, and 3 Nephi 22-25.

We can also measure the value of their effort when we read about what happened to the People of Zarahemla who were contemporaries of the Nephites, but who were not able to take their scriptures with them when they also fled Jerusalem a few years later. Their language eventually became corrupted, but more importantly, without the scriptures they lost their faith, as well.

If we desire the treasure of a testimony, we should ponder the declaration of the Savior: "These words are not of men nor of man, but of me; wherefore, you shall testify they are of me and not of man; For it is my voice which speaketh them unto you; for they are given by my Spirit unto you, and by my power you can read them one to another; and save it were by my power you could not have them. Wherefore, you can testify that you have heard my voice, and know my words." (D&C 18:34-36).

Some guidelines that should accompany our scripture study include the following:

Pray before beginning. We slow down our minds to free ourselves from the cares and concerns of the world. As we read, and as we have questions, we continue to pray for understanding.

Keep writing materials handy. Reading can be a stimulating activity, and often, ideas or original thoughts that we will want to develop later will creep into our minds. These may be fleeting, so we need to be ready to capture them on paper.

Go slowly. For a change, this study is not a race. We do not have to finish a prescribed number of chapters or verses each day. We linger over a single chapter or verse, turning the concepts over and over in our minds. We are amazed at the fresh perspectives that turn up.

Read topically. We search the scriptures to see what other prophets have said about the same subjects. As we memorize a scripture, neural pathways are created that will bloom with hidden meanings we hadn't been aware of.

Ask questions as you read. We turn scriptural statements into introspective questions and allow the Holy Ghost to illuminate our minds with answers, but only after we have posed good questions.

Stop your busy activities during the day. We make time to think about the scriptures we are currently studying. We let our minds work on their application to our lives' experiences, and as we relate to them more personally they assume an importance and relevance they might not otherwise have had.

Ponder and pray, rather than wander and play. The Savior said of the scriptures: "I leave these sayings with you to ponder in your hearts, with this commandment which I give unto you, that ye shall call upon me while I am near. Draw near unto me and I will draw near unto you." (D&C 88:62-63). God, Who cannot lie, has promised us that our eyes may be opened by the power of the Spirit, and our understandings enlightened, so as to see and understand the things of God. (D&C 76:12).

Believe that your study will make a difference. Ezra Taft Benson declared, "The Book of Mormon will change your life. It will fortify you against the evils of our day. It will bring a spirituality into your life that no other book will. It will be the most important book you will read in preparation for a mission and for life. A young man who knows and loves The Book of Mormon, who has read it several times, who has an abiding testimony of its truthfulness, and who applies its teachings will be able to stand against the wiles of the devil and will be a mighty tool in the hands of the Lord." (C.R., 4/1986).

Divide your time among all the Standard Works. Joseph Fielding Smith said of The Doctrine & Covenants: "In my judgment, there is no book on earth yet come to man as important as the book known as the Doctrine and Covenants, with all due respect to The Book of Mormon, and the Pearl of Great Price. The book of Doctrine and Covenants to us stands in a peculiar position above them all. This Doctrine and Covenants contains the word of God to those who dwell here now. It is our book. It belongs to the Latter-day Saints." ("Doctrines of Salvation," 3:198-199).

Acknowledge the power of the Bible to change your life. Victor Ludlow described how Latter-day Saints view the Bible: "The Bible stands at the foundation of The Church of Jesus Christ of Latter-day Saints. In 1820 a New Testament passage in the epistle of James prompted the young Joseph Smith to ask God about the religions of his time, and thereupon he received his first vision. Three years later, Old Testament and New Testament passages provided the principal scriptural foundation of Joseph's second major spiritual experience when the angel Moroni appeared to him and taught him from Malachi, Isaiah, Joel, Daniel, and other scriptures. After completing The Book of Mormon Translation and organizing the restored Church of Jesus Christ in 1830, the Prophet Joseph Smith thoroughly studied the Bible as instructed by the Lord and prepared the Joseph Smith Translation of the Bible (JST)." ("A Companion to Your Study of The Old Testament").

Determine to be scripturally literate. One who will not read is more pitiable than one who cannot read. President Benson declared: "Oh, my brethren, let us not treat lightly the great things we have received from the hand of the Lord. His word is one of the most valuable gifts He has given us. I urge you to recommit yourselves to a study of the scriptures. Read them in your families, and teach your children to love and treasure them. Then, prayerfully and in counsel with others, seek every way possible to encourage the members of the church to follow your example. If you do, you will find, as Alma did, that 'the word (has) a great tendency to lead people to do that which is just, yea, it (has) more powerful effect upon the minds of the people, than the sword, or anything else which (has) happened to them.'. (Alma 31:5).". (C.R., 4/1986).

If we desire the
treasure of testimony, we
should ponder the words of the Savior:
"These words are not of men nor of man, but
of me; wherefore, you shall testify they are of me
and not of man; For it is my voice which speaketh
them unto you; for they are given by my Spirit
unto you, and by my power you can read them
one to another; and save it were by my power
you could not have them. Wherefore, you
can testify that you have heard my
voice, and know my words."
(D&C 18:34-36).

Success Strategies

"I say unto you that ye shall
have hope through the atonement of
Christ and the power of his resurrection,
to be raised up unto life eternal, and
this because of your faith in him
according to the promise."
(Moroni 7:41).

Because they had already proven themselves in the crucible of adversity and temptation, the Master called His disciples to an even higher plane of spirituality and to a commitment by covenant to selfless consecration of effort. He advised them to "lay up for (themselves) treasures in heaven, where neither moth nor rust doth corrupt, and where thieves do not break through nor steal." (3 Nephi 13:19-20). To help them accomplish this task, He identified a number of strategies, the implementation of which would be key to overcoming telestial tendencies and maintaining stability in an uncertain world.

First, He inspired his disciples to lose themselves in service and to focus their attention on their less fortunate brethren. In doing so, He knew that they would eventually be brought into complete harmony with divine attributes. Patterning their lives after His would transform their nature as they assumed both the image and likeness of God. "And ye shall be even as I am, and I am even as the Father, and the Father and I are one," said the Savior. (3 Nephi 28:10). Secondly, He asked His disciples to exercise saving faith in Him and in His gospel. The standard of the world is: "Seeing is believing." is believing." But as Harold B. Lee taught: "You must learn to walk to the edge of the light, and then a few steps into the darkness; then the light will appear and show the way before you." ("B.Y.U. Today," 3/1991, p. 22-23). This is the way faith is developed and strengthened.

The Savior encouraged His disciples to exercise faith, rather than rely upon their own experience as the sole arbiter of all things. A classic definition of faith in the scriptures is that it "is not to have a perfect knowledge of things; therefore, if ye have faith ye hope for things which are not seen, which are true." (Alma 32:21). This is correct in the ultimate sense. In Alma's usage, the verse might more clearly read: "Faith is not to have a perfect knowledge of things gained through our own experience." Trust in the physical senses only is the rational approach that is the enemy of faith.

The Savior knew that the development of faith follows a natural progression, and that our success in life hinges upon a deeper and more abiding faith, "the substance of things hoped for, the evidence of things not seen." (Hebrews 11:1). This is true during the genesis of faith, as our desire to believe propels us out of darkness into the light. Then, under proper circumstances, when the stage has been set by our purposeful preparation, when the necessary groundwork has been laid, "by doing our duty, faith increases until it becomes perfect knowledge." (Heber J. Grant, C.R., 4/1934). Initially, faith is to believe what we do not see, and the reward of faith is to see what we believe, with clear understanding and perfect familiarity. Flawless faith implies ownership of the principle toward which our efforts have carried us. Its acquisition does not have a monetary cost and it cannot be purchased at any price. Instead, it carries a performance cost. It must be earned and then paid for by that which is of greatest worth. Those who desire to obtain it must not hold anything back. They must invest everything they have, including their trust, confidence, conviction, assurance, anticipation, and expectation in its ability to deliver on its promise.

Ultimately, our success or failure will be determined in the crucible of adversity, for we "receive no witness until after the trial of (our) faith." (Ether 12:6). It is important to remember that in matters of faith the Lord is not on trial. At the Bar of Justice, our previous acceptance or rejection of the evidence presented to the Judge will determine our reward or punishment. The trial of our faith is eminently fair.

Faith is an essential element in our success strategy because it is the foundation of our hope in Christ, with the assurance of peace and the comfort of our convictions that the momentum in our lives will carry us heavenward. As Mormon taught, hope is born of faith. He said that we should "have hope through the atonement of Christ and the power of his resurrection, to be raised up unto life eternal, and this because of (our) faith in him according to the promise." (Moroni 7:41). Hope is more than wishful thinking, misguided trust in promises that cannot be fulfilled, or a high stakes gamble based on statistical improbabilities. Hopeful people do not write checks they cannot cash. Their hope is the reasonable expectation of promised blessings that flow from obedience. It is the inevitable reward of well-founded faith, and is the interest earned on an investment made in their undeviating trust in God and in the principles of the gospel.

These success strategies ultimately carry us to a new dimension, that of charity, which is the supreme characteristic of faithful disciples. Mormon taught: "If a man be meek and lowly in heart, and confess by the power of the Holy Ghost that Jesus is the Christ," with a sure hope born of faith, "he must needs have charity." (Moroni 7:44).

Charity is patient and nurtures sensitivity toward others. It is empathic and is less concerned with telestial trinkets and is more focused on celestial sureties. It is humble and selfless, reflects poise under provocation, and has no secret agenda to follow. Repulsed by sin, it is drawn toward the light, and is continually open and receptive to that which is good.

Without it, we cannot progress, and our lives are empty shells of wasted efforts. As Paul said: "Though I speak with the tongues of men and of angels, and have not charity, I am become as sounding brass, or a tinkling cymbal." (1 Corinthians 13:1). Mormon confirmed: "If ye have not charity, ye are nothing, for charity never faileth. Wherefore, cleave unto charity, which is the greatest of all (the spiritual gifts), for all things must fail" without it. (Moroni 7:46). Because "charity is the pure love of Christ ... it endureth forever, and whoso is found possessed of it at the last day, it shall be well with him." (Moroni 7:47). By motivating us to Christian service, it prepares us to be like God. It is a gift of His grace, designed to reconfigure our carnality and elevate us to exaltation.

The Lord admonished us to be full of faith, to be bright with hope, to abound in charity, and to develop other noble character traits, such as "virtue, knowledge, temperance, patience, brotherly kindness, godliness, humility, (and) diligence." (D&C 4:6). We do this, Peter wrote: "That we might be partakers of the divine nature." (2 Peter 1:4). When God said: "Let us make man in our image, after our likeness," He meant not only that we should have the same physical qualities as our Parents, but the same spiritual characteristics as well. (Moses 2:26). When we are like-minded, we seek each other out, are drawn to each other, have a natural affinity for each other, stand by each other, comfort and encourage each other, and bring out the best in each other. "For this end was the law given," to prepare us to be Christ-like. When the Law illuminates these personality traits "we are made alive in Christ." (2 Nephi 25:25).

We cannot have sustained successes in life without the constant nourishment of the Holy Scriptures whose purpose is to testify of the Savior. Alma recognized the virtue of the word, or in other words, the incredible power of Christ to touch our hearts. Many examples from His life teach this principle. On one particular occasion, the multitudes were drawn to Him as they often were, because in Him their innermost yearnings were satisfied. Jesus, in turn, being a wellspring of the Spirit sensed each moment when need drew upon that source: "And a certain woman, which had an issue of blood twelve years ... when she had heard of Jesus, came in the press behind, and touched his garment. For she said, If I may touch but his clothes, I shall be whole. And straightway she felt in her body that she was healed. And Jesus, immediately knowing in himself that virtue had gone out of him, turned him about and said, Who touched my clothes?" (Mark 5:25-30).

This episode assures us that, in a wonderfully whole and complete manner, God is sensitive to our needs and to our prayers, however small or insignificant they may seem in the grand scheme. He does hear us, because in conformity to law, we draw upon the source of virtue that is the Spirit of God. Every time we call upon God, we are, in effect, touching His garment. How it is accomplished no-one can describe, for it must be directly experienced. "The wind bloweth where it listeth, and thou hearest the sound thereof, but canst not tell whence it cometh, and whither it goeth. So is everyone that is born of the Spirit." (John 3:8).

Spiritual fluency is facilitated by scriptural literacy, and both lead to direct experience with God. As the Lord explained in the Doctrine & Covenants: "These words are not of men, nor of man, but of me; wherefore, you shall testify they are of me and not of man. For it is my voice which speaketh them unto you; for they are given by my Spirit unto you, and by my power you can read them one to another; and save it were by my power you could not have them. Wherefore, you can testify that you have heard my voice, and know my words." (D&C 18:34-36). S. Dilworth Young said: "When I read a verse in the Doctrine & Covenants, I am hearing the voice of the Lord, as well as reading His words, if I hear by the Spirit." (C.R., 4/1963).

As Jacob put it: "No man knoweth of (God's) ways, save it be revealed unto him." (Jacob 4:8). "No matter what ability and talent we may possess, all must come under this rule if we wish to know the Father and the Son. If knowledge of them is not obtained through revelation it cannot be obtained at all." (John Taylor, "The Gospel Kingdom," p. 112). The light and knowledge we receive of God is given by personal revelation when truth speaks directly to our soul.

We easily observe the disastrous consequences of disregard for the Lord's success strategies. Particularly destructive are the habit patterns of those who are enslaved by drunkenness, selfish indulgence, or intemperance. "O God, that men should put an enemy in their mouths to steal away their brains! That we should...transform ourselves into beasts!" (Shakespeare, "Othello," Act 2, Scene 3).

"Wo unto them that rise up early in the morning, that they may follow strong drink, that continue until night, and wine inflame them!" (2 Nephi 15:11). Such people are blinded to the path of progress that is before them. "They regard not the work of the Lord, neither consider the operation of his hands." (2 Nephi 15:12). They are captive because their character is flawed. Their intemperance can never slake their spiritual thirst. On the contrary, both willful and ignorant misbehavior lead to inevitable consequences. As Isaiah prophesied, in the Last Days, even "honorable men (will be) famished, and their multitude dried up with thirst." (2 Nephi 15:13).

"Therefore, hell hath enlarged herself, and opened her mouth without measure; and their glory, and their multitude, and their pomp, and he that rejoiceth, shall descend into it. And the mean (or common) man shall be brought down, and the mighty man shall be humbled, and the eyes of the lofty shall be humbled. But the Lord of Hosts will be exalted in judgment, and God that is holy shall be sanctified in righteousness." (2 Nephi 15:14-16).

The Lord is patient and long-suffering. He is an eternal optimist with unflappable faith in His proven success strategies. He extends His arm of mercy long after the faint-hearted would have given up hope. When Elijah complained to the Lord: "The children of Israel have forsaken thy covenant, thrown down thine altars, and slain thy prophets with the sword; and I, even I only, am left; and they seek my life to take it away," the Lord responded: "Yet I have left me seven thousand in Israel, all the knees which have not bowed unto Baal, and every mouth which hath not kissed him." (1 Kings 19:14 & 18).

Satan's version of our success strategies is a recipe for disaster. His formula is the worst form of virulent infectious disease. When individuals venture onto his turf they are truly in the "Hot Zone." In fact, "the greatest crime in all this world is to lead men and women away from ... true principles" by recruiting them into the legions of the Adversary. (Joseph Fielding Smith, Jr., C.R., 4/1951). The bar must not be lowered by compromise or complacency to accommodate his ideology. There is a standard of human decency, concern, and brotherly kindness that is expected of each of us. It is part of the package we accepted when we sustained the Plan of Salvation.

Before Fiorello La Guardia became mayor of New York City, he was a magistrate. One day there appeared before him a man accused of stealing a loaf of bread. Upon questioning, the man explained that he'd committed the crime to feed his family, for they were starving. Whereupon, La Guardia dismissed the case, and sentenced all present in the courtroom to pay a fine for living in a city where a man must steal to feed his family.

The Lord illustrated the gospel principle of concern for the welfare of others when He said: "I am the bread of life: He that cometh to me shall never hunger; and he that believeth on me shall never thirst." (John 6:35). There will be for each of us an Eternal Court of Justice, where a penalty will be executed for our failure to provide others with the Bread of Life, or for feeding them only stale, or moldy, or otherwise unwholesome bread.

When we have internalized and personalized the success strategies taught by the Master, we will have a responsibility to strengthen others with these same principles. Thomas Carlyle said: "The mystic bond of brotherhood makes all men one." The family of man is, after all, "but one great city, full of beloved ones, divine and human, by nature endeared to each other." (Epictetus). We are an interdependent family, irrevocably committed and connected to each other. Our brotherhood "is an integral part of Christianity no less than the Fatherhood of God; and to deny the one is no less infidel than to deny the other." (Lyman Abbott).

Gospel links forge an unbreakable relationship with God. The covenants we make with Him are the keystones of our success strategies because they define the bounds and conditions describing how we can emulate Him. They reveal His nature and reflect His attributes. They address morality, chastity, charity, discipline, obedience, sacrifice, stewardship, and consecration. These parameters provide us with working definitions to make "eternal progression" a realistic goal.

God is perfect in every way. He could give us everything He has, but what He is, we must earn for ourselves, as we struggle to overcome adversity and gain self-mastery. Covenants help us to focus our efforts, and as we realize that it is possible to develop divine attributes, they become a vital part of our success strategy. The only motive strong enough to encourage us to exercise the self-control required by the covenants of the gospel of Jesus Christ is love. Hence, the Lord characterized our love of God and others as the two greatest commandments, and conceived success strategies interwoven into our covenants that would allow us to express love without at the same time either overstepping the bounds of propriety within the parameters of the Plan or jeopardizing our power to act independently.

There is a contrast between those who are stiff-necked and those whose faith gives them pliancy, plasticity, perception, and perspective allowing them to enjoy the companionship of the Holy Spirit or Holy Ghost, "which maketh manifest unto the children of men, according to their faith." (Jarom 1:4). Perhaps inflexibility prevents us from looking up to Heavenly Father for guidance, over to priesthood leaders for counsel, around to seek out those in need, or down in an attitude of humility. Such elasticity is a critical element of every success strategy.

Joseph F. Smith declared: "No man need fear in his heart when he is conscious of having lived up to the principles of truth and righteousness as God has required it at his hands, according to his best knowledge and understanding." (C.R., 4/1904, p. 97). When we are diligent in our obedience, our agency enjoys its greatest expression. This is one of the hardest things for the unconverted to understand.

Comforting words confirm the Lord's accessibility and receptivity: "Ask, and ye shall receive; knock, and it shall be opened unto you." (D&C 4:7). "Blessed are those which hunger and thirst after righteousness, for they shall be filled. (Matthew 5:6). Since receiving the Law of Christ is an ongoing process, wo unto those who do not feel the need for heavenly instruction. The Savior taught: "He that receiveth my law, and doeth it, the same is my disciple." (D&C 41:5).

As the Psalmist wrote: "Thou preparest a table before me in the presence of mine enemies; thou anointest my head with oil; my cup runneth over." (Psalms 23:5). While overindulgence is generally to be avoided, we cannot receive "too much of a good thing," if it is counsel and instruction from our Lord as He coaxes us to make success strategies habitual by internalizing gospel principles.

We need to look in the right places for our instruction and utilize the correct tools to achieve success. Anciently, the prophets repeatedly warned Israel against dalliances with magicians, sorcerers, witches, familiar spirits, astrologers, exorcists, and in participating in divinations, enchantments, and other activities that encourage or solicit the intervention of evil spirits. Isaiah mocked those who relied on such, when he said: "Thou art wearied in the multitude of thy counsels. Let now the astrologers, the stargazers, the monthly prognosticators, stand up, and save thee from these things that shall come upon thee. Behold, they shall be as stubble; the fire shall burn them; they shall not deliver themselves from the power of the flame; there shall not be a coal to warm at, nor fire to sit before it." (Isaiah 47:13-14).

Thousands of years later, the Prophet Joseph Smith asked: "Does it remain for a people who never had faith enough to call down one scrap of revelation from heaven, and for all they have now are indebted to the faith of another people who lived hundreds and thousands of years before them, does it remain for them to say how much God has spoken and how much he has not spoken?" (H.C. 11:17-18). Does it remain for them to ignorantly and erroneously define the very strategies for success that so maddeningly elude them?

Another time, he said: "We shall at last have to come to this conclusion, whatever we may think of revelation, that without it we can neither know nor understand anything of God, or the devil." ("Millennial Star," 19:275). The Book of Mormon attests to that fact. Within its pages, we learn truths about both God and the devil that are vital to our understanding if we are to negotiate the minefields of mortality in our quest for success.

Paul taught: The key to gospel knowledge of every sort is personal revelation, and "let him be accursed who preaches any other gospel." (Galatians 1:8-12). "That which is of God is light; and he that receiveth light, and continueth in God, receiveth more light: and that light groweth brighter and brighter until the perfect day." (D&C 50:24). Who could hope to be more successful than this?

God is the Author of the greatest
diversity on the planet earth. In fact, He created diversity
when He divided the light from the darkness, the waters from
the firmament, the heaven from the earth, the earth from the sea,
the day from the night, and when he created all manner of living
things, each to go forth and multiply after its own kind. His
quintessential act of creative diversity was when "male
and female created he them." (Genesis 1:27). He
may have even created Mars and Venus
specifically to be the habitation
of men and women,
respectively.

Symbols

"A good symbol is the best argument,
and is a missionary to persuade thousands."
(Ralph Waldo Emerson).

"And many signs, and wonders,
and types, and shadows showed he unto
them, concerning his coming."
(Mosiah 3:15).

A symbol is simply one thing that is the representation of something else. Because language is symbolic, when you process this essay you are reading letters that make up words that are only depictions of concepts with which you are familiar. Our minds grasp symbols from the simple to the profoundly complex. For example, the word GOD is made up of only three letters, but the symbolism behind the concept can be stirring. The ancient Hebrews, who dared not utter His sacred name, used the symbol YHWH ("Jehovah") instead, literally: "I am Who I Am." Such symbolism has no scope, depth, breadth, or height. It defies space and time and spans the eternities. Perhaps this is why God symbolically defines Himself as Alpha and Omega, the First and the Last, the Beginning and the End, and without beginning of days or end of years. At least superficially, we comprehend the symbols associated with God.

Symbols lubricate the flow of the scriptures. "In the beginning was the Word, and the Word was with God, and the Word was God." (John 1:1). We wrap our minds around the symbolism of entire bodies of scripture, such as in the Epistle of Paul to the Ephesians: "Put on the whole armour of God, that ye may be able to stand against the wiles of the devil. For we wrestle not against flesh and blood, but against principalities, against powers, against the rulers of the darkness of this world, against spiritual wickedness in high places. Wherefore take unto you the whole armour of God, that ye may be able to withstand in the evil day, and having done all, to stand. Stand therefore, having your loins girt about with truth, and having on the breastplate of righteousness; and your feet shod with the preparation of the gospel of peace; Above all, taking the shield of faith, wherewith ye shall be able to quench all the fiery darts of the wicked. And take the helmet of salvation, and the sword of the Spirit, which is the word of God." (Ephesians 6:11-17). We grasp the collective symbolism of the Old Testament. "Moreover, thou son of man, take thee one stick, and write upon it, for Judah, and for the children of Israel his companions; then take another stick, and write upon it, for Joseph, the stick of Ephraim, and for all the house of Israel his companions. And join them one to another into one stick; and they shall become one in thine hand." (Ezekiel 37:16-17).

Symbolism makes it possible to have faith in systematic organizations of religious tenets that are compartmentalized as Catholicism, or Evangelism, or "Mormonism." In a link entitled "Basic Beliefs," the church website (LDS.ORG) explains how symbols can create order in a chaotic world: "Your Heavenly Father knows you and loves you and wants to help you return to Him. Your life on Earth is part of His plan for you to gain a body, learn, grow, and find joy. Sometimes life is hard, lonely, or frightening, but your Heavenly Father is always there. He sorrows when you suffer and rejoices when you do what is right. He wants to communicate with you as you sincerely pray to Him, and He stands ready to give you comfort, peace, and guidance in your life. Jesus Christ taught that you must know the only true God to have eternal life. As His child, you must know who He is and what He is like to find greater peace and joy, both in this life and in the life to come."

Symbolism allows us to embrace an entire religious movement such as The restoration of the gospel. "The keys of the kingdom of God are committed unto man on the earth, and from thence shall the gospel roll forth unto the ends of the earth, as the stone which is cut out of the mountain without hands shall roll forth, until it has filled the whole earth." (D&C 65:2, See Daniel 2:45). On a grand scale, we maintain purposeful focus by using symbols to answer the questions relating to why we are here, where we came from, and where we are going. "And they who keep their first estate shall be added upon; and they who keep not their first estate shall not have glory in the same kingdom with those who keep their first estate; and they who keep their second estate shall have glory added upon their heads forever and ever." (Abraham 3:26). We define our divine purpose with symbols and call it The Plan of Salvation, the Plan of Redemption, and the Plan of Happiness, all centered on the Atonement of Jesus Christ. This takes us back to the being of God Himself, whom we simply call "Father."

Overlapping brain-maps enhance and potentiate our exteroceptive senses of sight, smell, taste, touch, hearing, and balance, the interoceptive senses of thermoception and nociception, and proprioception. Standing before the Christus on Temple Square, looking up in awe at the ceiling of the Sistine Chapel, or surrounded by the natural beauty of a sunset, we are enveloped in the experience. We are moved by inner stirrings that simply cannot be explained by the activation of neural pathways or hormonal secretions. When ecclesiastical leaders enter the Conference Center and we join with the choir singing "We Thank Thee O God for a Prophet," we are participating in a collective experience that cannot be explained by optic and auditory nerve stimulation alone. Such experiences have been described as tangible immersions in the element of the spirit. Symbolism is a catalyst for the emotions that permeate these experiences.

The ability of oral and written symbols to shape our minds is staggering. We have an incredibly powerful capacity to incorporate symbols into our collective consciousness. According to the Global Language Monitor (languagemonitor.com) there are 6,912 languages and dialects on earth. The various Chinese dialects utilize about 50,000 ideograms. In his complete works, Shakespeare used something on the order of 29,000 different words, about 1,700 of which he invented. There are about 20,000 different words in the King James Translation of the Bible, and a mind-boggling total of 995,112 words (give or take a few) in the English language.

Most of do reasonably well navigating through life, communicating with others, and personally interpreting the world around us through sensory input and perceptual processing (as long as we stick with our native tongue and don't stray into any of the other 6,911 languages and dialects). Albert Einstein's wife was once asked if she understood her husband's explanation of his theories of relativity. She said she understood the words, but not the sentences. That brings to mind another symbol, one that shaped the 20th Century: $E = MC^2$. There probably exists on earth no other expression that is so simple to articulate and yet is so complex, so universally recognized, and so little understood.

Another great mind, the brilliant theoretical physicist, Steven Hawking, wrote a watered-down version of his trail-blazing work on spacetime, entitled "A Brief History of Time," that attained a cult following and graced millions of coffee tables around the world. That it was seldom actually read, and rarely understood when it was, doesn't change the fact that it quickly became a symbol of our desire to recognize, acknowledge, and conceptually tackle some of the most challenging concepts that have flowed from the minds, pens, and computer programs of our academic icons. Each of us has created a personal learning laboratory in our own cerebral cortex. God has given us more than enough neural pathways to last a lifetime. Within our brains, each of our one hundred billion neurons has a direct connection via dendrites to sixty other neural axons. The possible combinations are literally endless (six thousand billion possible connections). Looking at it from a slightly different perspective, a one hundred forty-pound human being is made up of roughly ten trillion cells. Each cell is composed of twenty billion protein molecules. Each protein molecule has, on average, fourteen thousand atoms. Each atom has around forty-nine matter particles (nucleus, protons, electrons, etc.). Each of those average matter particles is composed of roughly one million photons, the basic units of electro-magnetic energy. The human body is one-billionth particle matter (composed of substance), and the rest is photons. Fundamentally, we are beings of light. We communicate on more than just a somatic level. The energy that drives us cannot be easily quantified, for we radiate with light. "Have ye spiritually been born of God?" asked Alma. "Have ye received his image in your countenances? Have ye experienced this mighty change in your hearts? If ye have experienced a change of heart, and if ye have felt to sing the song of redeeming love, I would ask, can ye feel so now?" (Alma 5:14&26). Those who draw upon this universal energy variously call it the Great Ocean of Thought, Ka, Teotl, the Force, Prana, Mana, the Great Spirit, Chakra, Yin/Yang, Ch'i, Tao, and the light of Christ.

We enter mortality as "children coming down like gentle rain through darkened skies, with glory trailing from our feet as we go, and endless promise in our eyes." (Doug Stewart, Saturday's Warrior). Truly did the poet observe: "Our birth is but a sleep and a forgetting. The soul that rises with us, our life's star, hath had elsewhere its setting, and cometh from afar. Not in entire forgetfulness, and not in utter nakedness, but trailing clouds of glory do we come, from God, Who is our Home." (Wordsworth). These inspiring words are true. We "are the sons (and daughters) of the living God." (Hosea 1:10). "The Spirit itself beareth witness with our spirit, that we are the children of God." (Romans 8:16).

The poets symbolically describe our place in the Cosmos that is at once intensely private, and, yet is molded by our communal interaction with our environment. But ultimately, we feather those nests that are uniquely our own. No-one is permitted to enter our inner sanctum without permission. Esau sold his birthright for a mess of pottage, evoking images that reflect far more than the forfeiture of a meal or personal possessions. In fact, he profaned a very special relationship and lost his identity as a chosen vessel of God.

Obviously, many symbols are peculiar to a given culture. These are idioms whose meaning "cannot be deduced from the literal definitions and the arrangements of their parts, but refers instead to a figurative meaning that is known only through common use." (Wikipedia). The operative words here are "common use." Sometimes, idioms leap across cultural boundaries through repetitive use. For example, we have commonality with the ancient Greeks because we study classical literature (even though their thoughts and expressions have been translated from Greek to English. Without such clarification, after all, it would be "Greek" to us). We understand Isaiah because we are students of the Bible and with the help of William Tyndale and the King James Translators we have become familiar with the nuances of Isaiah's unique style. Idiomatic expressions become ours as we study other cultures that coined terms or phrases that were once uniquely theirs.

Tyndale is a classic example of one who had the gift of inspired translation, and who has helped countless millions make the transition to a higher spiritual plane. He studied the New Testament in its original Hebrew and Greek in order to translate it into English. (He was fluent in French, Greek, German, Italian, Latin, and Spanish in addition to his native English). The results of his study were so spectacular that, in the following century, the 54 independent scholars revising the existing English translations of the Bible relied heavily upon his interpretations when creating the King James Translation. He became the mostly unrecognized translator of the most influential book in the world. He coined such beautiful and familiar phrases as: "let there be light, am I my brother's keeper, the salt of the earth, filthy lucre, the signs of the times, and fight the good fight." We can thank Tyndale for the expressions: "In the beginning, God created heaven and earth. The Lord bless thee and keep thee. The Lord make his face to shine upon thee and be merciful unto thee. The Lord lift up his countenance upon thee, and give thee peace. The spirit is willing, but the flesh is weak. In the beginning was the Word and the Word was with God and the Word was God. In him we live, move and have our being."

Plato used the contrasting symbols of light and darkness 2500 years ago, when he said: "The real tragedy in life is not children who are afraid of the dark, but men who are afraid of the light." The inherent symbolism moves us as much as it did the ancient Greeks. Such symbols possess layers of meaning, and as we would peel an onion, so we can move beyond simple symbolic recognition (think of Pavlov's dog salivating in anticipation of food at the sound of a bell) to profound comprehension.

The Savior relied on the same universal familiarity with light and darkness when He said: "Let your light so shine before men, that they may see your good works, and glorify your Father which is in heaven." (Matthew 5:16). He touched chords of commonality, rooting our faith in familiarity when He said: "Neither do men light a candle, and put it under a bushel, but on a candlestick; and it giveth light unto all that are in the house." (Matthew 5:15).

We easily slip into the use of metaphor and simile precisely because we are comfortable with symbolism. Isaac Newton said: "I was like a boy playing on the seashore, and diverting myself now and then finding a smoother pebble or a prettier shell than ordinary, while the great ocean of truth lay undiscovered before me." He was not talking as an adolescent, a lapidarist, or a mariner; rather, he was utilizing the power of metaphor clothed in symbolism to create a memorable statement of fact to the end that might motivate others to humble inquiry. Soapboxes are inherently symbolic. Those who stand on bully pulpits to promote social or political agendas gain the attention of the curious crowd by tantalizing them with the symbolism that is woven into their rhetoric. In the post-war era, sensing the shifting politics of the region, Winston Churchill warned: "Socialism is a philosophy of failure, the creed of ignorance, and the gospel of envy. Its inherent virtue is the equal sharing of misery." A literary invention of George Orwell, coined in 1948, has forever altered our view and symbolizes our mistrust of government: "Big Brother is watching you." ("1984").

Shakespeare employed symbolism to describe the evils of alcohol: "O God, that men should put an enemy in their mouths to steal away their brains! That we should with joy, pleasance revel, and applause transform ourselves into beasts!" (Cassio, "Othello," Act 2, Scene 3). Duke Orsino says: "If music be the food of love, play on. Give me excess of it; that surfeiting, the appetite may sicken, and so die." ("Twelfth Night," Act 1, Scene 1). Jacques reminds us: "All the world's a stage, and all the men and women merely players; they have their exits and their entrances, and one man in his time plays many parts, his acts being seven ages." ("As You Like It," Act 2, Scene 7). Richard laments: "Now is the winter of our discontent made glorious summer by this son of York; and all the clouds that low'r'd upon our house in the deep bosom of the ocean buried." ("Richard The Third," Act 1, Scene 1). Iago speaks of jealousy, "the green-ey'd monster, which doth mock the meat it feeds on." ("Othello," Act 3, Scene 3). And in Portia's estimation, the arrogant Prince of Aragon was "a blinking idiot." ("The Merchant of Venice," Act 2, Scene 9).

When describing his intimate familiarity with the mechanics of mathematical inquiry, Einstein employed equally powerful symbols: "A storm broke loose in my mind," he wrote. "A splendid light dawned on me." Of our own original ideas, we often simply say: "A light bulb went off in my head." When we have a stupor of thought, we declare: "I am having a brain freeze," or "a senior moment." If someone uses "gutter language," they aren't putting downspouts on their roofs, but on their tongues. We know instantly that we should avoid their company and conversation in order to remain free of the corruption created by their coarseness.

Our conversation is peppered with symbols and is particularly idiomatic, for example, when we say: "Lighten up, Dude!" As a matter of fact, when our speech is devoid of symbolism, it is often perceived as dry, uninteresting, and without passion. It figuratively falls flat on its face, short of its intended target. (Oh, there I go again, utilizing more symbolism to make my point.) Which one tugs at our heartstrings, a mathematical equation, or the poetry of Elizabeth Barrett Browning? $2 + 3 = 5$, $(x + 1)2 = x2 + 2x + 1$, or "How do I love thee? Let me count the ways. I love thee to the depth and breadth and height my soul can reach, when feeling out of sight for the ends of being and ideal grace. I love thee to the level of every day's most quiet need, by sun and candlelight. I love thee freely, as men strive for right; I love thee purely, as they turn from praise. I love thee with the passion put to use in my old griefs, and with my childhood's faith. I love thee with a love I seemed to lose with my lost saints! I love thee with the breath, smiles, and tears of all my life! And, if God choose, I shall but love thee better after death." ("Sonnets from the Portuguese"). Advertisers pay top dollar to find slogans that strike their audiences. Symbolism meets their demands: "Mr. Goodwrench." "Fly the friendly skies." "Put a tiger in your tank." "More bars." "Can you hear me now?" "Sharp minds, sharp products." "Welcome to the human network." "Think outside the bun." "So easy even a caveman can do it." "You deserve a break today." "Where's the beef?" "Are you in good hands?" "A diamond is forever." "It takes a licking and keeps on ticking." "Tang. It's a kick in the glass." "Do the Dew." "It's the pause that refreshes." "Breakfast of Champions." "Snap, crackle, and pop." "Sometimes you feel like a nut, sometimes you don't." "Born from jets." "Everything we do is driven by you." "Grab life by the horns." "Driven by passion." "When it pours, it reigns." "Loose lips sink ships." "Give a hoot, don't pollute." A fifteen-second sound bite (a symbol for an effective use of air-time) can be worth hundreds, of thousands of dollars to advertisers.

Today, we use symbols in ways we never before dreamed of: "It's all relative." We associate "The Twilight Zone" with inexplicable phenomena. We see symbols in movies like "The DaVinci Code" whose protagonist was a "religious symbologist." We take for granted "The Holy Grail" and "The Vitruvian Man." In "National Treasure," the secret lay with Charlotte. Its popular sequel was entitled: "The Book of Secrets," and it was chock-full of symbols. We even see symbols in nursery rhymes: "Ring around the rosie, a pocket full of posies, ashes, ashes, we all fall down." The poem has long been associated with the Plague or Black Death. A rosy rash was a symptom of plague, and posies of herbs were carried as talisman for protection from the dreaded disease. The victims' homes were burned to combat the disease, and of course, falling
down refers to death.

Even today, the symbolism of medieval fairy tales powerfully shapes our view of life. For example, when the people of Hamelin refused to pay the Pied Piper, he led the children away with his flute. This is a thinly veiled commentary on social values, family dynamics and personal psychology. Bedtime stories infused with images of mad hatters, Cheshire cats, fairy dust, pirate ships, talking frogs, wicked wolves who impersonate grandmothers, trolls in the forest, leprechauns, giants and beanstalks, geese that lay golden eggs, mermaids, lamps and genies, glass slippers and fairy godmothers, knights jousting with windmills, and magic carpets, dynamically influence our perspective on life.

Even common speech is symbolic. The word "man" can mean dozens of things, including any of these fifty, depending upon the context or even the inflexion of the voice, facial expression or body language: aide, ally, backup, being, body, boss, captain, con artist, character, creature, dad, deputy, earthling, fellow, fellow worker, folk, helper, hero, homo sapiens, human being, hunk, husband, individual, jock, lover, macho, man upstairs, man-about-town, master, master of the house, mentor, mortal, ordinary citizen, papa, person, personage, provider, soul, sir, spouse, stud, paterfamilias, patriarch, right-hand-man, superintendent, supervisor, top dog, valet, valiant, and vigorous.

"Woman" has even more symbolical emotional baggage attached to it, including these fifty: babe, beauty, broad, chick, cleaning lady, coquette, courtesan, cupcake, cutie, dame, damsel, doll, dowager, enchantress, female, filly, flirt, fox, gal, girl, girlfriend, hooker, household helper, hustler, kitten, lady, lass, lover, maid, mama, matron, mistress, model, old bat, old lady, partner, piece, pin-up, prostitute, seductress, servant, siren, socialite, spouse, sweetheart, tart, temptress, tomato, tootsie, vamp, wench, and wife.

Great orators have used symbolism. Shakespeare's Henry V exhorted his troops with the imagery of brotherhood before the Battle of Agincourt: "We few, we happy few, we band of brothers. For he today that sheds his blood with me shall be my brother, be he ne'er so vile. This day shall gentle his condition, and gentlemen in England now a-bed shall think themselves accursed they were not here, and hold their manhoods cheap whiles any speaks that fought with us upon Saint Crispin's day. ("Henry V," Act 4, Scene 3).

Abraham Lincoln addressed a severely divided nation in his First Inaugural Address by pleading: "We are not enemies, but friends. Though passion may have strained, it must not break our bonds of affection. The mystic chords of memory, stretching from every battlefield and patriot grave, to every living heart and hearthstone all over this broad land, will yet swell the chorus of the Union, when again touched, as surely they will be, by the better angels of our nature."

One day before his assassination, Martin Luther King, Jr. said: "I don't know what will happen now. We've got some difficult days ahead, but it doesn't matter with me now because I've been to the mountain top, and I don't mind. Like anybody, I would like to live a long life. Longevity has its place, but I'm not concerned about that now. I just want to do God's will. He's allowed me to go up to the mountain, and I've looked over and I've seen the Promised Land. I may not get there with you. But I want you to know tonight, that as a people we will get to the Promised Land. And I'm happy tonight. I'm not worried about anything. I'm not fearing any man. Mine eyes have seen the glory of the coming of the Lord." (Memphis, Tennessee, 4/3/1968). Before his fateful journey to Carthage Jail, Joseph Smith said: "I am going like a lamb to the slaughter, but I am calm as a summer's morning. I have a conscience void of offense towards God, and towards and all men." (D&C 135:4). His stirring words carried the church through difficult times and across harsh prairies to its own promised land. Spencer W. Kimball motivated another generation of Latter-day Saints when he encouraged them: "Lengthen your stride." In his book "Way to Be," President Gordon B. Hinckley outlined nine B's that can help us lead happy and productive lives: "Be Grateful," "Be Smart," "Be Involved," "Be Clean," "Be True," "Be Positive," "Be Humble," "Be Still," and "Be Prayerful."

In the 1950s, Premier Nikita Khrushchev told the West, "We will bury you." The symbolism of his tirade before the United Nations General Assembly marks the beginning of the Cold War even as it spurred the Free World to action. Then, on June 12, 1987, President Ronald Reagan spoke to the German people at the base of the Brandenburg Gate in West Berlin and challenged: "Mr. Gorbachev, tear down this wall!" That remark symbolized the end of the Cold War, because it fueled the fires of freedom within the Communist Block. Two years later the wall itself was physically dismantled, and the "Iron Curtain" fell. (The phrase "Iron Curtain" was coined by Winston Churchill, on March 5, 1946, in a speech delivered at Westminster College in Fulton, Missouri: "From Stettin in the Baltic to Trieste in the Adriatic, an iron curtain has descended across the Continent.") Freedom of expression and the ability to exercise free will is really a centuries-old process, aided along the way from the Founding Fathers who coined the expression "We the people" to Neal Armstrong, who declared in real time from the surface of the moon: "That's one small step for a man; one giant leap for mankind."

The following quote, attributed to Shakespeare and yet anonymous, recently made the rounds on the internet: "Beware the leader who bangs the drums of war in order to whip the citizenry into a patriotic fervor, for patriotism is indeed a double-edged sword. It emboldens the blood, but narrows the mind. For when the drums of war reach a fever pitch, the blood boils with hate, and minds have closed, the leader will have no need to seize the rights of the citizenry. Rather, the citizenry, infused with fear and blinded with patriotism, will offer up all of its rights to the leader, and gladly so. How do I know? For this is what I have done. And I am Caesar."

Winston Churchill rallied the British Empire when Fortress Europe and the German Wehrmacht were arrayed against it. He later acknowledged: "It was the nation and the race dwelling all round the globe that had the lion's heart. I had the luck to be called upon to give the roar." Imparting homespun wisdom, he once observed: "By swallowing evil words unsaid, no one has ever harmed his stomach." In each case, symbols helped him drive home the point. Today, we live in a world where information is dispensed in thirty-second sound bites and where teachers compete for the attention of students who are accustomed to six hours of television and video games every day. Children are influenced as they have always been by symbols, but when parents lose control of the connection that has been forged by culturally stable symbolism, the
results are disastrous.

The tools and trade of poets are symbols that are infused in their blood and find ready expression in their pens. "Lives of great men all remind us we can make our lives sublime, and, departing, leave behind us, footprints on the sands of time." (Longfellow). "With silent lifting mind I've trod the high untrespassed sanctity of space, put out my hand, and touched the face of God." (John G. Magee, Jr., "High Flight"). "Change comes like a flash of lightning and a clap of thunder. The people shrink in fear, but after the storm, flowers bloom." (I Ching). "Faith, the spiritual strong searchlight, illuminates the way, and although sinister doubts lurk in the shadow, I walk unafraid towards the Enchanted Wood where the foliage is always green, where joy abides, where nightingales nest and sing, and where life and death are one in the presence of the Lord." (Helen Keller). Symbols cast us off into a stream of revelation where we are carried along in the quickening currents of direct experience with God.

The media may find its greatest expression with symbols. "Mormons are like artichokes. At first encounter, you either like them or you don't. But those who have unfavorable first impressions often find that once the outer layers are peeled away, both Mormons and artichokes are most likable." ("Boston Globe," 1/22/1967). But it can be a two-edged sword. Spiro Agnew referred to the media, with whom he had an acrimonious relationship, as "the nattering nabob of negativism." (Address to the California Republican State Convention in San Diego on September 11, 1970).

Religious leaders frequently use the vivid imagery of symbolism. "The Priesthood is a robe of responsibility and not a cloak of comfort." (Thomas S. Monson, "Ensign," 7/2009). "The church is not an ecclesiastical country club situated on a narrow theological terrace." (Neal A. Maxwell, "New Era," 8/1971). "Lengthen your stride." (Spencer W. Kimball, "Ensign," 10/1974). "Don't be a pickle-sucker." (Gordon B. Hinckley, "B.Y.U. Devotional Address," 10/29/1974). "Much of what we do organizationally is scaffolding, as we seek to build the individual, and we must not mistake the scaffolding for the soul." (Harold B. Lee, "Stand Ye in Holy Places," p. 309). "Those who break windows to let in fresh air do not love fresh air so much as the sound of tinkling glass." (Richard L. Evans, quoted by James E. Faust, "B.Y.U. Devotional," 6/10/1975). "At the banquet of consequences there will not be much that is satisfying at the table, unless I am able to bow my head in reverence, not hang it in shame, in the presence of God who will be there." (Marion D. Hanks, (Marion D. Hanks, "B.Y.U. Address," 10/7/67). "The greatest exercise for the human heart is to reach down and lift another up." (Jon Huntsman, "Winners Never Cheat").

The scriptures are intensely idiomatic. In reference to both the mercy and justice of God, Genesis reports that He "drove out the man, and he placed at the east of the Garden of Eden Cherubims, and a flaming sword which turned every way, to keep the way of the tree of life." (Genesis 13:24). Isaiah described a seraph having "a live coal in his hand, which he had taken with the tongs from off the altar." (Isaiah 6:6). John beheld "a pale horse: and his name that sat on him was Death, and Hell followed with him." (Revelation 6:8). He described "a noisome and grievous sore upon the men which had the mark of the beast." (Revelation 16:2).

Even the oft' repeated phrase "and it came to pass" used hundreds of times in The Book of Mormon, could have symbolic antecedent. The Maya used a glyph with a similar meaning as a grammatical marker in their texts. Book of Mormon prophets could have also used a simple diacritical marker to do the same thing. This would have greatly facilitated the laborious task of engraving on plates of ore, while at the same time allowing the intended message to be easily conveyed and to flow freely.

Our Latter-day Saint tradition utilizes symbolism that is in "accord one with another – that which is earthly conforming to that which is heavenly." (D&C 128:9). As a matter of fact, of idiomatic speech the scriptures testify: "All things have their likeness, and all things are created and made to bear record of me." (Moses 6:63). We are all familiar with "another angel (who flew) in the midst of heaven, having the everlasting gospel to preach unto them that dwell on the earth, and to every nation, and kindred, and tongue, and people." (Revelation 14:6). We know exactly where, in the Last Days, "the mountain of the Lord's house shall be established, "and that it "shall be exalted above the hills, and all nations shall flow unto it." (Isaiah 2:2).

We immediately understand Who it is, of Whom Isaiah wrote: For unto us a child is born, unto us a son is given, and the government shall be upon his shoulder: and his name shall be called Wonderful, Counsellor, The Mighty God, The everlasting Father, The Prince of Peace. (Isaiah 9:6).

Other symbols are equally profoundly moving: "And out of the ground made the Lord God to grow every tree that is pleasant to the sight, and good for food, the tree of life also in the midst of the garden, and the tree of knowledge of good and evil." (Genesis 2:9). "But of the tree of the knowledge of good and evil, thou shalt not eat of it," Adam was commanded, "for in the day that thou eatest thereof thou shalt surely die." (Genesis 2:17). It has been argued that, at the time this commandment was given, "death" was a symbol with which Adam was completely unfamiliar.

"And the Lord God caused a deep sleep to fall upon Adam, and he slept: and he took one of his ribs, and closed up the flesh instead thereof; And the rib, which the Lord God had taken from man, made he a woman, and brought her unto the man." (Genesis 2:21-22). The scriptures go on to talk about the blood of lambs, scapegoats, winepresses, crosses, and bleeding from pores. They describe manna from heaven, wheat and tares, fertile and stony ground, sowers and reapers, bread, the staff of life, and wells of living water. They speak of talents, chariots of fire, cities set on hills, water pouring from rocks, burnt offerings, fire, smoke, whirlwinds, pavement of gold in color like amber, and voices as the sound of the rushing of great waters.

Sometimes, The Book of Mormon clarifies the symbolism of the Bible. "As he lifted up the brazen serpent in the wilderness, even so shall he be lifted up who should come." (Helaman 8:14). "And now, my son, I would that ye should understand that these things are not without a shadow … For behold, it is as easy to give heed to the word of Christ, which will point to you a straight course to eternal bliss, as it was for our fathers to give heed to this compass, which would point unto them a straight course to the promised land." (Alma 37:43-44).

This compass (the Liahoha) was a "type" of Christ that had symbolic significance as well as a literal meaning. There are repeated references to types in the Nephite record, for they are profoundly effective teaching tools. Outward observances without real meaning are only ceremonies. For example, when the bishop stands at the pulpit at the beginning of Sacrament Meeting, his greeting is a ceremony. His expression of thanks to the Aaronic Priesthood for a job well done after the administration of the Sacrament is a ceremony. The recognition of visitors to Relief Society and other meetings is largely ceremonial. These events pass without any lasting significance, and are only superficially acknowledged.

A rite that has a present spiritual meaning is a symbol. No one would dispute the symbolic significance of the bread and water used in the Sacrament; the prayer accompanying the ordinance reminds the participants of Christ's sacrifice and of their covenant relationship with Him. The ordinance of baptism is carried out in a font that is in similitude of the grave. In its waters, the repentant faithful symbolically wash away their sins, and emerge clean and pure in the sight of God. Christ Himself was baptized in Jordan, that is the lowest body of fresh water on earth, a river that flows into the Dead Sea at 1,385 feet below sea level. The symbolism cannot be lost on us: He figuratively and literally descended beneath us all.

In the font itself, both the officiant and recipient are dressed in white clothing that is symbolic of purity. The authority of the priesthood is vested in one who holds his right arm to the square in a symbolic gesture of the power of God. No one who has received a priesthood blessing when sick can deny the power of the rejuvenating symbolism of pure olive oil that has in turn been consecrated for the healing of the sick in the household of faith. There is symbolic significance in the olive tree itself. It is a living thing that produces good fruit and whose branch has always been associated with peace. But an olive tree cannot become productive by itself. It requires the grafting of a tame branch by a husbandman. Afterward, careful attention and pruning are required, because whenever the tree is neglected, it will begin to revert to the primitive, wild plant it once was. But once fruitful, it may remain so for centuries. In fact, new shoots from the root of the original tree may continue producing fruit for thousands of years.

It is interesting that, during the siege of Jerusalem (70 A.D.), the Romans symbolically cut down the olive trees, including those in the Garden of Gethsemane beside the Brook Kidron, outside the city walls. Then, three years later, the Romans built a three-foot high wall entirely around the mountain fortress of Masada, (a "line of circumvallation") symbolically demonstrating to the Jewish Zealots within that there could be no hope of escape.

In any event, when symbolism points to a future reality, conveying at the same time, by anticipation, the blessing that is yet to appear, it is a type. The brazen serpent raised up in the wilderness by Moses pointed Israel to the future ministry of Christ and to promised salvation. Our comprehension is enlarged beyond that which we would normally expect through mortal experience, and there emerges a powerful link between the secular and the divine.

This clarity expressed in types and shadows is particularly true of the writings of Isaiah, that may explain why his words were so loved by both the Nephite prophets and the Savior Himself. "Awake, awake, put on thy strength, O Zion; put on thy beautiful garments, O Jerusalem, the holy city; for henceforth there shall no more come into thee thy uncircumcised and the unclean. Shake thyself from the dust; arise, sit down, O Jerusalem; loose thyself from the bands of thy neck, O captive daughter of Zion." (2 Nephi 8:24-25). "Enlarge the place of thy tent, and let them stretch forth the curtains of thy habitations. Spare not. Lengthen thy cords and strengthen thy stakes." (3 Nephi 22:2).

The last two verses of Isaiah Chapter 4 were quoted to Joseph Smith in September 1823 by the Angel Moroni, who said the prophecies contained therein were soon to be fulfilled. Their symbolism must have been a comfort to him through long years of hardship, adversity, and persecution. "And the Lord will create upon every dwelling-place of mount Zion, and upon her assemblies, a cloud and smoke by day and the shining of a flaming fire by night." These are powerful symbols of God's Presence. "For upon all, the glory of Zion shall be a defense. And there shall be a tabernacle" or a wedding canopy for the bridegroom, that is another symbol of the Lord's Presence "for a shadow in the daytime from the heat, and for a place of refuge, and a covert from the storm and from rain." (Isaiah 4:5-6).

After almost two centuries of nurturing and development, L.D.S. cultural symbolism abounds. We take much of it for granted, but it does seem strange at times to non-members who hear their L.D.S. friends talk about the special significance of bread and water, consecrated oil, sealing rooms, new names, prophets, seers, and revelators, priesthood purposes, young women values, sunbeams, beehives, teachers, presidencies and counselors, home and visiting teachers, seminary, firesides, and roadshows. To them, our temples are shrouded in mystery (And why don't Stake Centers serve beef?) They hear that our missionaries call the scriptures "sticks," their door-approaches "tracting," and truth-seekers "investigators." Instead of parishes, or even congregations, we have "wards" that have political connotations for many unfamiliar with the ecclesiastical structure of the church. In some cultures, the conservative dress of our missionaries labels them as government agents. When our neighbors hear that we wear special underwear, raise our right hands to the square, have prayer circles, baptize dead people, and have special names for each-other (starting with "brother" and "sister"), they sometimes become confused and naturally so.

Because of our Latter-day Saint tradition, we are comfortable with such symbolism, and we are also at ease with the symbolism of the scriptures. The Parables of Jesus speak of fruitful and barren fig trees, stony and fertile ground, wise and foolish builders, sowers and reapers, sheep and goats, wheat and tares, pearls of great price, good Samaritans, the nets of fishermen, laborers in the vineyard, Pharisees and Publicans, little children and lost sheep, mustard seeds, salt that has lost its savor, lilies of the field, prodigal sons, wedding feasts, virgins, debtors, and unmerciful servants.

Think of the Book of Revelation and its beasts with seven heads, a woman clothed with the sun, four beasts all full of eyes with six wings apiece, a little book to be eaten which was bitter in the belly and yet sweet as honey in the mouth, two olive trees and two candlesticks standing in the streets, four and twenty elders, 144,000 ministers, a great red dragon, a woman given two wings with which she flies into the wilderness for 1260 days, marks in right hands or in foreheads, and the number 666.

Our icon of scriptural, spiritual, and symbolical fluency is Joseph Smith, who declared the Book of Revelation to be "one of the plainest books God ever caused to be written" ("Teachings," p. 290). Time Magazine, reflecting an equal and opposite stupor of thought, called it "that stunning piece of apocalyptic biblical literature that has fascinated and frustrated interpreters for nearly nineteen centuries." (1/8/1973, p, 42).

Both trivial matters and events that are nearest and dearest to us resonate with symbolism. As part of his revelation, John saw a symbolic vision of the War in Heaven and its continuation on earth. (Revelation 12). He learned that the Saints would overcome Satan through the Atonement of Jesus Christ. "And the great dragon was cast out, that old serpent, called the Devil, and Satan, which deceiveth the whole world: he was cast out into the earth, and his angels were cast out with him." (Revelation 12:9). "And his tail drew the third part of the stars of heaven, and did cast them to the earth: and the dragon stood before the woman (the church) which was ready to be delivered, for to devour her child (the church and kingdom of God) as soon as it was born." (Revelation 12:4). "And the dragon was wroth with the woman, (the church) and went to make war with the remnant of her seed, which keep the commandments of God, and have the testimony of Jesus Christ." (Revelation 12:17). "Therefore rejoice, ye heavens, and ye that dwell in them. Woe to the inhabiters of the earth and of the sea! for the devil is come down unto you, having great wrath, because he knoweth that he hath but a short time." (Revelation 12:12). To understand how the church and Kingdom of God will finally overcome Satan, we must once more vigorously employ the symbolism of the scriptures: "And they overcame him by the blood of the Lamb, and by the word of their testimony." (Revelation 12:11).

What better way to end, than to simply say that we comprehend and interpret ourselves and the world around us in the most intimately symbolic ways. Some time ago, I wrote the following of my wife, not particularly thinking of the symbols used, but rather of the feelings they evoked. "You are the rudder of my ship, guiding me past unseen rocks and reefs. You are my helm, holding steady when winds of adversity blow. You are my telltale, alerting me to impending storms. You are my keel, helping me to move against the current and the wind. You are my mainsheet, holding firmly with just enough pressure to prevent me from capsizing when I am heeled over. You are my safety-line, providing security when my footing is unsure, and the foaming sea is streaming across my deck. You are my compass, showing me the way, especially when the course is unclear. You are my chart, warning me of hidden dangers. You are my barometer, alerting me to impending storms. You are my lookout, standing as my sentinel when I am distracted by trivial concerns. You hold the line that trails in my wake, offering safety should I slip and fall overboard. You are the wind that fills my sails.

The sacred precincts that
are chosen by the faithful to study
The Book of Mormon have more to do with
how they live than where they conduct their
daily rituals. A holy place, then, is anywhere we
enjoy the presence of the Spirit. "Who shall ascend
into the hill of the Lord?" asked the Psalmist, "or who
shall stand in his holy place? He that hath clean hands,
and a pure heart; who hath not lifted up his soul unto
vanity, nor sworn deceitfully. He shall receive the
blessing from the Lord, and righteousness
from the God of his salvation."
(Psalms 24:3-5).

Talents

"After having had so much light and so
much knowledge given unto them of the Lord
their God; yea, after having been such a highly
favored people of the Lord ... having been visited by
the Spirit of God; having conversed with angels, and
having been spoken unto by the voice of the Lord; and
having the spirit of prophecy, and the spirit of revelation,
and also many gifts ... if this people, who have received so
many blessings from the hand of the Lor, should transgress
contrary to the light and knowledge which they do have ... if
they should fall into transgression, it would be far more
tolerable for the Lamanites than for them."
(Alma 9:19-23).

A talent is a stewardship or responsibility in the Kingdom of God. It is an aptitude, a gift, a capacity, a facility, and even an endowment. Paul taught that under the best of circumstances, we "are one body in Christ" with many individual gifts. (Romans 12:5-6). After we have linked our fortunes to the church, we "are no more strangers and foreigners, but fellow citizens with the saints, and of the household of God." (Ephesians 2:19-20). Within this vast congregation "are diversities of gifts." (1 Corinthians 12:4-31). The implication is that every member of the flock has talents that may be used to bless the lives of others living within the fold.

The Savior gave us the Parable of The Talents to teach us that we will be given greater responsibilities when we have served well in our stewardships. If we do not, that which has been entrusted to our care will eventually be taken from us and given to others. (See Matthew 25:14-30). But as we use our talents, constructively focus our energies, develop self-control, gain self-mastery, experience joy in service, exercise faith in God, and grow in humility, He will give us His strength to meet our challenges and to overcome adversity. (See Ether 12:27). As our partnership with God changes our perception of potential stumbling blocks, we will see them as stepping-stones to greater heights of individual and collective achievement.

Demosthenes overcame a lisp to become one of the greatest orators of all time. Beethoven composed some of his finest music after he had become deaf. Through many personal and political reversals of fortune, Abraham Lincoln yet said: "I will prepare myself, and some day my chance will come." Helen Keller triumphed over the silence and darkness in her life to finally write that "faith, the spiritual strong searchlight, illuminates the way, and although sinister doubts lurk in the shadow, I walk unafraid towards the Enchanted Wood where the foliage is always green, where joy abides, where nightingales nest and sing, and where life and death are one in the presence of the Lord." As a young man, Heber J. Grant couldn't carry a note. Later, after tireless effort and perpetual personal progress, he became well known for his singing abilities. Of his experience, he quoted Ralph Waldo Emerson, saying: "That which we persist in doing becomes easier for us to do; not that the nature of the thing is changed, but that our power to do is increased."

As we discover our talents and make efforts to improve and develop them, we would do well to remember the law of inertia. As we get moving, we need to sustain our momentum, remembering that if we always do what we always did, we'll always get what we always got. Even if we are on the right road, we're going to get run over if we just sit there.

Those who seek to improve their talents have high ideals, which "are like stars. We will not succeed in touching them with our hands. But, like the seafaring man in the desert of waters, we choose them as our guides, and following them, we will reach our destiny." (Carl Shurz, "B.Y.U. Studies," 16:4 (449).)

We must persevere in our efforts. Albert Einstein said: "The greatest tragedy in life is what dies in a man while he is alive." We must have faith. Harold B. Lee taught: "We must learn to walk to the edge of the light, and then a few steps into the darkness; then the light will appear and show the way before us." ("B.Y.U. Today," 3/1991). We must reach outward. for "love is never wasted, because at a minimum, it enlarges the capacity of the giver." (Neal A. Maxwell, "Press Forward," p. 37). We must share our talents with others, unlike the "very cautious man who never laughed or played; who never risked and never tried; who never sang or prayed. And when, one day, he passed away, his insurance was denied. For since he never really lived, they claimed he never died." (Anonymous).

Instead, we should conduct ourselves as if "our birth (were) but a sleep and a forgetting; (as if) the Soul that rises with us, our life's Star, hath had elsewhere its setting, and cometh from afar. (For) not in entire forgetfulness, and not in utter nakedness, but trailing clouds of glory do we come, from God, Who is our Home. (William Wordsworth, "Ode on Intimations of Immortality").

Teaching in The Church

"And it came to pass
that none received authority
to preach or to teach except it were by
him from God. Therefore, he consecrated
all their priests and their teachers; and none
were consecrated except they were just men."
(Mosiah 23:7).

Teaching in the church is multi-faceted as it is conducted on many levels and in many different settings. One style may be appropriate to one circumstance, while another approach may be tailor-made to fit a different situation. Church members are on many plateaus of spiritual development, and what may be effective for one may not be for another. The common denominator is that the Spirit must accompany all teaching. Without it we should not, and certainly cannot effectively, teach. (See D&C 42:14). But when our teaching is endowed with power, great changes may take place. (See D&C 43:16).

Teachers are vital to the spiritual well being of the church, because not everyone has every spiritual gift. "For there are many gifts, and to every man is given a gift by the Spirit of God. To some is given one, and to some is given another, that all may be profited thereby." For example, one individual may receive "the word of knowledge, that (others) may be taught to be wise and to have knowledge." A loving Father has given these gifts for the benefit of all of His children. (D&C 46:11-26).

Long ago, the Lord counseled the Saints that "as all have not faith, seek ye diligently and teach one another words of wisdom; yea, seek ye out of the best books words of wisdom; seek learning, even by study and also by faith." (D&C 88:118 & 109:7). In the society of the Saints, "people will gain knowledge and skill both by study and by faith, and will not confuse the two." (Chauncey Riddle, "B.Y.U. Studies," 16:4). We are on safe ground when the scriptures are the foundation of our gospel scholarship; indeed, as Mormon observed of Alma's efforts: "And now, the preaching of the word had a great tendency to lead the people to do that which was just; yea, it had had more powerful effect upon the minds of the people than the sword, or anything else." (Alma 31:5). But insightful books and commentaries, written by faithful Latter-day Saints with broad experience and background in the gospel, can be primers that also lead us to Christ. Knowledge of the gospel from the scriptures can provide a stable foundation of intellectual and spiritual unity. Coupled with and strengthened by a study of the expanding library of Latter-day Saint publications, a fortress of faith can be created. The glory of God is intelligence, by whatever avenue or vehicle that light and truth may come to us. Henry Thoreau, who was eclectic in his appreciation of the written word, echoed the prophets when he said: "Books are the treasured wealth of the world and the fit inheritance of generations and nations." ("Walden," Chapter 3).

The college portals in Moorish Granada (1300 - 1492) were inscribed with these lines: "The world is supported by four things: the learning of the wise, the justice of the great, the prayers of the good, and the valor of the brave." (Mohammed). Over 500 years later, the Lord was moved to observe of the Saints in Zion that they were "truly humble and (were) seeking diligently to learn wisdom and to find truth." (D&C 97:1). Today the quest continues, and the Lord has blessed us with more resources than the early Saints ever imagined could be possible, but with which we sometimes become complacent.

Written in an era of limited resources, the first issue of the Times and Seasons contained a lead editorial to the elders: "Be careful that you teach not for the word of God, the commandments of men, nor the doctrines of men. Study the word of God and preach it and not your own opinions, for no man's opinion is worth a straw." (Hugh Nibley, "Beyond Politics" p. 299). Throughout history, we have been counseled to trust in the Lord with all our heart and lean not unto our own understanding. (Proverbs). This is why B.H. Roberts "said after a coherent and vigorous presentation that he loved books; indeed, that in some degree books had made him. But then, in a most vehement way, he said 'But I am not dependent on books. I am dependent for what I really know and really trust, on the direct experience of God.'" ("Defender of The Faith" p. 374). It is our teaching, with all of its wonderful resources, that brings those within the sphere of our influence into the realm of direct experience with God. In fact, "we save ourselves by our teaching, and we save those who will get in tune with the same Spirit that we have, when we teach those truths." (Bruce R. McConkie, "The Foolishness of Teaching," 1981, Address given to religion instructors, seminary and institute teachers). Remember the wise counsel of Paul to Timothy: "The things that thou hast heard of me among many witnesses, the same commit thou to faithful men, who shall be able to teach others also." (2 Timothy 2:2).

All of us are teachers. As parents, we teach, consciously or unconsciously. When advising a friend, setting family rules for children, or counseling with our spouses, we are teachers. If we serve as a quorum our auxiliary leader, we are teachers. Our teaching should have such power that those whom we influence might say, as did the two disciples of Christ on the road to Emmaus, "Did not our heart burn within us, while he talked with us by the way, and while he opened to us the scriptures?" (Luke 24:32).

The vitality of the church is its strength, and it is alive with interactive communication with God. It is overflowing with an energy that reflects its joyous approach to life. "These currents and many more are part of the flowing fountain of the church. If we do not drink, if we die of thirst while only inches from the fountain, the fault comes down to us. For the free, full, flowing, living water is there." (Truman Madsen, "Christ and The Inner Life" p. 31). Latter-day Saints who are quickened by the Spirit will recognize the source of the life-giving water that is offered by wonderful teachers in the church. They will gratefully accept inspired insight from whomever has made sincere and humble efforts to be blessed with the Spirit. In every teaching moment, however, "we must not be caught in the bind of building a church and killing the articles of its faith, or permitting form to triumph over spirit. (Ultimately,) the church and kingdom of God is built by the ardor and conviction of its members." (Alvin R. Dyer, "A Foundation for Education"). There is no greater call than that of teaching.

Our best role models as teachers are the Sons of Mosiah, who "had waxed strong in the knowledge of the truth; for they were men of a sound understanding and they had searched the scriptures diligently, that they might know the word of God. But this is not all; they had given themselves to much prayer, and fasting; therefore, they had the spirit of prophecy, and the spirit of revelation, and when they taught, they taught with power and authority of God." (Mosiah 17:2-3).

Outstanding teachers have high ideals, which "are like stars. You will not succeed in touching them with your hands. But, like the seafaring man in the desert of waters, you choose them as your guides, and following them, you will reach your destiny." (Carl Shurz, "B.Y.U. Studies," 16:4). Great teachers persevere in their efforts. Albert Einstein said: "The greatest tragedy in life is what dies in a man while he is alive." We must have faith. Harold B. Lee taught: "You must learn to walk to the edge of the light, and then a few steps into the darkness; then the light will appear and show the way before you." ("B.Y.U. Today," 3/1991, p. 22-23). We must reach outward, for "love is never wasted, because at a minimum, it enlarges the capacity of the giver." (Neal A. Maxwell, "Ensign." 5/1982).

Influential teachers share their insights with others. We must not be like the "very cautious man who never laughed or played, who never risked, who never tried, who never sang or prayed. And when, one day, he passed away, his insurance was denied. For since he never really lived, they claimed he never died." (Mark Barsouna).

With humility, memorable teachers instill in others a sense that "our birth is but a sleep and a forgetting; The Soul that rises with us, our life's Star, hath had elsewhere its setting, and cometh from afar. Not in entire forgetfulness, and not in utter nakedness, but trailing clouds of glory do we come, from God, Who is our home." (William Wordsworth, "Ode: Intimations of Immortality").

Teaching in the church
and kingdom is multi-faceted as it
is conducted on many levels and in many
different settings. One style may be appropriate
to one circumstance, while another approach may be
tailor-made for different situations. Church members
are on many plateaus of spiritual development, and
what may be effective for one may not be for another.
The common denominator is that the Spirit must
accompany all learning. Without it, we should
not teach, for we cannot effectively do so.
But when our teaching is endowed
with power, profound change
may take place.

Teaching Key Doctrine

"They shall come to the
knowledge of their Redeemer and the
very points of his doctrine, that
they may know how to come
unto him and be saved."
(1 Nephi 15:14).

Printed on the front cover of the church publication "Gospel Principles" is the scripture: "They shall come to the knowledge of their Redeemer and the very points of his doctrine, that they may know how to come unto him and be saved." (1 Nephi 15:14). Every member of the church should be familiar with these basic principles so that they can better share the gospel with others and give them the tools necessary to save their own eternal lives.

It only takes about 8 years of higher education to become a dentist, but being an effective Sunbeam teacher or Sunday School teacher is an ongoing lifetime process. We can never learn enough that we can sit back on our laurels and relax in vacation-mode. Elder David Bednar shared with the Saints three elements of effective teaching that relate to core curriculum that each member should continually work on to be more effective. They are 1) teach key doctrine, 2) extend an invitation to action, and 3) describe promised blessings. This is exactly what Nephi and Lehi did to great effect in the Land of Zarahemla: They "knew concerning the true points of doctrine, having many revelations daily, therefore they did preach unto the people." (Helaman 11:23).

Learning about the translation of the City of Enoch is stimulating, but it is not key doctrine. Knowing about the theomorphic nature of man gives us a unique perspective relating to our place in the cosmos, but it is not key doctrine. Pinpointing the exact location of Kolob in relation to the earth does not address key doctrine. Familiarity with the symbolism of the rockwork on the exterior of the Salt Lake Temple is interesting, but it is not key doctrine. The first issue of The Times and Seasons contained a lead editorial addressed to the elders: "Be careful that you teach not for the word of God, the commandments of men, nor the doctrines of men. Study the word of God and preach it and not your own opinions, for no man's opinion is worth a straw."

B.H. Roberts loved books and felt that in some degree they had made him. But he said: "I am not dependent on books. I am dependent for what I really know and really trust, on the direct experience of God." If we turn to the scriptures for direct experience that relates to key doctrine, we need look no further than the Thirteen Articles of Faith. For example: "We believe that the first principles and ordinances of the gospel are first, faith in the Lord Jesus Christ, second, repentance, third, baptism by immersion for the remission of sins, and fourth, the laying on of hands for the gift of the Holy Ghost." (4th Article of Faith).

We can also teach key doctrine by taking more complex principles and reducing them to their lowest common denominators. For example, the Fall of Adam can be taught in the context of agency and opposition, the Atonement, and The Plan of Salvation. Lehi taught key doctrine relating to the circumstances in the Garden by simply stating: "Adam fell that men might be, and men are that they might have joy." (2 Nephi 2:25). Alma taught his son Corianton key doctrine by telling him: "Wickedness never was happiness." (Alma 41:10). Samuel the Lamanite taught key doctrine to the people of Zarahemla by declaring in the name of the Lord: "Blessed are they who repent for them will I spare." (Helaman 13:13). Moroni both warned and comforted us with key doctrine: "Despair cometh because of iniquity." (Moroni 10:22) and "Charity never faileth." (Moroni 7:46).

We are on safe ground when the scriptures are the foundation of our teaching of key doctrine. Indeed, as Mormon observed of Alma's efforts: "And now, as the preaching of the word had a great tendency to lead the people to do that which was just; yea, it had had more powerful effect upon the minds of the people than the sword, or anything else which had happened unto them – therefore Alma though it was expedient that they should try the virtue of the word of God." (Alma 31:5).

After teaching key doctrine, it follows that we should extend an invitation to action, and finally describe promised blessings that are linked to obedience. As an example, let's look at the duty of the priest, and how the Lord has proposed that we train young men to teach key doctrine, extend an invitation to action, and describe promised blessings. Their duty is to "preach, teach, expound, exhort" and then to baptize and administer the sacrament. (D&C 20:46). The pertinent key doctrine is to preach and teach the first principles and ordinances of the gospel, in that order; then expound upon the principles taught and extend an invitation to act upon the doctrine that has been presented. Finally, in the case of the duty of the priest, the promised blessings of obedience, namely baptism and the sacrament, are described.

Alvin R. Dyer referred to invitations to action that necessarily follow the introduction of key doctrine, when he said: "We must not be caught in the bind of building a church and killing the articles of its faith, or permitting form to triumph over spirit. The church and kingdom of God is built by the ardor and conviction of its members" to come unto Christ.

Our teacher/mentors from the scriptures all taught key doctrine, extended calls to action, and described anticipated blessings in ways that made the effort seem worthwhile. Think of the heroes from The Book of Mormon like Nephi, Jacob, Benjamin, Abinadi, Alma, Mormon, Moroni, and those from the Bible, like Isaiah, Paul, Peter, James, and John, and latter-day heroes like Joseph Smith, Brigham Young and today's General Authorities.

Of Joseph Smith, it has been said: "One of his greatest contributions was his knowledge of what is to come after death. He did much to clarify our understanding of heaven and to make it seem worth working for." He taught key doctrine, extended invitations to action, and described promised blessings in ways that made the effort seem worthwhile. The Apostle Peter did the same thing. "Now when they heard (him preach), they were pricked in their heart, and said unto Peter and the rest of the apostles, Men and brethren, what shall we do?" Repent, and be baptized every one of you in the name of Jesus Christ for the remission of sins, and ye shall receive the gift of the Holy Ghost" was his call to action and description of anticipated blessings. (Acts 2:37-38).

After teaching key doctrine in a masterful discourse, King Benjamin then extended an invitation to action, urging his people: "I would that ye should be steadfast and immovable, always abounding in good works." Next, he described the positive consequences or outcome of obedience, promising: "Christ, the Lord God Omnipotent, may seal you his, that you may be brought to heaven, that ye may have everlasting salvation and eternal life, through the wisdom, and power, and justice, and mercy of him who created all things, in heaven and in earth." (Mosiah 5:15).

Thomas S. Monson, ever the consummate teacher, may have had Benjamin in the back of his mind when he declared: "The goal of gospel teaching … is not to 'pour information' into the minds of class members. Its aim is to inspire the individual to think about, feel about, and then do something about living gospel principles" (C.R., 10/1970).

The blessings that are related to the doctrine of the kingdom are released when we act on our faith. Let's use The Proclamation on The Family as an example. The key doctrine woven into the message of The First Presidency is the reality that families can be together forever. Their invitation to action is to change our lives so that we will enjoy the blessing of an eternal family. The anticipated blessings will come when we participate in the sealing ordinances of the temple. When, in turn, we talk to our friends and neighbors and teach them key doctrine relating to their families, extend invitations to action, and describe the anticipated blessings related to obedience, they should feel as did the two disciples on the Road to Emmaus: "Did not our heart burn within us," they asked each other, "while he talked with us by the way, and while he opened to us the scriptures?" (Luke 24:32).

The key doctrine related to keeping the Sabbath day holy is simply that the Lord has set aside one day each week for worship. The invitation to action is equally straightforward: To attend our church worship services each Sunday. The anticipated blessing comes when we spiritually renew ourselves to prepare for the challenges of the week that lies ahead.

The key doctrine associated with the Word of Wisdom is that our bodies are holy temples. The invitation to action is to change one or more of our behaviors so that we might enjoy the anticipated blessings of better physical and spiritual health. "And all saints who remember to keep and do these sayings, walking in obedience to the commandments, shall receive health in their navel and marrow to their bones; and shall find wisdom and great treasures of knowledge, even hidden treasures. And shall run and not be weary, and shall walk and not faint. And I, the Lord, give unto them a promise, that the destroying angel shall pass them by, as the children of Israel, and not slay them." (D&C 89:18-21).

The key doctrine that is tied to The Law of the Fast is feeling the spirit and focusing the powers of heaven through the simple act of purposeful fasting. The invitation to action is to join the ward in a monthly fast. The anticipated blessing is that by learning to discipline our physical appetites and subjugate them to our spiritual nature, we will gain greater sensitivity as we allow the Holy Ghost to direct our lives.

The key doctrine related to the Law of Chastity is that obedience contributes to our sense of honor, love, and faithfulness to ourselves, our loved ones, and also to God. The invitation to action encourages us to avoid situations that might compromise our standards, and to engage in behaviors and activities that celebrate morality. The anticipated blessing is to enjoy the cherished companionship of the Spirit, for it will not dwell in an unholy tabernacle.

As teachers of key doctrine, we perform periodic self-diagnostic reality checks and ask if we view ourselves as servants of our Master. In our teaching efforts, we pour ourselves into the task so that we can be lifesavers. We focus on the doctrine of Christ and love those whom we teach as does our Heavenly Father. We make every effort to teach by the power of the Spirit and have such a passion for our message that those whom we teach find it hard to resist our invitation to action. We bear personal testimony that is based on our own experiences relating to the anticipated blessings, and make them seem worth working and fighting for.

We save others through our teaching of key doctrine. We must not be like the "very cautious man who never laughed or played, who never risked, who never tried, who never sang or prayed. And when, one day, he passed away, his insurance was denied, for since he never really lived, they claimed he never died." (Mark Barsouna). We know the doctrine. We have been called to action to strengthen the Saints and to bring others to the knowledge of the truth. We have the power to so teach that our brothers and sisters will fall down and kiss our necks for having brought them the anticipated blessings of hope and salvation.

Technological Traps

"O ye pollutions, ye hypocrites, ye teachers, who sell yourselves for that which will canker." (Mormon 8:38).

Technological traps are man-made devices used to detach us from reality and lead us into a state of vulnerability. Substitutes for the real thing, these paraphernalia are a poor counterfeit currency. They are an "artificial intelligence" that should alert us to the fact that they are not real. A lot can be done with binary code, but at the end of the day, it's just a lot of zeroes and ones. The sum of reality is more than that. It is at least the five physical senses with a metaphysical sixth sense thrown in for good measure, resulting in a tangible immersion in the spiritual element that sets us free to reach our potential.

Technological traps can lead to obsessive, addictive, irrational, and self-defeating behaviors. They can corrupt canon, distort doctrine, deform dogma, garble guidelines, interfere with ideology, pervert principles and twist thinking. They can be psychotropic drugs that nurture self-destructive lifestyles. They can be chemotherapeutics that upset the homeostatic balance of nature, or diet drugs that facilitate a flight from personal accountability and responsibility. They can be clothed in the robes of the false-priesthood, or cloistered in the ivory towers of academia. They are often the undesirable side-effects of otherwise worthwhile activities.

Technological traps can be disguised as TIVO, bundled in video games, and can be embedded in cell phones, text messaging, computers, Google, blogs, and Facebook. We go to great lengths to eliminate malware, spyware, and undesirable cookies from our computer code, but we rarely view the code itself as a threatening virus. Firewalls protect us from external threats, but do little to insulate us from the effects of a Trojan Horse that may lie within.

Technological traps can be electronic and online gambling, iPad, SnapChat, Twitter, and YouTube. We can become ensnared by technological traps when surfing the Web, never realizing that when the wave closes out, we'll have to either kick out or be pulverized by pounding breakers.

Technological traps can be an obsession with spectator sports and other competitive activities, credit cards, the Home Shopping Network, Powerball, catalog shopping and the allure of glossy ads promoting 50% off sales, push-up bras, or ripped abdominal muscles. They can be advertising slogans that promise to make life easier, bring the good things to life, and make our lives better through chemistry. When retailers promise: "It's the real thing," we can be sure it isn't. When they invite us to "reach out and touch someone," we can be certain that physical contact is not what they had in mind. When they admiringly declare: "You've come a long way, baby!" we'd better guard our valuables and values even more carefully. When they invite us to "double our pleasure, double our fun!" it's time to perform a self-diagnostic on our behavioral standards. If we swallow their suggestion that "a diamond is forever," we'd better hold on more tightly to our treasures that money can't buy.

Technological traps can be so insidiously enticing that we should basically avoid anything that can be purchased from the car by talking into a microphone, anything involving empty calories, sticky or glistening food, neon or bright lights, loud music, stars on sidewalks, fashion models, and anything with the name "Hollywood," "Thigh Master," or "Ab Cruncher" associated with it. Praise, recognition, applause, autograph books, fan mail, and monetary reward without commensurate effort should alert us to danger.

Technological traps are promoted in glossy tabloids and are disguised as "Reality T.V." They are frequently used to excess and extortion, and may involve 8 or 12 cylinders, the color red, and any vehicle with more than 400 horsepower or less than 18 miles per gallon. They are designed to disguise a transition from celestial-bound to telestial-torn individuals. They stimulate a metamorphosis that changes both our appearance and nature, and our image and likeness. He who is caught up in these traps walks "in his own way, and after the image of his own god, whose image is in the likeness of the world, and whose substance is that of an idol, which waxeth old and shall perish in Babylon, even Babylon the great, which shall fall." (D&C 1:16). These images are too often made of wood and stone, or in other words, silica, fiber-optic cables, semi-conductors and electrically charged ionized gas.

Isaiah foresaw our dangerous proclivity to participate in a lemming-like rush to the sea, in a frenzy to open the latest cargo container from China, when he wrote: "Every one that thirsteth, come ye to the waters, and he that hath no money; come ye, buy, and eat; yea, come, buy wine and milk without money and without price." (Isaiah 55:1). It is strange but true that the most valuable things in life aren't things and cannot be purchased. Strip away all of the technological accouterments of the modern age, and what is left is nothing less that the essence of a gospel Plan of Salvation that doesn't rely on the wisdom of the world to promote its agenda. To validate its worth it only asks that we try the virtue of the word. When we do, we will cry "with one voice, saying: Yea, we believe all the words which thou hast spoken unto us; and also, we know of their surety and truth, because of the Spirit of the Lord Omnipotent, which has wrought a mighty change in us, or in our hearts, that we have no more disposition to do evil, but to do good continually," and to avoid the technological traps that might otherwise ensnare us. (Mosiah 5:2).

(A) Testimony of Christ

"Behold, I have all things
as a testimony that these things
are true; and ye also have all things
as a testimony unto you that they are
true; and will ye deny them? Believest
thou that these things are true?
(Alma 30:41).

I believe in Christ. I belong to The Church of Jesus Christ of Latter-day Saints. The Book of Mormon is Another Testament of Jesus Christ. I am a Saint of the Most High God!

I testify of His ante-mortal existence and His foreordination to be the Redeemer of the world. The scriptures speak of His relationship with the Father, and of His divine investiture of authority. His appearances to His servants throughout history were many. The Book of Mormon, particularly, explains His condescension in taking a mortal body. Thus, I can better understand His temptations, and the power, might, dominion, and authority that typified His earthly ministry.

At His baptism, He demonstrated by example the way for me to follow. In His ministry, He taught with simplicity the truths of the gospel. In the Garden of Gethsemane, He revealed His strength and compassion. The crucifixion, then, was only an apostrophe, and His death but a pause allowing me to re-focus attention on His resurrection and ascension into heaven.

When He comes again, it will be in the clouds, accompanied by the Church of the Firstborn. His Second Coming will usher in His Millennial Reign. For a thousand years, His gospel will penetrate every soul and burn brightly in every bosom.

He is my Advocate with the Father and is the Bread of Life. He is the Cornerstone of my creation, and the foundation beneath my existence. He is the Creator of worlds without number and the Deliverer of the Covenant.

He is Emmanuel, for truly, God is with us. He is perfect in every detail and was the Firstborn of the Spirit Children of the Father. He is the Good Shepherd and the Judge of both the quick and the dead. As Lord, King, and Jehovah, He has all power to act as my Mediator and Messenger of the Covenant.

The Lamb of God, He is the Messiah, the Anointed One, and my Redeemer. He is my Rock and my Savior, the

Only Begotten Son of God in the flesh. He is the Son of Man of Holiness, and will become my Second Comforter. "Surely goodness and mercy shall follow me all the days of my life: and I will dwell in the house of the Lord for ever." (Psalms 23:6).

(A) Thirty Day Spiritual Fitness Program

"And now, as the preaching
of the word had a great tendency
to lead the people to do that which was
just – yea it had had a more powerful effect
upon the minds of the people than the sword, or
anything else, which had happened unto them –
therefore Alma thought it was expedient that
they should try the virtue of the word of
God." (Alma 31:5).

Week #1 – focus on prayer.
Week #2 – be perfect in your repentance.
Week #3 – develop more fully the capacity to love.
Week #4 – commit yourself to develop the habit of service.

Week #1 - Pray

First and foremost, remember that in a world where ponder and pray have largely been replaced with wander and play, our Father loves to hear us express our thanks in prayer. We focus on the positive in our prayers. We overlook the shortcomings of others because there is so much in ourselves that needs improvement. In our prayers, we try to be specific, ask questions, acknowledge answers, articulate why we are thankful, and orient ourselves toward repentance. As we do so, we can't help but receive the blessing associated with eternal law. We must "pray always, lest (we) enter into temptation and lose (our) reward." (D&C 31:12).

Especially in times of adversity, we express our gratitude in prayer. In our most difficult times, we can find much for which to be grateful. "Gratitude is not only the greatest of virtues, but the parent of all others." (Cicero). We even express our thanks for the "no" answers, knowing that in God's greater vision allows Him to say: "Whom I love, I also chasten." (D&C 95:1). As we develop humility, we come to realize that the 'no' comes as an answer to the "specifications set forth in our petitions."

Some people grumble that roses have thorns. Others are thankful that thorns have roses. The poet wrote: "Why is it, whenever I reach for the sky to climb aboard cloud nine, it evaporates and rains upon my dreams? Is it a matter of science, or simply a matter of fact, that not even a cloud with a silver lining can hold the weight of our dreams without some precipitation. I think I've found the answer to this dilemma. Keep on reaching for the sky, but don't forget your umbrella." (Susan Stephenson).

Unlike an indulgent father, God doesn't give us that which we don't deserve, nor does He submit to our pressure to give us that which we do not need. So, we resolve not to act like spoiled children in our prayers. We communicate with God as we would with our own fathers. Through His prophet, He revealed: "And whoso receiveth not my voice is not acquainted with my voice, and is not of me." (D&C 84:52). If we pray always, and don't lose faith, He will consecrate our performance unto us, insomuch that it will be therapeutic for our soul.

"Therefore, our faith in and thanksgiving for Heavenly Father, so far as this mortal experience is concerned, consists—not simply of a faith and gladness that he exists—but also includes faith and thanksgiving for his tutoring of us to aid our acquisition of needed attributes and experiences while we are in mortality. We trust not only the Designer but also his design of life itself—including our portion thereof!." (Neal A. Maxwell). "The Lord bless thee and keep thee," wrote Moses. "The Lord make his face shine upon thee, and be gracious unto thee. The Lord lift up his countenance upon thee, and give thee peace." (Numbers 6:24-26).

If we're not accustomed to prayers of thanksgiving, we shouldn't be discouraged. Instead, "rejoice and think of what an impression you will make on those who thought they knew you! Think of how delightfully surprised they will be!." (Joseph Wirthlin).

"The builder who first bridged Niagara's gorge, before he swung his cable, shore to shore, sent out across the gulf his venturing kite bearing a slender cord for unseen hands to grasp upon the further cliff and draw a greater cord, and then a greater yet, 'til at last across the chasm swung The Cable - then the mighty bridge in air. So may we send our little timid thoughts across the void, out to God's reaching hands; send our love and faith to thread the deep; thought after thought until the little cord has greatened to a chain no chance can break, and we are anchored to the infinite!." (Edward Markham).

Finally, remember that when your prayers lead to such a faith that you are convicted of your sins and you are moved to repent, keep right on praying!

Week #2 - Repent

"The first condition of happiness is a clear conscience." (President David O. McKay). In medical terms, before a wound can heal, it has to be clean. Anyone who has had a physician vigorously scrub out an ugly wound knows how carefully and thoroughly the task must be accomplished before sterile dressings may be applied and the healing process begins. The same principle applies to repentance. There is no room for dry rot and there can be no skeletons lurking in the closet. We cannot superficially whitewash our sins to cover them up. The Savior called the Scribes and Pharisees hypocrites, for they were "like unto whited sepulchres, which indeed appear beautiful outward, but are within full of dead men's bones, and of all uncleanliness." (Matthew 23:27).

The purpose of earth life is to grow and progress in stature, until we have developed both the image and likeness of our Heavenly Father. During the process, we will fail again and again in our efforts. This creates a problem because "no unclean thing can dwell with God," and yet it is human nature to repeatedly violate the commandments. Unfortunately, sin does stop our progress. God, however, provided the principle of repentance so that we may yet become holy. Therefore, we are commanded, "All men, everywhere, must repent." (Moses 6:57).

The great blessing of repentance is that it allows us to become clean in the sight of God, and get moving again on the pathway to perfection. After repentance, God will remember our sins no more. It is true that we might retain a remembrance of them, insofar as they increase our testimonies, strengthen us to become more stalwart, and better prepare us to positively influence others. But we will no longer feel the guilt or experience the withdrawal of the Spirit that is associated with unresolved sin.

Repentance, then, can satisfy a two-fold purpose. First, it allows us to be justified by the Spirit, become holy or sanctified, and qualified to enter the Presence of the Lord. Secondly, it serves to strengthen our testimony, which makes it more unlikely that we will yield to the same temptations in the future. For example, after his exhortation to them, King Benjamin's people "cried with one voice, saying ... the Spirit of the Lord Omnipotent ... has wrought a mighty change in us, or in our hearts, that we have no more disposition to do evil, but to do good continually." These people made a covenant to forsake their sins, and to keep the commandments, in order to be able to avoid the otherwise inevitable consequences of disobedient behavior. (Mosiah 5:2 & 5). But it is a path we can successfully negotiate.

Repentance that brings about such change requires great courage, much strength, many tears, unceasing prayers, and untiring efforts. "There is no royal road to repentance, no privileged path to forgiveness. Every man must follow the same course whether he is rich or poor, educated or untrained, tall or short, prince or pauper, king or commoner. There is only one way. It is a long road spiked with thorns and briars and pitfalls and problems." (Elder Spencer W. Kimball). But it is a path that can be successfully negotiated.

In order to repent, we must recognize our sins. This might at first sound like a trivial point, but we should remember Alma's wise counsel to his son that applies to us all: "Let your sins trouble you," he urged Corianton, "with that trouble which shall bring you down unto repentance. Do not endeavor to excuse yourself in the least point." (Alma 42:29-30).

We must feel sorrow for our sins. We must feel terrible about them. We must feel profoundly filthy. We must want to unload and abandon them. We must be almost obsessive-compulsive about cleansing our souls. We must be broken in heart, and have the spirit of contrition. A broken heart is softened to receive the things of the Spirit, and it is teachable. With spiritual preparation, when our faith has convicted us of our sins, we must be prepared to ask, as did those on the Day of Pentecost: "What shall we do?" The straightforward answer is to repent.

We must confess and forsake our sins. "By this ye may know if a man repenteth of his sins - behold, he will confess them and forsake them." (D&C 58:43). Confession can remove a heavy burden. The Lord has promised, "I, the Lord, forgive sins, and am merciful unto those who confess their sins with humble hearts." (D&C 61:2).

All sins must be confessed to God, but those that might affect our standing in the church should be confessed to the proper priesthood authority, as well. However, only the Lord can forgive sin. "The Son of man hath power on earth to forgive sins." (Matthew 9: He recognizes that even the righteous do not become perfect overnight. Therefore, He has promised, "as often as my people repent will I forgive them their trespasses against me." (Mosiah 26:30). Of those who will not repent, however, He said, "The same shall not be numbered among my people." (Mosiah 26:32).

We must make restitution, if possible. Wrongs must be righted, and fences mended. The fundamental truth is that restitution in its broad sense is personal for every individual, for "that which ye do send out shall return unto you again." (Alma 41:15).

We must forgive others. We may find that "enduring to the end" simply involves mastery of two principles: repentance for our own sins, and forgiveness of others. The Savior obtained forgiveness for the sins of mankind only after the most excruciating suffering on His part. Is it, then, too much for Him to ask us to forgive each other?. He recognized that without forgiveness, the Plan of Redemption is completely inoperative for both the penitent and he who has been wronged by another. The quality of our forgiveness is really a celestial barometer. Christ requires it of those who strive to be obedient to the Laws of His Kingdom so that they might feel comfortable living there. This is why He commanded Joseph Smith: "I, the Lord, will forgive whom I will forgive, but of you it is required to forgive all men." (D&C 64:10). Brigham Young put it a little more bluntly, when, echoing Confucius, he declared: He who takes offense when none was intended is a fool, and he who takes offense when one was intended is usually a fool." We are only fully repentant when we endure to the end in righteousness by being strictly obedient to the principle of forgiveness, and that door swings both ways.

When the process of repentance has been completed, the Plan of Salvation shifts into high gear and the Atonement becomes fully effective in our lives. The unique source of peace is our complete and all-encompassing repentance through the power of the Savior's Atonement, and our Heavenly Father's consequent forgiveness of our sins. As Parley P. Pratt declared: "I have received the holy anointing, and I can never rest until the last enemy (that is unresolved sin) is conquered, (spiritual) death destroyed, and truth reigns triumphant." From our perspective, this is accomplished when we conquer those self-defeating behaviors and character flaws that limit our progression. The Prophet Joseph Smith said, "Salvation consists in a man's being placed beyond the power of his enemies, meaning the enemies of his progression, such as dishonesty, greediness, lying, immorality, and other vices."

We should repent now, for this second week of our thirty-day spiritual fitness program "is the time for men to prepare to meet God." (Alma 34:32). It is difficult to learn a skill all at once, but it is easy if we repetitively practice every day until we gain mastery. Let us then be perfect in our repentance. Now that we're praying and repenting, we mustn't forget to keep doing so even as we begin to feel the stirrings of God's love in greater abundance.

Week #3 - Love

Love is the characteristic that underlies our quest for perfection, and having learned to pray and to repent, it is natural to feel the love of God and fellowmen swell our hearts. A heart that is "past feeling" is insensitive. It is wounded and cannot be easily nurtured. All of the qualities of a noble character need the softening influence of love before they become celestial qualities. Love is like an ether that allows us to catch a glimpse of heaven. It allows us to bridge the gulf between the world of everyday, and the land unpromised and unearned that is felt only with the Spirit.

The pure love of Christ is built upon the foundation of faith and hope, and is the supreme characteristic of every faithful disciple. Mormon taught "if a man be meek and lowly in heart, and confess by the power of the Holy Ghost that Jesus is the Christ," with a sure hope born of faith, "he must needs have charity." (Moroni 7:44).

This pure love is characterized by sensitivity toward others. It is more focused on celestial sureties and less concerned with telestial trinkets. It is humble and selfless, reflects poise under provocation and has no secret agenda to follow. It is repulsed by sin and is drawn toward the light, and is continually open to that which is good. It naturally follows prayer and repentance.

Without love, man is nothing, because his progression stops. "If ye have not charity, ye are nothing, for charity never faileth. Wherefore, cleave unto charity, which is the greatest of all (the spiritual gifts), for all things must fail" without it. (Moroni 7:46). "Charity … endureth forever, and whoso is found possessed of it at the last day, it shall be well with him." (Moroni 7:47). Charity can motivate us to Christian service, but it also prepares us to be like God, so that we will feel comfortable in His Presence. It is a gift of the Spirit that is bestowed upon the faithful by the grace of God.

We remember the noble quality of love, Peter wrote, "that we might be partakers of the divine nature." (2 Peter 1:4). When God said: "Let us make man in our image, after our likeness," He meant not only that man should have the same physical characteristics as his Parents, but the same spiritual characteristics as well. (Moses 2:26).

When we live in thanksgiving daily, are perfect in our repentance, and love ourselves, our fellowmen, and our Savior, we will see the glass as half full. No matter what life may throw at us, we will put a positive spin on our experiences. Then, our love and its companion attitudes will overpower our carnal nature, with its jealousies, malice, and prejudices, and carry us upward into the rarified atmosphere of heaven on earth.

Just remember: Don't stop praying, repenting, and loving when you start serving in week 4 of the Lord's Spiritual Fitness Program.

Week #4 - Serve

When we are in the service of our fellow beings, we are in God's service, but without love it is insincere and is often unappreciated or even resented. So, make sure your prayers, repentance, and love of your fellowmen translate into affirmative action. President Gordon B. Hinckley said: "My plea is that we stop seeking out the storms and enjoy more fully the sunlight. I am suggesting that as we go through life, we accentuate the positive. I am asking that we look a little deeper for the good, that we still our voices of insult and sarcasm, that we more generously compliment and endorse virtue and effort."

"God does notice us, and He watches over us. But it is usually through another person that He meets our needs. Therefore, it is vital that we serve each other. The abundant life is achieved as we magnify our view of life and expand our view of others and our own possibilities. Thus, the more we follow the teachings of the Master, the more enlarged our perspective becomes. We see many more possibilities for service that we would have seen without this magnification. There is great security in spirituality, and we cannot have spirituality without service." (President Spencer W. Kimball).

"But you were always a good man of business, Jacob." said Scrooge. "Business!" cried the ghost, wringing its hands again. "Mankind was my business. The common welfare was my business; charity, mercy, forbearance, and benevolence were all my business. The dealings of my trade were but a drop of water in the comprehensive ocean of my business. At this time of the rolling year," the spectre said, "I suffer most. Why did I walk through crowds of fellow-beings with my eyes turned down, and never raise them to that blessed Star which led the Wise Men to a poor abode? Were there no poor homes to which its light would have conducted me?." (Charles Dickens, "A Christmas Carol").

President Joseph Fielding Smith, Jr. Declared: "The greatest crime in all this world is to lead men and women away from the true principles." (C.R., April 1951). When we serve our brothers and sisters, we will guide them toward the light. The following story illustrates the level of human decency and concern that is expected of each of us. and particularly of members of the church.

Before Fiorello La Guardia became mayor of New York City, he was a magistrate. One day there appeared before him a man accused of stealing a loaf of bread. Upon questioning, the man explained that he'd committed the crime to feed his family, for they were starving. Whereupon, La Guardia dismissed the case, and sentenced all present in the courtroom to pay a fine for living in a city where a man must steal to feed his family.

The Lord illustrated the gospel principle of concern for the welfare of others, when He said: "I am the bread of life: He that cometh to me shall never hunger; and he that believeth on me shall never thirst." (John 6:35). In the Eternal Court of Justice, what will be the penalty for failure to provide others with the Bread of Life, or for feeding them stale, or moldy, or otherwise unwholesome bread?

Lyman Abbott said: "The brotherhood of man is an integral part of Christianity no less than the Fatherhood of God; and to deny the one is no less infidel than to deny the other." Truly, there is no brotherhood of man without the fatherhood of God. "The mystic bond of brotherhood," in fact, "makes all men one." (Thomas Carlyle). "The universe is but one great city, full of beloved ones, divine and human, by nature endeared to each other." (Epictetus).

President Spencer W. Kimball told those who urged him to slow down: "I am like an old shoe, to be worn out in the service of the Lord." His successor prophet, Gordon B. Hinckley, observed: "Too many of us die with wasted capacity." He was a self-effacing, humble man, who unconsciously worked harder than many retirees thirty years younger than he. We should all follow his tireless example, to defend the faith, follow the Plan of Salvation, express our thanks in prayer, reconcile ourselves to negative responses to our petitions, lay our lives on the altar of sacrifice, consistently repent, pattern our lives after the Savior, gain spiritual fluency, focus on the positive, forgive others, keep the commandments, endure to the end in righteousness, recognize the merits of the principles of righteousness, righteously exercise what power or authority we do possess, acknowledge Him as the sole source of our protection, determine to serve Him, recognize His majesty and power and that of His servants, see His presence in the earth around us, use our agency wisely to validate the wisdom of our self-government, indicate by our actions that we understand the true value of things and do not covet the profane things of the world, understand the relationship between commandments and blessings, multiply our talents and turn weaknesses into strengths, use our means wisely, manage our time carefully, keep our priorities in order, maintain our perspective even when our days seem purposeless, change our hearts through faith on His name, accept responsibility for our actions and use our agency wisely, use our opportunities for failure as learning experiences, bear adversity well, recognize the seeming detours and distractions in our lives as opportunities for personal growth, continue to express our gratitude in times of adversity, maintain a cheerful attitude, sacrifice (seemingly), be anxiously engaged, perform acts of quiet Christianity, open our arms to those around us, love our neighbors, do missionary work, acknowledge the qualities of goodness in others, express appreciation to others, recognize how precious our divine attributes are, read the scriptures, promote the cause of Zion, magnify our callings, shout Hosannas to the Lord, be valiant in our testimony of Jesus, worship God in the temple and honor our temple covenants, observe the Word of Wisdom, be temperate and not easily provoked to anger, have integrity, view education as a life-long process, know how to work, nurture family relationships, and take our responsibilities as teachers seriously.

We make a living by what we get, but we make a life by what we give. "Little people, like you and me," wrote C.S. Lewis, "if our prayers are sometimes granted beyond all hope and probability, had better not draw hasty conclusions to our own advantage. If we were stronger, we might be less tenderly treated. If we were braver, we might be sent, with far less help, to defend far more desperate posts in the great battle." ("The World's Last Night, p. 10-11).

"There is no man who ever made a sacrifice on the earth for the kingdom of heave except the Savior," declared Brigham Young. "I would not give the ashes of a rye straw for that man who feels that he is making sacrifices for God. We are doing this for our own happiness, welfare, and exaltation, and for nobody else's. What we do, we do for the salvation of the inhabitants of the earth, not for the salvation of the heavens, the angels, or God." (Brigham Young, J.D. 16:114).

We perform "acts of quiet Christianity," those charitable acts of service for which there is no recognition, recompense, or thought of reciprocation. As Joseph Smith observed: "A man filled with the love of God, is not content with blessing his family alone, but ranges through the whole world, anxious to bless the whole human race." On another occasion, he said: "Nothing is so much calculated to lead people to forsake sin as to take them by the hand, and watch over them with tenderness."

"I sought to see myself," wrote the poet. "Myself I could not see. I sought to know the Lord through prayer, but He eluded me. I sought to serve my fellow men, and I found all three." (Anonymous). "Next to the blessed sacrament itself, your neighbor is the holiest object presented to your senses. If he is your Christian neighbor he is holy in almost the same way, for in him also Christ is truly hidden and glorified." (C.S. Lewis). The first five books of the Old Testament speak of keeping the Sabbath day holy just once, but of respecting one's neighbors 30 times. When we seek to discover the best in others, we somehow bring out the best in ourselves.

In week 4 of our Spiritual Fitness Program, we have learned how to serve. Now we have a foundation built on the bedrock of the gospel, and we are firm and immovable. We have developed the habit of prayer and of repentance. We have learned how to love ourselves and our neighbors. We have experienced the joy of service, and we cannot be easily shaken in our testimonies, and we will surely spring up unto eternal life in the Celestial Kingdom of God

Those who have determined
to read The Book of Mormon with the goal in
mind of determining if it is true need to remember to
acknowledge the Lord's timetable during their endeavor.
The world insists on the instant satisfaction of its curiosity
as well as immediate gratification through the natural senses,
but those who would be disciples of Christ remove the latchets from
their shoes, realizing that they are standing on holy ground and are
in the presence of burning bushes, and they patiently wait upon the
Lord God to speak to them. Babylon, however, remains pre-occupied
with the occult, and with magic, diviners, and soothsayers. They
roll the dice and dream of the bounty that will be theirs if only
their lucky number comes up, while disciples are unaffected
by a world in motion that is unbalanced by commotion.
The stand in holy places and are not moved.

Thou Hast Done Wonderful Things

"I will proceed to do
a marvelous work among
this people, yea, a marvelous
work and a wonder."
(2 Nephi 27:26).

The prophet Isaiah did much of his teaching employing symbolic language that does not teach directly, so we must examine and ponder his words to discover the truths they convey. His most beautiful and profound symbolic language focused on the Savior, as, for example, this familiar expression: "For unto us a child is born, unto us a son is given, and the government shall be upon his shoulder, and his name shall be called Wonderful, Counselor, the mighty God, the everlasting Father, the Prince of Peace." (Isaiah 9:6).

He described how the Savior has the power to admit or exclude any person from Heavenly Father's presence: "And the key of the house of David will I lay upon his shoulder; so he shall open, and none shall shut; and he shall shut, and none shall open." (Isaiah 22:22). Nephi, who was a great admirer of Isaiah, expanded upon this theme: "Behold, the way for man is narrow, but it lieth in a straight course before him, and the keeper of the gate (of heaven) is the Holy One of Israel; and he employeth no servant there; and there is none other way (we can enter into Heavenly Father's presence) save it be by the gate; for he cannot be deceived, for the Lord God is his name." (2 Nephi 9:41).

Isaiah described how those who did not receive the gospel while on the earth, or who were not valiant in their testimonies while they were here, will go to a spiritual prison, of sorts, where the Savior will show them mercy. "And it shall come to pass in that day, that the Lord shall punish the host of the high ones that are on high, and the kings of the earth upon the earth. And they shall be gathered together, as prisoners are gathered in the pit, and shall be shut up in the prison, and after many days shall they be visited." (Isaiah 24:21-22).

Joseph F. Smith taught that the gospel was "preached to those who had died in their sins, without a knowledge of the truth, or in transgression, having rejected the prophets." (D&C 138:32). This makes clear Isaiah's prophetic message: "The Lord has called thee in righteousness, and will hold thine hand, and will keep thee, and give thee for a covenant of the people, for a light of the Gentiles; to open the blind eyes, to bring out the prisoners from the prison, them that sit in darkness out of the prison house." (Isaiah 42:6-7). "Say to the prisoners, Go forth; to them that are in darkness, Shew yourselves. They shall feed in the ways, and their pastures shall be in all high places. They shall not hunger nor thirst; neither shall the heat nor sun smite them: for he that hath mercy on them shall lead them, even by the springs of water shall he guide them." (Isaiah 49:9-10).

The Savior will be our sanctuary, our "strength to the poor and to the needy in his distress, a refuge from the storm, a shadow from the heat, when the blast of the terrible ones is as a storm against the wall. (Isaiah 25:4). He is "as an hiding place from the wind, and a covert from the tempest; as rivers of water in a dry place, as the shadow of a great rock in a weary land." (Isaiah 32:2).

"And in this mountain shall the Lord of hosts make unto all people a feast of fat things, a feast of wines on the lees, of fat things full of marrow, of wines on the lees well refined. And he will destroy in this mountain the face of the covering cast over all people, and the vail that is spread over all nations. He will swallow up death in victory; and the Lord God will wipe away tears from off all faces; and the rebuke of his people shall he take away from off all the earth: for the Lord hath spoken it. And it shall be said in that day, Lo, this is our God; we have waited for him, and he will save us: this is the Lord; we have waited for him, we will be glad and rejoice in his salvation." (Isaiah 25:6-9).

One interpretation of Isaiah 25:6-7, that is popular among Latter-day Saints, is that the mountain he described is a symbol for the temple. (See Isaiah 2:2 and D&C 58:8-9). The feast mentioned in Isaiah 25:6 could be a feast of the words and teachings of Christ. We know that the temple endowment can be like a feast. "And it shall come to pass in the last days, that the mountain of the Lord's house shall be established in the top of the mountains, and shall be exalted above the hills; and all nations shall flow unto it." (Isaiah 2:2).

A vail or veil is a thin covering. Symbolically it often represented the unbelief that prevented people from embracing the Savior. "And he beheld Satan; and he had a great chain in his hand, and it veiled the whole face of the earth with darkness; and he looked up and laughed, and his angels rejoiced." (Moses 7:26). The "vail" of darkness that is over the earth can only be dismissed by the power of the priesthood.

The Savior will comfort His children, and "swallow up death in victory; and the Lord God will wipe away tears from off all faces." (Isaiah 28:5). There is a sense of intimacy in this tender gesture that is shared only by people who love and trust each other completely.

The Savior will exercise the keys of the Resurrection. "Thy dead men shall live, together with my body shall they arise. Awake and sing, ye that dwell in dust: for thy dew is as the dew of herbs, and the earth shall cast out the dead." (Isaiah 26:19).

The Savior is the bedrock of our faith. "Thus saith the Lord God, Behold, I lay in Zion for a foundation a stone, a tried stone, a precious corner stone, a sure foundation." (Isaiah 28:16). "And now, my sons," Helaman clearly explained to Lehi and Nephi, "remember, remember that it is upon the rock of our Redeemer, who is Christ, the Son of God, that ye must build your foundation; that when the devil shall send forth his mighty winds, yea, his shafts in the whirlwind, yea, when all his hail and his mighty storm shall beat upon you, it shall have no power over you to drag you down to the gulf of misery and endless wo, because of the rock upon which ye are built, which is a sure foundation, a foundation whereon if men build they cannot fall." (Helaman 5:12). He is "the good shepherd, and the stone of Israel. He that buildeth upon this rock shall never fail." (D&C 50:44).

The Savior will restore the gospel to the earth. "And thou shalt be brought down, and shalt speak out of the ground, and thy speech shall be low out of the dust, and thy voice shall be, as of one that hath a familiar spirit, out of the ground, and thy speech shall whisper out of the dust." (Isaiah 29:4). In the process, a most remarkable thing will happen: "I will proceed to do a marvelous work among this people, even a marvelous work and a wonder: for the wisdom of their wise men shall perish, and the understanding of their prudent men shall be hid." (Isaiah 29:14). "They also that erred in spirit shall come to understanding, and they that murmured shall learn doctrine." (Isaiah 29:24).

The Savior, Who knows our trials and directs our paths, used the prophetic powers of one of His favorite servants to reveal how He will influence our lives in the Last Days. Isaiah clothed the Savior and His ministry with beautiful, symbolic expressions, showing us how He has done wonderful things for us.

The Savior, Who knows our trials and guides our paths, used the prophetic literary powers of one of His faithful servants to describe how He will influence our lives in the Last Days. Nephi clothed the Savior and His ministry with beautiful, symbolic vestments showing us how He has done wonderful things for us.
(See 1 Nephi 7:11).

(The) Thrill of Victory / The Agony of De Feet

"These are they who have published peace, who have brought good tidings of good, who have published salvation; and said unto Zion: Thy God reigneth! And O how beautiful upon the mountains were their feet! And again, how beautiful upon the mountains are the feet of those that are still publishing peace! And again, how beautiful upon the mountains are the feet of those who shall hereafter publish peace, yea, from this time henceforth and forever! And behold, I say unto you, this is not all. For O how beautiful upon the mountains are the feet of him that bringeth good tidings, that is the founder of peace, yea, even the Lord, who has redeemed his people; yea, him who has granted salvation unto his people.' (Mosiah 15:14-18).

Long ago, the Viking invaded Scotland. As the Danes crept up unawares on the sleeping Scottish forces, they inadvertently walked across a patch of sharp thistles that poked deep into the soles of their feet. Alerted to their presence by their cries of pain, the Scots rallied to drive off the enemy. To this day, the thistle has been the emblem of Scotland.

The foot soldier has been the bulwark of nearly every army since the dawn of history, but feet can also be a source of weakness. Not everyone is like the Kentucky hillbilly who never wore shoes. One evening, he came into the cabin and stood by the fireplace. His wife said, "I reckon you'd better move. You're standin' on a live coal." He replied, "Which foot?"

Most of us don't have feet that are so heavily calloused and insensitive. The weakness of the great warrior Achilles, after all, was his heel. A dog may be man's best friend, but we call our own feet "puppies," our comfortable shoes "hushpuppies," and we say "our dogs are tired." Sometimes, a swift kick (with the foot) in the rear is all it takes to get us moving. If we try to hold on for dear life, we "get a toehold." When we want to accomplish more, we "lengthen our stride." Things that are really easy are "a cakewalk." We "take a step back" to appraise a situation objectively, but if we're ready to go right now, we "step up to the plate." When we relinquish our position of authority, "we step down."

If we have "feet of clay," we have trouble getting things done. When we encourage someone, we tell them to put both their feet on the ground. If we haven't got a care in the world, we are "foot-loose and fancy-free." If someone's philosophical position is unsupportable, we say they "haven't got a leg to stand on." If we want to be upwardly mobile, we try to "get our foot in the door." If the shoe fits, wear it. If we stumble over our words and say something inappropriate, we've "put our foot in our mouth." When we venture into new territory, we are "getting our feet wet." If we are fully committed to a new course, we "jump in with both feet." If we are slow to adopt a policy, we are "dragging our feet." When we "kick the bucket," we are carried out "feet first." Then we are buried "six feet deep." If we are awkward, we have "two left feet." If we are true to our principles, "we toe the line." Because feet are sometimes seen as a liability, we see signs that read: "No bare feet allowed," or "No shirt, no shoes, no service." "Walks" and "runs" are integral to baseball. A "false step" might bring us to defeat, but putting "our best foot forward" could carry us to victory.

If we move recklessly forward, we call it a "misstep." But if we move quickly, "we step lively." If we are true to our principles, we "have our feet planted firmly on gospel soil." If we consciously try to make a good impression we "put our best foot forward." But sometimes, we "take a step backward." Distances are measured in feet. Light is measured in foot-candles, and power is measured in foot-pounds. If we are nimble, we are "sure-footed." If we are passive, we take timid, halting, or hesitant steps. When we dance around a dominant personality, we are "walking on eggshells." If someone faints, we elevate the feet to improve circulation. When we have had a long day, we "put our feet up."

When Neil Armstrong walked on the moon, he said: "That's one small step for a man, one giant leap for mankind." Ralph Waldo Emerson said: "Build a better mousetrap, and the world will beat a path to your door," presumably on foot. During Israel's exodus from Egypt, they walked through the Red Sea on dry ground. (The pursuing Egyptians should have followed their example. Instead, they and their horse-drawn chariots were drowned). Richard III cried, "A horse, a horse. My kingdom for a horse," presumably because he didn't think himself adequate to the task when afoot.

We talk about the steps of repentance. When we exercise unrighteous dominion, we overstep our bounds. If we carelessly put our feet down without forethought, they are sometimes caught in a snare. Depending upon our perspective, obstacles in our path can be seen as stepping-stones or stumbling-blocks.

The stage-lights that illuminate a set are called "footlights." The journey of a thousand miles begins with one step. We maintain our forward momentum by continuing to put one foot in front of the other. If a tennis player crosses the service line too quickly, he commits a foot-fault. A gentleman's servant is called a footman.

In the advanced stages of diabetes, peripheral circulation is so poor that all feeling may be lost in the feet. When this happens, there is a tremendous risk of infection from even minor irritations that go unnoticed. Stepping on a nail, for example, can have devastating consequences if we are "past feeling." There are spiritual equivalents that are equally devastating that can be traced back to the feet. The feet can take us on detours so that before we realize it, we are walking around in our summer home in Babylon.

In the humid climate of Viet Nam, keeping the feet clean and dry was of paramount importance to the U.S. Forces stationed there. Clean socks were as necessary as clean weapons. An entire army would have been brought to its knees, if basic hygiene relating to the feet had been neglected.

In the Revolutionary War, the colonial troops often went barefoot for lack of boots, or wrapped their naked feet in bloody rags. It was said bloodstains in the snow marked route the army had taken. The protection of the feet was of great concern to George Washington and his staff officers, for the fortunes of war swung on the health of the feet of their soldiers.

Feet are one of the miracles of creation. Leonardo daVinci called them "a masterpiece of engineering and a work of art." They contain one quarter of the bones in our bodies. The average person by age 55 has walked the equivalent of two and a half times around the world. In all our perambulating, the "lives of great men all remind us we can make our lives sublime, and departing leave behind us footprints in the sands of time." (Longfellow).

"Aha!" said the cartoon philosopher Pogo. "Here we have someone paying for the sin of excess. The hobnailed boots of indiscretion's marathon dancer tap a rowdy two-step across the terracotta of his consciousness. Excess was his master. Reason was cast into the rumble seat of his libidinous juggernaut. Now the piper must be paid!" Any way you look at it, feet play a major role in our lives.

John said: "One mightier than I cometh, the latchet of whose shoes I am not worthy to unloose." (Luke 3:16). He was speaking of the Lord Jesus Christ, whose feet are mentioned over two dozen times in the New Testament. Feet are referenced over 150 times in the Old Testament and 75 times in the New Testament, suggesting that they were simply more conspicuous in a world without modern transportation, and where sandals were the most popular form of footwear. It was natural to bring the blind and the infirm to the feet of Jesus, that He might heal them. It makes perfect sense that He caused the lame to walk as a consequence of their faith. To be able to do so gave them a new lease on life.

Our feet can be used as weapons against evil. "The God of peace shall bruise Satan under your feet," wrote Paul. (Romans 16:20). He encouraged the Ephesians: "Put on the whole armour of God, that ye may be able to stand against the wiles of the devil…. And your feet shod with the preparation of the gospel of peace." (Ephesians 6:11 & 15). As weapons of spiritual warfare, our feet strategically conquer territory that is under Satan's power and liberate the captives under his control. God Himself, we are told, "hath put all things under his feet." (Ephesians 1:22). As His disciples, we consciously sit at the feet of the Savior, in order to be positioned to promote the cause of Zion.

The devil, in the meantime, is as Ozymandias, of whom Shelley wrote: "I met a traveler from an antique land who said: Two vast and trunkless legs of stone stand in the desert. Near them, on the sand half sunk, a shattered visage lies, whose frown and wrinkled lip and sneer of cold command tell that its sculptor well those passions read, which yet survive. Stamped on these lifeless things, the hand that mocks them and the heart that fed; and on the pedestal these words appear: 'My name is Ozymandias, King of Kings; Look on my works, ye mighty, and despair!' Nothing beside remains. Round the decay of that colossal wreck, boundless and bare, the lone and level sand stretched far away."

Of contemporary royalty, it was similarly written: "And it came to pass, when they brought out those kings unto Joshua, that Joshua called for all the men of Israel, and said unto the captains of the men of war which went with him, Come near, put your feet upon the necks of these kings." (Joshua 10:24). This symbolic demonstration of domination was not lost on either the conquerors or the vanquished.

If we want to have the greatest success in life, we must sit at the feet of Jesus because His footprints have changed the course of history. He never strayed more than a hundred miles or so from His birthplace, but everywhere he went on foot has become a place of great interest, and we undertake pilgrimages at great effort and expense just to be there to share, even in a small way, a common experience.

The feet are very sensitive. Helen Keller once gave a speech, and at its conclusion the crowd gave her a thunderous round of applause. When asked how she knew what the reaction of the audience had been, she said she felt their appreciation through the vibrations in her feet. This sheds understanding on the statement of the Prophet Joseph Smith who said after receiving revelation: "My whole body was full of light, and I could see even out at the ends of my fingers and toes." Perhaps this is why the angel Moroni hovered in the air when he was visiting Joseph. He wanted to see better, for he could see even out of his toes. "And if your eye be single to my glory, your whole bodies shall be filled with light, and there shall be no darkness in you; and that body which is filled with light comprehendeth all things." (D&C 88:67).

The feet can feel not only pleasure, but pain as well. Certainly, Jesus felt both. He was thankful for the concern Mary showed to Him when she washed his feet after a long and dusty journey, but He also felt the pain as the nails of His crucifiers were driven through his feet.

Those who washed His feet showed by their actions that love is not something you say, but something you do. Service can sometimes be very costly, and the feet bear the burden. How often do we say after a particularly hard day: "My feet are killing me," or "Oh, my aching feet." The feet carry us wherever we can render the best service.

His feet carried Him to the far corners of Galilee and Judea, performing acts of service. To minister to the needs of others, His feet needed attention, and so His disciples washed them and cared for them as sacred instruments. He was unlike "the young lady of Crete, who was so exceedingly neat. When she got out of bed, she stood on her head to make sure of not soiling her feet." (Bennet Cerf).

Shakespeare referred to the feet of the Savior, when he wrote of "those holy fields over whose acres walked those blessed feet which, fourteen hundred years ago were nailed for our advantage on the bitter cross." (Henry IV).

Doubting Thomas said: "Except I shall see in his hands the print of the nails, and put my finger into the print of the nails, and thrust my hand into his side, I will not believe." (John 20:25). But to skeptics in all ages, the Savior responded: "Behold my hands and my feet, that it is I myself.... And when he had thus spoken, he shewed them his hands and his feet. (Luke 20:39-40). It is sobering to ponder the thought that because of His wounds, we may use our own feet to walk in a newness of life, and that one day they may be used to explore every nook and cranny in the Celestial Kingdom.

When the Savior said: "Go ye into all the world and preach the gospel" the command could not be carried out without the feet. (Mark 16:15). Isaiah recognized this when he wrote: "How beautiful upon the mountains are the feet of him that bringeth good tidings, that publisheth peace; that bringeth good tidings of good, that publisheth salvation." (Isaiah 57:2).

Except for the one time Jesus entered Jerusalem on the back of a donkey (in fulfillment of prophecy), He went everywhere on foot. There are over 100 references in the Gospels to his walking. You cannot fully appreciate His ministry without a conscious consideration of His feet. His invitations to "Come, follow me," and "Go ye therefore into all the world," had specific references to the feet, even though there will never be a beauty contest that focuses on the feet.

In the scriptures, many parts of the human anatomy have been related to behavior. We read of strong backs, eyes and ears, and hearts, hands, and feet. When President Spencer W. Kimball said: "I am like an old shoe, to be worn out in the service of the Lord," he was utilizing vivid imagery about themes with which we can all relate.

Tithing

"Will a man rob God? Yet ye have
robbed me. But ye say: Wherein have
we robbed thee? In tithes and offerings. Ye
are curse with a curse, for ye have robbed me,
even this whole nation. Bring ye all the tithes into
the storehouse, that there may be meat in my house;
and prove me now herewith, saith the Lord of Hosts,
if I will not open you the windows of heaven, and
pour you out a blessing that there shall not
be room enough to receive it."
(3 Nephi 24:8-10).

The temple is a beacon that orients mankind toward the path leading back home. Accordingly, attending the temple regularly is one of the most important things we can do while on the earth. When Moroni asked us to "come unto Christ" (Moroni 10:32), it was a plea to enter into the ordinances of His priesthood and make temple covenants that would bind us forever to our families. That is the essence of the gospel of Jesus Christ. Therefore, it makes no difference on which principle of the gospel we may be focusing, the distance to the temple where we ultimately take our bearing on eternity is measured in faith, and not in miles. It may have been with this in mind that, in 1881, obedience to the law of tithing became a requirement for temple attendance for those with an income. (J.D. 22:207-208). Payment of a full tithe is a good barometer of our spiritual maturity, and is an easy measurement of our core testimony temperature.

"Those who have been thus tithed shall pay one-tenth of all their interest annually; and this shall be a standing law unto them forever, for my holy priesthood, saith the Lord." (D&C 119:4). Of course, we know that tithing has been a part of the gospel since the time of the Patriarchs, but it has been firmly re-established as a foundation principle of the latter-day Restoration. The History of the church records that in 1834 Joseph Smith and Oliver Cowdery pledged one-tenth of all that the Lord should give them as an offering for the poor. (H.C. 2:174-75). "The term 'tithing' had been used in some revelations before 1838 (e.g., D&C 64:23; 85:3; & 97:11-12) but the term connoted all free-will offerings or contributions, whether they were more or less than 10 percent. Then, in 1838, the Prophet received the definitive law that would be binding upon the church. (D&C 119).

Prior to this revelation on tithing, an adaptation of the law of consecration of property was practiced by the Saints to care for the poor, to purchase lands, and to build church facilities. (D&C 42:30-39). The declared spiritual objective of that law was to "advance the cause" of "the salvation of man" (D&C 78:4-7) by creating equality in both "earthly things" and "heavenly things." This proved too difficult at the time, especially under the disruptive conditions suffered by church members in Missouri, and the practice was temporarily suspended in 1840. (H.C., 4:93). The law of tithing was given in part to fulfil material needs and to prepare the membership of the church to live the temporal aspects of the law of consecration at some future time. Tithing has variously been described as the donation of (1) a tenth of what people owned when they converted; (2) a tenth of their "increase" or income each year; and (3) one workday in ten of their labor, teams, and tools to public projects. Today, tithe payers pay a tenth of their "increase," or income, consistent with the direction given in D&C 119.

A 1970 letter from the First Presidency stated that notwithstanding the fact that members should pay one-tenth of their income, "every member of the church is entitled to make his own decision as to what he thinks he owes the Lord and to make payment accordingly" (March 19, 1970). Hence, the exact amount paid is not as important as that each member feels that he or she has paid an honest tenth." ("Encyclopedia of Mormonism").

In the Church today, tithing money is basically used to support the three-fold mission of the Church, to preach the gospel, redeem the dead, and perfect the Saints. "The collection of tithing is the responsibility of the bishop in each ward. Tithes are presented confidentially to him or to his counselors. He forwards the tithes collected locally to church headquarters, where a committee consisting of the First Presidency, the Presiding Bishopric, and the Quorum of the Twelve Apostles supervises the distribution and expenditure of tithing funds. (D&C 120). These are used for such purposes as the building and maintenance of meetinghouses, temples, and other facilities, as well as for the partial support of the missionary, educational, and welfare programs of the church." ("Encyclopedia of Mormonism").

Matthew Cowley gave a marvelous address that beautifully illustrates the relationship God can have with His children when they are obedient to His laws. He said: "God is a wonderful partner, isn't he. I would like to be in business with somebody like that, having my partner come up to me and say 'Here, I'll furnish all the capital to start the business. I will furnish all the blessings. Then, you look after the business. Don't forget me. When the increase comes, you keep ninety percent, and turn over to me ten percent. You use your ninety percent any way you want to, and I'll put my ten percent right back into the business.' Wouldn't that be wonderful? That's just the kind of partner we have in this church. We keep the ninety percent and use it anyway we wish. We give him the ten percent, and here stands a temple, (and there) stands a tabernacle. He puts it all right back into the business, into his business. God will finance the church, brothers and sisters, if you will obey the principles of the gospel." ("Matthew Cowley Speaks," p. 76-77).

Finally, Heber J. Grant bore testimony of the promise given by Malachi when that prophet spoke in the name of the Lord, declaring: "Prove me now herewith, saith the Lord of hosts, if I will not open you the windows of heaven, and pour you out a blessing, that there shall not be room enough to receive it." (Malachi 3:10). "I bear witness," Elder Grant said, "that the men and women who have been absolutely honest with God, who have paid their one-tenth (have received) wisdom whereby they have been able to utilize the remaining nine-tenths, and it has been of greater value to them, and they have accomplished more with it than they would if they had not been honest with the Lord." (C.R. 4/1912).

The Lord also declared, through Malachi, that he would "rebuke the devourer for your sakes, and he shall not destroy the fruits of your ground." (Malachi 3:11). This promise becomes increasingly important in the Last Days, as events are played out and the struggle with Spiritual Babylon intensifies. We must obey this law, said the Lord, "to prepare (ourselves) against the day of vengeance and burning," (D&C 85:3), when the wicked who do not obey the will of God will be visited with "sore affliction, with pestilence, with plague, with sword, with vengeance, (and) with devouring fire." (D&C 97:26). "Nevertheless, let it be read this once . that if (Zion) sin no more, none of these things shall come upon her. And I will bless her with…a multiplicity of blessings upon her, and upon her generations forever and ever, saith the Lord your God." (D&C 97:27-28).

It is not unusual to hear members of the church bear personal testimony of the blessings that come through their obedience to the Law of Tithing. It is a wonderful law, conceived in royal courts above, and designed to give God's children a means to taste the riches of eternity. It allows faithful members of the church to be junior partners of the Lord in His work, that began even before our birth, which is to bring about our immortality and eternal life. (See Moses 1:39). It adds a whole new layer of meaning to the Savior's question: "Wist ye not that I must be about my Father's business?" (Luke 2:49). It adds depth to the question: "What think ye of Christ?" (Matthew 22:42). It adds poignancy to the Savior's plea: "Will ye also go away?" (John 6:67).

It establishes a measure of equality to temporal circumstances that seem, at times, to be wildly out of balance. Obedience allows every faithful member to labor in the traces, yoked equally to the Master. It gives them a chance to wipe the sweat from their foreheads, and to acknowledge talents and capacities that have come from God. The Law of Tithing transports its adherents through time to the altars of the ancient temple, there to offer sacrifice with the Levitical priests, and to feel the stirrings of a spiritual reality from beyond the veil. It gives them the means to measure the fruits of their labor, and when their offerings are put to use, to experience confirmation of the immutable law that relates blessings to obedience. It is with tithing donation slips that faithful members bank the fires of their testimonies, and warm themselves beside their glowing embers. The Law of Tithing provides a bellows that fans the flames of their resolve, as they plunge themselves directly into the white-hot crucible of faith.

It asks the same of those who have been blessed with the Midas Touch, those who have been tenderly caressed by the hand of fate, and those who were born with silver spoons in their mouths, as well as of those who are enrolled in the school of hard knocks, whose mortal curriculum seems to be filled with elusive goals, cancelled classes, cranky professors, daunting tuition, exhausting prerequisites, repetitive lower-level classes, dismaying learning laboratories, demoralizing homework assignments, intimidating term papers, unfulfilled dreams, and one crisis of confidence after another.

The circumstances might have been exceptional, but when the Lord sent Elijah to the Widow of Zarephath, he saw her "there gathering of sticks: and he called to her, and said, Fetch me, I pray thee, a little water in a vessel, that I may drink. And as she was going to fetch it, he called to her, and said, Bring me, I pray thee, a morsel of bread in thine hand. And she said, As the Lord thy God liveth, I have not a cake, but an handful of meal in a barrel, and a little oil in a cruse: and, behold, I am gathering two sticks, that I may go in and dress it for me and my son, that we may eat it, and die. And Elijah said unto her, Fear not; go and do as thou hast said: but make me thereof a little cake first, and bring it unto me, and after make for thee and for thy son. For thus saith the Lord God of Israel, The barrel of meal shall not waste, neither shall the cruse of oil fail, until the day that the Lord sendeth rain upon the earth. And she went and did according to the saying of Elijah: and she, and he, and her house, did eat many days. And the barrel of meal wasted not, neither did the cruse of oil fail, according to the word of the Lord, which he spake by Elijah. (1 Kings 17:7-16).

The Lord helps those in need through the tithes and offerings of the Saints, and He has re-established the law that the door might swing both ways. We are both blessed, and our capacity to bless the lives of others increases, when we pay our tithing. "When we put God first, all other things fall into their proper place or drop out of our lives. Our love of the Lord will govern the claims for our affection, the demands on our time, the interests we pursue, and the order of our priorities. May God bless us to put Him first and, as a result, reap peace in this life and eternal life with a fulness of joy in the life to come." (Ezra Taft Benson).

The law was conceived, because "all are alike unto God." (2 Nephi 26:33). It allows Him to apply a fine line to stewardship, and to measure our devotions without ambiguity. It creates a celestial standard that permits Him to be fair and impartial in His dealings with His children, without risking accusations of favoritism given to one or to another. It provides a way for both the rich and the poor to participate equally in the expansion of the temporal and spiritual assets of the church and Kingdom. It eliminates class distinction by evenly dividing the weight of responsibility among all the members of the church, regardless of their individual temporal circumstances. Its objective is to make both princes and paupers feel that they are "fellowcitizens with the saints, and of the household of God." (Ephesians 2:19).

Those who pay their tithes are blessed with an exalted view of the kingdom of God on the earth. They are empowered with the spirit of anticipation. When they live in strict conformity to the other laws of the gospel, they are blessed to participate in temple ordinances, and are prepared to kneel at holy altars to make sacred covenants of consecration with God. Tithe payers are blessed with both the temporal and spiritual means to do all that is required to bring to pass a new heaven and a new earth. As their lives spin out joyfully, the price, once paid so dearly, is recalled in gladness. They receive full value. Brigham Young, in his inimitable way, said: "I never count the cost of anything. I just find out what the Lord wants me to do, and I do it." He knew from whence his blessings came. (See Mormon 5:10).

"Act now, before it is too late!" urged Spencer W. Kimball. "Now is the time to chart the course of action you will follow tomorrow, and next week, and next year. Now is the time to commit yourself to be as Abraham...to begin to keep those commandments you have been failing to live. Determine now to...pay your tithing faithfully. ...Here, then, is the challenge the Lord gives ... every single man and woman ... in the church: "Go ye, therefore, and do the works of Abraham." (D&C 132:32). ("The Example of Abraham").

Too Good to be True

"The Spirit speaketh the truth and lieth not. Wherefore, it speaketh of things as they really are, and of things as they really will be; wherefore, these things are manifested unto us plainly."
(Jacob 4:13).

In early September 2009, my daughter Tara decided to visit her sister Kathryn in New York City. She got on the Internet and went to her favorite airline's website to book a ticket. To her surprise and delight, she found a fare that seemed too good to be true. It was one that suited her travel plans perfectly. Because she was in a hurry to nail it down, she quickly entered her credit card information, hit the "Purchase" option, and then turned her attention to other preparation details relating to the trip.

The departure date was only a week or so away, and plans had to be made regarding the care and feeding of her family in her absence. Everything was made ready without difficulty, however, leaving her time to work with Kathryn, who made reservations at a fun restaurant, scouted venues for activities, and stocked her refrigerator with goodies in excited anticipation.

The morning of her flight, Tara had her bag packed with clothes picked out especially for a late summer visit to The Big Apple. The bag was already tucked in the trunk of the car, in fact, when Tara sat down at her computer to print out her boarding pass. But the message that popped up on the screen in front of her read: "Boarding passes can only be obtained within 24 hours of departure."

With a bit of impatience, Tara first thought to call the airline to seek help in straightening out this glitch in her plans. But then, she looked more carefully at the date of departure. "What's this?" she asked herself, as her pulse rate quickened. " NOVEMBER 15? But today is SEPTEMBER 15." (Oops!)

What was to be done?. She thought she would call the airline, plead stupidity, and see if they would let her fly. (in two hours). "Yes," the agent told her. "No problem. Just pay the difference in fare. It's about $1,000.00." "I guess I should have dug into the details of the reservation a little more deeply," she told me later. With a sheepish grin, she sighed: "It just seemed too good to be true."

What should we do when we are faced with opportunities in life that just seem too good to be true?. Sometimes, the very "deceitfulness of riches choke(s) the word," and we are blinded to our characteristic good judgment, insomuch that we act irrationally. (Matthew 13:22). That is to say, the temptation of a screaming deal can cloud our vision and compromise our ability to make a correct and prudent choice.

Every day we are blitzed by any number of offers to spend obscene amounts of money so we can save big-time, (where is the logic in that?) and it is only natural to assume that some of the purveyors of promises "too good to be true" lie in wait to "falsify the balances by deceit." (Amos 8:5). They prowl the media, and like sharks cruising near the shore, wait for the unwary to move out of their safety zones into dangerously deep water. They disguise their evil purposes with tinsel, and invite the innocent to gamble away their fortunes and forfeit their birthright for a mess of pottage. Like the tangled Christmas lights of confusion, they play upon our innate trust and the better angels of our nature, twisting the truth into caricatures of reality. By this time, our heads are spinning so wildly that just about any outlandish offer would seem too good to be true.

These exaggerations stretch our comprehension of credibility, causing us to stand unsteadily on our spiritual tippy toes, roll the dice, and leave our destiny in the hands of lady luck. When things seem too good to be true, it may be that the source is the great deceiver himself, for Alma clearly taught: "Whatsoever is good cometh from God, and whatsoever is evil cometh from the devil." (Alma 5:40). To narrow our search parameters, however, and to steer us back on course, Paul reminded us:. "If there is anything virtuous, lovely, or of good report or praiseworthy, we seek after these things." (Philippians 4:8).

Paraphrasing the Apostle Paul, we should abhor that which seems too good to be true, and instead cleave to that which a reasonable person would presume to be true. (See Romans 12:9). Paul was all too familiar with those who sowed false hope. He wrote: "For they that are such … serve their own belly; and by good words and fair speeches deceive the hearts of the simple." (Romans 16:18). Such deceivers have sharpened their pencils and honed their skills as consummate con-men.

When confronting such swindlers, we cannot descend to their comfort level of the lowest common denominator. Instead, we should yearn, as Paul did, for the light that will disperse their darkness, "that we henceforth be no more children, tossed to and fro," as flotsam and jetsam on the sea of life, "and carried about with every wind of doctrine, by the sleight of men, and cunning craftiness." (Ephesians 4:14). Paul's simple counsel was" "Let no man deceive you with vain words." The trouble with vanity is that it relies on false hope and its strength is built upon false premises. It is a pyramid scheme that cannot deliver on its promises. It writes checks it cannot cash because its spiritual reserves are running on empty, and it is forever teetering on the brink of bankruptcy. In its worst form, it is an abomination because it thwarts God's very Plan of Happiness. No wonder Paul counseled: "Beware lest any man spoil you through philosophy and vain deceit, after the tradition of men, after the rudiments of the world." (Colossians 2:8). Not only can our travel plans be spoiled, but also the direction of our life's journey can be detoured when we succumb to offers that just seem too good to be true.

Jacob taught: "The Spirit speaketh the truth and lieth not. Wherefore, it speaketh of things as they really are, and of things as they really will be; wherefore, these things are manifested unto us plainly." (Jacob 4:13). When faced with claims that seem too good to be true, we should remember that God's reality is the only one that really matters. If we are in synch with Him, then our objectives will be obtainable because our perceptions are faultless. Thus, Moroni tells us: "Come unto Christ, and be perfected in him, and deny yourselves of all ungodliness; and if ye shall deny yourselves of all ungodliness, and love God with all your might, mind and strength, then is his grace sufficient for you, that by his grace ye may be perfect in Christ." (Moroni 10:32).

By the grace of God, we are perfected in Christ to the end that we "shall know the truth, and the truth shall make (us) free." (John 8:32). We will be free to make good choices based on accurate information and observations. Perhaps when David O. McKay said: "Spirituality is the consciousness of victory over self, and of communion with the Infinite" he meant it opens up opportunities to live abundantly, no matter what curves life throws at us or what our temporal circumstances may be.

Little wonder that Moroni, who saw our day and knows our challenges, would urge us: "Wherefore, I beseech of you, brethren, that ye should search diligently in the Light of Christ that ye may know good from evil." (Moroni 7:19). His broader application was that when things seem too good to be true, "by the power of the Holy Ghost (we) may know the truth of all things." (Moroni 10:5). He could make that promise with confidence, because we all intuitively understand that "whatsoever is light is good because it is discernible, therefore (we) must know that it is good." (Alma 32:35).

Our Heavenly Father has not left us alone as we negotiate the minefields of mortality. He has shown us in myriad ways how we can safely reach our destination. He is like the able mariner who can read the weather like a book, can focus his nautical skills and use his navigational equipment to trim his sails and set a course that will lead him unerringly to safe harbor. The same wind that might cause another vessel to founder fills the sails of the vessel whose helmsman is a skilled seafarer.

That sailor may not see the port that is his destination. Sometimes, it is over the horizon, and sometimes the tack of the vessel appears to be taking the ship away from its objective. But if correct principles are followed, the landfall is always sure.

The best Mariner of all, and the One in control of the elements around Him, was the Savior. The scriptures tell us: "When he was entered into a ship, his disciples followed him. And, behold, there arose a great tempest in the sea, insomuch that the ship was covered with the waves; but he was asleep. And his disciples came to him, and awoke him, saying, Lord, save us; we perish. And he saith unto them, Why are ye fearful, O ye of little faith? Then he arose and rebuked the winds and the sea; and there was a great calm. But the men marvelled, saying, What manner of man is this, that even the winds and the sea obey him!". (Matthew 8:23-27).

When things seem too good to be true, we should remember the counsel of Alma, who taught: "For behold, it is as easy to give heed to the word of Christ, which will point to you a straight course to eternal bliss, as it was for our fathers to give heed to this compass, which would point unto them a straight course to the promised land." (Alma 37: 44). As it was for Alma and his people, so it is for us. With our Liahona, we will find that no wind can blow except it fills our sails and carries us ever closer to our intended destination, without delay or interruption, and without extra cost, loss, or sacrifice.

Feet are two of the miracles of creation. Leonardo da Vinci called them "a masterpiece of engineering and a work of art." The feet contain one quarter of the bones in our bodies. By age 55, we have walked the equivalent of over two and a half times around the world. In all of our perambulating, we are reminded that "we can make our lives sublime, and departing, leave behind us footprints on the sands of time." (Longfellow). Our feet can feel not only pleasure, but pain as well. Certainly, Jesus felt both. He was thankful for the concern Mary showed to Him when she washed His feet after a long and dusty journey, but later, He also felt pain as the nails of His crucifiers were driven through His feet.

(The) Tools of The Trade

"Because of your diligence
and your faith and your patience
with the word in nourishing it, that it
may take root in you, behold, by and by ye
shall pluck the fruit thereof, which is most
precious, which is sweet above all that is sweet,
and which is white above all that is white, yea, and
pure above all that is pure; and ye shall feast upon
this fruit even until ye are filled, that ye hunger
not, neither shall ye thirst. Then, my brethren,
ye shall reap the rewards of your faith, and
your diligence, and patience, and
(your) long-suffering."
(Alma 32:42-43).

Joseph, whose trade was carpentry, mentored Jesus from His youth. He must have developed considerable skill using the tools of Joseph's trade to craft many of the household items that would have made life in Israel more tolerable. Among other things, He surely learned three simple lessons from Joseph.

First, He learned to "measure twice and cut once." With the scarcity of wood in ancient Israel, Joseph couldn't afford to make mistakes. His example showed Jesus that He must know exactly what He was doing, why He was doing it, proceed carefully, delegate responsibility, accept accountability, earn trust, delight in appreciation, and feel satisfaction. Measuring twice and cutting once, Jesus would understand by inference that proper prior priesthood planning prevents poor performance.

Secondly, He learned to "use the right tool for the job." In His youth, Jesus would have learned when and how to use chisels, drills, hammers, nails, pegs, and clamps. He would have learned how much pressure to apply with His adze, in order to shape either hard or soft wood, and how to deal with knots and other imperfections in the materials with which He was working. He would also have trusted His instincts, and relied upon relationship tools such as appreciation, benevolence, concern, empathy, encouragement, forgiveness, friendship, gentleness, humility, kindness, patience, persuasiveness, sincerity, tolerance, and understanding.

Thirdly, He would have learned that "by taking care of the tools of His trade, they would take care of Him." He would have learned how to use these tools without abusing or damaging them, how to get the most out of them, and how to maintain them so that they would reliably provide for the temporal needs of His family. He would also have learned to use the spiritual tools of conviction, devotion, fasting, holiness, meditation, prayer, purity, reverence, scripture study, self-control, wisdom, and worship. In short, He would have learned to use both His head and his hands under the watchful eye of Joseph, but He would also have learned to use His heart, as His capacity for compassion and unconditional love expanded.

As His carpentry skills developed, He would have discovered a confidence born of the Spirit that would spill over into every other aspect of His life, for "he spake not as other men, neither could he be taught; for he needed not that any man should teach him." (J.S.T. Matthew 3:25). He would have mastered the innovative and original utilization of tools relating to priesthood keys, that confirms what He said through His prophet Isaiah: "My thoughts are not your thoughts, neither are your ways my ways." (Isaiah 55:8). In the process, He would have nurtured in the armory of His own thoughts the devices to build bastions of joy and the strategies of strength and peace. These tools would help Him to become the shaper of condition, environment, and destiny, and the author of salvation. (See Hebrews 5:9).

The Carpenter of Nazareth also utilized simple tools that relate to healthy and provident living. He knew that "when health is absent, then wisdom cannot reveal itself, culture cannot become manifest, strength cannot fight, and intelligence cannot be applied." (Heraclitus - Philosopher of the Golden Age of Greece). Truly, had Isaiah declared: "They that wait upon the Lord shall renew their strength, they shall mount up with wings as eagles, they shall run, and not be weary, and they shall walk, and not faint." (Isaiah 40:31). Isaiah recognized the tools that nurture our dependent relationship between obedience to the commandments and physical and spiritual well-being.

Even trivial trappings can resonate with symbolism, and so the Carpenter of Nazareth used the simple telestial tools with which we are familiar to promote His celestial agenda. He used the color white as the symbol of purity. White bandages bind up our wounds. Flags of submission are white. Wedding dresses are white. Our venerable elders have white hair. When a wound has been cleaned with hydrogen peroxide, the flesh turns white. The linens used in the burial of the dead are white. The light at the end of the tunnel is a dazzling white. It may be no coincidence that our eyes are calibrated to see the stars in the heavens as a blaze of white light across the night sky that we call the Milky Way. Puffy white clouds stand out against blue skies and herald spring days filled with fields of beautiful white daisies. Healthy teeth are white. A bright, white smile is the universal language and may be our best form of communication. The Lone Ranger and all the good cowboys have worn white hats. Satan tries to pervert white as the symbol of purity, and rationalizes falsehoods as nothing more than "white lies."

The Carpenter of Nazareth used "that for which all virtue now is sold, and almost every vice – almighty gold" as a symbolic tool, as well. (Ben Jonson, "Epistle to Elizabeth, Countess of Rutland"). While the desire for gold can obviously corrupt, the bright, shiny metal that cannot be corroded is also a symbol of purity that turns our thoughts to the inestimable worth of the celestial kingdom. Gold that has been heated in the crucible of the refiner's fire turns a dazzling white, and when the earth attains its celestial glory, the streets of its cities will be "pure gold, as it were transparent glass." (Revelation 21:21).

The Carpenter of Nazareth had at His disposal enough tools and to spare to build the incomparable Emerald City of Oz. We pat ourselves on the back and think that we have created palatial surroundings fit for kings with our telestial tools, but these temporal trappings provide nothing more than second-class accommodations in lodgings illuminated by a single bare bulb suspended from the ceiling by a frayed cord. Contrast that bleak existence with the experience of entering the prototype of heaven itself, the celestial room in the temple.

As breathtaking as that chamber in the House of the Lord might be, as much as it might orient our thoughts to eternity, it was still built by craftsmen utilizing corrupt tools with which we are largely familiar: hammers, nails, saws, levels, and tape measures. The celestial room is only a type or a shadow of the heavenly home that beckons to us, and that will be built with tools of a more enduring substance: faith, and charity, repentance and forgiveness, covenants and obedience, contrition and humility, ordinances and priesthood, and mercy and atonement.

We realize that these spiritual tools provided by the Carpenter of Nazareth have such power to influence our destiny that our growth and development are meant to be of generation, and not just of maturation. We can be born again as new creatures in Christ by a mystical transformation utilizing otherworldly tools that we can scarcely explain. (See 2 Corinthians 5:17). The dismantling of our earthly clay may be traumatic, accomplished with the figurative equivalents of sledgehammers and crowbars, and the occasional small explosive, but through the lingering dust kicked up into the air we can see that God is up to something. The run-down cottage we had been living in is slowly being transformed by a celestial craftsman who visualizes the construction of a tabernacle fit to be the eternal dwelling place of our souls. We realize that Heavenly Father is using tools that run on the power of the priesthood, that have an infinite supply of energy from rechargeable batteries, that have been designed to create an environment for us that will be so much more than just an overnight stay in a cheap hotel.

The course of our development may involve costly change-orders, but the objective of the Master Carpenter is a remodel that will create a spiritual figure that is the embodiment of our "perfect frame." The accounting of cost overruns will be measured only in terms of contrition, and will be swallowed up in humility. During construction, He will put the tape measure around our hearts, and not our heads. He will use blueprints that call for the use of tools upon which a monetary value cannot be placed. His workplace safety standards will far exceed those established by OSHA. The premium for Workman's Comp will be paid for with the tool of repentance, and the insurance policy of the Atonement will provide the benefit of forgiveness.

During the process, not a hair of our heads will be lost. Our struggle to achieve the spiritual equivalent of cardiovascular fitness will be measured in soul-sweat, and somehow we will be able to call upon our bodies to produce more red blood cells. Their greater oxygen carrying capacity will enable us to go the second mile, to receive the tool of spiritual independence that eliminates our insensitivity to our destiny. The Savior's program of spiritual aerobics will allow us to run and not be weary, and to walk and not faint. Our capabilities will be expanded, and an organic transformation will bind us, not to red blood cells, but to the life-generating tools of oaths and covenants, and promises and ordinances.

To facilitate our progression, the Carpenter of Nazareth will use a tool known as The Word of Wisdom. Its principles have been given to the Saints because of the particularly persuasive and well-entrenched influence of wickedness in our society, and "in consequence of the evil and designs which do and will exist in the hearts of conspiring men in the Last Days." (D&C 89:4). The Carpenter of Nazareth has leveled the playing field by giving us this important tool to combat the adversary. It nurtures our enjoyment of moral agency, while allowing its exercise to rule without abatement. The truth be told, we are given some wiggle room relating to our obedience to the laws of health, even as we are given pointed and specific tools to identify the pathway to happiness. Thus, is preserved the lynchpin of the Plan "that every man may act in doctrine and principle pertaining to futurity, according to the moral agency which (God has) given unto him, that every man may be accountable for his own sins in the day of judgment." (D&C 101:78).

In general, we are quite pleased with ourselves and with the sophisticated tools we use in our approach to Twenty-first century health care. The 1950s saw medical advances like the heart-lung machine that enabled surgeons to perform open-heart procedures that had been heretofore unthinkable. And yet, even today coronary artery disease remains one of our most daunting health care challenges. We prescribe a cornucopia of therapeutics like blood thinners, high blood pressure medications, and statin drugs, but these stopgap measures are largely ineffective tools that only skirt the real issues that concern a change of heart. The world has a ready diagnosis, but the gospel of Jesus Christ is a virtual war chest of tools that provide effective therapy for cold, stony, and hard hearts. The Atonement is the tool of choice for reconciliation, of which the Carpenter of Nazareth said: "If they harden not their hearts, and stiffen not their necks against me, they shall be converted, and I will heal them." (D&C 112:13).

Over time, we may build up cholesterol deposits in our arteries that choke the very lifeblood from our hearts. Arteriosclerosis can threaten our physical lives. However, when we use gospel carpentry tools as the antidotes to the spiritual sclerosis jeopardizing our eternal stability, we become pliable clay in the hands of the Master Potter. The virtue of the massive collection of tools collectively known as the Plan of Salvation is its incredible power to touch our hearts, to change our nature, to soften us and to humble us, and to mold us as little children, to the end that our eternal happiness is secured.

We work hard to avoid physical obesity, but the Carpenter of Nazareth is a personal trainer with celestial certification, Who encourages us to avoid the sugar-coated temptations that contribute to spiritual obesity and flabbiness. They might taste good, but they pile on the calories of corruption. Indulgence makes delayed gratification more difficult, interferes with our awareness of personal responsibility and accountability, distorts healthy self-esteem, and damages the development of interpersonal relationships. The Carpenter's tools to combat the obsession of our society with self-absorption include faith, divine nature, individual worth, knowledge, choice and accountability, good works, integrity, and virtue. (See: Young Women Values).

"Aha!" said the cartoon philosopher Pogo, who might have been talking about the reckless, self-centered, and self-destructive behavioral tools of the adversary. "Here we have someone paying for the sin of excess. The hobnailed boots of indiscretion's marathon dancer tap a rowdy two-step across the terracotta of his consciousness. Excess was his master. Reason was cast into the rumble seat of his libidinous juggernaut. Now the piper must be paid!"

Indulgence in the self-defeating behaviors that neglect the tools of the Sabbath day, tithing, fasting, and prayer is accompanied by a heavy cost. For every physical regulation relating to our bodies, the Carpenter of Nazareth has provided tools that are their spiritual counterparts. To Him, a tool is a tool; He sees no distinction between the spiritual and the physical sides of our nature. (See D&C 29:34).

As we learn to use the tools of His trade, we will find "wisdom and great treasures of knowledge, even hidden treasures." (D&C 89:19). These include increased faith, spiritual power, and testimony. We will catch a glimpse of how Daniel must have felt in the worldly court of Darius, when he received the tools of "knowledge and skill in all learning and wisdom," and "understanding in all visions and dreams." (Daniel 1:17).

We live in the midst of Spiritual Babylon, adjacent to the wilderness of worldliness and the stench of sin, but we must not compromise our standards, yield to the rising tide of mediocrity, or be swayed by the siren song of Satan's sentinels. The tools of the Savior's gospel trade allow us, as His disciples, to hold fast to the undeviating standard of celestial bound souls. Our eyes are fixed on the prize, because "vice is a monster of so frightful mien, as to be hated needs but to be seen; Yet seen too oft, familiar with her face, we first endure, then pity, then embrace." (Alexander Pope, "Essay on Man, Epistle 2").

In the physical world, we have learned that if we do not ingest enough iron, we will become anemic. But there are also trace elements that are required to avoid spiritual anemia. The Carpenter of Nazareth employs metaphysical mechanisms as tools of His trade, that enable the Spirit to be bound to the blood flowing through our veins.

If pregnant women are deficient in folic acid, their babies will be at risk of neural tube defects, or serious spinal cord anomalies. Just so, if we do not consistently include in our diet the folic acid of faith, we will suffer spiritual spina bifida. We will be "unstable in all our ways. (See James 1:8). We will be double-minded, and subject to spiritual anencephalia. For all practical purposes, a major portion of our brain, that would have otherwise meticulously regulated all aspects of our spiritual development, will be missing.

Just so, if the octane rating of the fuel that fires our faith is too low, we may limp along with our engines misfiring badly. Our fear will diminish our discipleship. The Carpenter of Nazareth has perfected a fuel additive that is designed to add needed horsepower during our push to the finish line. For example, He was able to power the performance of Paul, who provided us with the familiar endorsement: "I have fought a good fight, I have finished my course, I have kept the faith." (2 Timothy 4:7).

In the 1970s, a medical procedure was perfected to remove impurities from the bodies of those suffering from kidney failure. Today, those who go to dialysis centers do so to have contaminants removed from their blood, because their kidneys cannot accomplish the task on their own. The natural man is the spiritual equivalent of one who is in acute kidney failure, who "is an enemy to God, and has been from the fall of Adam, and will be, forever and ever, unless he yields to the enticings of the Holy Spirit…and becometh as a child, submissive, meek, humble, patient, full of love, willing to submit to all things which the Lord seeth fit to inflict upon him, even as a child doth submit to his father." (Mosiah 3:19). He is the stubborn individual who will not use the tools that have been providentially provided for him, who strikes out on his own, and fashions works of his own hands, worshipping "gods of wood or of stone," desperately clinging to the indefensible position that they are somehow the keys to his salvation. (Abraham 1:11).

The Sacrament has been provided as a tool so that we can remove impurities from our hearts. "Though your sins be as scarlet," counseled Isaiah, "they shall be as white as snow; though they be red like crimson, they shall be as wool." (Isaiah 1:18). There are gospel tools that effectively treat hostility, gall, rancor, and even bad blood. The Plan provides the gurney of the Sacrament service, where we may go to seek relief, where we may be given transfusions of the spiritual element to keep us going, at least until in a week's time it becomes necessary to repeat the process. The Carpenter of Nazareth learned that to be a master of His trade, He would need to be the servant of all, and for as long as we frequent His gospel blood-bank, we will be both recipients and donors, beneficiaries and benefactors.

The liver removes toxins from our bodies, but the tool of repentance removes the stain and the stench of sin from our souls. Reconciliation through the Atonement "detoxifies" us from the cares and the conditioning influences of the world, and from the process of homogenization that occurs as we are ground down by the vicissitudes of life.

Epinephrine secreted by the adrenal glands helps us to deal with everyday stress. The tool of prayer helps us to deal with the stress that is built into mortality. The pituitary has been called the master gland that secretes hormones that regulate many of the vital functions of our bodies. As we draw closer to the Carpenter of Nazareth, its spiritual equivalent, the Holy Ghost, will comfort us and help us to maintain our overall spiritual equilibrium.

We give little thought to our autonomic nervous system, that regulates the day-to-day physical activities of our bodies. The Light of Christ nurtures our spirits, but most of us give it equally little attention. But as we study matters out in our own minds preparatory to receiving answers to our prayers, we become actively, rather than passively, involved in the process of inquiry. We dust off the tool of agency, and actually use it as it was envisioned. We move beyond the rusted tools of control, coercion, compulsion, intimidation, and external influence to the bright and shiny precision instruments of friendly persuasion and independence of action. We expand our capabilities, as we exercise the gifts, resources, and reserves provided by the perfect Plan of Salvation. President Kimball promised: "If there be eyes to see, there will be visions to inspire. If there be ears to hear, there will be revelations to experience. If there be hearts which can understand, know this: that the exalting truths of Christ's gospel will no longer be hidden and mysterious, and all earnest seekers may know God and his program." (C.R., 10/1966).

We have the 5 physical senses of sight, hearing, smell, taste, and touch. But there is a spiritual sixth sense that is a tool of inestimable worth. The Holy Ghost is like a "Leatherman," the original multi-tool. Lorenzo Snow recalled the cascade of feelings that poured forth at his baptism: "It was a tangible immersion in the heavenly principle or element, the Holy Ghost; and even more real and physical in its effects upon every part of my system than the immersion by water; dispelling forever, so long as reason and memory last, all possibility of doubt or fear in relation to the fact handed down to us historically, that the Babe of Bethlehem is truly the Son of God." ("Biography and Family Record of Lorenzo Snow," p. 7-9).

Our spiritual sixth sense is a tool that allows us to see beyond the limited horizon of our vision, and to be touched by the virtue of the word of God so that we can savor eternal life with taste buds that are sensitive to eternal worlds. Our spiritual sixth sense helps us to smell the sweet fragrance of celestial gardens and hear its harmonic melodies, not just with our ears, but also with our joints and sinews. When we walk in the light and grasp the principles of truth, we brim over with charity as we find luxurious accommodations in the household of faith. We let virtue garnish our thoughts unceasingly. We cultivate a comfortable, contented, and confident companionship with the Spirit, and the doctrine of the priesthood washes over our minds as the dews from heaven. We celebrate the light, and the Plan becomes a talisman of truth that is interwoven into the fabric of our being until its expression bursts forth as a coat of many colors. Its principles become elements of a tapestry that is everlasting, and without compulsion or coercion we become independent agents with the freedom to embrace our destiny and claim our eternal reward. (See D&C 121:45-46).

But for the Carpenter of Nazareth, discomfort can also be a useful tool. It can even be our friend. Our pain receptors have practical purposes and tangible benefits. Diabetics are at real risk of injury because they cannot feel pain. Perhaps the Savior wanted us to be able to feel and deal with physical and emotional distress because we need to develop empathy for His sacrifice. Perhaps growing pains are necessary to really comprehend the Atonement.

The Carpenter of Nazareth uses perspiration as a tool to teach us about fortitude. We all experience "soul sweat." If we can't stand the heat, we are admonished to get out of the kitchen! "I would thou wert hot or cold," said the Savior. (Revelation 3:14). The application of heat is an essential element in the process of purification. It ramps up our metabolism, gets our juices flowing, and stimulates us to move along on the path of progression. "Then flew one of the seraphims unto me," wrote Isaiah, "having a live coal in his hand, which he had taken with the tongs from off the altar. And he laid it upon my mouth, and said, Lo, this hath touched thy lips; and thine iniquity is taken away, and thy sin purged." (Isaiah 6:6-7).

The Carpenter of Nazareth judiciously uses the tool of friendly persuasion. The word "beseech" is used in the scriptures 118 times, 65 times in the New Testament alone. When working with homeowners who didn't have a clear vision of what they wanted, or needed, to make their house a home, Joseph had to be a psychologist as well as a carpenter. He had a lot more experience than his neighbors when it came to crafting fine furnishings, and his suggestions would have been based not only on their perceived needs, but also on what would actually be the best fit for them, given their circumstances. Joseph would have been a good mentor to his Son, the Carpenter of Nazareth, as he groomed Him to become a motivational speaker who could change the world with the tools at hand, one Galilean at a time.

The Carpenter of Nazareth uses the tool of fatigue. Joseph must have had deadlines to meet, and customers with unreasonable expectations, but his work ethic kept him in his shop no matter what, until their orders had been successfully completed. We never read in the scriptures about their dissatisfaction, or about careless or shoddy workmanship on his part. Jesus must have learned from Joseph that we can push ourselves to the point that we feel we have no more to give. But then, we read His admonition: "Whosoever shall compel thee to go a mile, go with him twain," and we realize that He took His responsibilities to another level. (Matthew 5:41). The tool of fatigue can teach us a lot about ourselves, and about who we really are, especially when everything is on the line and all eternity hangs in the balance. Then, like the footprints in the sand, when we have utterly exhausted our own resources, the Carpenter of Nazareth will step up and carry our burdens for us. He will descend below any sacrifice we could ever make, and is in a league all His own. (See D&C 122:8). His compassion is not something anyone could have taught Him, but it probably was to His advantage that He wasn't born with a silver spoon in His mouth.

The Carpenter of Nazareth uses the tool of testimony. All of us have been faced with times when withdrawals have needed to be made from our spiritual bank accounts. If we are fortunate, we have beforehand faithfully and consistently made deposits, in order to be prepared in our moment of need with a cushion of confidence that flows from our own courage and commitment, as well as from the condescension and compassion of our Creator. Testimony can be a financial tool to make sure we are not writing checks that cannot be cashed.

There is no financial stipend associated with the Plan of Salvation, but it does provide us with the tools of the trade, that we might by the sweat of our brow earn enough money to secure our own accommodations, pay our bills on time, and occasionally indulge ourselves with some of the finer things of life. Interestingly, just as Millennials do in their relationships with their earthly parents, the Plan anticipates that eventually we'll return Home to move back in with our Heavenly Parents, and live under one roof, as we did at first.

One day, we may show up at Their doorstep in the same condition as the Navy pilot who barely made it back to his ship. As the story goes, this World War II aviator had left the security of his aircraft carrier to undertake a dangerous mission over hostile territory. True to the predictions of his superior officers, he endured bad weather, flack from enemy anti-aircraft fire, and engaged in lethal dogfights with adversaries whose sole purpose was to kill him. His craft was hit numerous times by machine gun fire that riddled his fuselage, and by shrapnel that tore away parts of his wings. His Plexiglas canopy was shattered, and he could hardly see through blood-splattered goggles to navigate back to his ship.

As he came in for a landing in the midst of a storm on the pitching deck of the carrier, his controls were nearly useless, his descent was too steep, and his angle was wrong. He was frantically waved off by the crewman on deck who was guiding him in, but he figured he had only one chance, and he would take it. With a sickening thump, he pancaked his aircraft on the deck, its fuel tank burst into flame, and the tail hook failed to engage the cables that would have jerked him to a halt. As he careened into the safety net at the far end of the deck, what was left of his plane crumpled into twisted metal.

A rescue crew in asbestos suits rushed to his aid, smothered the wreckage in fire-retardant foam, clamored up to the cockpit, unsnapped his safety harness, grabbed him by the shoulders, yanked him out of the plane, and dragged him to safety. Doctors and nurses attended to his wounds even before he arrived at sickbay. Due to their skill and attention, as well as to his unconquerable spirit, he made a remarkable and full recovery. For his heroism and gallantry during action, he was awarded the Distinguished Flying Cross, and given thirty days' leave for rest and recuperation. This is how most of us will return from our mortal mission to the presence of our Father. God-speed to us all. (Paraphrased from an address given by Boyd K. Packer).

We'll probably hear Him tell us that all our trials and tribulations have given us experience, and have been for our good. (See D&C 122:7). We will all be together again, busily engaged in the family business, utilizing the tools of the trade that have become familiar to us all.

After Jacob Chapter 5, Alma Chapter 5 is the second longest chapter in The Book of Mormon. It reads very much like a General Conference address. A careful study of this chapter teaches us that it is easy to mechanically spit out pat answers, but it is much more difficult to articulate good questions. In Alma's discourse to the people of Zarahemla, we find many such questions.

Touching His Garment

"They did fast and pray oft,
and did wax stronger and stronger
in their humility, and firmer and firmer
in the faith of Christ, unto the filling their
souls with joy and consolation, yea, even to
the purifying and the sanctification of their
hearts, which sanctification cometh because
of their yielding their hearts unto
God." (Helaman 3:35).

"And a certain woman, which had an issue of blood twelve years, and had suffered many things of many physicians, and had spent all that she had, and was nothing bettered, but rather grew worse, when she had heard of Jesus, came in the press behind, and touched his garment. For she said, If I may touch but his clothes, I shall be whole. And straightway the fountain of her blood was dried up; and she felt in her body that she was healed of that plague. And Jesus, immediately knowing in himself that virtue had gone out of him, turned him about in the press, and said, Who touched my clothes?." (Mark 5:25-30).

The Mortal Messiah was filled with the Spirit of God, and the spiritually hungry came to Him to satisfy their yearnings. Jesus, in turn, being a wellspring of the Spirit, sensed every moment when a need drew upon that source.

This story in Mark gives us assurance that God is sensitive to our needs, and does hear our prayers. In conformity to some spiritual law, we can tap into and draw upon the life force that is the Spirit of God. When we do so, we are, in effect, touching His garment.

One of President David O. McKay's favorite poem reads: "The builder who first bridged Niagara's gorge, before he swung his cable, shore to shore, sent out across the gulf his venturing kite, bearing a slender cord for unseen hands to grasp upon the further cliff and draw a greater cord, and then a greater yet; til at last across the chasm swung The Cable - then the mighty bridge in air!. So may we send our little timid thoughts, across the void, out to God's reaching hands. Send our love, and faith, to thread the deep, thought after thought, until the little cord, and we, are anchored to the Infinite!." (Edward Markham).

This is the process of sanctification by which we are cleansed from the effects of sin. It happens when the gospel has driven the law into our inward parts (Jeremiah 31:33) and we become "firmer and firmer in the faith of Christ." (Helaman 3:35). "Sanctify yourselves," He commands us, "that your minds become single to God, and the days will come that you shall see him; for he will unveil his face unto you." (D&C 88:68). Thus spiritually renewed, we stand prepared to enter His presence.

Tough Questions
(Alma Chapter 5)

"Verily I say unto you,
whatsoever things ye shall ask
the Father in my name shall be given
unto you. Therefore, ask, and ye shall receive;
knock, and it shall be opened unto you; for he that
asketh, receiveth; and unto him that knocketh,
it shall be opened." (3 Nephi 27:28-29).

Alma Chapter 5 is the second longest chapter in The Book of Mormon, after Jacob Chapter 5, and reads very much like a General Conference address. A careful study of this chapter teaches us that it is easy to mechanically spit out pat answers, but it is more difficult to embrace good questions. In Alma's discourse to the People of Zarahemla, we find many such questions. They are summarized below.

Alma asked if his people had sufficiently retained in remembrance the hardships that their fathers had endured due to their spiritual bondage. He was saying that history is prologue. He longed for his people to learn from the experiences of their fathers. He knew from his own troubled youth the sadness that can result from ignoring or rejecting counsel from one's elders.

He questioned if his people remembered how merciful and long-suffering Heavenly Father is toward those who are groping about in spiritual darkness? Isaiah in particular among the prophets of the Old Testament reminded the people "His arm is stretched out still." In other words, He is always willing to forgive those who repent. Alma must have remembered the patience that his own father had exercised during the years of his rebellion.

Alma wondered if his people remembered that Heavenly Father's Plan will deliver from the Spirit Prison of the Unjust those who there accept the gospel?. (See D&C 76:13, 23, & 73, 138:8 & 28, Isaiah 61:1, 1 Peter 3:19, & Moses 7:57). His mercy even breaks the barrier of death, and offers the hope of eternal family life to all who have ever lived on the earth. God is absolutely non-discriminatory as He deals with His children. Sooner or later, all will have the opportunity to accept or reject the offer of a covenant relationship with God. Therefore, Alma asked, would Heavenly Father really destroy those who are, at present, spiritually ignorant? Because His Perfect Plan is Infinite and Eternal, He would not.

Alma answered this question with another. Has God, then, broken the bands of death and the chains of hell, which have bound these unfortunate individuals, in contrast to Satan who is unable to support his disciples at the Day of Judgment? Of course, for God is the Master of all circumstances. Every provision of the Plan has been carefully thought out before its implementation, and harmonizes perfectly with its companion principles.

Continuing on this track, Alma asked on what condition is mankind saved? No matter that God sets those conditions, for His Judgments are always just. On what grounds, then, does one have hope of salvation? It is the Atonement that establishes the firm foundation. Any other conditions are only corollaries to the Atonement and to the covenants that relate to it.

How is it, Alma questioned, that mankind has been loosed from the bands of death and the chains of hell? It is because the Lamb slain from the foundation of the world is the Author of Salvation and the very Savior of the world; He is our Mediator. His sacrifice is central to the Plan of Salvation.

Years earlier, the words of Abinadi had greatly impressed Alma's father. Did not this mighty prophet prove that the power of the word is mightier than the sword? Was not Abinadi a prophet of God? The Spirit testifies that this is true. Did not Abinadi speak the words of God?. His message touched the receptive heart of the Elder Alma, the hearts of generations of Nephites and Lamanites to come, and it continues to inspire many in the Last Days, especially those still in the infancy of their faith, as well as those who are in the midst of trials that test their seasoned faith.

So, Alma asked his people if they had been spiritually born of God. Mormon hoped that his labor to abridge the words of Alma would not be in vain. Those efforts are only worthwhile if his message is able to span the centuries to touch the hearts of the readers of The Book of Mormon in the Last Days. The very last words that Mormon wrote in our Book of Mormon were these: "For behold, this (book) is written for the intent that ye may believe ... And if it so be that be believe in Christ, and are baptized, first with water, then with fire and with the Holy Ghost, following the example of our Savior, according to that which he hath commanded us, it shall be well with you in the day of judgment." (Mormon 7:9 & 10).

Alma's next question penetrates the barriers of time and place. He asked if his people had received the image of the Lord in their countenance. When they had, he assured them, their faces would reflect the Light of Christ. He knew that a mighty change in their hearts would change their very nature; it would change the inner man. The world seeks change from the outside, and fails miserably. The gospel changes man from the inside, and succeeds brilliantly. Man is thus created to reach his potential in both the image and likeness of God his Father.

He asked if they exercised faith in the redemption of Him who had created them? Being changed in the inner man, their testimonies would be the foundation for sustained, saving faith. Then they would look forward with an eye of faith to stand one day before God to be judged according to their works. Saving faith gives one confidence to stand in the presence of God, before His Pleasing Bar.

He asked if they could imagine that they heard the voice of the Lord saying to them: "Come unto me ye blessed, for behold, your works have been the works of righteousness." Alma knew by personal experience that God's Rest is reserved for the righteous, and so this principle became a cornerstone of his message.

Alma wondered if his people thought that they could lie to the Lord in the Day of Judgment, saying that they had been righteous, so that God would thereby save them. Beware, he cautioned, lest they think that they could fool God. During His mortal ministry, the Lord had particularly harsh words for such hypocrites.

He continued, asking if they could imagine themselves before the Judgment Bar of God, with their souls filled with guilt and remorse, and a remembrance that they had set themselves in defiance to the commandments. When one's true nature is revealed and it is found wanting, the inevitable consequences are frightening. Could they hope to look up to God at that day with a pure heart and clean hands? The prophet Isaiah had unequivocally warned, "Be ye clean that bear the vessels of the Lord." (Isaiah 52:11).

Knowing that dedicated disciples assume the nature of their mentor, he asked if the image of God had been engraven upon their countenances. Contrast this description of permanence with the fickle visage of those characterized as hypocrites. We cannot be hypocritical when we follow the Savior. The word "hypocrite" is from the Greek that describes the mask used by actors. A hypocrite, then, is someone who professes to be one thing, when actually it is a charade; he is an entirely different person behind his mask.

Could they think of being saved when they had yielded themselves to become subject to the devil? The very thought defies all logic. "Here is the agency of man, and here is the condemnation of man; because that which was from the beginning is plainly manifest unto them, and they receive not the light." (D&C 93:31).

How might we feel, Alma asked, standing before the Bar of God, clothed in garments stained with filthiness? The stirrings of religious recognition within us would at that very moment convict us of our sins. How much better to have achieved purity through the Atonement by washing our garments in the blood of the Lamb?

Of what do these things testify, Alma questioned? The record of one's life is engraven indelibly in the sinews. Might that record testify of guilt for all manner of wickedness? The Holy Spirit cannot lie. Alma wondered if the unrepentant sinner could comfortably sit down in the Kingdom of God? After all, water seeks its own level.

Alma knew that those who listened to his words had, at one time, experienced a change of heart. He wondered if they could feel so at that moment as well. He knew that the Word could penetrate their innermost parts to touch their spiritual sensitivities. His people should have felt indescribable stirrings, for every gospel principle carries within itself its own witness of its truthfulness.

Elder Hugh B. Brown described his relationship with the Spirit in these words: "Sometimes during solitude I hear truth spoken with clarity and freshness. Uncolored and untranslated it speaks from within myself in a language original but inarticulate, heard only with the soul." ("Eternal Quest," p. 435).

Alma knew that the gospel Plan enables Christ's disciples to walk blamelessly before God, because it successfully addresses all of life's challenges and compensates for the weaknesses of mortality. He wondered if his people could say, if they were called to die at that moment, that they had been sufficiently humble. For it is the meek who shall inherit the celestialized earth.

Alma wanted his people to take advantage of the Atonement of Christ, which is of no power or effect for those who will not accept the Lord as their personal Savior. He hoped that his people were stripped of pride, for he knew that nothing will keep us out of Zion more surely than the feeling of superiority over our neighbors. Nothing will kill the Spirit faster than pride. In all of its insidiously and horribly mutated forms, such as envy, flattery, vanity, selfishness, haughtiness, and covetousness, it is equally damaging.

Alma asked if any of his people mocked or in any other way persecuted their brethren. The gospel teaches that the worth of souls is great in the sight of God, Who esteems all mankind as one and is no respecter of persons. This means that He values all his children as equally precious. Therefore, there is no justifiable circumstance in which any one of His children may be treated unkindly or unfairly.

C.S. Lewis once observed that "it is a serious thing to live in a society of possible Gods and Goddesses - to remember that the dullest and most uninteresting person you talk to may one day be a creature which, if you saw it now, you would be strongly tempted to worship. It is in the light of these overwhelming possibilities, it is with the awe and the circumspection proper to them, that we should conduct all our dealings with one another ... all friendships, all loves, all play all politics. There are no ordinary people. You have never talked to a mere mortal-- it is immortals whom we joke with, work with, marry, snub and exploit ... Our charity must be a real and costly love, with deep feeling for the sins in spite of which we love the sinner ... no mere tolerance or indulgence which parodies love as flippancy parodies merriment. Next to the blessed sacrament itself, your neighbor is the holiest object presented to your senses. If he is your Christian neighbor he is holy in almost the same way, for in him also Christ is truly hidden and glorified."

Alma knew that man cannot serve two masters. The questions thus posed to each individual are, "If you are not of the fold of the Good Shepherd, of what fold are you? Who can deny that if you are not of His fold, you are of the devil's?"

Alma asked the congregation if it supposed that he knew these things of himself. He explained to his people that he was just as they were, endowed with the same earthly gifts with which our Heavenly Father blesses each of His children. Without interfering with our agency, these gifts are sufficient to guide us to behavior consistent with celestial principles. God wants each of us to succeed and to pass the individual tests of mortality. He has given us the tools with which to accomplish this, and the guidelines, which will allow us to move on in a partnership with Deity, having satisfied the entrance requirements for admittance to the Celestial Kingdom.

Alma bore testimony of these principles to his people, asking in effect: "How do you suppose that I know of their surety? Can you withstand these sayings? Just how powerful is the voice of the Spirit? Can you lay aside these things, and trample the Holy One under your feet? Would you make a mockery of your own Savior? How can you be so puffed up in the pride of your hearts? Will the cares of the world, and your insatiable desire for worldly goods, cloud your vision? Will you still set your hearts upon the vain things of the world, and upon your riches? Do you not yet understand that all is vanity? Will you persist in supposing that you are better than other people? Do you think that your accumulation of worldly goods establishes your superiority over others of less substantial means? Will you continue to persecute your brethren who humble themselves and walk after the Holy Order of God? Will you turn your backs upon the poor? Will you withhold your substance from them?" Today, members of the church have the obligation to consider these same questions.

Travel at The Speed of Thought

"Behold,
I know your thoughts."
(3 Nephi 28:6).

In the television series "Star Trek: The Next Generation," the Traveler, whose real name was unpronounceable by humans, was a native of Tau Alpha C, who had the power to alter space, time, and warp fields with his mind. He could phase in and out of time and dimension, based on his ability to focus the energy of thought.

We are not there yet, but give us time, no pun intended. The universe is 13.7 billion years old. On its journey to earth, photons from the most distant stars have been traveling across space, at a constant speed of 5.8 trillion miles per year. That's 5.8 thousand billion miles each and every year, for as many as 13.7 billion years. To put things in perspective, just 4,000 years ago, when the starlight just now reaching our eyes was a mere 23,200 trillion miles from earth, our ancestors were still fashioning tools out of stone, so we haven't been players on the universal stage for very long. Early civilizations somewhere out there could have had well over three million times as long as we have had to figure things out. What wondrous technologies might alien civilizations have developed within a time span that is almost three and a half million times as long as 4,000 years!

Nevertheless, what we do have going for us is impressive, at least by our own standards. Since the 1970s, the Information Age, also known as the Digital Age, Computer Age, or New Media Age, has blessed our lives with a shift from industrialization to information computerization and a knowledge-based society embedded within a global economy. Amazon and Google are good examples of the practical benefits related to the explosion in information-based technology. The transition by society to the use of technology in daily life has been dramatic, with no end in sight, and is nowhere more profound than in the sphere of the acquisition and utilization of knowledge.

In 1900, at the dawn of the 20th century, it had taken 150 years to double all human knowledge. Today it takes only around 12 months, and soon it will be every 12 hours, according to reliable estimates. Where will we be in 10, 50, or 100 years? Maybe the sky is not the limit. (We've already been there, after all). Our brains (the same ones that are "boggled" by the aforementioned numbers) contain several billion petabytes of information. (One petabyte is 1,000 terabytes, 1 terabyte is 1,000 gigabytes and 1 gigabyte is 1,000 megabytes). Perhaps we just have to organize the information in our brains more efficiently, in order to utilize its resources to greater potential. We have the Internet to compare it with, which is arguably not very well organized either, as presently constituted. All of the information on the World Wide Web is currently estimated to be just 5 million terabytes (TB) of which Google has indexed roughly 200 TB or just .004% of its total storage capacity.

Just consider transportation technology. Caesar rode a horse, but so did George Washington, 2,000 years later. As a matter of fact, the gauge of railroad track in the Nineteenth Century was initially determined by the width of a horse's rear, specifically a Roman chariot horse's rear. (Verified by Snopes). In 1592, Richard III was prompted to exclaim: "A horse! A horse! My kingdom for a horse!" (Shakespeare, Richard III, Act, 5, Scene 4). Until the invention of the steam engine, which was the driving force behind the Industrial Revolution, the horse defined the absolute speed limit at which we could travel in a horizontal direction. Henry Ford is said to have remarked: "If I had asked people what they wanted, they would have said faster horses."

In the next 100 years, there were amazing advances in transportation technology, with train travel in 1900 achieving a top speed of about 40 mph. In the next 50 years, transportation technology took another giant leap forward. On July 23, 1949, the De Havilland Comet became the first commercial jet aircraft, with a cruising speed of 460 mph.

In the next 25 years, transportation technology took a quantum leap forward. The Saturn 5 rocket that propelled humans to the moon weighed 6.5 million pounds and had a payload capacity of 260,000 pounds. It developed almost 8 million pounds of thrust for eight and a half minutes, achieving a speed of 7 miles per second, or 24,593 miles per hour.

In the next 12.5 years, the Voyager 1 spacecraft launched by NASA on September 5, 1977, achieved the fastest heliocentric recession speed of any man-made object: 10.72 miles per second (38,592 miles per hour). It has sustained that speed for over 35 years, and has now left our solar system and entered interstellar space.

To put things in perspective, the Internet has made communication lightning fast, and the search bar on computer screens has become "the Sippy Cup of culture." Information technology is approaching light-speed.

On September 10, 2008, scientists created the Large Hadron Collider, the world's largest and most powerful particle accelerator. It was built in collaboration with over 10,000 scientists and engineers from over 100 countries, as well as hundreds of universities and laboratories, and remains the largest and most complex experimental facility ever built. At a cost of over 7.5 billion Euros, it is arguably the most expensive scientific instrument ever made. It consists of a 27-kilometer ring of superconducting magnets with a number of accelerating structures to boost the energy of the particles along its path. Inside the accelerator, two particle beams approach the speed of light, or 186,200 miles per second. The data collected from the operation of the Large Hadron Collider consists of tens of petabytes of information per year. It is being analyzed by the world's largest computing grid, comprising over 170 computing facilities in a worldwide network in 36 countries. As of this writing, fears of the "doomsday phenomenon" (particle collisions causing black holes) have proven to be unfounded. This is fortunate, inasmuch as their creation would have resulted in the annihilation of the earth.

As we approach the cosmic speed limit, perhaps we should re-write the laws of physics to allow warp speed. Warp drive is a hypothetical faster-than-light propulsion system. A spacecraft equipped with a warp drive has been theorized to be able to travel at speeds greater than that of light by many orders of magnitude, (Warp 1 – Warp 10), while circumventing the relativity problem of time dilation. If warp drive technology were to create an artificial "bubble" of normal space-time surrounding the spacecraft, the vehicle would be able to maintain interaction with objects in normal space. A theoretical solution for faster-than-light travel that models the warp drive concept was formulated by physicist Miguel Alcubierre in 1994, and NASA scientists have begun preliminary research to learn more about the practical applications of the technology.

But what of the aforementioned Traveler, and his ability to alter space, time, and warp fields? In the "Star Trek: The Next Generation" episode entitled "Where Silence Has Lease," Captain Jean Luc Picard says: "Considering the marvelous complexity of the universe, its clockwork perfection, its balances of this against that, such as matter, energy, gravitation, time, and dimension, I believe that our existence must go beyond Euclidean or other practical measuring systems, and that it is part of a reality beyond what we understand now."

After warp speed's wrinkles have been ironed out, will the next level be travel at the speed of thought, like the Traveler? Perhaps so, if mathematical equations can be formulated to embrace a time-space-thought continuum, as described by Prot, in the movie "KPax." He told the scientists examining his claims of extraterrestrial origin and travel at thought-speed: "Einstein never said that nothing can travel faster than the speed of light." What he did say is that something traveling slower than light is slower in all frames of reference, and cannot therefore accelerate to a speed above the cosmic speed limit.

Perhaps "gravitational waves that propagate at the speed of thought," a concept first suggested by the physicist Arthur Stanley Eddington, in 1922, will allow us to jump past that limit. If we can somehow come to a meeting of the minds between the abstract reality that emerges from mathematics, and the warm body of nature that we can see and touch, we just might be able to ride the exponential expansion of knowledge to a destination that reveal the answers we are looking for, that relate to travel at the speed of thought.

If we are somehow able to hammer out a reconciliation between the deterministic corporeality that emerges from rational thought and the esoteric reasoning that we encounter throughout The Book of Mormon and that we feel not so much by the head as by the heart, we just might be able to ride out the exponential expansion of knowledge in these Last Days to reach a faith-based destination that will reveal the answers we are looking for, and that will open up to our view the vistas that reach all the way from here to eternity.

(The) Twelve Tribes of Israel

"And verily, verily, I say unto you that I have other sheep, which are not of this land, neither of the land of Jerusalem, neither in any parts of the land round about whither I have been to minister. For they of whom I speak are they who have not as yet heard my voice (nor) have I at any time manifested myself unto them. But I have received a commandment of the Father that I shall go unto them, and that they shall hear my voice, and shall be numbered among my sheep, that there may be one fold and one shepherd." (3 Nephi 16:1-3).

I can't take credit for all of the scholarship that went into this description of the Twelve Tribes of Israel, although I have significantly editorialized my sources, which include the scriptures, Josephus, Wikipedia, and LDS.org, to name just a few. I have collated and organized diverse materials in an attempt to bring coherence to holy writ, doctrine, and historical, apocryphal, and Pseudepigraphical accounts that have proven to be confusing to many students of the scriptures. My objective in studying the Twelve Tribes was simply to gain greater familiarity with my roots. I hope this collection of resources helps you to do just that, whether you are a literal or adopted member of the House of Israel. At the end, is a short discussion of the Ten Lost Tribes of Israel that is solely my own work.

"Now the sons of Jacob were twelve: The sons of Leah; Reuben, Jacob's firstborn, and Simeon, and Levi, and Judah, and Issachar, and Zebulun: The sons of Rachel; Joseph, and Benjamin: And the sons of Bilhah, Rachel's handmaid; Dan and Naphtali: And the sons of Zilpah, Leah's handmaid; Gad and Asher." (Genesis 35:22-26).

Leah: Reuben, Simeon, Levi, Judah, Issachar, and Zebulun. Rachel: Joseph (Ephraim and Manasseh / a double portion), and Benjamin, Bilhah (Rachel's maid): Dan and Naphtali, Zilpah (Leah's maid): Gad and Asher.

Reuben

Until the creation of the first Kingdom of Israel around 1050 B.C., Reuben was part of a loose confederation of Israelite tribes. No central government existed, and in times of crisis the people were led by leaders known as Judges.

With the threat of Philistine incursions, however, the twelve Israelite tribes formed a centralized monarchy (made up of the Kingdoms of Israel in the north, and Judah in the south) to meet the challenge. The new kingdom was called the United Monarchy, with Saul as its first king. After his death, all the tribes, with the exception of Judah in the south, remained loyal to the United Monarchy / Kingdom of Israel in the north. After the death of Saul's son and successor to the throne, Reuben joined the ten other northern Israelite tribes in making David, who was then the king of Judah in the south, the king of a reunited Kingdom of Israel.

According to the Book of Chronicles, Reuben aided David in conquering the Jebusite City of David, which paved the way for the establishment of Jerusalem as the seat of Israelite religion. However, when David's grandson Rehoboam took the throne around 930 B.C., the northern tribes split from the House of David/Kingdom of Israel/United Monarchy to re-form the Northern Kingdom. Reuben then remained part of the Northern Kingdom until it was conquered by Assyria around 723 B.C. The tribes of the Northern Kingdom were deported, and from that time, Reuben was lost to history as one of the Ten Lost Tribes of Israel.

Simeon

Following the conquest of Canaan by the Israelites around 1200 B.C., Joshua allocated the land among the twelve tribes. At its height, the territory occupied by Simeon was in the southwest of Canaan, which was an insignificant rural backwater. Simeon was considered one of the less significant tribes in the Kingdom of Judah.

Simeon was the second son of Jacob and of Leah. Following the death of Joshua, the Israelites asked the Lord which tribe should be first to occupy its allotted territory, and the tribe of Judah was chosen. Judah invited Simeon to fight with it in an alliance, in order to secure each of their allotted territories.

Simeon had been one of the strongest tribes during the wandering in the desert. But afterwards, the tribe seems to have dwindled in size, which was divine punishment for its reaction to the rape of Dinah.

As part of the kingdom of Judah in the south, what remained of Simeon was ultimately subjected to the Babylonian captivity, and when it ended, all remaining distinctions between Simeon and the other tribes in the Kingdom of Judah had been lost, in favour of a common identity as "Jews." The apocrypha claims that Simeon was deported by the Babylonians to Ethiopia. A few modern-day groups claim descent from the tribe of Simeon, with varying levels of academic and rabbinical support.

Levi

The Levites were the high priests of the Israelites, and descended from Levi, who was the third son of Jacob and Leah. Moses and his brother Aaron were both Levites. When Joshua led the Israelites into the land of Canaan, the Levites were the only tribe that received cities but not land, "because the Lord the God of Israel Himself (was) their inheritance." (Deuteronomy 18:2). The Levites had both religious and political responsibilities. In return, the landed tribes were expected to give tithes to the Levite priests who served in the temple. As Paul taught: "They that are of the sons of Levi, who receive the office of the priesthood, have a commandment to take tithes of the people according to the law." (Hebrews 7:5).

Samuel, Ezekiel, Ezra, and Malachi were all Levites. The descendants of Aaron, who was the first Levite high priest of Israel, continued in the priestly class. Even today, there are family dynasties within the tribe of Levi that have been integrated into Jewish and Samaritan societies.

When John the Baptist conferred the Aaronic Priesthood upon Joseph Smith and Oliver Cowdery, on April 15, 1829, he pronounced a blessing, saying: "Upon you my fellow servants, in the name of Messiah, I confer the Priesthood of Aaron, which holds the keys of the ministering of angels, and of the gospel of repentance, and of baptism by immersion for the remission of sins; and this shall never be taken again from the earth, until the sons of Levi do offer again an offering unto the Lord in righteousness." (D&C 13:1).

In an epistle to the Saints dated September 6, 1842, Joseph Smith wrote: "Behold, the great day of the Lord is at hand; and who can abide the day of his coming, and who can stand when he appeareth? For he is like a refiner's fire, and like fuller's soap; and he shall sit as a refiner and purifier of silver, and he shall purify the sons of Levi, and purge them as gold and silver, that they may offer unto the Lord an offering in righteousness." (D&C 128:24).

Judah

Judah was the fourth son of Jacob and of Leah. The Tribe of Judah, its conquests, the centrality of its capital in Jerusalem, and the worship of Yahweh figure prominently in the books of Deuteronomy through 2 Kings. According to the Book of Joshua, following a partial conquest of Canaan by Israel shortly before 1200 B.C., Judah's divinely ordained inheritance encompassed most of the southern portion of the Land of Israel, including the Negev, the Wilderness of Zin, and Jerusalem.

In the Book of Judges, Judah is identified as the first tribe that was allowed to occupy the Promised Land. According to the Book of Judges, Judah invited Simeon to fight with it to secure their allotted territories.

The Book of Samuel describes God's repudiation of a budding monarchy initiated by the northern Tribe of Benjamin. That honor was then bestowed upon the Tribe of Judah for all time in the person of King David. In Samuel's account, after the death of Saul, all the tribes other than Judah remained loyal to the House of Saul, while Judah chose David as its king. However, after the death of Saul's son and successor to the throne of Israel, all the other Israelite tribes backed David, who was then the king of Judah, as the king of a reunited Kingdom of Israel. Ultimately, the Savior would come through David's line.

The Book of Kings follows the expansion and unparalleled glory of a united monarchy under David's son Solomon. However, with the accession of Solomon's son Rehoboam, around 930 B.C., the ten Northern Tribes, under the leadership of Jeroboam from the Tribe of Ephraim, split from the House of David to create the Northern Kingdom. The Book of Kings is uncompromising in its low opinion of its larger and richer neighbor to the north, and portrays its conquest by Assyria in 722 B.C. as divine retribution for that Kingdom's return to idolatry.

Judah and Benjamin remained loyal to the House of David. These tribes formed the Kingdom of Judah, , which existed until the Babylonian captivity around 586 B.C. when the population was deported.

Judah was the leading tribe of the Kingdom of Judah. David belonged to the tribe, and the royal line continued after the fall of the Kingdom of Judah. The traditional Jewish belief was that the Messiah would be of the Davidic line, based on the Lord's promise to David of an everlasting throne for his offspring.

Many Jewish leaders and prophets claimed membership in the tribe of Judah. For example, Isaiah, Amos, Habakkuk, Joel, Micah, Obadiah, Zechariah, and Zephaniah all belonged to Judah. Later, after the Babylonian exile ended, Zerubbabel, who was the leader of the first Jews to return, was also said to be of the Davidic line, as was Nehemiah.

By lineage, Jesus was a member of the tribe of Judah. (Matthew 1:1-6 and Luke 3:31-34). Because it was part of the

Kingdom of Judah in the south, the tribe of Judah survived the destruction of Israel (the Northern Kingdom) by the Assyrians, only to be later subjected to the Babylonian captivity. When Judah and Benjamin returned from that Babylonian exile, tribal affiliations were abandoned, probably because of the impossibility of reestablishing previous land holdings. Only the special religious role of the Levites was maintained. Jerusalem became the sole place of worship and sacrifice among the returning exiles, northerners and southerners alike. The distinction between tribes was lost in favor of a common identity that has endured to this day. Since Simeon and Benjamin had been very much the junior partners in the Kingdom of Judah, it was Judah that gave its name, that of the Jews, to this identity.

After the fall of Jerusalem to the Babylonians, Babylonia became the focus of Jewish life for a thousand years. The first Jewish communities in Babylonia started with the exile of the Tribe of Judah to Babylon in 597 B.C., as well as after the destruction of the Temple in Jerusalem in 586 B.C.

Ethiopian tradition asserts descent from Israelites of the tribes of Dan and Judah, who returned with the Queen of Sheba after her visit to King Solomon in Jerusalem. Hence the phrase "The Lion of the Tribe of Judah has conquered," that is found in the Book of Revelation.

Haile Selassie was the emperor of Ethiopia from 1930 to 1974. His full title in office was "By the Conquering Lion of the Tribe of Judah, His Imperial Majesty Haile Selassie I, King of Kings of Ethiopia, Elect of God." This title reflects Ethiopian dynastic traditions, which hold that all monarchs must trace their lineage to the offspring of King Solomon and the Queen of Sheba.

Latter-day revelation describes how "the children of Judah may begin to return to the lands which (the Lord) didst give to Abraham, their father." (D&C 109:64). It also demands: "Let them who be of Judah flee unto Jerusalem, unto the mountains of the Lord's house." (D&C 133:13). Then, "they also of the tribe of Judah, after their pain, shall be sanctified in holiness before the Lord, to dwell in his presence day and night, forever and ever." (D&C 133:35). This corroborates Paul's teaching: "Behold, the days come, saith the Lord, when I will make a new covenant with the house of Israel and with the house of Judah." (Hebrews 8:8).

Dan

Dan and Naphtali were the sons of Jacob and Bilhah, Rachel's maidservant. The tribe of Dan was the second largest Israelite tribe, after Judah. Until the formation of the first united Kingdom of Israel around 1050 B.C., Dan was a part of a loose confederation of Israelite tribes. No central government existed, and in times of crisis the people were led by leaders known as Judges.

Following the conquest of Canaan by the Israelites around 1200 B.C., Dan was the last tribe to receive its inheritance, a small enclave in the central coastal area. Members of the Tribe of Dan were seafarers, which was unusual for an Israelite tribe. Its territory, not very extensive initially, was further diminished by the incursions of its dangerous Philistine neighbors. The most celebrated Danite was Samson, who figured prominently in tales of conflict with the Philistines.

All twelve Israelite tribes formed a strong centralized monarchy (made up of the Kingdoms of Israel in the north, and Judah in the south) to meet the challenge from the Philistines. The new kingdom was called the United Monarchy, with Saul as its first king.

After the death of Saul, all the tribes except Judah remained loyal to the House of Saul, but after the death of his son and successor to the throne of Israel, the Tribe of Dan joined the other northern Israelite tribes in making David, who was already the king of Judah, the monarch of a re-united Kingdom of Israel.

However, on the accession of David's grandson Rehoboam, around 930 B.C., the Northern Tribes split from the House of David to re-invent a Kingdom of Israel known as the Northern Kingdom. The territory of Dan was conquered by the Assyrians, and exiled Dan was lost to history, as one of the Ten Lost Tribes of Israel.

Today, Ethiopian Jews claim descent from the Tribe of Dan, claiming that its members migrated into the Kingdom of Kush, now Ethiopia and Sudan, along with members of the tribes of Gad, Asher, and Naphtali, , after the destruction of the Temple of Zerubbabel.

Naphtali

Following the completion of the conquest of Canaan by the Israelite tribes around 1200 B.C., Joshua allocated the land among the twelve tribes. Naphtali's inheritance was along the Lower Galilee. In this region was the highly fertile plain of Gennesaret, that brought prosperity to the region.

Naphtali was the second son of Jacob and Bilhah, Dan being the first. Militarism figured prominently in Naphtali's history. In the Gideon narrative Naphtali is one of the tribes that joined in an attack against Midianite invaders.

Until the formation of the first Kingdom of Israel around 1050 B.C., Naphtali was a part of a loose confederation of Israelite tribes. No central government existed, and in times of crisis, the people were led by leaders known as Judges. With the threat of Philistine incursions, the Israelite tribes decided to form a strong centralized monarchy to meet the challenge, and Naphtali joined the new kingdom with Saul as the first king. After his death, all the tribes other than Judah remained loyal to the House of Saul, but after the death of Saul's son who was successor to the throne of Israel, the Tribe of Naphtali joined the other northern Israelite tribes and made David, who was then the king of Judah, the king of a re-united Kingdom of Israel. However, on the accession of David's grandson Rehoboam, around 930 B.C., the Northern Tribes split from the House of David to re-create a Kingdom known as the Northern Kingdom.

Around 732 B.C., Naphtali, one of the most northern tribes, was one of the first to be conquered and then deported by Assyria. With its exile, it was lost to history. The Kingdom of Israel continued to exist until around 723 B.C., when it was again invaded by Assyria and the balance of the population deported. From that time, the Tribe of Naphtali has been counted as one of the Ten Lost Tribes of Israel. There has been speculation that the Bukharian Jews living in Central Asia today are descendants of Naphtali.

Gad

Gad was the seventh son of Jacob, one of the two descendants of Zilpah, his handmaid, the second being Asher.

After the Exodus from Egypt, and following the conquest of Canaan by the Israelites around 1200 B.C., Joshua allocated the land among the twelve tribes. Gad settled near the Jordan River, on land the tribe desired as soon as it saw it, before it had even crossed the Jordan. However, the location was never secure from invasion and attacks, since to the south it was exposed to the Moabites, and like the other tribes east of the Jordan, it was exposed on the north and east to the Assyrians.

Until the formation of the first Kingdom of Israel around 1050 B.C., Gad was a part of a loose confederation of Israelite tribes. No central government existed, and in times of crisis, the people were led by leaders known as Judges.

With the threat of Philistine incursions, the Israelite tribes decided to form a strong centralized monarchy to meet the challenge, and Gad joined the new kingdom with Saul as the first king. After his death, all the tribes other than Judah remained loyal to the House of Saul, but after the death of Saul's son and successor to the throne of Israel, Gad joined the other Northern Tribes in making David, who was then the king of Judah, the king of a re-united Kingdom of Israel.

However, on the accession to the throne of Rehoboam, David's grandson, around 930 B.C., the Northern Tribes split from the House of David to re-create a Kingdom of Israel as the Northern Kingdom. Gad was a member of that kingdom until it was conquered by Assyria around 723 B.C. The population was deported, and thereafter lost to history. It is now counted as one of the Ten Lost Tribes of Israel.

In the Talmud, it is Gad, along with the tribe of Reuben, that is portrayed as being the first tribe to be carried away by the Assyrians. Some members of Gad may have escaped and settled in southern Spain. The ancient name of the city of Cadiz was Gadir, which means city of Gad, and the people in Cadiz still call themselves Gaditanos, which means Gadites. The word Gad, which is Guad in Spanish, is found all over southern Spain. Written on the coat of arms of Cadiz is its Latin name, which is Gadium, or the city of Gad.

Asher

The tribe consisted of descendants of Asher, the eighth son of Jacob. Asher was one of the two descendants of Zilpah, a handmaid of Leah, the other being Gad.

Following the completion of the conquest of Canaan by the Israelites around 1200 B.C., Joshua allocated the land among the Twelve Tribes. To Asher, he assigned western and coastal Galilee, a region with cool temperatures and plentiful rainfall, making it some of the most fertile land in Canaan. It boasted rich pastures, wooded hills, and orchards. Consequently, Asher was particularly prosperous, and was known for its production of good quality olive oil.

Until the formation of the first Kingdom of Israel around 1050 B.C., Asher was a part of a loose confederation of Israelite tribes. No central government existed, and in times of crisis, the people were led by leaders known as Judges. With the threat of Philistine incursions, the Israelite tribes decided to form a strong centralized monarchy to meet the challenge, and Asher joined the new kingdom with Saul as the first king. After his death, all the tribes other than Judah remained loyal to the House of Saul, but soon thereafter, Asher joined the other northern Israelite tribes in making David, who was then the king of Judah, the king of a re-united Kingdom of Israel.

On the accession of Rehoboam, David's grandson, around 930 B.C., the Northern Tribes split from the House of David to re-form a Kingdom of Israel known as the Northern Kingdom. Asher was a member of that kingdom until it was conquered by Assyria around 723 B.C., when the population was deported. From that time, Asher was lost to history and became one of the Ten Lost Tribes of Israel. Interestingly, we learn in the New Testament that Anna the prophetess, and her father, Phanuel, belonged to the Tribe of Asher.

Despite appearing to have had close contact with the markets of Phoenicia, Asher appears to have been fairly disconnected from the other tribes of Israel. Additionally, it seems to have taken little part in the antagonism between the Canaanites and the other tribes of Israel.

Issachar

Issachar was the ninth son of Jacob, and the fifth son of Leah, his wife. Traditionally, Issachar was dominated by religious scholars. Jewish religious scholars seem to have been either Levites, or from the Tribe of Issachar.

Following the completion of the conquest of Canaan by the Israelites around 1200 B.C., Joshua allocated the land among the twelve tribes. Issachar's territory stretched from the Jordan River in the east, to the coast in the west. This region included the fertile Esdraelon plain.

Since the members of the tribe of Zebulun were traditionally seen as merchants, and Issachar as religious teachers, Issachar and Zebulun were benefitted by a mutually advantageous relationship, whereby Issachar would devote its time to the study and teaching of Torah, while Zebulun would provide financial support in exchange for a share of Issachar's spiritual reward. Such was the tradition of this symbiosis, that anyone engaged in such a partnership became termed Issachar and Zebulun respectively, even to this day.

As part of the Kingdom of Israel, the territory of Issachar was conquered by the Assyrians, and the tribe was lost to history, it becoming one of the Ten Lost Tribes of Israel.

Zebulun

Following the conquest of Canaan by the Israelite tribes, Joshua allocated the land among the twelve tribes. Zebulun's territory was at the southern end of the Galilee. The tribe consisted of descendants of Zebulun, the sixth son of Jacob and Leah. At the division of the land of Israel among the seven tribes not yet provided for, the lot of Zebulun was third. Jesus was raised within the territory of Zebulun.

In Jewish tradition, the tribe of Zebulun was considered to have a mutually advantageous relationship with the tribe of Issachar. Issachar's devotion to the study and teaching of the Torah, was financially supported by Zebulun in exchange for a share of the spiritual reward gained from such learning. The terms Issachar and Zebulun came to be used by Jews for anyone engaged in such a symbiotic relationship.

Zebulun played an important part in the early history of Israel. At the census of the tribes while in the Desert of Sinai during the second year of the Exodus, Zebulun numbered 57,400 men fit for war. Later, among those that followed David to Hebron to make him king were 50,000 fully armed men of Zebulun. (1 Chronicles 12:33).

Joseph

The Tribe of Joseph was descended from Joseph, the son of Jacob and Rachel. Joseph was the brother to Benjamin, the other son of Rachel and Jacob. The sons of Joseph were Ephraim and Manasseh, and together they traditionally constituted the tribe of Joseph. Consequently, Joseph is sometimes not listed as one of the tribes, in favor of Ephraim and Manasseh in its place. The Tribe of Joseph is often termed the House of Joseph, or the "two half-tribes of Joseph." Scholars believe that Joseph was originally considered a single tribe, and only split into Ephraim and Manasseh later.

Joseph's inheritance in the land of Canaan was one of the most valuable parts of the country, and the House of Joseph became the most dominant group in the Northern Kingdom of Israel. Eventually, the territories of both Ephraim and Manasseh were conquered by the Assyrians, and the tribe was exiled and thereafter lost to history. Despite a familial connection to Ephraim, Benjamin associated with the southern tribes and became part of the Kingdom of Judah. As a result, its people escaped Assyrian captivity, and were only subjected to the later Babylonian exile. When these exiles were allowed to return, the distinction between Benjamin and the other tribes in the kingdom of Judah was lost in favor of a common identity as "Jews."

Despite both Ephraim and Manasseh being led away as two of the Ten Lost Tribes of Israel, several modern-day groups claim descent from them, with varying levels of academic and rabbinical support. The Yusufzai tribe (literal translation The Sons of Joseph) in Afghanistan and Pakistan, have a long tradition connecting them to the exiled Kingdom of Israel. The Samaritans claim descent from these tribes, as do many Persian Jews. In Northeast India, the Mizo Jews claim descent from Manasseh. Similar traditions are held by the Telugu Jews in Southern India, who claim descent from Ephraim.

Considered less plausible by academic and Jewish authorities are the claims of western Christian groups. Many members of The Church of Jesus Christ of Latter-day Saints identify themselves as descended from Ephraim and Manasseh, believing that the lost tribes will be restored in the latter days as prophesied by Isaiah. Some Mormons believe that this would be the fulfillment of part of the Blessing of Jacob, that states that Joseph is a fruitful bough, even a fruitful bough by a well; whose branches run over the wall, with the interpretation that the wall is the ocean. In fact, The Book of Mormon teaches: "Behold, our father Jacob also testified concerning a remnant of the seed of Joseph. And behold, are not we a remnant of the seed of Joseph?" (3 Nephi 10:17).

Benjamin

The tribe consisted of descendants of Benjamin, the youngest son of Jacob and Rachel. The temple in Jerusalem was traditionally said to be partly in the territory of the tribe of Benjamin, with the balance of it in that of Judah.

After the conquest of the Promised Land promised land until the formation of the first Kingdom of Israel around 1050 B.C., Benjamin was a part of a loose confederation of Israelite tribes. No central government existed, and in times of crisis the people were led by leaders known as Judges.

Following the conquest of Canaan by the Israelites around 1200 B.C., Joshua allocated the land among the twelve tribes. To Benjamin, he assigned the territory between that of Ephraim to the north and Judah to the south. The westward boundary of the tribe of Benjamin stretched as far as the Mediterranean Sea.

Responding to a growing threat from the Philistines, the Israelite tribes formed a strong, centralized monarchy. Its first king was Saul, from the Tribe of Benjamin, which at the time was the smallest of the tribes. He reigned for 38 years. After his death, all the tribes other than Judah remained loyal to the House of Saul, but after the death of his son and successor to the throne of Israel, the Tribe of Benjamin joined the northern Israelite tribes in making David, then king of the Southern Kingdom of Judah, king of the united Kingdom of Israel and Judah. On the accession of Rehoboam, David's grandson, around 93 B.C., the northern tribes split from the House of David to re-form a Kingdom of Israel. Benjamin remained a part of the Southern Kingdom of Judah, until it was conquered around 586 B.C., and the population deported to Babylonia.

The tribe of Benjamin is described in the Bible as being taught to fight left-handed, so as to be able to wrong-foot its enemies. (See Judges 3:15-21 & 20:16, & 1 Chronicles 12:2).

The Book of Judges recounts how the rape of a concubine who belonged to a member of the tribe of Levi, by members of the tribe of Benjamin resulted in a battle at Gibeah, in which the other tribes of Israel sought vengeance, and during which the members of Benjamin including women and children, were systematically slaughtered. With Benjamin nearly wiped out, it was decided that the tribe should be allowed to survive, and its 600 surviving men were married off to women who were descended from Manasseh, whose men had been killed when it was discovered that they had not participated in the war against Benjamin. (So much for a Band of Brothers!)

Initially, although Jerusalem was in the territory allocated to the tribe of Benjamin, it remained under the independent control of the Jebusites, until it was finally conquered by David in the 11th century B.C., and made the capital of the United Kingdom of Israel. After the breakup of that United Monarchy, Jerusalem continued as the capital of the Southern Kingdom of Judah.

After the dissolution of the United Kingdoms of Israel and Judah around 930 B.C., Benjamin joined Judah as a junior partner in the Kingdom of Judah, or the Southern Kingdom. The Davidic dynasty, which had roots there, continued to reign in Judah. As part of the Southern Kingdom of Judah, Benjamin survived the destruction of Kingdom of Israel by the Assyrians, only to be later subjected to the Babylonian captivity. When that captivity ended, the distinctions between Benjamin and Judah was lost in favor of a common identity as Israel, though as late as the time of Jesus of Nazareth, Paul still identified himself by his Benjamite ancestry. "I also am an Israelite,' he wrote, "of the seed of Abraham, of the tribe of Benjamin." (Romans 11:1).

Manasseh and Ephraim were of the House of Joseph (A Double Portion).

Manasseh (the older of the two brothers)

Along with Benjamin, Joseph was the son of Jacob and Rachel. Joseph's sons Ephraim and Manasseh received "a double portion," and together they are often described as being of the "House of Joseph."

Until the formation of the first Kingdom of Israel around 1050 B.C., the Tribe of Manasseh was part of a loose confederation of Israelite tribes. No central government existed, and in times of crisis the people were led by leaders known as Judges. With the threat of Philistine incursions, the Israelite tribes decided to form a strong centralized monarchy to meet the challenge, and Manasseh joined the new kingdom with Saul as its first king. After his death, all the tribes other than Judah remained loyal to the House of Saul, but after the death of Saul's son and successor to the throne of Israel, Manasseh joined the other northern Israelite tribes in making David, who was then the king of Judah in the south, king of a re-united Kingdom of Israel. However, on the accession of Rehoboam, David's grandson, around 930 B.C., the northern tribes split from the House of David to re-form a Kingdom of Israel as the Northern Kingdom. Manasseh was a member of that kingdom until, around 723 B.C., it was conquered by Assyria and the population deported. From that time, Manasseh has been numbered among the Ten Lost Tribes of Israel, although some modern groups claim descent from the tribe.

We do know from The Book of Mormon that, "Aminadi was a descendant of Nephi, who was the son of Lehi, who came out of the land of Jerusalem, who was a descendant of Manasseh, who was the son of Joseph who was sold into Egypt by the hands of his brethren." (Alma 10:3).

Ephraim (the younger of the two brothers)

The Tribe of Ephraim was one of the Tribes of Israel. The Tribe of Manasseh, together with Ephraim, formed the House of Joseph. The descendants of Joseph became two of the tribes of Israel, whereas each of the other sons of Jacob was the founder of only one tribe. In the Blessing of Jacob, Ephraim and Manasseh are treated as a single tribe, making it likely that originally Ephraim and Manasseh were considered one tribe, that of Joseph.

Following the completion of the conquest of Canaan by the Israelites around 1200 B.C., Joshua allocated the land among the twelve tribes. The territory given to the Tribe of Ephraim was at the center of Canaan. The region later named Samaria consisted mostly of Ephraim's territory. The area was mountainous, giving it protection, and also highly fertile, providing an opportunity for prosperity.

Ephraim was the second son of Joseph and Asenath. Contrary to tradition, Ephraim received the birthright blessing from his grandfather Jacob, that was the blessing of the firstborn, instead of Manasseh. Although Manasseh was the elder son, Jacob had foreseen that Ephraim's descendants would be greater than his brother's. In some accounts, Ephraim is portrayed as domineering, haughty, discontented, and jealous, but in classical rabbinical literature, the biblical founder of the tribe is described as being modest and unselfish. These rabbinical sources allege that it was on account of modesty and selflessness that Jacob gave Ephraim precedence over Manasseh, the elder of the two. In these sources, God upholds the blessing in honor of the righteousness of Jacob, and makes Ephraim the leading tribe.

Ephraim became the progenitor of the tribe of Ephraim. In the Last Days, their privilege and responsibility is to bear the priesthood, take the message of the restored gospel to the world, and raise an Ensign to gather scattered Israel. The children of Ephraim will crown with glory those from the north countries who will return in the Last Days. (See D&C 133:26-34).

A written record of one group from the tribe of Ephraim that was led from Jerusalem to America about 600 B.C. is described in the scriptures as the stick of Ephraim or Joseph, commonly called The Book of Mormon. It and the stick of Judah, which is the Bible, form a unified testimony of the Lord Jesus Christ, His resurrection, and His divine work among these two tribes (Joseph and Judah) of the house of Israel.

According to Joseph Smith, a branch of Ephraim will be broken off and will write another testament of Christ. (See J.S.T. Genesis 50:24-26 & 30-31). The stick of Judah and the stick of Joseph will become one in the Lord's hand. (See Ezekiel 37:15-19). The writings of Judah and of Joseph shall grow together. (See 2 Nephi 3:12). In The Book of Mormon, the keys of power or control over the record of the stick of Ephraim were committed to the prophet Moroni. (See D&C 27:5).

Ephraim is often seen as the tribe that embodied the entire Northern Kingdom, and the royal house resided in its territory, just as Judah was the tribe that personified the Kingdom of Judah to the south, and provided its royal family.

From the end of the conquest of Canaan by Joshua, who himself was a descendant of Ephraim, the Tribe of Ephraim was a part of a loose confederation of Israelite tribes. No central government existed, and in times of crisis the people were led by leaders known as Judges. With the threat of Philistine incursions, the Israelite tribes decided to form a strong centralized monarchy to meet the challenge, and the Tribe of Ephraim joined the new kingdom, with Saul as the first king. After his death, all the tribes other than Judah remained loyal to the House of Saul, but after the death of Saul's son and successor to the throne of Israel, the Tribe of Ephraim joined the other northern Israelite tribes and made David, who was then the king of Judah in the south, king of a re-united Kingdom of Israel.

However, on the accession of Rehoboam, David's grandson, around 930 B.C., the northern tribes split from the House of David to form the Northern Kingdom of Israel. Its first king was Jeroboam, who came from the Tribe of Ephraim. (See 1 Kings 1:26).

The accents of the tribes were distinctive enough, even at the time of the confederacy, so that when the Israelites of Gilead, under the leadership of Jephthah, fought the Tribe of Ephraim, their pronunciation of "shibboleth" as "sibboleth" was considered sufficient evidence to single out individuals from Ephraim, to be punished with immediate death at the hands of the Israelites of Gilead.

Ephraim remained a member of the Northern Kingdom until it was conquered by Assyria around 723 B.C. and the population deported. From that time, the Tribe of Ephraim was lost to history and has been counted as one of the

Ten Lost Tribes of Israel. In The Book of Mormon, the Savior revealed something about these lost tribes: "And verily, verily, I say unto you that I have other sheep, which are not of this land, neither of the land of Jerusalem, neither in any parts of that land round about whither I have been to minister. For they of whom I speak are they who have not as yet heard my voice; neither have I at any time manifested myself unto them. But I have received a commandment of the Father that I shall go unto them, and that they shall hear my voice, and shall be numbered among my sheep, that there may be one fold and one shepherd; therefore, I go to show myself unto them." (3 Nephi 16:1-3).

Ephraim was the most dominant of the tribes in the Northern Kingdom of Israel, which led to "Ephraim" becoming a synonym for the entire kingdom. As part of that kingdom, the territory of Ephraim was conquered by the Assyrians, and the tribe exiled; the manner of their exile led to their further history being lost. However, several modern-day groups claim descent, with varying levels of academic and rabbinical support. The Church of Jesus Christ of Latter-day Saints believes that a significant portion of its members are descended from, or have been adopted into, the tribe of Ephraim. They argue that they are charged with restoring the lost tribes in the latter days as prophesied by Isaiah, and that the tribes of both Ephraim and Judah will play important leadership roles for covenant Israel in the Last Days. Some believe that this would be the fulfilment of part of the Blessing of Jacob, that states that Joseph is a fruitful bough, even a fruitful bough by a well; whose branches run over the wall, interpreting the "wall" as the ocean. (See Genesis 49:22).

"And it shall come to pass in that day that the Lord shall set his hand again the second time to recover the remnant of his people which shall be left, from Assyria, and from Egypt, and from Pathros, and from Cush, and from Elam, and from Shinar, and from Hamath, and from the islands of the sea. And he shall set up an ensign for the nations, and shall assemble the outcasts of Israel, and gather together the dispersed of Judah from the four corners of the earth. The envy of Ephraim also shall depart, and the adversaries of Judah shall be cut off; Ephraim shall not envy Judah, and Judah shall not vex Ephraim." (2 Nephi 21:11-13).

In The Church of Jesus Christ of Latter-day Saints, patriarchal blessings include a declaration of lineage, typically stating that the person is of the house of Israel and a descendant of Abraham, belonging to a specific tribe of Jacob. Many Latter-day Saints are of the tribe of Ephraim, the tribe given the primary responsibility to lead the latter-day work of the Lord. Because each of us has many bloodlines running in us, two members of the same family may be declared as being of different tribes in Israel. It does not matter if a person's lineage in the house of Israel is through bloodlines or by adoption. Church members are counted as descendants of Abraham and an heir to all the promises and blessings contained in the Abrahamic covenant.

The Ten Lost Tribes of Israel

According to the Bible, the Kingdom of Israel (or Northern Kingdom) was one of the successor states to the older United Monarchy (also called the Kingdom of Israel), which came into existence around 930 B.C., after the northern Tribes of Israel rejected Solomon's son Rehoboam as their king. Nine landed tribes formed the Northern Kingdom: the tribes of Reuben, Issachar, Zebulun, Dan, Naphtali, Gad, Asher, and Ephraim and Manasseh through Joseph. In addition, some members of Tribe of Levi, who had no land allocation, were found in the Northern Kingdom. The Tribes of Judah and Benjamin remained loyal to Rehoboam, and formed the Kingdom of Judah in the south, sometimes called the Southern Kingdom.

Nephi said: "There are many who are already lost from the knowledge of those who are at Jerusalem. Yea, the more part of all the tribes have been led away; and they are scattered to and fro upon the isles of the sea; and whither they are none of us knoweth, save that we know that they have been led away." (1 Nephi 22:4-5).

Nevertheless, he prophesied: "The Lord God will proceed to make bare his arm in the eyes of all the nations, in bringing about his covenants and his gospel unto those who are of the house of Israel. Wherefore, he will bring them again out of captivity, and they shall be gathered together to the lands of their inheritance; and they shall be brought out of obscurity and out of darkness; and they shall know that the Lord is their Savior and their Redeemer, the Mighty One of Israel." (1 Nephi 22:11-12).

In order to accomplish this, "the Lord shall utterly destroy the tongue of the Egyptian sea; and with his mighty wind he shall shake his hand over the river, and shall smite it in the seven streams, and make men go over dry shod." (2 Nephi 27:15).

The Lord revealed to Joseph Smith: "And they who are in the north countries shall come in remembrance before the Lord; and their prophets shall hear his voice, and shall no longer stay themselves; and they shall smite the rocks, and the ice shall flow down at their presence. And an highway shall be cast up in the midst of the great deep." (D&C 133:26-27).

When speaking of Israel, most people think of the Jews, and when referring to the Gathering of Israel, they have in mind the return of the Jews to the land of Jerusalem. It should be remembered, however, that the Jews represent but one of the Twelve Tribes of the House of Israel. "For lo ... I will sift the house of Israel among all nations." (Amos 9:9).

Isaiah spoke of the Last Days, when the Lord would set His Hand a second time to gather His people. The first time was either during the Exodus from Egypt, or during Israel's return from the Babylonian captivity, depending upon one's point of view. As Isaiah saw it, the House of Israel would return from the seven known countries of his day, "from Assyria, and from Egypt, and from Pathros (or upper Egypt), and from Cush (or Ethiopia), and from Elam (east of Babylonia), and from Hamath (Northern Syria), and from the isles of the sea (the rest of the world)." (2 Nephi 21:11).

The apocryphal writer Esdras recorded this version of the escape of the Ten Lost Tribes of Israel from Assyria: "Those are the ten tribes, which were carried away prisoners out of their own land in the time of Hosea the king whom Shalmaneser the king of Assyria led away captive, and he carried them over the waters, and so came they into another land. But they took this counsel among themselves, that they would leave the multitude of the heathen, and go forth unto a further country, where never mankind dwelt, that they might there keep their statutes, which they never kept in their own land. And they entered into Euphrates by the narrow passage of the river. For the most High then shewed signs for them, and held still the flood, till they were passed over. For through that country there was a great way to go, namely, of a year and a half: and the same region is called Arsareth. Then dwelt they there until the latter times; and now when they shall begin to come, the Highest shall stay the stream again, that they may go through." (Apocrypha, 2 Esdras 13:40-47).

Interestingly, Esdras declared that the Ten Tribes determined to keep the statutes of the Lord, even though they had not kept them when they were living in the Northern Kingdom. Other scriptures attest to the facts that these tribes were led away by the Lord, have since been continually preserved by Him, have had their own prophets minister among them, had the Savior Himself visit them after His resurrection, have kept their own scriptures and records, keep the statutes of God, and will be led out of the North Country by His power to help build the New Jerusalem.

Types, Rites, Ceremonies, and Symbols

"Is there not a type
in this thing? For just a
surely as this director did bring
our fathers, by following its course,
to the promised land, shall the words of
Christ, if we follow their course, carry
us beyond this vale of sorrow into
a far better land of promise."
(Alma 37:45).

This compass (the Liahona) was a "type" of Christ that had symbolic significance as well as a literal meaning. There are repeated references to types in the Nephite record, for they are profoundly effective teaching tools. Outward observances without real meaning are only ceremonies. For example, when the bishop stands at the pulpit at the beginning of Sacrament Meeting, his greeting is a ceremony. His expression of thanks to the Aaronic Priesthood for a job well done after the administration of the Sacrament is a ceremony. The recognition of visitors to Relief Society and other meetings is largely ceremonial. These events pass without any lasting significance, and are only superficially acknowledged.

A rite that has a present spiritual meaning is a symbol. No one would dispute the symbolic significance of the bread and water used in the Sacrament; the prayer accompanying the ordinance reminds the participants of Christ's sacrifice and of their covenant relationship with Him. The ordinance of baptism is carried out in a font that is in similitude of the grave. In its waters, the repentant faithful symbolically wash away their sins, and emerge clean and pure in the sight of God. Christ Himself was baptized in the Jordan River, which happens to be the lowest body of fresh water on earth. It flows into the Dead Sea at 1,385 feet below sea level. The symbolism cannot be lost on us: He figuratively and literally descended beneath us all.

In the font itself, both the officiant and recipient are dressed in white clothing that is symbolic of purity. The authority of the priesthood is vested in one who holds his right arm to the square in a symbolic gesture of the power of God. No one who has received a priesthood blessing when sick can deny the power of the rejuvenating symbolism of pure olive oil that has, in turn, been consecrated for the healing of the sick in the household of faith. There is symbolic significance in the olive tree itself. It is a living thing that produces good fruit and whose branch has always been associated with peace. But an olive tree cannot become productive by itself. It requires the grafting in of a tame branch by a husbandman. Afterward, careful attention and pruning are required, because whenever the tree is neglected, it will begin to revert to the primitive, wild plant it once was. But once fruitful, it may remain so for centuries. In fact, new shoots from the root of the original tree may continue producing fruit for thousands of years.

It is interesting that, during the siege of Jerusalem (70 A.D.), the Romans symbolically cut down the olive trees, including those in the Garden of Gethsemane beside the Brook Kidron, outside the city walls. Then, three years later, the Romans built a three-foot high wall entirely around the mountain fortress of Masada, (a "line of circumvallation") symbolically demonstrating to the Jewish Zealots within, that there could be no possibility of escape.

In any event, when symbolism points to a future reality, conveying at the same time, by anticipation, the blessing that is yet to appear, it is a type. The brazen serpent raised up in the wilderness by Moses pointed Israel to the future ministry of Christ and to promised salvation. Our comprehension is enlarged beyond that which we would normally expect through mortal experience, and there emerges a powerful link between the secular and the divine.

This clarity expressed in types and shadows is particularly true of the writings of Isaiah, that may explain why his words were so loved by both the Nephite prophets and the Savior Himself. "Awake, awake, put on thy strength, O Zion; put on thy beautiful garments, O Jerusalem, the holy city; for henceforth there shall no more come into thee thy uncircumcised and the unclean. Shake thyself from the dust; arise, sit down, O Jerusalem; loose thyself from the bands of thy neck, O captive daughter of Zion." (2 Nephi 8:24-25). "Enlarge the place of thy tent, and let them stretch forth the curtains of thy habitations. Spare not. Lengthen thy cords and strengthen thy stakes." (3 Nephi 22:2).

Unity

"They were one,
the children of Christ,
and heirs to the kingdom
of God. And how blessed were
they! For the Lord did bless them
in all their doings." (4 Nephi
1:17-18).

Who in the church, or which office, do you think is the most important? The Apostle Paul compared the members of the church to the parts of the body. "For the body is not one member, but many... And the eye cannot say unto the hand, I have no need of thee: nor again the head to the feet, I have no need of you." (1 Corinthians 12:14-21). Just as the eye, the hand, the head, and the feet are important in their unique functions, so are all members of the church important with their different skill sets and talents.

During the Apostolic ministry, the church grew rapidly, which was cause for great rejoicing, but it also created some challenges. As congregations became more numerous and with the increasing burdens of the work of the ministry, the Apostles needed the help of others in their efforts to build and nurture the kingdom. So, they called seven men of honest report, full of the Holy Ghost and wisdom, who were appointed (or set apart) to focus on day-to-day administrative responsibilities. "And in those days, when the number of the disciples was multiplied, there arose a murmuring of the Grecians against the Hebrews, because their widows were neglected in the daily ministration. Then the twelve called the multitude of the disciples unto them, and said, It is not reason that we should leave the word of God, and serve tables....And (so) they chose Stephen, a man full of faith and of the Holy Ghost, and Philip, and Prochorus, and Nicanor, and Timon, and Parmenas, and Nicolas a proselyte of Antioch: (seven in all) Whom they set before the apostles: and when they had prayed, they laid their hands on them" and set them apart. As a consequence, "the word of God increased; and the number of the disciples multiplied in Jerusalem greatly; and a great company of the priests were obedient to the faith." (Acts 6:1-7).

Then, as now, when the diversity among members was recognized and handled appropriately, it enriched and strengthened the church. Today, we find that Zion comes in many different colors. It speaks Aymara, Dutch, Fijian, French, Mandarin, Russian, Slovene, Zulu, and dozens of other languages. It lives in nearly 3,000 stakes (2,818 as of April 2009), in practically every country in the world, from Argentina to Zimbabwe. It has over 13 million members (13,508,509 as of April 2009) who are red, yellow, brown, black, and white. Zion wears a sarong, a grass skirt, a blue collar, a tupeno, a kilt, and a business suit. It lives in igloos, huts, and high-rises. Most important of all, it shares a common testimony that Jesus is the Christ, and that His love, indeed, makes the world go 'round. Today it is more important than ever to remember the words of President Harold B. Lee, who reminded us in General Conference that "there is no United States of America in heaven." The great equalizer in the sight of God is the obedience of His children to His will, so they may all be at-one with Christ.

How can we differ from each other, living in strikingly different cultures as we do, and still be unified? Coast redwoods are among the largest living things. The tallest tree reaches a height of over 360 feet, weighs hundreds of tons, and has been living for well over 2,000 years. But, curiously, while most other trees of massive size have deep roots to support their great weight, the root system of the redwood is very shallow. The key to its survival is the intertwining of the roots of one tree with those of several of its neighbors. Redwoods live in groves; they cannot stand alone. Interdependence is critical to the stability and longevity of each individual tree.

In a similar fashion, the structure and organization of the church helps in many ways to unify its members. They are a lot like snowflakes, at the other extreme from coast redwoods and one of nature's most fragile creations. Although delicate in structure, look at what they can do when they stick together. As in the case of either redwoods or snowflakes, so it is with the church, which "hath need of every member," that the whole may be kept in perfect working order, and so that all individuals within the organization may expand their capabilities to the level of their potential. (D&C 84:110).

As He did during the Apostolic ministry, the Lord has inspired latter-day church leaders to make organizational changes as the church has grown, to help meet the needs of individual members in wards, branches, stakes, and missions throughout the world. There are now 9 Quorums of the Seventy and 28 Areas presided over by Presidencies. Seventeen training centers throughout the world help missionaries prepare for the field. Area Conferences address the cultural needs of members in the far corners of the world. 128 temples (18 more have been announced as of April 2009) serve the needs of the members on 6 continents and the isles of the sea. The ordinances performed in these temples create a unifying backdrop to the worldwide tapestry that is being woven by the 50,000 + members of the Army of God as they seek out and find the elect, and draw them into the Fold.

By their actions, new converts and well-established church members alike echo Paul, who declared to the Romans: "We, being many, are one body in Christ." (Romans 12:5). This spiritual unification is confirmed by striking evidences. For example, in spite of the scores of translations of The Book of Mormon used by members worldwide, (including Arabic, Burmese, Efik, Farsi, Georgian, Navajo, Pohnpeian, Sesotho, and Tshiluba), there is remarkably little disagreement as to their meaning. The scriptures provide a gospel "standard." In fact, they are called "The Standard Works" with good reason, inasmuch as they are the foundation for the actions of the Lord's worldwide priesthood government and are every member's personal "Handbook of Instructions." They are not of private interpretation. Their meaning is discerned by the Spirit that is universally accessible to the members who have been endowed by priesthood ordinance with the Gift of the Holy Ghost.

I personally witnessed this unity when I attended the Munich Area Conference in 1973. (This was the second Area Conference to be held. The first was a year earlier in Mexico City). As the closing hymn was being sung, I made my way to a central station within the Olympic Sports Area to return my audio headsets. As I passed by the Saints who had gathered from all over Europe, I could hear them singing "The Spirit of God" in their native languages. On the stage, the Mormon Tabernacle sang each of the four verses in a different language. It was quite moving, specifically because the words (in English) were unimportant. Instead, we were collectively carried by the Spirit to a higher plane where the common bonds of shared experience made us one.

In church organization and church government, ecclesiastical leaders enjoy similar harmony in spite of individual cultural, social, political, and economic circumstances. The ordinances of the gospel, from baptism to the endowment in the temple, are universally understood and faithfully administered by Latter-day Saints whose identity as brethren in the Priesthood of God overshadows any perceived or superficial differences.

We are living in a time when the church is growing rapidly. The Lord wants each of us to serve in His kingdom as it grows. Even as we recognize and appreciate our unique qualities, talents, and experiences we also know that we are bound in ways that bridge any cultural gulfs that might otherwise separate us.

With this understanding, as a church we can squarely face even our most stubborn challenges. We can be unified, even as we celebrate our diversity. We can move from dependence, through independence, to interdependence. We can enjoy unity and conformity without giving up our individuality. We can go into all the world and spread the Lord's message, who invites "all to come unto him and partake of his goodness; and he denieth none that come unto him, black and white, bond and free, male and female; and he remembereth the heathen; and all are alike unto God, both Jew and Gentile." (2 Nephi 26:33). We can collectively stand independent above all creatures, for our sum is far greater than our parts.

In our own day, as it did so many times in The Book of Mormon, the church is expanding rapidly. Then as now, the Lord wants each of us to find opportunities for service in the kingdom. (See 2 Nephi 2:3, & Mosiah 2:17). Even as we discover our unique talents, and we have individual experiences, we will also find that the gospel binds to each other in ways that bridge any cultural gulfs that might have, in less fortuitous circumstances, separated us.

Updates are Ready

"I will give unto the children of men
line upon line, precept upon precept, here a
little and there a little, and blessed are they who
hearken unto my precepts, and lend an ear unto my
counsel, for they shall learn wisdom; for unto him that
receiveth I will give more, and from them that shall say, We
have enough, from them shall be taken away even that which
they have. Cursed is he that putteth his trust in man, or maketh
flesh his arm, or shall hearken unto the precepts of men, save their
precepts shall be given by the power of the Holy Ghost. Wo be unto
the Gentiles, saith the Lord God of Hosts! Fore notwithstanding
I shall lengthen out mine arm unto them from day to day,
they will deny me; nevertheless, I will be merciful
unto them, saith the Lord God, if they will
repent and come unto me."
(2 Nephi 28:30-32).

Apple Terms and Conditions

Adam and Eve were the first ones not to read these terms, although they were thoroughly explained to them.
"I, the Lord God commanded the man, saying: Of every tree of the garden thou mayest freely eat, but of the tree of the knowledge of good and evil, thou shalt not eat of it, nevertheless, thou mayest choose for thyself, for it is given unto thee; but, remember that I forbid it, for in the day thou eatest thereof thou shalt surly die." (Moses 3:16-17, See Abraham 5:12-13).

But then, "Satan put it into the heart of the serpent, (for he had drawn away many after him,) and he sought also to beguile Eve, for he knew not the mind of God, wherefore he sought to destroy the world. And he said unto the woman: Yea, hath God said - Ye shall not eat of every tree of the garden? (And he spake by the mouth of the serpent.) And the woman said unto the serpent: We may eat of the fruit of the trees of the garden; But of the fruit of the tree which thou beholdest in the midst of the garden, God hath said—Ye shall not eat of it, neither shall ye touch it, lest ye die. And the serpent said unto the woman: Ye shall not surely die; For God doth know that in the day ye eat thereof, then your eyes shall be opened, and ye shall be as gods, knowing good and evil." (Moses 4:6-11).

Checking for New Software

Everyone needs an automatically recurring schedule that checks for new software. One member of the church who developed such an agenda said: "I felt I had received some (new software) before. However, I saw that random (updates were) not sufficient. To be a rock, a bastion of surety, (updates) must be something on which one can count and receive in every occasion of real need. I began to seek (them) actively. I prayed, I fasted, I lived the gospel as best I knew. I was faithful in my church duties. I tried to live up to every scruple which my conscience enjoined upon me. And dependable (updates) did come. Intermittently, haltingly at first, then steadily, over some years (they) finally came to be a mighty stream of experience. I came to know that at any time of day or night, in any circumstance, for any real need, I could get help. (The new software) came in the form of feelings of encouragement when things seemed hopeless. It came in ideas to unravel puzzles that blocked my accomplishment. It came in priesthood blessings which were fully realized. It came in whisperings of prophecy which were fulfilled. It came in support and even anticipation of what the General Authorities of the church would say and do in general conference. It came in the gifts of the Spirit, as the wonders of eternity were opened to the eyes of my understanding. That (new software) is today for me a river of living water that nourishes my soul in every situation. It is the most important factor of my life. If it were taken away, all that I have and am would be dust and ashes. It is the basis of my love, life, understanding, hope, and progress." (Chauncy Riddle).

Your Software is Up-to-Date

In the very best of circumstances, when our software is up to date, we quietly go about our Father's business. We make His thoughts our thoughts, and His purposes are reflected in our actions. Because the latest version of software guides us unerringly by principle, the temptation to act in a manner contrary to His will would never enter our minds. Our faith is action whose foundation is built upon the solid rock of binary code.

Checking for new software through the ordinance of the Sacrament is strong motivation to commit ourselves to higher levels of achievement. The Sacrament frees Heavenly Father to bring our software up to date, so that potential stumbling blocks can become stepping-stones, and mortality can become the vital growth experience it was designed to be.

New Software is Available

If we take advantage of new software whose code has been written by the Senior Systems Analyst, our operating system will run more smoothly and at an optimal level. Listening to the Conference Addresses of His prophets, seers, and revelators will alert us to the availability of new software. Its functionality will justify the performance cost that must be paid to utilize it. As the father of King Lamoni prayed: "I will give away all my sins to know thee." (Alma 22:18). When he learned that new software was available, it was his desire to do a system re-boot and utilize not just the update, but also embrace an entirely new operating system.

We cannot allow ourselves to be seduced by pirated software that carries the risk of fatal flaws hidden within its code. Our new software should carry genuine registration barcode data that authenticates its compatibility with the operating system. As he knelt in prayer near an "Apple" tree in the Sacred Grove, Joseph Smith was told that he must not purchase counterfeit software, for it was "wrong, and the (Senior Systems Analyst) who addressed (him) said that all their (code) was an abomination in his sight; that (the software engineers of his day) were all corrupt." (J.S.H. 1:9). In reality, the abomination of their software was that it was all form and no substance, the sizzle without the steak. Superficially, it appeared to function seamlessly with the hardware then available to the general public. But insult was added to injury because hypocrisy had become a part of a humanized, spiritually impotent data stream with the software support of systems analysts who did not really believe in the integrity of their existing software, but only professed to appreciate its value. They revealed their true character, as they were "lifted up in the imagination of the thoughts of (their) heart(s), being only evil continually." (Moses 8:22).

The software available to Joseph Smith's contemporaries had become corrupted, inasmuch as the power by which the various networks operated had been transferred to those who professed to be the Senior System Analyst's earthly software representatives, but who were really only commercial vendors competing for market share. They mechanically distributed outdated disks, with regard for neither the relevancy of programs therein, nor the qualifications of their recipients. The operating manual itself had become a magical book in the eyes of many, ostensibly conveying power and knowledge without the need for accurate translation from the original computer language in which it was written. Moroni saw that there would be many in the Last Days who had "transfigured the holy word of God," or who had arrogantly and contemptuously changed the appearance and substance of the operating system, and had so brought damnation upon their souls. (Mormon 8:33).

Update Now

We believe all that the Senior Systems Analyst has revealed, all that He does now reveal, and that he will continue to reveal many great and important things pertaining to the operating system to help it run smoothly and efficiently in our behalf. He does this to prevent "bugs" from compromising its integrity. We cannot be computer-literate if we are saddled with diminished capacity. We cannot hope to deal with Twenty-first Century challenges utilizing code that was written in the Middle-Ages, with code that was written for others living in times distant from ours, or with code that is unreliable because its accuracy cannot be confirmed. Updates streamline our code to help us to dream big, formulate clear goals, accept responsibility, dedicate ourselves to service, develop the love to work, cultivate optimism, be honest, enjoy a reputation for dependability, possess single-minded concentration, focus on success, and persist until we succeed.

There are a variety of sources available for regular updates, and they are all freeware. As Isaiah wrote: "Every one that thirsteth, come ye" to the internet cafe, "and he that hath no money; come ye, buy, and eat; yea, come, buy (software updates) without money and without price." (Isaiah 55:1). Updates cannot be purchased for money, but they may be better classified as "shareware," or software that is provided without cost only on a trial basis. Ultimately, however, behavioral changes will occur that satisfy the cost. Shareware updates include Conference addresses and instructions from local leaders, sacrament meeting talks, personal prayer, temple attendance, and church media, to name a few.

System Restore

If our computer crashes and we lose important data, we can do a system restore by typing in the word "repentance," and then following the prescribed instructions. Regaining full functionality within the operating system may not be instantaneous. A series of steps will likely stretch the process out over a period of days, weeks, or even months. This can cause serious, but reversible, anxiety as full functionality is regained. For obvious reasons, computer crashes should be avoided at all costs.

When taught by knowledgeable technicians, those who have been computer illiterate may be given the opportunity to "update" to an entirely new operating system by way of baptism. When contemplating this significant lifestyle change, it is important to have the proper authority provide the necessary service to your CPU so that your hardware infrastructure is built on a solid foundation.

Time Machine

Those with Apple Leopard may enjoy the benefits of Time Machine, a feature that allows the user to return to the date of baptism and start afresh. This program flexibly adapts to the circumstances and wishes of individual users. One program or the entire operating system may be selected. A handy shortcut is included with this software, wherein partaking of the Sacrament provides an alternative to selecting the entire Time Machine System Restore.

Remind Me Later

We cannot afford to be reminded later to update with software that is now available. Procrastination siphons away power that is critical to the enhancement of the operating system. If we take time now to sharpen the saw, to plan, prioritize, and focus our energies, we will not need to be reminded later. Clearing our desktop eliminates the clutter that might otherwise distract us from updating now. It helps us to avoid the spinning wheels of crisis management, first putting out one fire and then another, but never focusing our energies on the relevant tasks at hand. (iCal would be a handy application to have, or even sticky notes). Developing organizational skills, being tidy in our affairs, and keeping our discs out of harm's way and in their protective cases will keep them free of the contamination that so insidiously compromises essential code.

The operating system was designed to be universally recognized, accepted, and utilized. Therefore, the "Remind Me Later" prompt has applicability when used on behalf of those who are not currently ready to upgrade.

Accept

Hopefully, with our hand on the mouse and in control of the movement of the cursor, we will have the courage to click on the correct key, to say "to the man who stood at the gate of the year 'Give me a light that I may tread safely into the unknown.' And he replied 'Go into the darkness and put your hand into the hand of God. That shall be to you better than light and safer than a known way.' (Minnie Louise Haskins).

To accept the update is a tangible manifestation of our determination to discipline ourselves "in doctrine and principle pertaining to futurity, according to the moral agency" given to us by the Lord and it is an acknowledgement that 'we are accountable." (D&C 101:78). The integrity and worth of the operating system is validated by our determination to accept the invitation to "Update Now." But if we do not carry out our responsibilities within the context of the Software Licensing Agreement, the gift of the unbridled freedom to do so may lead to tyranny. We are free to choose, but we cannot choose to escape the consequences of our poor choices. Brigham Young was surely thinking up "Accepting" updates, when he said we are "in progress either to an endless advancement in eternal perfections or back to dissolution. There is no period in all the eternities wherein organized existence will become stationary that it cannot advance in knowledge, wisdom, power and glory."

Do Not Accept

Satan will try to get us to hit the "Do Not Accept" key. He will use diversionary tactics and will flatter us with deceptions and distractions. "And thus, he goeth up and down, to and fro in the earth, seeking to destroy the souls of men" by influencing them to reject available updates. (D&C 10:27). Even now, his ideology requires blind obedience to a counterfeit and unworkable operating system whose power is derived from compulsion. The code that he so carelessly wrote would actually have put us in the untenable position of being able to press neither the "Accept" nor the "Do not Accept" key. No software patch has ever been written that would remedy that dilemma. It is a conundrum of cosmic proportion. Thus, he was a liar from the beginning who promoted a bogus operating system reminiscent of Windows Millennium. (And we all remember what a disaster that was!) Today, his program is equally untenable, and the enthusiastically ignorant who embrace it ultimately find themselves dumbly staring at a flashing question mark or a sad-faced emoticon.

The cursor's blinking on the "Accept" box alerts Satan that he must act decisively to deal with disaster. His immediate strategy is to cut the power to the keyboard's illumination and to create confusion. Then he exerts just enough pressure to move the monitor from brilliant, dazzling white, through every shade of grey, to fathomless black. He induces panic in the software marketplace by creating a carefully constructed prospectus that is crafted to confuse us with its cunning. He seeks to minimize in our minds the consequences of indecisiveness and he forces us into carelessly conceived and hasty decisions relating to our choice of operating systems, without regard for their long-term negative consequences. His flattery is a deception designed to distract us from our recognition of genuine updates. His pandering plays to our vanity, so that he might weaken the moral fiber and humility that are necessary prerequisites to a check of the "Accept" box. The Master Software Engineer told Joseph Smith such misguided individuals would one day lament: "The harvest is past, the summer is ended, and my soul is not saved," for I rejected the software updates that were before me. (D&C 56:16). With weeping, and wailing, and gnashing of teeth, those who are cast down into a bottomless pit littered with useless code will cry, as it were:. "Why did I settle for Windows 95, when I could have had Apple Leopard 10.6.1?"

I Understand and Agree to the Software Licensing Agreement

That we are here testifies that we both understand and have agreed to the Software Licensing Agreement. In fact, when it was first introduced, we were among "the morning stars (who) sang together, (when) all the sons of God shouted for joy." (Job 38:7). Intimate familiarity with the SLA propelled us from our first estate to a condition where we might be "added upon" as we are introduced to unlimited opportunities for the expansion of our hard drive capability. (Abraham 3:26). In the Garden of Eden after the Fall, "the Lord God said, Behold, the man is become as one of us," To know both PC and MAC. (Genesis 3:22). He was not speaking of Gigabyte, Terabyte, or Petabyte potential. Instead, He was envisioning infinite possibilities because His perspective is that of a mainframe supercomputer with unlimited processing capabilities.

We have the responsibility to have read and to have understood the SLA before checking the "I Agree" box at the bottom of all the pages of fine print. (Yes. This does include a familiarity with the Isaiah chapters in The Book of Mormon). The alternative would be to have the entire operating system crash because we had "Performed an Illegal Operation" in consequence of a superficial understanding of the SLA, notwithstanding that we might have raised our right arm to the square in acknowledgement of its provisions.

Restart Now

It is time to act once we have made the commitment to do so. Joseph Fielding Smith, Jr. cautioned, "Before you (turned on your laptop) you stood on neutral ground. When the (operating system was introduced), good and evil were set before you. You could choose either or neither. There were two opposite masters inviting you to serve them. You left the neutral ground, and you can never get back on to it." King Benjamin told his people: "Because of (your willingness to check the "Restart Now" box,) ye shall be called the children of Christ, his sons and his daughters, for behold, this day he hath spiritually begotten you; for ye say that your hearts are changed through faith on his name; therefore, ye are born of him and have become his sons and his daughters. And under this (operating system and in no other) ye are made free." (Mosiah 5:7-8).

As Alma told his people who stood beside The Waters of Mormon: "If this be the desire of your hearts, what have you against (checking the "Restart Now" box), as a witness before him that ye have entered into a covenant with him, that ye will serve him and keep his commandments, that he may pour out his Spirit more abundantly upon you," and immediately upgrade you to a brand new operating system?. (Mosiah 18:10). These people did commit to "Restart Now," to change their lives, and so Alma did an entire network system reboot, "and they were in number about two hundred and four souls" who were filled with a whole new appreciation of their enhanced computing capabilities. (Mosiah 18:16).

Virus Detection Software

"Restarting Now" has all to do with choice, change, and accountability. We are charged with the responsibility to be obedient, and we cannot afford to procrastinate. The risk of damage from an existing undetected virus is just too great. Using version 1.0 when version 10.5.1 is available creates compatibility issues that wreak havoc with our ability to cope with new and unforeseen challenges. Without virus protection software capability, we might also be susceptible to hidden cookies and other clutter that could cause a significant slow-down in data processing or even memory. Fonts might not be recognized, and graphics and video cards might not function at all. In a worst-case scenario, our data could become corrupted or even unusable. Our computing capability could be effectively destroyed in a fiery cauldron of anguish.

Restart Later

Satan has a PhD (Philosophy of the Devil) in computer science, and is very good at hacking into and compromising the integrity of our most basic systems. His spyware can not only monitor how we are using our existing software, but without our knowledge it can also change our settings, resulting in frustratingly slow connections to sites we visit often. We might even be misdirected to a site that bears no resemblance to the one we wished to enter. Sometimes his spyware creates a debilitating compromise of the functionality of the very programs that control our feelings, our attitudes, and even our basic life-support. This malware may disguise itself as any number of self-defeating behaviors that subtly influence us to Restart Later.

The righteous face challenges equivalent to those of the Pentagon, whose computer systems are under cyber-attack over 2 million times a day. Shawn Henry, assistant director of the FBI's cyber division, told a conference in New York:. "Other than a nuclear device or some other type of destructive weapon, the threat to our infrastructure, the threat to our intelligence, the threat to our computer network is the most critical threat we face." (January 7, 2009). We need spiritual firewalls and effective virus detection software (available from the Senior System Analyst or His representatives) that are constantly being updated to bolster our resistance to satanic cyber-attacks that are mounted against our defenses and which occur more frequently that we care to admit. (In fact, studies have shown that many breaches of our firewalls go unreported, due to ignorance, embarrassment, or unawareness).

Are You Sure You Want to Perform This Function?

Calvin Coolidge said: "We cannot do everything at once, but we can do something at once." In fact, we can do a lot more than something at once, but we have to commit ourselves to want to perform the required upgrades to our systems that allow us to do so. We can do many things at once, and we can do them well. Our internal operating system is capable of performing myriad tasks at the same time, although our focus of attention (at least for now) can be on only one thing at a time. The complexity of our brains is miniscule in comparison to the Mainframe Supercomputer, even though He has created a cerebral cortex that contains over a hundred billion neurons, with the number of possible connections exceeding the number of particles in the known universe. (Read: infinite). The computing power of the human mind may be beyond comprehension, but the capacity of God is infinite. "My thoughts are not your thoughts," reported His publicist, "neither are your ways my ways, saith the Lord." (Isaiah 55:8).

As Carl Satan so whimsically put it: "There is an idea, strange, haunting, evocative, one of the most exquisite conjectures in science or religion. It is entirely undemonstrated, and it may never be proven. But it stirs the blood. There is, we are told, an infinite hierarchy of universes, so that an elementary particle, such as an electron, in our universe, would, if penetrated, reveal itself to be an entire closed universe. Within it, organized into the local equivalent of galaxies and smaller structures, are an immense number of other, much tinier elementary particles, which are themselves universes at the next level, and so on forever, an infinite downward regression, universes within universes, endlessly. And upward as well. Our familiar universe of galaxies and stars, planets and people, would be a single elementary particle in the next universe up, the first step of another infinite progress. Poised at the edge of forever, we would jump off" into the infinite reaches of eternity. ("Cosmos," p. 262-267). For that is the next logical step in our software update progression.

Move to Trash / Empty Trash

Remember that success comes by design, and we experience it largely through the strength of our own will and as a result of our reliance on the Senior Systems Analyst. In order to move forward purposefully, it will be necessary to drag to the trash whatever is not compatible with our overall objective of maintenance of the operating system. We might feel that we lack conscious control of updates even as they transform our operating system, but we can deliberately control personal outcomes and personal consequences. Therefore, during the updating process, even while our computer allows us to simultaneously perform other unrelated functions, we cannot capitulate our destiny to forces that we only believe to be beyond our control. Regularly emptying the trash allows nonessential code to quietly disappear into cyberspace.

Epilogue

Bill Gates is famously quoted as having said: "640 K should be enough for anybody." The statement illustrates that computing power expands exponentially, relentlessly, and unremittingly. It also suggests that we characteristically underestimate ourselves and our potential. We rarely appreciate both the breathtaking simplicity and the astonishing complexity of The Plan of Salvation. Just like our computer software, we are constantly updating our internal operating system in a quest for perfection, and every day of our lives, we figuratively and literally jump off into the infinite reaches of eternity in order to regain the glory of our former home. "I have warmed both hands before the fire of life," wrote Sir William Mulock. "The rich spoils of memory are mine. Mine, too, are the precious things of today. The best of life is always further on. Its real lure is hidden from our eyes somewhere behind the hills of time." So go ahead. Updates are ready.

"Now, what do we hear? ... A voice of gladness! A voice of mercy from heaven, and a voice of truth out of the earth." (D&C 128:19). The Book of Mormon speaking out of the dust! (2 Nephi 26:16, & Moroni 10:27). Joseph Smith said that "Cumorah" in the Nephite language means "the place of light and truth" In either a Meso-American or a North American context, the history of the Nephites, and now of the Latter-day Saints, completely validates that translation.

Walk in The Light of The Lord

"O house of Jacob,
come ye and let us walk in
the light of the Lord."
(2 Nephi 12:5).

Walking in the light of the gospel endows us with a greater capacity to love the Savior, His work, and His children. As we embrace its principles, the Lord is good to us. Enlightenment dissipates the cobwebs of doubt, smooths out the rough edges of our testimonies, builds our self-confidence to tackle tough questions, and provides the self-assuredness we need to exercise our agency wisely. Light bestows upon us the gifts of peace, comfort, and a clear conscience. It illuminates the gospel as the ultimate measure of truth. The light exerts a liberating influence, as it frees us from apprehension, despair, doubt, fear, ignorance, timidity, unsteadiness, and worry. It empowers us to keep that which we hold near and dear safe from those rodents who scurry about in the shadows, waiting for opportunities to ransack our treasury.

Light also energizes our ability to manage the gift of time. We learn to take time with discipline, bide our time with patience, make time with diligence, find time with care, spend time with thoughtfulness, invest time with wisdom, and share time with pleasure. Shedding light on the weightier matters of the law infuses us with a liberating sense of independence, as we learn something new every day. Our hearts and our minds are illuminated with a breathtaking expansion of understanding. As our learning style embraces the Spirit, we discover a pattern that soon becomes the norm.

The genius of the Plan is that in order to increase our understanding of the truth, further light and knowledge are available to create an atmosphere that is conducive to teaching by the Spirit. Truth bears its own independent witness, and it builds with steadiness on its own solid foundation. It requires no external warrant.

When we walk mildly and quietly in the light, we embrace truth. (See D.B.Y., p. 65). "The wisdom that is from above is first pure, then peaceable, gentle, and easy to be entreated, full of mercy and good fruits, without partiality, and without hypocrisy." (James 3:17). As the world grows increasingly noisy, we remember that inspiration comes more easily in peaceful settings. A quarter of a century ago, Boyd K. Packer lamented: "Clothing and grooming and conduct are looser and sloppier and more disheveled. Raucous music characterizes the drug culture, with obscene lyrics blasted through amplifiers, while lights flash psychedelic colors. This trend to more noise, more excitement, more contention, less restraint, less dignity, less formality is not coincidental nor innocent nor harmless. The first order issued by a commander mounting a military invasion is the jamming of the channels of communication of those he intends to conquer. Irreverence suits the purposes of the adversary by obstructing the delicate channels of revelation in both mind and spirit." (C.R., 10/1991).

As we embrace the light we establish a prayerful attitude. Spencer W. Kimball promised: "The Lord is eager to see our first awakening desires and our beginning efforts to penetrate the darkness. Having granted freedom of decision, he must permit us to grope our way until we reach for the light. But when we begin to hunger, when our arms begin to reach, when our knees begin to bend and our voices becomes articulate, then and not till then does our Lord push back the horizons, draw back the veil, and make it possible for us to emerge from dim uncertain stumbling to sureness, in heavenly light." (Munich Germany Area Conference, 8/1973).

Light is like a deep-tissue massage that strengthens our core, stimulates our fast-twitch muscle fibers, and increases our elasticity. Light warms up our juices, channels them, gets them flowing, and raises our testimony temperature. The Prophet Joseph is our example, and his experiences underscore several basic principles relating to light and knowledge. What he did in preparation for his theophany in the Sacred Grove is our pattern, as well. His "mind was called up to serious reflection and great uneasiness." His "feelings were deep and often poignant," and he "attended... meetings as often as occasion would permit." His "mind at times was greatly excited" to understand the will of God. He wondered to himself: "How shall I know it" to be true?" and the light guided him along a path that led to spectacular answers. (J.S.H. 1:8-10).

As we embrace the light, we establish a prayerful attitude. As we study matters out in our own minds preparatory to receiving answers to our prayers, we become actively, rather than passively, involved in the process of inquiry. We dust off our agency, and actually use it as it was envisioned. We move beyond control, coercion, compulsion, intimidation, and external influence to friendly persuasion and independence of action. We expand our capabilities, as we exercise the gifts, resources, and reserves provided by the perfect Plan of Salvation. President Kimball promised: "If there be eyes to see, there will be visions to inspire. If there be ears to hear, there will be revelations to experience. If there be hearts which can understand, know this: that the exalting truths of Christ's gospel will no longer be hidden and mysterious, and all earnest seekers may know God and his program." (C.R., 10/1966).

If we want to walk in the light, our vocal prayers will summon the angels with the power to unlock the doorway that opens into heaven. The example of Joseph Smith in the Sacred Grove teaches us how to pray with emotion, intensity, and the power of concentration. As he knelt in humility and offered up the desires of his heart, when necessity required it, he exerted all his resources to call upon God. (J.S.H. 1:13-16). Later, the Lord spoke through him to those who followed his example: "Blessed art thou for what thou hast done; for thou hast inquired of me, and behold, as often as thou hast inquired thou hast received instruction of my Spirit." (D&C 6:14).

"Do you offer a few trite words and worn-out phrases, or do you talk intimately to the Lord?" asked Spencer W. Kimball. "Do you pray occasionally when you should be praying regularly, often constantly? When you pray, do you just speak, or do you also listen? Do you give thanks or merely ask for favors?" ("New Era," 3/1978).

If we want to walk in the light, we must prepare ourselves to recognize truth when it comes. As long as we stick to the Plan, "by the power of the Holy Ghost (we) may know the truth of all things." (Moroni 10:5). "Most recorded revelations in the Doctrine and Covenants were a consciousness of direction from above. This is the sort of revelation individuals often have for their own needs." (Spencer W. Kimball, "Faith Precedes the Miracle," p. 30). The light illuminates our deep impressions, gives them breadth depth, and width, fine-tunes our perception, and kindles the sparks of recognition that allow us to make the vital distinctions between revelation and its worldly counterparts. The Lord provided counsel to Oliver Cowdery that confirms what President Kimball taught: "Did I not speak peace to your mind concerning the matter?" He asked. "What greater witness can you have than from God?" (D&C 6:22-23).

Have we not all experienced similar peace that has been spoken to our minds, concerning matters of great personal importance?

When we walk in the light, we eschew implicit denial of the revelations of the Lord. (See 3 Nephi 29:6). "Many people expect that if there be revelation it will come with awe-inspiring, earth-shaking display. For many it is hard to accept revelations as deep, unassailable impressions settling down on the mind and heart as dew from heaven or as the dawn dissipates the darkness of night. Expecting the spectacular, (they) may not be fully alerted to the constant flow of revealed communication" that we receive on a daily basis. (Spencer W. Kimball, "Instructor," 8/1960).

Those who walk in the light carefully cultivate their church attendance and treasure their fellowship with the Saints. They see the Sacrament service as a channel of power and the ordinance a mighty tool enabling them to approach Heavenly Father so that His promises might be fully realized. They have experienced the truth in Elder Melvin J. Ballard's declaration that "the road to the Sacrament table is the path of safety for the Latter-day Saints."

Those who walk in the light exercise devotion to their callings. Having been set apart to do a particular work in the church, they understand that it no longer belongs to anyone else, and no-one else has a right to it. They claim ownership of the position and realize that if they don't do the job, it will not be done. Therefore, they accept positions with the intention to carry out the associated responsibilities as though their life depended on it, as indeed it does. Their constant prayer is that after they have been "set apart," everyone within the circle of their influence will be enriched because His work was given into their hands. Therefore," said the Lord, "Let every man stand in his own office, and labor in his own calling, that the system may be kept perfect." (D&C 84:109-110).

Those who walk in the light listen to the counsel of their priesthood leaders, and read the scriptures daily. As Dallin Oaks explained: "We do not overstate the point when we say that the scriptures can be a Urim and Thummim (translation: "lights and perfections" or "revelation and truth," or "doctrine and truth") to assist each of us to receive personal revelation. Because we believe that scripture reading can help us receive revelation, we are encouraged to read the scriptures again and again." ("Ensign," 1/1995).

Those who walk in the light expand upon the counsel of Nephi, and view it in a larger context. "Wherefore, ye must press forward (with complete dedication and) steadfastness (or confidence and a firm determination) in Christ, having a perfect brightness of hope, and a love of God and of all men. (If we do this,) feasting upon the word of Christ, (or receiving strength and nourishment from the scriptures,) and endure to the end (in righteousness), behold, thus saith the Father: (We) shall have eternal life," which is the greatest gift He may bestow upon us. (2 Nephi 31:20).

Those who walk in the light emulate the righteous example of others. As Chauncey Riddle reflected: "I felt I had received some revelation before. However, I saw that random revelation was not sufficient. To be a rock, a bastion of surety, revelation must be something on which one can count and receive on every occasion of real need.

I began to seek it actively. I prayed, I fasted, I lived the gospel as best I knew. I was faithful in my church duties. I tried to live up to every scruple which my conscience enjoined upon me. And dependable revelation did come. Intermittently, haltingly at first, then steadily, over some years it finally came to be a mighty stream of experience. I came to know that at any time of day or night, in any circumstance, for any real need, I could get help.

That help came in the form of feelings of encouragement when things seemed hopeless. It came in ideas to unravel puzzles that blocked my accomplishment. It came in priesthood blessings which were fully realized. It came in anticipation of what the General Authorities of the church would say and do in general conference. It came in the gifts of the Spirit, as the wonders of eternity were opened to the eyes of my understanding.

That stream of spiritual experience is today for me a river of living water that nourishes my soul in every situation. It is the most important factor of my life. If it were taken away, all that I have and am would be dust and ashes. It is the basis of my love, life, understanding, hope, and progress.

My only regret is that though this river is so wonderful, I have not been able to take full advantage of it as yet. My life does not yet conform to all that I know. But now I do know; I do not just believe." ("Sunstone," 5/1988).

Our sole objective when we walk in the light is to find out what the Lord has revealed, and then to believe, and finally to act accordingly. This is reminiscent of a statement attributed to Brigham Young: "I never count the cost of anything. I simply find out what the Lord wants me to do, and I do it."

Those who walk in the light and have grasped the principles of truth, brim over with charity as they find comfortable accommodations in the household of faith. They let virtue garnish their thoughts unceasingly. They cultivate a contented and confident companionship with the Spirit, and the doctrine of the priesthood washes over their minds as the dews from heaven. They celebrate the light, and the Plan becomes a talisman of truth that is interwoven into the coat of many colors that is the fabric of their being. Its principles become elements of a tapestry that is everlasting, and without compulsion or coercion they become independent agents with the freedom to embrace their destiny and claim their eternal reward. (See D&C 121:45-46).

(Our) Weaknesses

"Fools mock, but they shall mourn;
and y grace is sufficient for the meek,
that they shall take no advantage of your
weakness." (Ether 12:26).

God grants to His obedient children an extra measure of discipline to see things through to their successful conclusion, and especially in the case of challenges, their resolution based on gospel principles. He knows that our fortunes depend largely upon our response to our weaknesses, and that our character is shaped by how we handle them. We may allow them to impede our progress; on the other hand, we may use weaknesses as stepping-stones to higher achievement.

The Lord said: "And if men come unto me, I will show unto them their weakness. I give unto men weakness that they may be humble; and my grace is sufficient for all men that humble themselves before me; for if they humble themselves before me, and have faith in me, then will I make weak things strong unto them." (Ether 12:27).

The process of overcoming weakness has intangible benefits. It makes our faith robust, our testimonies stalwart, our convictions sturdy, and our actions fruitful. When we pattern our lives after that of the Savior, internalize gospel principles, are obedient to priesthood covenants, develop strong bodies and spirits, and are decisive, resolute, and purposeful, we can do all things. "What a piece of work is a man!" declared Hamlet. "How noble in reason, how infinite in faculty, in form and moving how express and admirable, in action how like an angel, in apprehension how like a god - the beauty of the world, the paragon of animals! (Shakespeare, "Hamlet," Act 2, Scene 2).

But we are not lights unto ourselves. When we ignore the Lord's helping hand, we invite disaster. Truly, pride goeth before a fall. (See Proverbs 16:28). "For which of you, intending to build a tower, sitteth not down first, and counteth the cost, whether he have sufficient to finish it? Lest haply, after he hath laid the foundation, and is not able to finish it, all that behold it begin to mock him, saying, This man began to build, and was not able to finish." (Luke 14:28-30).

Heber J. Grant said: "I do not believe that any man lives up to his ideals, but if we are striving, if we are working, if we are trying, to the best of our ability, to improve day by day, then we are in the line of our duty. If we are seeking to remedy our own defects, if we are so living that we can ask for light, for knowledge, for intelligence, and above all, for His Spirit that we may overcome weakness, then, I can tell you, we are in the straight and narrow path that leads to life eternal." (Gospel Standards, p. 184-5). It is the love and concern of the Savior that allows us to rise above our imperfections. The great equalizing influence is obedience to the will of the Father. As we work through our weaknesses, we may be at-one with Christ, perfected in the ultimate sense and in the spirit of the Atonement.

The power of the church rests in the full faith and fellowship of its worldwide membership. Alvin R. Dyer warned that its fortunes rise and fall on the tide of its common witness. The Kingdom of God is built by the ardor and conviction of its members. But "we must be alert to the expansion of its assets at the cost of lost conviction," he said. "When buildings or institutions grow bigger and bigger, let us be fearful lest the Spirit will thin out." ("A Foundation for Education").

The growth experiences we share as members of the church are subtly interwoven into the fabric of the gospel, and the resultant tapestry is resplendent with a vitality and power to change our lives. As members of the church continue to "witness of God at all times and in all things, and in all places," the foundation of the Kingdom of God is planted in bedrock. (Mosiah 18:9). A story illustrates the point: An Irishman built a wall around his farm that was five feet high and eight feet thick. When asked why he built it so thick, he replied that if the wind ever blew so hard that it toppled the wall, it would still be five feet thick. The church is such an organization. Redundancy built into its programs is a shield and a protection not only against the winds of adversity, but also to ensure that its diverse members move steadily forward in spite of individual imperfections. This is one of the keys to the worldwide applicability of the gospel plan. It collectively appeals to the needs of the common man.

In language plain and simple, Paul expressed the universality of God's love for all of his children, regardless of their position along the path of progress. In the Lord's church, he said "there is neither Jew nor Greek, there is neither bond nor free, there is neither male nor female: for (we) are all one in Christ Jesus." (Galatians 3:28). At another time, he expressed his hope and desire for unity to his Thessalonian brethren, saying: "We were gentle among you, even as a nurse cherisheth her children. So being affectionately desirous of you, we were willing to have imparted unto you, not the gospel of God only, but also our own souls, because ye were dear unto us." (1 Thessalonians 2:7-8). Truly, "no man is an island; no man stands alone." (John Donne, "Meditation 17"). We are bound together in unity to power through our weaknesses to perfection.

Were There Two Cumorahs?

"I, Mormon, wrote an epistle unto the king of the Lamanites, and desired of him that he would grant unto us that we might gather together our people unto the land of Cumorah, by a hill which was called Cumorah, and there we could give them battle." (Mormon 6:2).

The Book of Mormon, in Alma chapters 17-26, records that Ammon journeyed from the Land of Zarahemla with his brethren to bring the gospel to the Lamanites living in the Land of Nephi. While in the wilderness separating those two population centers, he encountered a group of Nephites who were living in subjection to the Lamanites. These were the people of Limhi, descendants of Zeniff who had left Zarahemla two generations earlier to return to the Land of Nephi. (Mosiah 7:9).

Ammon stayed with these people and re-introduced them to the gospel. During this time, Limhi asked Ammon if he could interpret languages. It seems that some time around 121 B.C., Limhi had dispatched a party into the wilderness to see if contact might be reestablished with the Nephites back in Zarahemla. The specific mission of this group had been to seek assistance from the Nephites for relief from their bondage to the Lamanites in the Land of Nephi. (Mosiah 8:7).

Limhi's party had become "lost in the wilderness for the space of many days," finally stumbling upon a land to the northwest of Zarahemla "covered with bones of men, and of beasts, and with ruins of buildings." (Mosiah 8:8, See Omni 1:22). They had accidentally found the remains of the Jaredite civilization but mistakenly "supposed it to be the land of Zarahemla.". (Mosiah 21:26). "And they brought" back "a record with them, even a record of the people whose bones they had found, and it was engraven on plates of ore." (Mosiah 21:27).

Although they didn't yet realize it, this was the very journal that had been kept by Ether, the great Jaredite prophet. (See superscript to Ether Chapter 1). Ether had completed his record as the last of the Jaredites fell to the earth. "And the Lord spake unto Ether, and said unto him, Go forth" and hide the records "in a manner that the people of Limhi (should later) find them." (Ether 15:33). Limhi's search party did find them, and now he was desirous of Ammon to take this record back to Zarahemla, because he had learned that its king, Mosiah, "had a gift from God, whereby he could interpret such engravings." (Mosiah 21:28). So, this is the background and the cultural milieu in which we ask the question: "Were there two Cumorahs?"

To answer this question, we must consider just how far Limhi's search party might have traveled before finding the last great battlefield of the Jaredites. Nearby was the hill called Ramah by the Jaredites and Cumorah by the Nephites. A single parenthetical editorial remark by Moroni in the Book of Ether inextricably ties the two hills together: "And it came to pass that the army of Coriantumr did pitch their tents by the hill Ramah; and it was that same hill where my father Mormon did hide up the records unto the Lord, which were sacred." (Ether 15:11, See Mormon Chapter 6). Surely, Limhi's party had not wandered +/- 3,000 miles from the Land of Nephi through the wilderness to the Hill Cumorah near what is now Palmyra, New York, and then back all over again. If Alma's group had taken twenty days to travel from the Land of Nephi to the Land of Zarahemla, to make up for any difference in position as compared with Limhi's people, they would only have traveled about four hundred miles, at the rate of twenty miles per day. (Mosiah 23:3). We cannot escape the obvious conclusion that Moroni's Land of Cumorah must have been in Meso-America, probably within a few hundred miles of both the Land of Nephi and the Land of Zarahemla.

At the time of the Restoration, then, there must have been two Cumorahs, one where Mormon and Moroni hid the records, and one where the Lord arranged for Joseph Smith to miraculously find them near his home in Palmyra, New York. Additional evidence within The Book of Mormon supports this conclusion. When Alma's little flock of church members fled before the advancing armies of King Noah, sometime between 145 and 121 B.C., they traveled 8 days into the wilderness. (Mosiah 23:3). It is unclear in what direction they were headed, but after they left the Land of Helam, it only took them twelve more days to reach Zarahemla. (Mosiah 24:25).

By comparison, it had taken Ammon 40 days traveling in the opposite direction to reach the Land of Nephi from Zarahemla. (Mosiah 7:5). Then, on the return trip, his larger party spent "many days in the wilderness" between Nephi and Zarahemla. (Mosiah 22:13). But on this leg of the journey, Ammon was burdened down with the responsibility of guiding the slower-moving body of Limhi's people, who had taken with them "their flocks and their herds...and all their gold, and silver, and their precious things, which they could carry, and also their provisions with them." (Mosiah 22:11-12). Analyzed together, these geographical references linking landmarks to travel time indicate that Nephi and Zarahemla were not more than six weeks' journey from each other. Cumorah, which was "many days' travel" (Mosiah 8:8) from Nephi, is thus joined both geographically and temporally to both Nephi and Zarahemla.

A comparison between travel in the jungles of Meso-America and travel in Medieval Europe may help us to better understand just how arduous a task it must have been in either circumstance to make much progress. "The Dark Ages were stark in every dimension," wrote William Manchester. "Surrounding (the villages of Europe) was the vast, menacing, and at places impassable forest, infested by boars, by bears, by the hulking medieval wolves who lurk so fearsomely in fairy tales handed down from that time, by imaginary demons, and by very real outlaws. One consequence of medieval peril was that people huddled closely together in communal homes. They married fellow villagers and were so insular that local dialects were often incomprehensible to men living only a few miles away." Could life have been much different in Pre-Columbian Meso-America?. "In the early 1500s, in Western Europe, one could hike through the woods for days without encountering a settlement of any size. Between 80 and 90% of the population lived in villages of fewer than a hundred people, fifteen or twenty miles apart, surrounded by endless woodland. They worked in the fields between their huts and the great forest." (William Manchester, "A World Lit Only by Fire," p. 5-6 & 50-51).

Considering the references in The Book of Mormon that provide clues to possible locations for Cumorah, it is reasonable to assume that the hill called "Cumorah" by Book of Mormon prophets, in which Mormon hid the records of the Nephites, was not the hill that was adjacent to Joseph Smith's boyhood home in western New York, 3,000 odd miles to the northeast of Book of Mormon lands.

As indicated above, when King Limhi's search party found the land covered with bones of men and beasts, ruins of buildings, and remains of weapons of war, they did not yet realize that this was the last battlefield of the Jaredite civilization. (Mosiah 8:7-11). That it was, is made more certain by the fact that among the ruined remains was found the twenty-four gold Plates of Ether that had been expressly hidden by that Jaredite prophet in such a way that the men of Limhi might find them. (Mosiah 8:9, & Ether 15:33).

Also, as cited above, the last battlefield of the Jaredites was in the vicinity of the Hill Ramah/Cumorah. If that hill were located in the state of New York, it would have been necessary for Limhi's men to have traveled about six thousand miles altogether in their attempts to find the Land of Zarahemla. This is a completely unreasonable distance, considering the account of Alma's group of wandering refugees from religious persecution. He had brought his group of Zeniff's descendants from the Land of Helam to the Land of Zarahemla in just twelve to twenty days. (See Mosiah 24:23-25). Additionally, for the nearby Hill Ramah/Cumorah to be located in western New York, we must accept yet another unreasonable assumption. Not only both the Jaredites and Nephites would have had to travel there to fight their last battles, but also, Coriantumr, the last survivor of the Jaredites, would have had to limp, broken and bleeding, from the Hill Ramah/Cumorah to Zarahemla, there to die of his wounds 8 months later. (Omni 1:21).

In view of these facts, it is reasonable to assume that the Hill Cumorah (Ramah to the Jaredites) around which the last great battles of both the Nephites and Jaredites took place was in Meso-America, somewhere in the conservative range of 400 to 500 miles from Zarahemla. Wherever the hill may have been where Moroni physically deposited the records of the Nephites around 421 A.D., the Lord arranged for Joseph Smith to find these same records 1,400 years later near his home in Palmyra, New York.

As the Lord revealed through his prophet Isaiah: "My thoughts are not your thoughts, neither are your ways my ways." (Isaiah 55:8). When, in The Book of Mormon, the Lord described the great destruction in the New World that accompanied His crucifixion, he repeatedly used the phrase, "I caused." (3 Nephi 9:4, 6, 7, 8, 9, 10, 12). When the Lord is involved, things do not just happen by chance or circumstance. He causes things to happen, and it is not always in ways that are recognizable, reasonable, or rational to man. Remarkably, new stars shine in the heavens, waters are parted, the sun stands still, bushes burn but are not consumed, a few loaves and fishes feed thousands, angels appear to shepherds, voices are heard beside still waters, donkeys speak, handwriting appears on walls, men have dreams, manna is discovered in morning light, drinking water bursts forth from rocks and it also turns into wine, rivers turn to blood, rain is withheld, chariots of fire ascend into heaven, rams are discovered tangled in thickets and city walls crumble at the sound of their horns, lights and angels appear in darkened chambers, and stone boxes filled with sacred records are deposited in hillsides.

The important thing is to believe The Book of Mormon came forth by the gift and power of God and that "as your Lord and your God liveth it is true." (D&C 17:6). He Who was ultimately responsible for the care of the records declared: "Behold I am Moroni, and were it possible, I would make all things known unto you." (Mormon 8:12). One day, we will have the opportunity to ask him how he pulled it off, for he wrote on the last leaf of the record: "And now I bid unto all, farewell. I soon go to rest in the paradise of God, until my spirit and body shall again reunite, and I am brought forth triumphant through the air, to meet you before the pleasing bar of the great Jehovah,. (Moroni 10:34).

He was understandably preoccupied with more pressing matters when he said of the Lamanites: "Their wars are exceedingly fierce among themselves; and because of their hatred they put to death every Nephite" survivor of the conflict "that will not deny the Christ. And I, Moroni, will not deny the Christ; wherefore, I wander whithersoever I can for the safety of mine own life." (Moroni 1:2-3). For the rest of his days, he was a fugitive living on the run. But it is unlikely that he traveled thousands of miles, during the course of 36 years, (385 A.D. – 421 A.D.) burdened down with "many wagon loads" of records, his life constantly in peril.

We have learned from Brigham Young that "Joseph did not translate all of the plates; there was a portion of them sealed. When Joseph got the plates, the angel instructed him to carry them back to the hill Cumorah, which he did. Oliver says that when Joseph and Oliver went there, the hill opened, and they walked into a cave, in which there was a large and spacious room. ...They laid the plates on a...large table that stood in the room. Under this table there was a pile of plates as much as two feet high, and there were altogether in this room more plates than probably many wagon loads. They were piled up in the corners and along the walls." (Brigham Young, J.D., Address delivered in Farmington, Utah, 6.17/1877).

As the Lamanites hunted him, Moroni wrote: "I even remain alone to write the sad tale of the destruction of my people." His sacred commission was only to "write and hide up the records in the earth." (Mormon 8:3-4). He did not have the means to create new plates. He would have written more, if, as he recorded, "I had room upon the plates, but I have not; and ore I have none, for I am alone." (Mormon 8:5). He wrote these words in 400 A.D., and he would linger for another 21 years, sporadically returning to Cumorah where the plates had been deposited for safekeeping, to add meagerly, and yet significantly, to the record. "Wherefore, I write a few more things, contrary to that which I had supposed." (Moroni 1:4). But there is no evidence that the Spirit ever prompted him to gather up the plates and carry them through hostile Lamanite territory on a 3,000-mile journey to re-deposit them near what would later be the Joseph Smith, Sr. homestead.

How much better, he must have decided, to leave that task to the Lord and not worry about the details. As Nephi had written: "Then shall the Lord God say...I am able to do mine own work." (2 Nephi 27:20). The Lord had reassured Nephi: "I speak forth my words according to mine own pleasure." (2 Nephi 29:9). In many ways, He has used miraculous means to bring about the Restoration. The Sacred Grove Theophany itself defies logic. Successive visits of the Angel Moroni to Joseph in darkened chambers paint a portrait whose parameters lie outside the boundaries of mortal experience. The Pentecostal manifestations witnessed by hundreds at the dedication of the Kirtland Temple describe rushing winds, angelic voices, and translated beings. The appearances of the Savior to Joseph and Sidney Rigdon, recorded in D&C 76, and angelic visits to the Witnesses of The Book of Mormon are also modern-day miracles that by very definition defy rational explanation.

The Lord has always crafted the circumstances that would create an environment best suited to the success of the endeavor. Isaiah wrote: "And thou shalt ... speak out of the ground, and thy speech shall be low out of the dust, and thy voice shall be, as of one that hath a familiar spirit, out of the ground, and thy speech shall whisper out of the dust." (Isaiah 29:4). What better setting to do so than from within soil purchased with the blood of patriots, in the land of the free and the home of the brave?

We know that no matter where Book of Mormon prophets hid the record of their people, "none can have power to bring it to light save it be given him of God; for God wills that it shall be done with an eye single to his glory, or the welfare of the ancient and long dispersed covenant people of the Lord." (Mormon 8:15). We know that Joseph Smith was raised up for a specific purpose, and that it was prophetically foretold that he would "bring this thing to light; for it shall be brought out of darkness unto light, according to the word of God; yea, it shall be brought out of the earth, and it shall shine forth out of darkness, and come unto the knowledge of the people; and it shall be done by the power of God." (Mormon 8:16).

It is our testimony that angels have flown "in the midst of heaven, having the everlasting gospel to preach unto them that dwell on the earth." (Revelation 14:6). These angelic messengers have literally "brought" the gospel to those who were then entrusted with its dissemination. "Now, what do we hear in the gospel which we have received? A voice of gladness! A voice of mercy from heaven; and a voice of truth out of the earth." (D&C 128:19). Joseph Smith said that "Cumorah" in the Nephite language means "the place of light and truth." In both Meso-American and North American contexts, the history of the Nephites and of the Latter-day Saints completely validates that translation.

What Think Ye of Christ?

"More blessed are they
who shall believe in your
words because that ye shall
testify that ye have seen me, and
that ye know that I am. Yea, blessed
are they who shall believe in your words,
and come down into the depths of humility
and be baptized, for they shall be visited with
fire and with the Holy Ghost, and shall receive
a remission of their sins."
(3 Nephi 12:2).

When "the Pharisees were gathered together, Jesus asked them, saying, What think ye of Christ? Whose son is he?" Sadly, their sluggish response, "The Son of David," was tendered with little feeling or emotion. (Matthew 22:41-42). Although it was technically correct, it lacked spiritual horsepower. Its dearth of traction was obvious, its inability to generate spontaneity was palpable, its lack of energy to engage enthusiasm was noticeable, its incapacity to spark vitality was evident, and its failure to candidly acknowledge the powerful relationship that can exist between man and God was clear. Following the Savior's rebuke of their hesitancy and equivocation, none of the Pharisees were thereafter "able to answer him a word, neither durst any man from that day forth ask him any more questions." (Matthew 24:46). They had been weighed in the balances and had been found wanting, for they were spiritually bankrupt on an institutional scale. (See Daniel 5:27).

And yet, with adequate preparation, thinking about Christ could have generated the energy to lift them heavenward on a groundswell of emotion. Their example should be motivation enough for us to elevate the level of our worship to something more dynamic than the simple mechanical observance of a multiplicity of ceremonial rules, and to help us to avoid the pit into which the Pharisees fell. Thinking about the Savior should be more than a repetitive exercise to be performed only by the numbers. As the daily antidote to our tendency toward pride, selfishness, and self-reliance, it should help us to catalyze feeling, capture emotion, contour attitude, crystallize thought, congeal passion, compartmentalize action, and convey sentiments that lead to our spiritual revitalization.

Since those were, perhaps, among the most important and penetrating questions that could have been asked of anyone, at any time in history, or at any place on earth, we can be sure that the Pharisees were not the Savior's only intended respondents. He cast a much wider net. The Master, Who expounded all scripture in one, demands that you and I answer, as well, that we might also have the opportunity to squirm under the microscope of His scrutiny.

It matters little whether we identify with the Pharisees or the Sadducees, with Buddha, Confucius, Guru Nanak, Zoroaster, or with gods of wood and stone. We may concur with the monotheism of Islam or the Bahá'i, the pantheistic theology of Hinduism, Shintoism, or Taoism, with secular humanism or irreligion, with Catholicism or Eastern Orthodoxy, with evangelicals, fundamentalists, or Protestants, or with the existential nihilism of the postmodern world. Paul observed of the Athenians, who were not so very different from us, that they were inclined to bow down before unknown gods, whom, therefore, they ignorantly worshipped. It is in the hope that this essay will help you to stand independently in your witness of the true and living God, that "him declare I unto you." (Acts 17:23, see 1 Thessalonians 1:9).

You may be a trusting Timothy or a doubting Thomas, a spiritual giant or a philosophical naturalist, of a ready wit or resoundingly dull, earnestly enlightened or frivolously facetious, casually indifferent or energetically enthusiastic, a dedicated disciple or a distracted detractor, a true believer, an agnostic, or an atheist. In a moment of despair, you may have thrown up defensive dross designed to disregard, deflect, discourage, or disparage the question: "What think ye of Christ?" If you have wandered into disbelief, you may have deferred or deterred your response to the question: "Whose son is he?" If that day has already come, or if it looms large on your horizon, you can be sure that your stammering apologies will be unceremoniously swept aside when your true feelings are finally revealed.

In every case, no matter that you are a defender of the faith or an ambassador of the adversary, all of heaven will hold its collective breath as time stands still and your fate hangs in the air as a dandelion seed caught in the doldrums of a hot summer afternoon. How you answer will define you or destroy you, for your response will delineate your dreams, as it describes your destiny and determines how, where, and with whom you will spend eternity. I hope this essay can help you to prepare for that great and dreadful day when you will be asked to stand and give your sworn deposition before God, angels, and witnesses, to be counted among the sheep or the goats, on His right hand or His left hand.

To ensure that your answers might be animated with energy, to have no regrets, and to avoid the fate of the Pharisees, you have been given the Light of Christ. It proceeds from His throne as a powerful influence for good that is intended to groom you to receive the Holy Ghost. It is a gift that miraculously multiplies even as it divides within a universe populated with individuals whose actions are governed by free will. It is given, the Lord revealed, "that every man may act in doctrine and principle pertaining to futurity, according to the moral agency which I have given unto him." (D&C 101:78, see D&C 93:31).

It has been benevolently bestowed upon all of us by One Whom we can be sure "denieth none that come unto him, black and white, bond and free, male and female; and he remembereth the heathen; and all are alike unto (him), both Jew and Gentile." (2 Nephi 26:33). The Light of Christ stimulates our soul-sweat as it works on our conscience, our sense of duty, and our scruples. It provides a shield of protection against the corrosive spatter of perspiration cast off by the destroyer, who is insidiously and persistently working overtime to damage our doctrinal defenses, dull our spiritual sensitivities, diminish our charitable capacity, deplete our bountiful reservoirs of sympathy, and destroy our devotions, even as we labor with an equal but opposite intensity to deify our work on the earth.

The Light of Christ exerts a nurturing influence, as well. Although we must daily travel farther from the East, we are nevertheless oriented toward the radiant glow emanating from that distant horizon. It provides us with the regularly recurring reassurance of a religious recalibration that autocorrects with fortuitous frequency and celestial precision. It envelops us in an intuitive appreciation of where we came from, why we are here, and where we are going. As in a heavenly language that is rhythmical, melodious, soothing to our ears, and calming to our souls, when we hear the Spirit quietly whisper: "You're a stranger here," we are comforted by the realization that we have "wandered from a more exalted sphere." (Eliza R. Snow). The Light of Christ examines what it means to be anxiously engaged, inspires us to plumb the depths of our commitment to the Savior, sensitizes us to the nobility of His work, expands upon the visions of immortality, and makes us more acutely aware of His glory, as it brings eternal life within our purview.

In a way, thinking about the Savior can be likened to a primer on midwifery, because one of its purposes is to facilitate the arduous process of our spiritual rebirth, by contributing to our preparation to answer with conviction the questions that were first posed to the Pharisees so long ago: "What think ye of Christ?" and "Whose son is he?" When we feel the urge to push His agenda, the Light of Christ can be our labor coach, providing us with just the right amount of encouragement to successfully deliver our witness of the Savior without being overbearing.

One exciting element of the manifestation of the Light of Christ is the constant stream of inspiration and revelation that cascades down from above. This ensures that all may walk along illuminated pathways, and that no individual or institution may legitimately claim or have a monopoly on divine guidance. It exerts a leveling influence that is the great equalizer, giving each of us the same privileges to use our faculties of mind, intellect, and spirit to our best advantage, that we might discern between truth and error, no matter upon what spiritual plateau we might be currently relaxing. It permits us to listen with sensitivity and to be receptive to the cries of the downtrodden and oppressed, to see with a lucidity that allows us to be responsive to our environment, and to be benevolently blind to the shortcomings of others.

The Light of Christ provides us with a nurturing influence that makes it easier to have lips that have learned to articulate only positive expressions of speech and never speak guile, shoulders that have developed the strength to bear the burdens of those who have been battered and bruised by the vicissitudes of life and who may be faltering under the heavy weight of sorrow or sin, backs that have become sturdy enough to brace us against the fierce winds of adversity and the subtle wiles of the adversary, hearts that have become the receptacles of pure and virtuous principles upon which we may draw in times of need, bowels that are moved to compassion for those who are struggling with misfortune, hands that have become accustomed to lifting those who are in need of support, and feet that have been conditioned to speedily carry us to those who are imprisoned by poor choices, bad habits, or unfortunate circumstances.

Even now, heavenly messengers who minister by the Light of Christ are nursemaids to the nations of the earth, and use its power as a resource to reach out and caress those among them who are poor in spirit. Men and women of all persuasions feel that angels are watching over them. Witness countless newlyweds who are certain that their match was made in heaven before the world was. Others sense that they have been assisted by acts of providence, are the beneficiaries of divine intervention, have been touched by angels, are moved to compassion, or have been otherwise blessed to "walk in the light of the Lord." (Isaiah 2:5).

Guidance in the form of spiritual promptings and impressions are more common that many would suspect. Powerful intuitive communicators strongly influence nearly all of us to move in the direction of our dreams, toward a greater appreciation of the majesty and power of our Creator. Truly, He "is no respecter of persons" Who causes the sun to shine on the wicked, as well as on the just. (Acts 10:34). Therefore, we must venture forth out of the shadows, even beyond the direction we receive from the Light of Christ and the ministration of angels, if we want to begin to appreciate the special familiarity that the Lord enjoys with those whom He has characterized as "the children of light." (John 12:36). The more we think about Christ, the easier it is to craft with words the sensations that naturally flow to each of us as a result of the stirrings of those feelings of intimacy.

As we think about Christ, we realize how heavily we have borrowed from the towering examples of those who, over the years, have been our mystical mentors, our sensible chaperones, our spiritual guides, our surrogate saviors, as well as our compassionate critics. They are our avatars, who have shown us the way, strengthened our testimonies, taught us humility, been there to steady and nurture us, applied the Balm of Gilead and bound up our wounds, provided both tangible and immaterial support, emboldened us with words of encouragement, and cheered us on with wise counsel. When think of this multitude of angels thinly disguised as our family, friends, and peers, we remember the words of Sir Isaac Newton, who, when pressed to reveal the great secret behind his accomplishments, simply replied: "I stood on the shoulders of giants."

If we are fortunate, we are privileged to do so, as well. As we think about our Savior, we draw upon the faith, testimony, and spiritual insight of the General Authorities and lay members of The Church of Jesus Christ of Latter-day Saints, as well as numerous playwrights and poets, philosophers and humanitarians, authors, journalists, essayists, classicists, religious scholars of all persuasions, statesmen, sages, mystics, stoics, and the composers and lyricists with whom we are familiar. Our friends and family are often more influential than they could ever imagine. We are fortunate if we have been blessed with such wonderful traveling companions during our journey through mortality. Such gurus and guides can touch our lives with profound influences that help us to shape the tender feelings that we clothe in words, as we think about the Savior.

In the end, however, we sometimes need to ask for the pardon of our traveling companions when they are confronted by the literal and figurative blemishes, the idiosyncratic foibles, and the objective and subjective imperfections that too often subtly work their way into our character, if we are not vigilant. Whenever we take poetic license with foundation principles, or add needless ecclesiastical embroidery to gospel truths, we beseech the indulgence, and the forgiveness, of our peers. If our passion clouds our vision or overpowers our zealous intentions, if the syntax of our speech seems tortuous, too bland, or too spicy, if our feelings are understated or if we have been given over to hyperbole, or even if we appear to drift over the line separating true doctrine from baseless speculation, we beg for the forbearance of our contemporaries, that they might take a step back and allow our expressions to simmer for a while before returning to sample anew their flavor. The reduction sauce of time may enhance the palatability of our perspective.

In any case, as the congealed distillate of our life experiences, our thoughts and feelings relating to the Savior stand revealed as our innocent attempts to yoke our emotions to language. We hope that others will find them refreshing, and will use them as food for thought.

We dream that we might feel the gentle caress of the touch of the Master Potter, as He turns our lives with the hand of time. We want Him to mold us and shape us as the Artisan of our destinies. "As the clay is in the potter's hand, so are ye in mine hand," said the Lord to His prophet. (Jeremiah 18:6). As Isaiah declared: "O Lord, thou art our father; we are the clay, and thou our potter; and we all are the work of thy hand." (Isaiah 64:8). We hope and pray that as our thoughts to turn to the Savior, we may remain pliable and impressionable to the things of the Spirit.

All of us need to learn to utilize the divinely designed accouterments of the matchless and multi-talented Carpenter of Nazareth, Who will help us to construct the stages upon which will be enacted the drama of our lives. We can imagine that our efforts will be validated by appreciative applause from the audience, and an occasional bouquet of red roses thrown at our feet. But it will be even more satisfying to remain as His poor understudies, and to give our best efforts to supporting roles in off-Broadway performances that count for more than mere entertainment.

His Plan does not require that we be the stars of the show. Our path of progress to perfection is a process, and not a point. We do not need top billing to fulfil our dreams. We do not seek to garner a People's Choice Award. Rather than becoming the objects of attention of an adoring paparazzi, we foresee ourselves being enveloped instead in dazzling clouds of divinely directed diamond dust that glitters with thousands of points of light, and becoming the participants in daily dramas that far surpass the pomp and circumstance of any "American Idol" production.

Ours will be performances exhibiting displays of celestial energy worthy of notice from above. As fire in the sky, the air in the theater of life will be charged with an electricity that represents the inevitable merger of the universal encouragement of the Light of Christ with the pointed and providential guidance provided by the Holy Ghost. When these influences streak in tandem across the heavens, their trajectories will coalesce to trace a flaming trail that sparkles over a vast cosmic ocean of thought. Over the ebb and flow of its tide, the Spirit will create an effectual bridge of understanding that is buttressed by the cohesive influence of the mighty foundation of faith.

Our innermost longings to apprehend these visions of the eternal world are epitomized in our triumphant realization of dreams fulfilled. Our emotions are painted by words that depict our progression toward distant mileposts along the well-marked paths that lie before us. Our quest for the Holy Grail is defined as much by the obstacles we have encountered, as it is by the hurdles we have yet to face. We are molded by personal victories and by our commemoration of the achievement of our goals, but we are also refined by our frustrated plans, and shaped by our preparations to address challenges that lie just around the next bend in the road.

In the learning laboratory of life, experience is the active ingredient in a fertile matrix carefully created by God as He meticulously prepares the personalized petri dishes that are best suited to our individual circumstances. This rich culture medium becomes just the agar we need in order to nurture our metamorphosis, as we are transformed, not by maturation but by generation, into the full stature of our spirits. The infusion of a heavenly element readies us to receive with equanimity whatever might come during an incubation process that was designed to be just as challenging as it would be rewarding.

All this leads back to our basic objective, which is to keep the Savior in our thoughts, that we might encourage a daily atmosphere of reflection, maintain an eternal perspective, initiate positive change, and harmonize our behavior with His charitable example. Our determination to do so comes, in part, thanks to Moroni, whose words stir our souls as a voice whispering from out of the dust. On one occasion, he wrote: "I speak unto you as if ye were present, and yet ye are not. But behold, Jesus Christ hath shown you unto me, and I know your doing." (Mormon 8:35).

Because we will one day be asked to give accountability reports to the Savior, we try to heed King Benjamin's ancient but apropos warning to watch ourselves judiciously, to be the meticulous guardians of our thoughts, the scrupulous custodians of our words, and the prudent caretakers of our deeds, to fastidiously observe the commandments of God, and to continue evenly in the faith. (See Mosiah 4:30). As we hesitantly inch our way through mortality, this admonition invigorates us with renewed energy, and instills in us the desire to redouble our efforts to know the Savior better.

We persist because the simple questions: "What think ye of Christ?" and "Whose son is he?" should make a difference to each of us. These inquiries demand that we dig deeply within ourselves before we tender our responses, because it is all too easy to superficially retreat into colorless and insipid verbiage as the easy way out. If we casually and carelessly steer a course away from Him with offhand, dismissive, and inconsiderate remarks, until He is conveniently out of sight and far from our minds, we can realistically expect in return no more than a stupor of thought. Any fleeting, albeit faux, feelings of liberation from the constraints of conscience will soon give way to an inner emptiness that cannot be satisfied with the poor imitations of the settled conviction in our minds of the peace that surpasses understanding, that could have been ours. If, in our knee-jerk reactions to the healthy opposition that stimulates our growth, we kick against the pricks, we will surely further estrange ourselves from the Spirit, until we are left with neither root nor branch. We will be tossed to and fro by every wind of doctrine, as flotsam and jetsam on the sea of life.

None of us would choose to perish because of our willful neglect of the things that matter most, or to lead marginalized lives because we had intentionally become spiritually depleted on a personal or an institutional level. We persevere because we do not want to die of spiritual starvation, doctrinal dehydration, or intellectual inhibition, while only inches away from the living bread that would have satisfied our hunger, or from the healing fountains of truth that could have slaked our thirst. We elect to think about our Savior in positive and meaningful ways that lead us to green pastures and still waters. The process draws us into the warmth of His embrace, where we are permitted to enjoy an intimacy that allows us to pause for a moment to feel the touch of His garment, before His strident call to action reawakens within us a sense of our duty that quickens the pace of the inexorable journey back to our beginnings.

Precious few "self-help" books address the issues of self-denial, meekness, and charity, or ask that we surrender to the greater good our desire for self-actualization, self-renewal, self-determination, self-fulfillment, or self-aggrandizement. Not often are we taught to concentrate our efforts on the quality of self-control that honors God's design, rather than some twisted temporal theory of emotional or spiritual well-being that lacks an upward thrust. But that is exactly what we must do. We must "let go and let God." Only then, will we catch a religious fever that elevates our testimony temperature enough to get our juices flowing with an appreciation of Who He really is. Only then, will we experience the earth shaking and mind-bending theophany that we are His spiritual offspring, and will we recognize the potential of our position. The precious emanation of familiar and soothing oscillations of energy resonating from within the limitless reserves that are selflessly shared by the Holy Ghost will carry us along on rolling waves of the spirit toward a more sure witness of the Savior's divinity. That is why we must keep Him in our thoughts.

This pulsing arpeggio ignites our souls with passion, and may have been the catalyzing influence that was missing from the pedantic model of righteous behavior that was adopted, almost by default, by the Pharisees. We want our preparation for the performance of our lives to include fast scale runs through more than half a dozen octaves on all 88 of the glistening black and white ivory keys of experience. As we rehearse in our minds our witness that Christ is our Savior, we want to be accompanied by a celestial symphony that has been scored for every instrument. We want to expand our repertoire to include, not only inspiring artistic compositions representing every epoch of musical literature, but also our own original and signature harmonic inventions.

But most of all, in the orchestration of life, we want the Senior Recital that showcases our command of pitch, rhythm, dynamics, timbre, and texture, to be worthy of His approbation. Along the way, we want to find our way back to the Source of our inspiration, that we might one day enjoy master classes as we sit at the feet of the Maestro Who first created musicality by matching movement and form to the melody and mood of His celestial creations. We want to become reacquainted with our perfect fit. Then, when we have finally completed our dissertation on life, we hope that our composition may be recognized as our magnum opus. After we have successfully defended our thesis, we would like to be able to express our thanks at the exercises that not only celebrate our lives, but that also observe and honor our commencement. We hope to gratefully acknowledge our devotion to the one who became our doctoral advisor, who was none other than "the Christ, the son of the Living God." (Matthew 16:16).

We want to have a yearning to consecrate our lives to Him, and to throw ourselves upon an altar of faith that is of our own construction, whose foundation is buttressed by a supernal display of divine direction. We want to enjoy an unwavering confidence that drives us relentlessly forward so that we might one day squarely and unflinchingly meet His penetrating gaze with clear eyes, that His power to save might thereby be unleashed in our behalf, and that it might flow over our wounds as a healing balm.

When we look around, we want to find ourselves among those who have been Born Again, who are "called the children of Christ, his sons, and his daughters." (Mosiah 5:7). We want to experience the thrill of being spiritually begotten of

Him, and of having our hearts changed through faith on His name. We want Him to be ever before us so that, without distraction, our thoughts might turn to Him, that we might feel His energy building within us until it lifts us to the zenith of experience where the lines distinguishing mortality from eternity blur, and we find ourselves consumed in the fire of everlasting burnings.

We want to be able to resoundingly declare that we have been born of God, and have received His image in our countenances; that we have experienced a mighty change in our hearts. (See Alma 5:14 & 26). Only then, through saving faith, will we be prepared to respond to the questions that loom before us: "What think ye of Christ?" and "Whose son is he?" As we ponder our relationship with the Savior, our proper prior preparation will prevent our poor presthood performance. It will nudge us off our complacency plateaus, away from the trendy cafés situated along the broad avenues of Idumea, and transport us as on the wings of eagles beyond the boundaries of our self-imposed limitations, right to the edge of eternity, where "forever" will finally stand revealed before us.

At that moment, as the power fueling our actions charges our spiritual batteries and energizes our sight with infinite perspective, there will be created a pulsing stream of inspiration whose flow has no temporal or spatial boundary. We will be swept up by quickening currents into the direct experience of a holy communion with God. Although the heavens will always be higher than the earth, His thoughts will somehow have become our thoughts, and His ways our ways. (See Isaiah 55:8-9). We will be caught up in His work and His glory, and finally understand that "the universe is a machine for the making of gods." (Henri Bergson)

The doctrine of translation is quite peculiar to The Church of Jesus Christ of Latter-day Saints. Only with the perspective of companion scriptures to the Bible, latter-day revelation, the teachings of modern prophets, and the understanding that comes from the Holy Ghost, can we understand its importance and relevance to our personal participation in the Plan of Salvation.

Wherefore and Therefore

The Book of Mormon is a marvelous work and a wonder, no less because of its consistent use of words that, at the very least, pique our interest to invite further inquiry. Most of us blow right past these words without considering their potential to provide significant evidence supporting Joseph's claim that the book was translated by the gift and power of God.

Beginning with the abridgement by Mormon (that is loosely called The Plates of Mormon) there is an abrupt shift in the use of "wherefore" versus "therefore" in The Book of Mormon. The Small Plates of Nephi overwhelming prefer the use of "wherefore," while the books that are an abridgement by Mormon prefer the use of "therefore" (including the record that was written by Moroni, comprising chapters 8 and 9 of The Book of Mormon, and the book of Moroni, excluding chapters 7-9 that were written by his father Mormon).

The exception to this pattern is the Book of Ether. But this is where it gets interesting. Ether 4:17-18 is a message from God, that is quoted by Moroni from memory: "Therefore, when ye shall receive this record ye may know that the work of the Father has commenced upon all the face of the land. Therefore, repent all ye ends of the earth, and come unto me, and believe in my gospel, and be baptized in my name; for he that believeth and is baptized shall be saved; but he that believeth not shall be damned; and signs shall follow them that believe in my name."

It is a commandment that is directed to those in the last-days, that they must repent and be baptized. Unlike previous references to baptism in The Book of Mormon, where Lehi's descendants were repetitively commanded to be baptized, this time, the commandment is specifically pointed at those in the last days.

Prior to this commandment to be baptized, the Book of Ether contains 13 instances of the word "therefore" and 7 instances of "wherefore." After the commandment, Ether contains 11 instances of "therefore" and 54 instances of "wherefore." So, what may have happened to precipitate the shift?

Lucy Mack Smith stated in her history: "One morning ... they sat down to their usual work, when the first thing that presented itself to Joseph was a commandment from God that he and Oliver should repair to the water, and each of them be baptized." ("The Revised and Enhanced History of Joseph Smith By His Mother." Chapter 27). The only verse in The Book of Mormon that fits this description is Ether 4:18, and that fits the timeline of where Joseph would have been in the process of translation at the time of his baptism.

Now consider the impact Joseph says his baptism had on him. "Immediately on our coming up out of the water after we had been baptized, we experienced great and glorious blessings ... Our minds now enlightened, we began to have the scriptures laid open to our understandings, and the true meaning and intention of their more mysterious passages revealed unto us in a manner which we never could attain to previously, nor ever before had thought of." ("Joseph Smith History." 1:73-74).

For whatever reason, Joseph's baptism may have had a subtle, yet significant impact on the way he "viewed" the text of the plates from which he was translating the record, and if that is the case, he may have unconsciously modified his use of the words "therefore" and "wherefore."

One more observation is that the variation between "wherefore" and "therefore" cannot be discussed without considering larger questions of narrative structure, for example, those that address the use in The Book of Mormon of the words "whoso" and "whosoever." "oft" and "often", and "privily" and "secretly" to name a few.

The Book of Mormon is a marvelous work and a wonder, no less because of its consistent use of words that, at the very least, pique our interest and invite further inquiry. Most of us blow right past these words without considering their potential to provide significant evidence supporting Joseph's assertion that the book was translated by the gift and power of God.

(A) Whirlwind into Heaven

"Behold, the heavens
were opened, and they were
caught up into heaven, and saw
and heard unspeakable things. And
it was forbidden them that they should
utter; neither was it given unto them power
that they could utter the things which they saw
and heard And whether they were in the body or
out of the body, they could not tell; for it did seem
unto them like a transfiguration of them, that they
were changed from this body of flesh into an immortal
state, that they could behold the things of God."
(3 Nephi 28:13-15).

The doctrine of translation is peculiar to The Church of Jesus Christ of Latter-day Saints. Only with the perspective of companion scriptures to the Bible, latter-day revelation, the teachings of modern prophets, and the understanding that comes from the Holy Ghost, can we understand its importance and relevance to our personal participation in the Plan of Salvation.

We gain most of our scriptural understanding of translation from The Book of Mormon account of the post-mortal ministry of Jesus Christ among the Nephites. At a meeting in Zarahemla with His twelve special disciples, the Savior asked: "What is it that ye desire of me, after that I am gone to the Father?" (3 Nephi 28:1). Nine of them begged for a speedy resurrection to eternal glory in the Celestial Kingdom after the completion of their mortal ministry. The three remaining disciples may have felt their own request to be selfish, or perhaps they were embarrassed to ask, and so "they sorrowed in their hearts." (3 Nephi 28:5). But the Master knew their thoughts were the same as those of John the Beloved who had asked that he might remain on the earth until the Second Coming, in order to "prophesy before nations, kindreds, tongues and people," and to bring souls unto Christ. (John 21:22, Revelation 10:11, & D&C 7:3-4).

Thus, the stage was set for Jesus to introduce the doctrine of translation to the Nephites. Direct references in the Bible are meager, such as in Hebrews 11:5, where we read Paul's explanation that "by faith, Enoch was translated that he should not see death; and was not found, because God had translated him: for before his translation he had this testimony, that he pleased God." In his letter to the Colossians, Paul described how, through faith, certain of the Saints had been "delivered ... from the power of darkness, and (had been) translated ... into the kingdom" of the Lord Jesus Christ. (Colossians 1:13).

Generally, though, there are only oblique references to biblical translation. For example: "Enoch walked with God: and he was not; for God took him." (Genesis 5:24). This account is often ignored or overlooked by scholars, because without the illumination of additional scriptural insight, it just doesn't make much sense. However, D&C 107:49 clarifies the brief account in Genesis, explaining that Enoch "saw the Lord, and he walked with him, and was before his face continually; and he walked with God three hundred and sixty-five years, making him four hundred and thirty years old when he was translated." The Pearl of Great Price further clarifies the teaching that Enoch's City of Zion, "in process of time, was taken up into heaven." (Moses 7:21, See v. 23, 31 & 47). "And Enoch and all his people walked with God, and he dwelt in the midst of Zion; and it came to pass that Zion was not, for God received it up into his own bosom; and from thence went forth the saying, Zion is Fled." (Moses 7:69). Latter day revelation testifies that "Enoch and his brethren ... were separated from the (telestial) earth, and were received unto (the Lord as translated beings) - a city reserved until a day of righteousness shall come - a day which was sought for by all holy men." (D&C 45:11-12).

Joseph Smith explained that God reserved Enoch "unto Himself, that he should not die at that time, and appointed unto him a ministry unto terrestrial bodies, of whom there has been but little revealed. He is a ministering angel ... to those who shall be heirs of salvation ... Many have supposed that ... translation was a doctrine whereby men were taken immediately into the presence of God, and into an eternal fullness, but this is a mistaken idea. Their place of habitation is that of the terrestrial order, and a place prepared for such characters He held in reserve to be ministering angels ... and who as yet have not entered into so great a fullness as those who are resurrected from the dead." (H.C. 4:209-210).

The Savior confirmed to Joseph Smith: "I am the same which ha(s) taken the Zion of Enoch into mine own bosom and verily I say, even as many as have believed in my name." (D&C 38:4). "The purpose of granting to prophets (and others) this great blessing," said Joseph Fielding Smith, Jr., "is that they may minister upon the earth." He believed that "the Lord, of necessity, has kept authorized servants on the earth bearing the priesthood from the days of Adam to the present time." ("Answers to Gospel Questions," 2:245). In explaining that need, he said: "There has never been a moment of time since the Creation but what there has been someone holding the priesthood on the earth to hold Satan in check." (Quoted by Harold B. Lee, in "The Place of The Living Prophet, Seer, and Revelator," 7/8/1968). In between gospel dispensations, translated beings have assumed this responsibility.

Perhaps the best known of the prophets of the Old Testament who were translated were Moses and Elijah. To biblical scholars, however, the fate of both is a mystery. The account in Deuteronomy simply states: "Moses the servant of the Lord died there in the land of Moab, according to the word of the Lord. And (the Lord) buried him in a valley in the land of Moab, over against Bethpeor: but no man knoweth of his sepulchre unto this day." (Deuteronomy 34:5-6). From The Book of Mormon account, however, we know that "the Lord took Moses unto himself," in the sense that he was translated. (Alma 45:19).

As for Elijah, the Doctrine and Covenants simply states that he "was taken into heaven without tasting death." (D&C 110:13). Those who witnessed his translation recorded that "there appeared a chariot of fire, and horses of fire, and parted them both asunder; and Elijah went up by a whirlwind into heaven." (2 Kings 2:11). "Elijah and Moses were preserved from death because they had a mission to perform, and it had to be performed before the crucifixion of the Son of God, and it could not be done in the spirit. They had to have tangible bodies." (Joseph Fielding Smith, Jr. "Doctrines of Salvation," 2:110-111).

It was on the Mount of Transfiguration that their mission was revealed. Matthew tells us that "after six days Jesus taketh Peter, James, and John his brother, and bringeth them up into an high mountain apart, and was transfigured before them: and his face did shine as the sun, and his raiment was white as the light. And, behold, there appeared unto them Moses and Elias (Elijah) talking with him." (Matthew 17:1-3). "Christ is the first fruits of the resurrection; therefore, if any former prophets had a work to perform preparatory to the mortal mission of the Son of God, or during the dispensation of the meridian of time, it was essential that they be preserved to fulfil that mission in the flesh." (Joseph Fielding Smith, Jr. "Doctrines of Salvation," 2:110-111). These two translated beings then bestowed upon Peter, James, and John the keys that they had held as the priesthood leaders of their respective gospel dispensations. To Joseph Smith, the Savior reconfirmed that "the keys of the kingdom ... belong always unto the Presidency of the High Priesthood," or The First Presidency. (D&C 81:2, See Matthew 16:19). After the performance of their duties, Moses and Elijah "were with Christ in His resurrection." (D&C 133:55). They had been changed from mortality to immortality in the twinkling of an eye. D&C 133:54-55 suggests that all those who had been translated from the time of Adam to the resurrection of Christ were also resurrected at that time. In addition, Matthew reported that the graves of the dead "were opened, and many bodies of the saints which slept arose, and came out of the graves after his resurrection, and went into the holy city, and appeared unto many." (Matthew 27:52-53).

Thus, when Moses and Elijah appeared to Joseph Smith and Oliver Cowdery in the Kirtland Temple on Sunday, 4 3, 1836, they did so as resurrected beings. There, Moses "committed unto (them) the keys of the gathering of Israel from the four parts of the earth, and the leading of the ten tribes from the land of the north. After this, Elias (Elijah) appeared, and committed the dispensation of the gospel of Abraham, saying that (through the priesthood) all generations ... should be blessed." (D&C 110:11-12).

Prophets have always sought for the state of happiness described in the scriptures as Zion. Its inhabitants enjoy peace and rest from the cares of the world, which puts them in a position to preach the gospel, build the kingdom, and bring souls unto Christ. So it was that "Enoch beheld angels descending out of heaven, bearing testimony of the Father and Son; and the Holy Ghost fell on many, and they were caught up by the powers of heaven into Zion." (Moses 7:27). When Enoch was translated, so were the inhabitants of his city, who became the prototypical model for all who desire to enter into God's Rest. We have no idea how many others were translated during the first four thousand years of the temporal existence of the earth, but there may have been many of whom the scriptures are silent.

As the close of His mortal ministry approached, the Savior said of the faithful who had lived during the Dispensation of the Meridian of Time: "There be some standing here, which shall not taste of death, till they see the Son of man coming in his kingdom." (Matthew 16:28). We have it on the authority of the Savior, no less, that translated beings are yet among us. Those who have been translated since His resurrection will "be changed in the twinkling of an eye," when Jesus comes to earth as the Millennial Christ. (3 Nephi 28:8).

From modern revelation, we learn that translated beings are as angels of God, and that "there are no angels who administer to this earth but those who do belong or have belonged to it." (D&C 130:5). "We may be sure that any messenger coming before the resurrection of Jesus who had a tangible body was a translated being who had lived on the earth and had been translated to become a messenger to those on the earth. Such would evidently be the case in the visitors who came to Abraham, and the personage who wrestled with Jacob." (Joseph Fielding Smith, Jr., "Answers to Gospel Questions," 2:44). As Paul cautioned the Saints: "Be not forgetful to entertain strangers: for thereby some have entertained angels (meaning translated beings) unawares." (Hebrews 13:2).

Of the aforementioned Three Nephites, the Savior promised them that, as translated beings, they should never taste of death. "Translated beings are still mortal," explained Joseph Fielding Smith, Jr., "and will have to pass through the experience of death, although this will be instantaneous. ("Answers to Gospel Questions," 1:165, 2:46). They will continue to live as mortals, and will eventually die, but will "never endure the pains of death," but when Christ comes in His glory, they will "be changed in the twinkling of an eye from mortality to immortality." (3 Nephi

28:8). Since "the sting of death is sin" (1 Corinthians 15:56), they will be able to avoid the unpleasant side effects that accompany the transition of the disobedient from mortality to immortality. "Millennial man," said Bruce R. McConkie, "will live in a state akin to translation. His body will be changed so that it is no longer subject to disease or death, as we know it, although he will be changed in the twinkling of an eye to full immortality when he is a hundred years of age." ("The Millennial Messiah," p. 644). Isaiah prophesied that during the Millennium, "there shall be no more thence an infant of days: for the child shall die an hundred years old." (Isaiah 65:20).

The Savior told the Three Nephites: "Ye shall not have pain while ye shall dwell in the flesh, neither sorrow save it be for the sins of the world." (3 Nephi 28:9). These gifts would help them to focus on the commission they had received from the Savior to "bring the souls of men unto (Him) while the world (should) stand." (3 Nephi 28:9). In other words, missionary work without distraction was to be the focus of their attention until the Second Coming.

A fulness of joy comes only in the Resurrection, but missionary work can point us in that direction. The Savior told the three Nephite missionaries: "And for this cause ye shall have fulness of joy; and ye shall sit down in the kingdom of my Father; yea, your joy shall be full." (3 Nephi 28:10). There is no mistaking the importance of missionary work in the eyes of Jesus Christ. Because of their desire to continue their missions while the earth should stand, He said: "Therefore, more blessed are ye." (3 Nephi 28:7). Their continuing concern for their less fortunate brethren would eventually bring them into complete harmony with the attributes of their Father in Heaven, whose stated mission is "to bring to pass the immortality and eternal life of man." (Moses 1:39). "And ye shall be even as I am," promised the Savior, "and I am even as the Father, and the Father and I are one." (3 Nephi 28:10).

After the Savior departed, the Three Nephites were "caught up into heaven, and saw and heard unspeakable things." (3 Nephi 28:13). They had received an endowment of spiritual and priesthood power and "whether they were in the body or out of the body, they could not tell, for it did seem unto them like a transfiguration." which is a special change in appearance and nature wrought upon a person by the power of God. (3 Nephi 28:15). This transformation is from a lower to a higher state of being, resulting in a more exalted, impressive, and glorious condition.

The Eleventh Hymn of the Dead Sea Covenanters of Qumran declared: "Behold, for mine own part I have reached the intervision, and through the spirit thou has placed within me, come to know Thee, my God." (Preston Robinson, "Christ's Eternal Gospel," p. 111). In similar fashion, Moses wrote: "But now mine own eyes have beheld God; but not my natural, but my spiritual eyes, for my natural eyes could not have beheld; for I should have withered and died in his presence; but his glory was upon me; and I beheld his face, for I was transfigured before him." (Moses 1:11). Thus, a difference between transfiguration and translation is that the former seems to be of a temporary nature.

Exodus records that when Moses ascended the mountain to speak with Jehovah, "the glory of the Lord abode upon mount Sinai ... And the sight of the glory of the Lord was like a devouring fire on the top of the mount in the eyes of the children of Israel." (Exodus 24:16-17). And "when Moses came down from mount Sinai ... behold, the skin of his face shone." (Exodus 34:29-30). Fire and smoke are frequently cited in the scriptures to depict the glory of God. In the language of Joseph Smith: "God Almighty Himself dwells in eternal fire; flesh and blood cannot go there, for all corruption is devoured by that fire. Our God is a consuming fire. Immortality dwells in everlasting burnings." ("Teachings," p. 367). We must be transfigured or translated in order to endure the "consuming fire that is God." (Hebrews 12:29). Surely, none of us "hath seen God at any time in the flesh, except quickened by the Spirit of God" in an attitude of transfiguration or translation. (J.S.T. John 1:18, See D&C 67:11).

The scriptures testify that "eye hath not seen, nor ear heard, neither have entered into the heart of man, the things which God hath prepared for them that love him." (1 Corinthians 2:9). The Nephites to whom the Savior ministered testified that "no tongue can speak, neither can there be written by any man, neither can the hearts of men conceive so great and marvelous things as we ... saw." (3 Nephi 17:7). It seems that the wonders of heaven may be revealed to transfigured or translated beings in the most marvelous manner.

To Mormon, as he abridged the account made by Nephi, it seemed that the Three Nephites "were changed from this body of flesh into an immortal state, that they could behold the things of God." (3 Nephi 28:15). Then Mormon added a postscript that explains what the Lord told him in response to the question he had posed about the temporal status of the three Nephite disciples. Mormon had inquired to know their state of existence, and was told: "There must needs be a change wrought upon their bodies, or else it needs be that they must taste of death." (3 Nephi 28:37). In other words, the Lord confirmed to Mormon that although they were mortal, translated beings were, indeed, different from the rest of us.

"Therefore, that they might not taste of death there was a change wrought upon their bodies, that they might not suffer pain nor sorrow save it were for the sins of the world." (3 Nephi 28:38). Not only would they not grow older, but also while tarrying in this special state they would not experience the challenges of adversity normally associated with mortality.

Mormon explained: "This change was not equal to that which shall take place at the last day; but there was a change wrought upon them, insomuch that Satan could have no power over them, that he could not tempt them; and they were sanctified in the flesh, that they were holy, and that the powers of the earth could not hold them." (3 Nephi 28:39). Indeed, to describe them as mortal would be a gross understatement.

To this day, they remain in their sanctified state, endowed with the power of God to dominate Satan. However, they will not interfere in the course of human events to change history, but will always allow agency to rule. Their mission is to bring souls unto Christ. They will not allow Satan to thwart that mission as long as those to whom they minister do not willfully rebel and reject their invitations.

And so, the Three Nephites "did go forth upon the face of the land, and did minister unto all the people, uniting as many to the church as would believe in their preaching; baptizing them, and as many as were baptized did receive the Holy Ghost." (3 Nephi 28:8). In a demonstration of their power over evil, when "they were cast into prison by them who did not belong to the church ... the prisons could not hold them, for they were rent in twain. And they were cast down into the earth; but they did smite the earth with the word of God, insomuch that by his power they were delivered out of the depths of the earth; and therefore, they could not dig pits sufficient to hold them." (3 Nephi 28:19-20).

Because Satan clearly understood the power and potential influence of the Three Nephites, even before their special call he had tried desperately to prevent their ministry. Perhaps they had been foreordained to this mission under the hands of Heavenly Father Himself, while yet in the pre-earth existence. If so, then perhaps Satan knew of the potential impact of their future ministry from that time, and so caused the people to stone to death Nephi's brother Timothy, who at that time was one of the Nephite Twelve. (3 Nephi 19:4 & 3 Nephi 7:19).

But even that despicable and cowardly act was futile, for there was no power on earth that could destroy them. Timothy was raised from the dead by the power of the priesthood. We do not know the names of the Three Nephite disciples who tarried, nor do we know if Timothy was one of them. But we do know that three times were they 'cast into a furnace and received no harm. And twice were they cast into a den of wild beasts; and behold they did play with the beasts as a child with a suckling lamb, and received no harm." (3 Nephi 28:21-22).

The Three Nephites ministered to those who needed the gospel the most. Even though they had been mistreated and abused, they did not lose sight of their mission statement, which was to bring all unto Christ, so that they might enjoy the blessings of the gospel, participate in the ordinances of salvation and exaltation, partake of His divine nature, and be perfected in Him.

Therefore, "they did go forth among all the people of Nephi, and did preach the gospel of Christ unto all the people upon the face of the land, and they were converted unto the Lord, and were united into the church of Christ, and thus the people of that generation were blessed, according to the word of Jesus." (3 Nephi 28:23). Once again, we see that the Savior rarely intervenes directly in our affairs, but instead gives priesthood assignments to His faithful servants, and allows them to do the work on behalf of their own brethren. As the scriptures testify: "After much tribulation come the blessings." (D&C 58:4). The Three Nephites are to remain on the earth as translated beings "until the judgment day of Christ; and at that day they (are) to receive a greater change," to be resurrected "into the kingdom of the Father to go no more out, but to dwell with God eternally in the heavens." (3 Nephi 28:40).

Mormon's experience with the Three Nephites was more than anecdotal. It was direct and personal, for he wrote: "I have seen them, and they have ministered unto me." (3 Nephi 28:26, See Mormon 8:11). Perhaps they revealed to Mormon that they would minister to the Gentiles, for he recorded that among them "a great and marvelous work (would be) wrought by them, before that judgment day." (3 Nephi 28:27 & 32).

Mormon also learned that they would minister among the Jews and among "all the scattered tribes of Israel, and unto all nations, kindreds, tongues and people, and (would) bring out of them unto Jesus many souls, that their desire (might) be fulfilled, and also because of the convincing power of God which (would be) in them." (3 Nephi 28:28-29). "And they are as the angels of God, and if they shall pray unto the Father in the name of Jesus they can show themselves unto whatsoever man it seemeth them good. Therefore, great and marvelous works shall be wrought by them." (3 Nephi 28:30-31). Their ministry, it would seem, has known no bounds, as it has ranged over the earth through twenty centuries. It is thrilling to think that Heavenly Father loves us so much that He might even send strangers among us who might minister to our needs without even our conscious awareness.

Who is Packing Your Parachute?

"Turn ye unto the Lord;
cry mightily unto the Father
in the name of Jesus, that perhaps
ye may be found spotless, pure, fair,
and white, having been cleansed by the
blood of the Lamb, at that last and
great day." (Mormon 9:6).

Some activities need to be accomplished with precision and efficiency, and with unerring accuracy. Skydiving is one of those. When a parachute deploys during a jump, it must function properly 100% of the time, without error. For example, it needs to deploy with reliability, so the entire parachute inflates correctly. It needs to deploy with consistency, so the skydiver will know exactly what to expect when the parachute opens. It needs to deploy without twisting, so the skydiver is facing in the right direction after the deployment of the chute. It needs to deploy without tangling the lines, for obvious reasons. And it needs to deploy at the right pace to avoid damaging the equipment or injuring the jumper as it does so.

Skydiving mirrors our life experiences. We approach our potential when we conduct our lives so that we function properly 100% of the time, without error. To be at full capacity, we should begin every day with a focus on reliability, so that the day unfolds before us without glitches. Our conduct must be consistent, so others will know generally and specifically what they can expect of us, no matter the situation. It is best if our day unfolds with us facing in the right direction, so we can move forward without unnecessary course corrections that waste valuable time and resources. If we build upon proven foundation principles, we will avoid the tangled web created by those whose actions are influenced by convenience, situational ethics, and expediency. If we purposefully act rather than being acted upon, we will find ourselves in the right place, at the right time, moving at the right speed, remembering that the Lord commanded: "Do not run faster or labor more than you have strength." (D&C 10:4). In skydiving as well as in life, we do not want to plummet through space at terminal velocity, particularly because the expression has such a note of finality!

There are figurative connotations associated with "terminal velocity" as well. Objects in free-fall are subject to the opposite forces of gravity and drag. When they are equal, the falling object will have zero acceleration. It will have achieved terminal velocity. Those who are moving forward do not want to have "zero acceleration." Of course, they will be subject to the force of gravity, particularly insofar as it draws them nearer to their spiritual core, and as it grounds them to unchanging principles.

But "drag" in their lives will just slow them down. Friction unnecessarily heats them up and wears on them. Of course, they do not want to be gliding smoothly and effortlessly through life, because when we do that we are generally going downhill. Instead, they want to be steadily improving, moving upward as they encounter and conquer opposition. They dream big. They have developed spirituality. They are known as persons of character, with clearly defined realistic goals. They do not procrastinate, but accept responsibility. They do what they love to do, and establish priorities and stick with them. They are understanding, and consciously choose their habits. They have single-minded concentration, but remain flexible in their approach to problem-solving. They never consider the possibility of failure. They are honest, and dedicated to service. They are leaders and not just managers, and recognize and act upon the switch-points in their lives. They love to work and are dependable. They have a clear vision of who they are, and they persist at tasks until they succeed. They seize the moment. They are unified, and are teachers and mentors.

In skydiving, as we plan our jump, the chute prevents us from sustaining terminal velocity during our descent. The best way to make sure everything happens as planned is to pack the chute carefully and meticulously follow the manufacturer's instructions. Most experienced skydivers pack their own chutes, and have gotten so good at it that they can do it in 10 or 15 minutes.

Joseph Smith, when asked how he could govern so many people, simply said, "I teach people correct principles, and they govern themselves." If we listen to our file leaders and follow their counsel, we can act independently within our sphere of influence, and we will live life abundantly. This course entails risk, but it is God's ordained way. He declared to Adam while he was yet in the Garden: "Nevertheless, thou mayest choose for thyself, for it is given unto thee." (Moses 3:17). If we choose unwisely, we may forfeit our agency and no longer be free. Packing our chute carelessly or thoughtlessly may result in catastrophic consequences.

During a jump, when the chute has been deployed, the first thing the skydiver should do is look up to see that everything is okay. Only then should he grab the toggles and steer toward the landing site.

Jumping out of an airplane with a backpack stuffed with 15 pounds of silk mirrors our every day life experiences. Each 24-hour segment has its ups and downs with unanticipated challenges. Our experience in the church teaches us to be flexible so that we can adapt to evolving circumstances without compromising our standards. We meet our challenges the same way skydivers do. We respond to crises without panicking. We apply established protocols to deal with emergencies. We live in an imperfect world but deal with eternal progress the same way; one day at a time, even one hour at a time, and each minute brings us tangibly closer to our intended destination.

When Alice was in Wonderland, she asked the Cheshire Cat: "Would you please tell me which way I ought to go from here?" The Cat responded: "That depends a good deal on where you want to go." Alice acknowledged: "I admit, I don't much care where." To which the cat retorted: "Then it doesn't matter which way you go." Alice implored: "Just so I go somewhere!" The cat observed: "Oh, you are sure to do that, if you only walk far enough."

Sometimes, a skydiver may realize that something has gone terribly wrong with the main canopy during deployment. It may have never come out of the bag, or if it did, it might not have inflated properly. It may have become tangled in the lines, some of the lines may have broken, or the canopy may have ripped during deployment. It may have only partially inflated. It is of great comfort to skydivers to know that there are backup systems in place that can handle the emergency if the necessary steps are taken to address the situation.

In life, the list of the things that can and do go wrong is much longer. In fact, it is probably endless. Fortunately, the Atonement of Christ makes it possible for us to enjoy mortality without making mistakes that are ultimately and irreversibly spiritually fatal. Elder Boyd K. Packer once told the story of a World War II naval aviator, who left the security of his aircraft carrier for a dangerous mission. True to the predictions of his superior officers, he endured enemy anti-aircraft fire and engaged in lethal dogfights. His plane was hit numerous times by flack that tore away parts of his wings. His Plexiglas canopy was shattered, and he could hardly see through blood-splattered goggles to navigate back to his ship. As he came in for a landing on the pitching deck of the carrier, his controls were nearly useless, his descent too steep and his angle wrong. He was frantically waved off by the crewman on deck who was guiding him in, but he figured he had only one chance and this was it, and he would take it. With a sickening thump he pancaked on the deck, the fuel tank burst into flame, and the tail hook failed to engage the cables that would have brought him to a halt. As he careened into the safety net at the end of the deck, what was left of his plane crumpled into twisted metal. A rescue crew in asbestos suits rushed to his aid, smothered the wreckage in fire-retardant foam, clamored up to the cockpit, unsnapped his safety harness, grabbed him by the shoulders, and dragged in to safety. Doctors and nurses attended to his wounds even before he arrived at sickbay. Due to their skill and attention, as well as to his unconquerable spirit, he made a remarkable and full recovery. This, Elder Packer suggested, is how most of us will return from our mortal mission to the presence of our Father.

In skydiving, if your main chute has failed, the canopy cannot be used to land safely, so it needs to be cut away before deploying the reserve chute. This is not difficult to do, but your mind needs to be clear about how to correctly pull the ring that simultaneously releases the lines on both risers. When this has been accomplished, you will be in free-fall once again. A static line then automatically deploys the reserve chute. As this happens, many skydivers pray that it works.

We act the same way in life. We take two steps into the darkness, and then faith shows us the way. Helen Keller recorded a moving expression of her faith, writing: "I believe that no good shall be lost, and that all man has willed or hoped or dreamed of good shall exist forever. I believe in the immortality of the soul because I have within me immortal longings. I believe that the state we enter after death is wrought of our own motives, thoughts, and deeds. I believe that my home there will be beautiful with colour, music, and speech of flowers and faces I love. Without this faith, there would be little meaning in my life. I should be a mere pillar of darkness in the dark. Observers in the full enjoyment of their bodily senses pity me, but it is because they do not see the golden chamber in my life where I dwell delighted; for dark as my path may seem to them, I carry a magic light in my heart. Faith, the spiritual strong searchlight, illuminates the way, and although sinister doubts lurk in the shadow, I walk unafraid towards the Enchanted Wood where the foliage is always green, where joy abides, where nightingales nest and sing, and where life and death are one in the presence of the Lord." ("Midstream").

Because there is very little room for error in skydiving, jumpers also have an Automatic Activation Device that deploys the chute if you lose consciousness, or fall too far without deploying your main chute. It will also deploy your reserve chute if it is needed.

In life, if we lose our way, the Spirit will "deploy our chute," as well. "I will go before you and be your rearward;" promised the Lord, "and I will be in your midst, and you shall not be confounded." (D&C 49:27). The Savior is our Jumpmaster and our Flight Instructor. He is the Canopy over our head, and our Reserve Chute. With trust in Him, (and with a little bit of pixie dust), we can fly!. (Peter Pan). That magical formula allows us to "be like a bird, that pausing in her flight a while on boughs to light, feels them give way beneath her, and yet sings, knowing that she hath wings." (Victor Hugo). Then we will "fly away as an eagle toward heaven." (Proverbs 23:5).

As the power fueling our
actions charges our spiritual batteries
and energizes our sight with an infinite
perspective, we will experience a pulsing stream
of inspiration whose flow has no temporal or spatial
boundary. We will be swept up by quickening currents
into the direct experience of a holy communion with God.
Although the heavens will always be higher than the
earth, His thoughts will somehow have become our
thoughts, and His ways our ways. We will be
caught up in His work and His glory,
as we finally understand that the
universe is a machine for the
making of gods.

Why Do We Laugh?

"Men are that they might have joy," according to God's
great plan of happiness." For "if there be no righteousness,
there be no happiness ... which is prepared for the saints.
(2 Nephi 2:25, Alma 42:8, & 2 Nephi 21:13 & 9:43).

1. We laugh when we are happy.

The capacity for laughter that is consistent with The Plan of Happiness is within the reach of every one of God's children, no matter what their cultural, social, political, or economic circumstances might be. The key to such laughter is interwoven into every gospel principle and is intrinsic in every gospel teaching. On our own we can do pitifully little to influence our circumstances. It is only the infinite, continuing, uninterrupted, uncorrupted, and unfathomable grace of God that has the capacity to put a smile on our face.

In the end, we will find that when we enjoy "that happiness which is prepared for the saints" our lives will be filled with laughter. (2 Nephi 9:43). The Savior revealed: "Abundance is multiplied unto (the Saints) through the manifestations of the Spirit." (D&C 70:13). Our righteous objectives stay in focus only when we pay constant attention to spiritual guideposts. We will find that our senses and sensitivities will be sharpened, when we obtain the perspective on life that comes from a gospel-centered orientation.

2. The source of genuine laughter is born of contrast.

Our natural inclination is to seek relief from discomfort and we are quick to "laugh it off." Rarely do we recognize that in order to experience the happiness that is the soulmate of laughter, we must also experience its opposite. When Adam and Eve realized this, their eyes were opened. Too frequently, ours seem to be closed.

When people don't believe they have opposition in their lives, they may be particularly vulnerable to depression and unhappiness, the very things they seek so desperately to avoid. Opposition can actually precipitate laughter. But if we homogenize our experiences by smoothing out all the rough edges, we may inadvertently be neutralizing the very things that would have contributed most significantly to our happiness. If we have a one-dimensional view of life, we might find ourselves running to and fro seeking fulfilment in a world without genuine laughter. Our distorted perceptions may influence us to engage in self-defeating behaviors in a desperate attempt to interface with reality. Chemicals cooked up in a meth lab will definitely change our perception of reality, but endorphins are a better choice if we want to experience the real-world emotions that precipitate laughter.

3. Laughter may stem from want.

If someone continually gluts himself in order to experience gratification, he will eventually diminish his capacity for enjoyment. He may exhibit a waning smile, but for the wrong reasons. Progressively greater enhancements will be required to elicit the same level of satisfaction. Perhaps this is why happiness cannot be found in serial relationships that focus on physical attraction but have no emotional connection. As with the adulterer, greater and greater stimulation is necessary to achieve the same level of excitement, until there is a final retreat into a shallow core whose expression is a permanent frown.

4. Laughter can also be precipitated by excess.

One of the greatest challenges our society faces is the meaningless laughter that accompanies the insatiable desire for pleasure, immediate gratification, and repetitive waves of greater and greater stimulation. "Being affluent, we strangle ourselves with what we can buy, things whose opacity obstructs our ability see what is really there." (Gretel Erlich). As our culture demands escalating criteria to maintain an unsustainably false standard of comfort and entertainment, we are blinded to the sobering comparison to a heroin addict's progressive tolerance and destructive reliance on his own false gods of wood and stone.

5. We laugh when we are obedient to the commandments.

Our laughter betrays our happiness when "we pursue the path that leads to it; and this path is virtue, uprightness, faithfulness, holiness, and keeping all the commandments of God." (Joseph Smith). Lehi simply stated: "If there be no righteousness there be no happiness." (2 Nephi 2:13).

6. We laugh when we share the gospel with others.

To the Latter-day Saints, the Lord promised: "If it be so that you should labor all your days in crying repentance unto this people, and bring, save it be one soul unto me, how great shall be your joy with him in the kingdom of my father." (D&C 18:15). Quite obviously, the Lord wants us to be happy, and it is equally clear that He wants us to share the gospel because it is His universal formula for happiness. The smiles that light up our faces and the laughter that accompanies the gospel message, (literally "the good news"), are at the foundations of a universally recognized language.

7. We laugh because we are thoroughly committed to our covenants.

President Kimball recognized this eternal principle when he urged members of the church to lengthen their stride. In doing so, "he knew that the spirituality of the members would be intensified. Christ urged the man in bondage to go the second mile, to receive a gift of spiritual independence that removes the veil of insensitivity to a destiny." (Richard L. Gunn). It is in the second mile when endorphins kick in and our laughter is genuine and independent of external influences.

8. We laugh when our motives are pure, and we rise above the crowd.

Internalizing gospel principles softens our telestial tendencies, and covenants create an impenetrable shield of faith. By gaining an eternal perspective, we are able to discern between the polarized opposites of happiness and its worldly counterfeits that are so prevalent in our world today. The message of the Restoration strikes familiar chords within us, even as we feel disquieted by Satan's smudgy fingerprints on the idols with which he tempts us to keep us from the truth. Faithful disciples of Christ choose their laughter much more carefully, and their compassion for others brings them to tears more often than it brings them to laughter.

9. We laugh when we immerse ourselves in culturally stimulating environments.

The sturdiest plants that bear the best fruit are those that have deep roots in good, rich, nurturing soil. So, to be truly happy, and to share our happiness with others, we must surround ourselves with the best that can be provided in music and art, conversation, example, decency, virtue, and honor. Then our spirits will grow freely, even as we send down taproots in gospel soil to secure our solid footing.

In so doing, we commit the 13th Article of Faith to our lifestyle as well as to our memory. That will stimulate our tendency to laugh for appropriate reasons. "If there is anything virtuous, lovely, or of good report or praiseworthy, we seek after these things." To the extent that we do this, we may expect to blossom enthusiastically with the "fire of God." If we don't, we may experience hell while yet on earth, for that mental anguish may simply be the conscious recognition of lost opportunities, or the unconscious sense of dread that accompanies the stupor of thought when we have made Satan our bedfellow.

10. Sometimes, we laugh because we are sad.

In Proverbs, we read: "Even in laughter the heart is sorrowful; and the end of that mirth is heaviness." (Proverbs 14:13). In our quest, we sometimes forget that with nurturing rain we are also going to have to deal with mud, and that we all must negotiate potholes and other obstacles on rocky roads that are uphill most of the way. After all, "the dark threads are as needful in the weaver's skillful hand as the threads of gold and silver, in the pattern he has planned." (Anonymous).

11. We laugh in our ignorance.

Those who are as "children, tossed to and fro, and carried about with every wind of doctrine, by the sleight of men, and cunning craftiness" (Ephesians 4:14) do not understand that "fame is a vapor, and popularity is an accident, and that those who laugh with you today may deride you tomorrow. In the end, the only thing that endures is character." (Anonymous).

Even Abraham, when told that his wife would conceive, "fell upon his face, and laughed, and said in his heart, Shall a child be born unto him that is an hundred years old? And shall Sarah, that is ninety years old, bear?." (Genesis 17:17).

12. We laugh when we embrace life at its deepest levels.

We cannot find happiness without an appreciation of its value, or if we experience life superficially. That appreciation may come in our moments of greatest difficulty, distress, or sadness. Even in those circumstances, we can find things about which we can smile.

13. We laugh at ourselves.

It's best not to take ourselves too seriously. Once in a while, self-deprecating laughter can be like a pressure-release valve that brings us back down to earth.

14. We laugh at the irony in life.

When there is incongruity between what has happened to us, and what we would have expected to happen, when reality seems absurd, sometimes the best therapy is to just sit back and smile with sardonic humor. In our busy and complex world, we may see through a glass darkly and find that it is very difficult to discover just what formula will bring us happiness. Does beauty have the advantage, or does the beast? We cannot tell if it is fame or anonymity, poverty or wealth, sickness or health, worldly influence or obscurity.

15. We laugh because, in our vanity, we perceive that something is "funny."

The Preacher wrote: "I said in mine heart, Go to now, I will prove thee with mirth, therefore enjoy pleasure: and, behold, this also is vanity. I said of laughter, It is mad: and of mirth, What doeth it?." (Ecclesiastes 2:1-2). We also read: "For as the crackling of thorns under a pot, so is the laughter of the fool: this also is vanity." (Ecclesiastes 7:6).

16. Sometimes, our ostentatious display of self-importance prompts us to laugh.

Our pomp and circumstance cloud the spiritual independence that removes the veil of insensitivity to our destiny. If we are focused on latter-day idols of any kind, we will neither be happy, nor will we be in a position to engage in healthy laughter. If our faith is flawed, we will be blinded to the reality that the objects of our desires have no power to deliver on their promises or to provide a vigorous catalyst to laughter. Sooner or later, the master pretender will reveal his true character as the father of the lie, and in our misery we will find "no joy in Mudville."

17. Sometimes, we retreat into laughter as a defense mechanism for self-preservation.

If we feel confused, abandoned, disillusioned, or if we despair as a consequence of our focus on worldly pleasure, we will be like those of whom the Savior declared: "They seek not the Lord to establish his righteousness, but every man walketh in his own way, and after the image of his own god, whose image is in the likeness of the world, and whose substance is like that of an idol, which waxeth old and shall perish in Babylon, even Babylon the great, which shall fall." (D&C 1:16).

18. We laugh because we treat lightly things that are actually very serious.

Through Joseph Smith, the Saints were admonished: "Your minds in times past have been darkened because of unbelief, and because you have treated lightly the things you have received." (D&C 84:54). If we want to laugh with the Saints, we cannot book a vacation in Idumea as a pleasant respite from life on the strait and narrow path. Such diversions are only detours on life's journey that inevitably delay our progress toward our determined destination. When we delve into these distractions, we lose power, purpose, and focus, and our vocal cords strain with the effort to laugh.

19. We laugh when something unpleasant happens to someone else.

The Savior said that it is the devil who "laugheth, and his angels rejoice, because of the slain of the fair sons and daughters of my people." (3 Nephi 9:2). Such laughter can build into harmonic waves with the power to undermine the foundations of relationships and institutions. It is a cowardly act, often conducted anonymously or behind a cloak of secrecy, but its effect is felt publicly. Those who laugh at the expense of others are seeking a tangible return without having made a legitimate initial investment.

20. We laugh when we brush up against "evil."

Paul warned the Ephesian Saints about "filthiness [and] foolish talking, [and] jesting, which are not convenient." (Ephesians 5:4). Those of weak character frequently laugh as they experience worldly pleasures. They do so unconsciously, confusing wickedness with happiness, and thinking that when they are in a state of nature they are somehow at their best. But when base behavior seamlessly harmonizes with worldly standards, the resulting false sense of security is unsustainable in times of hardship. Laughter that accompanies evil is harsh, for although opposition in all things was a condition for the operation of the Plan, without active, conscious participation that carries us upward and forward on a path of progress, life can be a cruel joke with a punch line that elicits no laughter. Instead, it ultimately stabs at the heart when we are confronted by the utter futility and hopelessness of the predicament we have created for ourselves.

21. We laugh when the cold face of evil overpowers us.

As long as individuals shut out the Light of Christ, they may live an illusion and laugh when influenced by evil. But sooner or later the discrepancy between marginal behavior and foundation principles will become so great that short-lived mirth in worldly ways evaporates as morning dew in the full light of day. The only laughter then will be the forced giggle that barely escapes vocal chords that have been strained by fear. The Lord will not always suffer the wicked "to take happiness in sin." (Mormon 2:13). They can only conduct their lives in opposition to the laws of heaven for so long, before "critical mass" is reached. At that point, a readjustment is required, bringing errant individuals back into harmony with nature. (No more laughter, then!)

22. We laugh when we mock someone.

Alma reported of the people of Ammonihah: "They laughed us to scorn." (Alma 26:23). Even the Savior experienced the laughter of those who derided Him for His miracles. When he raised the daughter of Jairus from the dead, "He said unto them, Give place: for the maid is not dead, but sleepeth. And they laughed him to scorn." (Matthew 9:24). We mock others when we treat them with scorn or contempt, when we deliberately annoy or irritate them, when we make fun of them either playfully or maliciously, when we cast them in a light that is intended to make them appear silly or ridiculous, when we arouse in them hope with no intention of giving satisfaction, when we throw obstacles in their path in ways that cause them frustration or humiliation, when we play them for fools in order to amuse ourselves or others, or when we ridicule them for any reason whatsoever.

There is a fine line between a facetious observation and a sarcastic comment. The one is intended to be humorous and not to be taken seriously, but when one crosses the line, it can be silly or inappropriate. The other is consciously intended to be disparaging and inflicts pain. Laughter can light a fire under a facetious remark and unconsciously transform it into sarcasm.

23. Occasionally, our laughter is best confined to the locker-room.

If we have to be behind closed doors to "get a laugh," we probably should be throwing open the shutters and letting in some sunlight.

24. We laugh when we are "chatting over the back fence."

Such laughter often accompanies mindless chatter that feeds voraciously on rumor, hearsay, second-hand information, innuendo, and vanity. Left unchecked, it may build into a self-perpetuating chain reaction leading to a whole series of unfortunate, yet inevitable, consequences. Such careless laughter suggests that the vocal cords have been put in gear before the brain has been brought on-line. In fact, "there is so much good in the worst of us, and so much bad in the best of us, that it hardly behooves any of us to laugh about the rest of us." (Anonymous).

25. We laugh because we are blind to the reality of a situation; we are ignorant of the consequences of our or other's actions.

Sooner or later, "the Lord shall utter his voice, and all the ends of the earth shall hear it; and the nations of the earth shall mourn, and they that have laughed shall see their folly." (D&C 45:49). Sometimes our laughter is a nervous response to our awareness of impending doom. If we lighten up, we feel that we can somehow mitigate a bad situation. But life is all a stage, and when the bouquets are thrown at the feet of the cast and they are summoned for a curtain call after the final act, it will only be the faithful and true who receive a standing ovation. This is why Samuel the Lamanite charged the people of Zarahemla: "Ye have sought all the days of your lives for that which ye could not obtain, and ye have sought for happiness in doing iniquity, which thing is contrary to the nature of that righteousness" which is in God. (Helaman 13:38).

On the other hand, The Lord asks us to ground ourselves in the bedrock of gospel principles, and to express ourselves with emotions that are building blocks, and not bullets. The laughter of His disciples is sometimes a therapeutic tool, but never a weapon. Such laughter avoids assumptions, speculation, and second-guessing. It plumbs the depths, rather than skims the shallows, of issues. Those who laugh with the Saints are good listeners, and when they laugh, they do so more with purpose than with frivolity or levity. They value trust in relationships, and then literally laugh in good faith and with confidence, preferring substance over superficiality.

26. We laugh because we enjoy the "double meaning, the "play on words" or the "double entendre." (This is deceit).

Paul taught: "Likewise must the deacons be grave [and] not double tongued." (1 Timothy 3:8). We find it easy to laugh on brightly lighted stages filled with the appreciative applause and laudatory comments of supportive audiences. But cast in challenging roles when no understudy is available, when there have been no preparatory fortifying rehearsals, and there are no positive peer pressures to sustain us, it is far easier to brush aside standards and laugh at things that would normally abhor us.

27. Sometimes, we laugh in groups at things that we would never dream of laughing about if we were alone, or with our loved ones.

"You tell on yourself by the friends you seek, by the very manner in which you speak, by the way you enjoy your leisure time, by the use you make of dollar and dime. You tell who you are by the things you wear and in the way you wear your hair; by the kinds of things that make you laugh, by the records you play on your phonograph. You tell who you are by the way you walk, by the things in which you delight to talk; by the books you choose from a well filled shelf. In these ways and more, you tell on yourself." (Anonymous).

28. We laugh at cleverness.

When we do so, we throw dirt, and when we do that, we lose ground. With revulsion, we have all witnessed flies passing over healthy parts of the body to collect only at open sores to feed and to lay their eggs. We must not laugh at things that should shock our spirits with loathing.

29. We laugh inappropriately because we lose our resolve and our will to be valiant.

In our day, there seems to be a full-scale assault on appropriate laughter. Too often, it is pushed aside or crowded out by the media, especially television sit-coms with live audiences guffawing and belly-laughing, and canned laughter waiting to fill in the blanks. Many social conventions and customs snicker at our attempts to maintain our standards. It is precisely because our capacity for appropriate laughter is so frequently threatened that we need to recommit ourselves to a behavioral lifestyle that reinforces laughter that is the companion of righteous activities. This will protect us from the worldly influences that encroach on the fortress of our spiritual security and symmetry. It becomes a question of context.

30. We laugh when we accept the invitation to "try the virtue of the word of God." (Alma 31:5).

Alma's invited us to open our senses to the matchless realm of joy, and even laughter, available only through obedience to gospel principles. Today, we share the fruits of the gospel with our friends and neighbors because these divine characteristics are the very things that will make us happy. They will bring us joy. They will make us smile. They will be a catalyst to laugh with our brothers and sisters in the gospel as we contemplate the matchless gifts of our Father.

We should always be ready to give courage and hope, to speak kind words that come from the heart, and to awaken our souls to cheerfulness, "'til heart meets with heart and rejoices in friendship that ever is true." ("Let Us Oft Speak Kind Words," L.D.S. Hymnal).

31. We laugh when we contemplate the Plan of Happiness.

We laugh as we did "when the morning stars sang together, and all the sons of God shouted for joy." (Job 38:7).

Our goal should be to be the kind of person our dog thinks we are, to extend ourselves in our efforts to treat others as we would have them treat us. For when it becomes our nature to laugh as we think about the Plan, we will discover that the key to theology is found in kind and thoughtful words, and even in the laughter that unlock the door leading to the riches of eternity.

32. We will laugh with joy when we return Home and have a wonderful reunion with our loved ones.

At that homecoming, "He that sitteth in the heavens shall laugh." (Psalms 2:4-5). "Here you are, home from your mission. It seems like it was such a short time. Think of the people you met, the people you helped. Think of how you have grown spiritually. It seems like you were a child, so immature, when you left home such a short time ago. There is mother waiting to embrace you, standing just a bit behind father, who is bursting with pride. Are those tears of happiness on mother's cheeks?. Father first strikes hands with you, and then embraces you warmly. You know this is where you belong. This is a real homecoming, one that will surely be resonant with laughter. Home to Heavenly Father and Mother." (Anonymous).

Profoundly important questions are asked by The Book Mormon. Is the endowment of the Spirit among our most prized possessions? Has our work led us to the Holy Ghost? Is He our constant companion? Does our moral compass point us toward righteousness and truth, are the fruits of our obedience an everlasting dominion, and without compulsory means will heaven's blessings be showered down upon our heads?

Words of Mormon

"After I had made an abridgement
from the plates of Nephi, down to the reign
of this king Benjamin, of whom Amaleki spake,
I searched among the records which had been delivered
into my hands, and I found these plates, which contained
this small account of the prophets from Jacob down to the reign
of this king Benjamin, and also many of the words of Nephi."
(Words of Mormon 1:3).

Even though Mormon's abridgment of the Book of Lehi, from the Large Plates of Nephi, was included with all the other records, he must have known that Joseph Smith's manuscript translation up to the Book of Mosiah would be corrupted in some way. Therefore, he went to great pains to include this transitional book on the last leaf of the record comprising the Small Plates of Nephi.

Speaking of the loss of the manuscript translation of the Book of Lehi, the Lord declared to Joseph Smith that "the works, and the designs, and the purposes of God cannot be frustrated, neither can they come to naught." (D&C 3:1). He can prepare for any eventuality, inasmuch as He is omniscient. He knows all things. (See 2 Nephi 9:20). He knows the end from the beginning. (See 1 Nephi 9:6). He is the same yesterday, today, and forever. (See 1 Nephi 10:18). Past, present, and future are ever before His eyes. (See D&C 130:7). "With God, all things are possible." (Matthew 19:26).

Mormon taught that God the Father knows all things, "being from everlasting to everlasting." (Moroni 7:22). From our perspective, eternity spans the time from when we were unorganized intelligence, through our spiritual development as children of our Heavenly Father, on into mortality, and finally to our reunion with Him in the resurrection. Faith, hope, and charity define His attributes in absolute perfection. If we were to model our behavior after any individual, it would be Christ, Who in every quality is One with the Father. This is why Mormon taught: "In Christ there should come every good thing." (Moroni 7:22)

We are completely helpless to alter the progress or affect the outcome of any of God's activities. It was when Moses realized his utter dependence upon Him that he exclaimed: "Now, for this cause, I know that man is nothing, which thing I never had supposed." (Moses 1:10). Our debt to God is total and complete. King Benjamin asked his people: "Can ye say aught of yourselves? I answer you, nay. Ye cannot say that ye are even as much as the dust of the earth; yet ye were created of the dust of the earth; but behold, it belongeth to him who created you." (Mosiah 2:25).

Jesus Christ counseled: "Remember that it is not the work of God that is frustrated, but the work of men." (D&C 3:3). Joseph Fielding Smith, Jr. declared: "No power on earth or hell can overthrow or defeat that which God has decreed. Every plan of the adversary will fail, for the Lord knows the secret thoughts of men, and sees the future with a vision clear and perfect, even as though it were in the past." Jacob clearly understood this, when he wrote: "Oh, how great the holiness of our God. For he knoweth all things, and there is not anything save he knows it." (2 Nephi 9:20). Else He would cease to be God, and we could not have faith in Him.

Joseph Smith explained to John Wentworth: "No unhallowed hand can stop the work from progressing. Persecutions may rage, mobs may combine, armies may assemble, calumny may defame, but the truth of God will go forth boldly, nobly, and independent, until it has penetrated every continent, visited every clime, swept every country, and sounded in every ear; till the purposes of God shall be accomplished, and the Great Jehovah shall say: The work is done." (H.C. 4:540). "The truth is, that after the thousands of attacks, and scores of books that have been published, not one criticism has survived, and thousands have borne witness that the Lord has revealed to them the truth of this marvelous work." (Joseph Fielding Smith, Jr.).

At the opening of every dispensation of the gospel, Satan has made a frontal attack against the restoration of truth. He deceived the sons and daughters of Adam and Eve in the First Gospel Dispensation. At the beginning of the Mosaic Dispensation, "Satan came tempting him saying: Moses, son of man, worship me." (Moses 1:12). In the Dispensation of the Meridian of Times, Satan attacked the Master Himself. (Luke 4:1-13). We learn from the Prophet Joseph Smith that Satan was also present and contested the opening of the Dispensation of The Fulness of Times. (J.S.H. 1:15).

Certainly, he tried very hard to frustrate the work of translation of the plates delivered into the hands of Joseph Smith. He knew that The Church of Jesus Christ could not be organized until the publication of The Book of Mormon. "The loss of 116 pages of manuscript translated from the first part of The Book of Mormon, that was called The Book of Lehi, must have seemed a serious blow at first, to Joseph Smith. The Prophet had reluctantly allowed these pages to pass from his custody to that of Martin Harris, who had served for a brief period as scribe in the translation of The Book of Mormon." (Superscript to D&C 3). But the Lord had provided a duplicate record, in the form of the Small Plates of Nephi.

Mormon was about to deliver to his son Moroni the record that he had been making. He had finalized his abridgment of the Large Plates of Nephi from the Book of Lehi through The Book of Mormon, chapter 7. This was a comprehensive effort that chronicled almost 1,000 years of Nephite history. Mormon had witnessed the last great battles between the Nephites and the Lamanites, and the record of his people was completed, having been abridged by him from the Large Plates of Nephi onto the Plates of Mormon.

Mormon recorded: "And it came to pass that when we had gathered in all our people in one to the land of Cumorah. I made this record out of the plates of Nephi, and hid up in the hill Cumorah all the records which had been entrusted to me by the hand of the Lord, save it were these few plates which I gave unto my son Moroni." (Mormon 6:6).

Mormon hoped that his son Moroni would be able to document the outcome of the final conflict between the Nephites and Lamanites. "And it is many hundred years after the coming of Christ that I deliver these records into the hands of my son," he wrote, "and it supposeth me that he will witness the entire destruction of my people. But may God grant that he may survive them, that he may write somewhat concerning them, and somewhat concerning Christ, that perhaps some day it may profit them." (V. 2).

Mormon continued: "And it came to pass that my people, with their wives and their children, did now behold the armies of the Lamanites marching towards them; and with that awful fear of death which fills the breasts of all the wicked, did they await to receive them." (Mormon 6:7). What a contrast this was to the description of the experience of the righteous, who also stared death in the face, but did so without flinching: "And it shall come to pass that those that die in me shall not taste of death, for it shall be sweet unto them." (D&C 42:46). "They shall never die the second death and feel the torment of the wicked, when they come face to face with eternity." (Joseph Fielding Smith, Jr.). Better than anyone, the righteous know that "death hath passed upon all men to fulfil the merciful plan of the Great Creator." (2 Nephi 9:6).

When the work of death at Cumorah had been completed, Mormon confirmed: "All my people, save it were ... twenty and four who were with me, and also a few who had escaped into the south countries, and a few who had deserted over unto the Lamanites, had fallen." (Mormon 6:15). "And they that die not in me, wo unto them, for their death is bitter." (D&C 42:47). Such are unprepared to meet God. (See Alma 48:23). "Do not procrastinate the day of your repentance until the end," pleaded Alma, "for after this day of life, which is given us to prepare for eternity, behold, if we do not improve our time while in this life, then cometh the night of darkness wherein there can be no labor performed." (Alma 34:33).

The wish of Mormon that his son Moroni might survive the conflict to record the destruction of the Nephites was granted, and his writing was preserved on the Plates of Mormon, and now comprise Mormon chapters 8 and 9, as well as the entire Book of Moroni. The Doctrine & Covenants validates the efforts of Mormon and Moroni: "And for this very purpose are these plates preserved, which contain these records - that the promises of the Lord might be fulfilled, which he made to his people." (D&C 3:19).

In the Words of Mormon, the prophet explained his intention to write an appendage to the Small Plates of Nephi, which he had only recently discovered among all the other plates in the library of the Nephite prophets. "After I had made an abridgment from the (Large) plates of Nephi, down to the reign of this king Benjamin, of whom Amaleki spake, I searched among the records which had been delivered into my hands, and I found these plates, which contained this small account of the prophets, from Jacob down to the reign of this king Benjamin, and also many of the words of Nephi." (V. 3). Mormon also wanted to add a few historical notes, in order to bring the narrative of the Small Plates of Nephi to the precise point at which the Book of Mosiah, abridged from the Large Plates, began on the Plates of Mormon.

It has been explained that the portion of the Large Plates of Nephi concerning Nephite history to the reign of Benjamin was called The Book of Lehi. This book covered the same time period as the whole of the Small Plates of Nephi, but was probably much more detailed. (See v. 3). The Book of Mosiah, which followed the Book of Lehi on the Large Plates of Nephi, inaugurated a combined religious and secular history, that continued until the time of Mormon. The entire record of the Large Plates of Nephi was then abridged onto the Plates of Mormon, and was deposited with the other records in the sanctuary at the Hill Cumorah.

It was Joseph Smith's 116-page manuscript translation of Mormon's abridgment of the Large Plates (down to the reign of King Benjamin) that was lost by Martin Harris. This required the translation of the entire record of the Small Plates of Nephi, that was a record of the same period of Nephite history ("a small account of the prophets") as that which had been lost.

When Mormon was yet a child, the body of plates of all the Nephite prophets had been deposited for safekeeping by Ammaron, who, "being constrained by the Holy Ghost, did hide up ... all the sacred records which had been handed down from generation to generation." (4 Nephi 1:48). Mormon was of such spiritual stature that he was charged with the responsibility to care for these plates when only 10 years of age. "And Ammaron said unto (Mormon): I perceive that thou art a sober child, and art quick to observe. Therefore, when ye are about twenty and four years old I would that ye should ... go to the land Antum, unto a hill which shall be called Shim; and there have I deposited unto the Lord all the sacred engravings concerning this people." (Mormon 1:3).

Fourteen years later, Mormon "did go to the hill Shim, and did take up all the records which Ammaron had hid up unto the Lord." (Mormon 4:23). By this time, "wickedness did prevail upon the face of the whole land." (Mormon 1:13). The entire fabric of Nephite society was unraveling, and it must have taken extraordinary powers of concentration for Mormon to focus on his responsibilities as prophet-historian.

He related that after he had made an abridgment from the (Large) Plates of Nephi, he discovered within the Small Plates of Nephi much that was pleasing to him, "because of the prophecies of the coming of Christ." (V. 4). Therefore, he chose these plates as the vehicle to finish his record. (V. 5). Following the engravings of Amaleki, Mormon wrote his last few words (The Words of Mormon) in what little space remained on the Small Plates of Nephi.

When Mormon declared: The "remainder of my record I shall take from the (Large) Plates of Nephi," he meant that, in order to write an understandable transitional narrative that would maintain flow and continuity from the Small Plates to his abridgment of the Large Plates (which had already been completed), he would need to make a brief account on the Small Plates of the life of King Benjamin, using as his reference text the Large Plates of Nephi. (V. 5).

Mormon's statement that he could not "write the hundredth part of the things of (his) people" is tantalizing to the mind. (V. 5). Jacob had said the same thing, and both Mormon and Moroni repeated this observation in various places in their abridgments. (V. 5, See Jacob 3:13, Helaman 3:14, 3 Nephi 5:8 & 26:6, & Ether 15:33).

Mormon took the Small Plates of Nephi and deposited them with the remainder of his own abridgment, called the Plates of Mormon. This was done "for a wise purpose." (V. 7). A thousand years earlier, Nephi had also been commanded by the Lord to make a duplicate record "for a wise purpose" known only to the Lord. (1 Nephi 9:5). The reason would only become apparent when, in 2,400 years, the translation by Joseph Smith of the abridgment of the Large Plates of Nephi, concerning Nephite history from Lehi down to the reign of King Benjamin, and comprising 116 pages of handwritten manuscript, would be lost by Martin Harris, to whom it had been temporarily entrusted. (See D&C 3 & 10).

In verse 8, we once again encounter the expanding circle of concern by the prophets, as faith, hope, and charity are manifested in Mormon's thoughts, words, and deeds. Remember that he had just witnessed "almost all the destruction of (his) people." (V. 1). Nevertheless, he wrote: "My prayer to God is concerning my brethren (the Lamanites), that they may once again come to the knowledge of God, yea, the redemption of Christ; that they once again be a delightsome people." (V. 8, See Moroni 7:44-48).

Nephi had reported that the Lord cursed the Lamanites "because of their iniquity. For behold, they had hardened their hearts against him, that they had become like unto a flint; wherefore, as they were white, and exceedingly fair and delightsome, that they might not be enticing unto my people the Lord God did cause a skin of blackness to come upon them." (2 Nephi 5:21). This is the only reference in the entire Book of Mormon where a definite color adjective is used to refer to this mark, or to describe the curse. All other references call it a "skin of darkness" or "a dark skin." Interestingly, in Hebrew, the terms "blackness" and "darkness" are interchangeable.

Those who repent and become the Lord's disciples are also described in the scriptures as "white, fair, and beautiful." (1 Nephi 13:15). Moroni used the terms "spotless, pure, fair, and white." (Mormon 9:6). Such individuals are cleansed by the blood of the Lamb, in a rite of purification. As Isaiah said: "Though your sins be as scarlet, they shall be as white as snow. Though they be red like crimson, they shall be as wool." (Isaiah 1:18).

When verse 8 is read with frequent reference to Mormon's masterful discourse on faith, hope, and charity, that his son Moroni thoughtfully included in his Book of Moroni, it becomes a powerful witness to his total commitment to Jesus Christ and His teachings. (Moroni 7:25-48). At every opportunity, it seems that Mormon unconsciously demonstrated the qualities of a true disciple.

Mormon' sermon stresses that no teaching is of worth unless it is connected to Christ. Without the Atonement, we are lost, or as Mormon put it: "All things which are good cometh of Christ; otherwise, men were fallen, and there could no good thing come unto them." (Moroni 7:24).

Faith and repentance lead us to the strait gate of baptism. Those who pass through this gate will obtain a remission of sins, gain membership in the church, and open the door leading to personal sanctification through repentance and receipt of the Holy Ghost. We may then find ourselves on the path of eternal progression leading to the Celestial Kingdom. That way is strait and narrow. The gospel standard is undeviating, with no room for rationalization or compromise. There is no latitude in God's declaration, when He said: "For I the Lord cannot look upon sin with the least degree of allowance." (D&C 1:31).

"This seems a harsh scripture, for it clearly states that God cannot tolerate sin or sinfulness in any degree. He can't wink at it, or ignore it, or turn and look the other way. He won't sweep it under the rug or say, 'Well, it's just a little sin. It'll be all right.' God's standard, the celestial standard, is absolute, and it allows no exceptions. There is no wiggle room. Many people seem to have the idea that the Judgment will somehow involve weighing or balancing, with their good deeds on one side of the scales and their bad deeds on the other. If their good deeds outweigh their bad, or if their hearts are basically good and outweigh their sins, then they can be admitted into the presence of God. This notion is false. God cannot, and will not, allow moral or ethical imperfection in any degree whatsoever to dwell in His presence. He cannot tolerate sin with the least degree of allowance. It is not a question of whether our good deeds outweigh our sins. If there is even one sin on our record, we are finished. The celestial standard is complete innocence, pure and simple, and nothing less than that will be tolerated in the kingdom of God." (Stephen Robinson, "Believing Christ," p. 1-2).

In the discourse preserved for us by his son in the Book of Moroni, Mormon taught the foundation principles of faith, hope, and charity that will lead us to the celestial kingdom (Moroni 7:25-48). God provided his Spirit, that we would be able to begin "to exercise faith in Christ" and thus to lay hold upon every good thing. (Moroni 7:25). This he did by the ministering of angels and by proving the spoken and written word through His priesthood servants.

The "children of men," referred to in Moroni 7:24, receive by faith the power to "become the sons of God." (Moroni 7:26). These are they who "will cleave unto every good thing," as Mormon had taught them to do. (Moroni 7:28, See Moroni 7:5-24). As they do, Christ becomes their Advocate before the Father at the pleasing bar of justice. (See Moroni 7:28). As Christ taught his disciples in Judea: "I am not come to call the righteous, but sinners to repentance." (Matthew 9:13).

He does this in every way that will build faith among the people. Angels, who are the servants of Christ, are commissioned to the work. "And the office of their ministry is to call men unto repentance, and to fulfil and to do the work of the covenants of the Father, which he hath made unto the children of men, to prepare the way among the children of men, by declaring the word of Christ unto the chosen vessels of the Lord, that they may bear testimony of him." (Moroni 7:31).

The Lord told Joseph Smith: "To some it is given by the Holy Ghost to know that Jesus Christ is the Son of God, and that he was crucified for the sins of the world. To others it is given to believe on their words, that they also might have eternal life if they continue faithful." (D&C 46:13-14). This would apply to non-members, children, and to church members in general who listen to the General Authorities of the church bear testimony. "And by doing so, the Lord God prepareth the way that the residue of men may have faith in Christ, that the Holy Ghost may have place in their hearts." (Moroni 7:32).

Consequently, the Twelve Apostles and other General Authorities of the church today declare with boldness their witness of the truth, that faith might be increased in the hearts of those who hear their testimony. Hence the following representative sampling from the General Authorities of the church: "I know Him. I testify that He is real. I testify as a witness." (Enzio Busche). "I know that God lives, for as in the words of my predecessor, John Taylor, I have seen Him." (Spencer W. Kimball). "I know of the divinity of the Lord Jesus Christ, for it has been revealed to me in a most interesting, complete, and beautiful way." (L. Tom Perry). "I leave you with that special witness which is mine to bear, for I have witnessed it with my own eyes, and heard it with my own ears." (L. Tom Perry). "In a coming day I shall feel the nail marks in his hands and in his feet and shall wet his feet with my tears. But I shall not know any better then than I know now that he is God's Almighty Son, that he is our Savior and Redeemer, and that salvation comes in and through His atoning blood and in no other way." (Bruce R. McConkie).

The spark of faith is struck off the Divine Anvil of God. It ignites the flame of resolve in individuals, and endows them with the "power to do whatsoever thing is expedient" or right to do, under the circumstances. That thing, said the Savior, is to "repent all ye ends of the earth, and come unto me, and be baptized in my name, and have (more) faith in me, that ye may be saved." (Moroni 7:34). This is the fruits of faith, that is, to be saved in the Celestial Kingdom of God. It is the very reason for the ministry of Christ and His servants among the children of men.

The Savior will continue the ministry, and work miracles among the children of men, as "long as time shall last, or the earth shall stand, or there shall be one man upon the face thereof to be saved." (Moroni 7:36, See Moses 1:39). Under the terrible circumstances in which this sermon was delivered to the Nephites, Mormon condemned his people for their lack of faith. He said: "Wherefore, if these things have ceased, wo be unto the children of men, for it is because of unbelief, and all is vain." (Moroni 7:37). All around his congregation, after all, "there were sorceries, and witchcrafts, and magics, and the power of the evil one was wrought upon all the face of the land" because of the lack of faith among the people. (Mormon 1:19).

The gifts of the Spirit were effectively absent among the Nephites of Mormon's day, which led him to declare: "Awful is the state of man, for they are as though there had been no redemption made." (Moroni 7:38). As Alma put it: "For behold, if ye have procrastinated the day of your repentance even until death (or if you have waited to develop saving faith until you were spiritually dead to the Light of Christ), behold, ye have become subjected to the spirit of the devil, and he doth seal you his (because you can no longer make the vital distinction between good and evil or light and darkness); therefore, the Spirit of the Lord hath withdrawn from you, and hath no place in you, and the devil hath all power over you (for you have voluntarily surrendered your agency to act independently), and this is the final state of the wicked," for there is no recovery, and it will be as if there had been no redemption made for such individuals who refuse to repent. (Alma 34:35, See Mosiah 16:5, Alma 11:41 & 12:18, & Helaman 14:18).

A powerful verse follows, in which Mormon exhorted his congregation to rise to the occasion. He said: "But behold, my beloved brethren, I judge better things of you, for I judge that ye have faith in Christ because of your meekness; for if ye have not faith in him then ye are not fit to be numbered among the people of his church." (Moroni 7:39). He was like wise old Tevya, who told his daughters: "In Anatevka, God knows who you are, and what you may become." ("Fiddler on The Roof").

Mormon's judgment that his people were capable of choosing the better part revealed his belief that they had a hope in

Christ. For "how is it that ye can attain unto faith, save ye shall have hope?" (Moroni 7:40). Later, his son Moroni would voice the same sentiment: "Wherefore, there must be faith; and if there must be faith, there must also be hope." (Moroni 10:20).

When we have hope in Christ, we enjoy the assurance of peace, that the direction of our lives is on track, and that the Lord is pleased with our efforts. As Mormon said, hope is born of faith. "Behold, I say unto you that ye shall have hope through the atonement of Christ and the power of his resurrection, to be raised up unto life eternal, and this because of your faith in him according to the promise." (Moroni 7:41). The hope to which he referred is not trust in some wildly improbable promise, nor is it a high stakes gamble. It is the inevitable result of well-founded faith, when we are "meek and lowly of heart," and in complete control of our desires and emotions. (Moroni 7:43).

With a foundation of faith and hope, Mormon was ready to reveal how charity follows these two qualities as the supreme characteristic of faithful disciples. (Moroni 7:44-48). He taught: "If a man be meek and lowly in heart, and confess by the power of the Holy Ghost that Jesus is the Christ," with a sure hope born of faith, "he must needs have charity." (Moroni 7:44, See 2 Nephi 33, & Ether 12:32).

The similarity of these verses concerning charity to the counsel given by the Apostle Paul and recorded in the New Testament (1 Corinthians 13:4-8) has raised a question in the minds of some relating to the origin of the sentiment. Perhaps both Mormon and Paul had access to the same or similar ancient records dealing with faith, hope, and charity. Or, the Holy Ghost could have revealed the same ideas to each prophet in essentially the same language. Or, the impressions received by Joseph Smith as he translated the record by the power of the Spirit could have been recorded by the prophet in the biblical language with which he was familiar.

Moroni 7:45 reads: "And charity suffereth long (or is the quality of patience, from God's perspective, toward people and circumstances), and is kind (or is characterized by sensitivity toward others, and is empathic), and envieth not (or is less concerned with telestial trinkets and more focused on celestial sureties), and is not puffed up, seeketh not her own (or is selfless), is not easily provoked (but reflects poise under provocation), thinketh no evil (or has no secret agenda to follow), and rejoiceth not in iniquity, but rejoiceth in the truth (and is repulsed by sin), beareth all things, believeth all things, hopeth all things, endureth all things," or is drawn toward the light, and is continually open to that which is good.

When God said: "Let us make man in our image, after our likeness," He meant that we should have not only the same physical characteristics as our parents, but also the same spiritual characteristics. (See Moses 2:26). Like-minded individuals seek each other out, are drawn to each other, and have a natural affinity for each other. Without these God-like qualities, our progression must stop. "If ye have not charity, ye are nothing, for charity never faileth. Wherefore, cleave unto charity, which is the greatest of all (spiritual gifts), for all things must fail" without it. (Moroni 7:46). It is the greatest of all the qualities of God Himself, Whose character encompasses all spiritual gifts.

"Charity is the pure love of Christ, and it endureth forever, and whoso is found possessed of it at the last day, it shall be well with him." (Moroni 7:47). Charity motivates us to Christian service, but it also prepares us to be like God, that we might one day feel comfortable in His Presence. It is a gift of the Spirit that is bestowed upon the faithful by the grace of God.

Only when we carefully and prayerfully read and ponder this masterful discourse on faith, hope, and charity, can we comprehend the summary statement made in Moroni 7:48. It is all the more meaningful when it is understood in the context of the turmoil existing in Zarahemla around the year 385 A.D. "Wherefore, my beloved brethren, pray unto the Father with all the energy of heart, that ye may be filled with this love, which He hath bestowed upon all who are true followers of His Son, Jesus Christ; that ye may become the sons of God; that when He shall appear we shall be like Him, for we shall see Him as He is; that we may have this hope; that we may be purified even as He is pure. Amen."

Mormon also expressed his hope for his brethren the Lamanites in the Words of Mormon, at about the same time he wrote his discourse on faith, hope, and charity. Finally, he wrote: "And now I ... proceed to finish out my record, which I take from the (Large) plates of Nephi; and I make it according to the knowledge and the understanding which God has given me." (V. 9).

When Mormon attached these words to the last leaf of the Small Plates of Nephi, he had already completed his abridgment of the Large Plates of Nephi, and had also recorded his testimony in The Book of Mormon inclusive of chapter 7. The knowledge and understanding with which he accomplished this came by the Spirit. "And now come, saith the Lord, by the Spirit, unto the elders of his church, and let us reason together, that ye may understand." (D&C 50:10).

With the completion of the Words of Mormon, the records of the Nephite people were reconciled. After King Benjamin had received the Small Plates from Amaleki, he put them with the Large Plates, and from that point on, they were kept together by the Nephite kings and by the prophets who wrote exclusively upon the Large Plates of Nephi. But it was left to Mormon to fashion the bridge that would connect them as a part of the restoration of the gospel.

From verse 12 to the end of the Words of Mormon, we are provided with a brief summary of the reign of King Benjamin: "And now concerning this king Benjamin," wrote Mormon. (V. 12). He knew that those who would read The Book of Mormon would not have access to the account of the whole life of King Benjamin that was contained in the Book of Lehi, for that was lost with the 116 pages of manuscript translation that was mishandled by Martin Harris.

In the Book of Omni, only 3 verses concern King Benjamin, and what Mormon had written about him in his abridgment of the Book of Mosiah was confined to the last 3 years of the king's life. Nevertheless, what we do know of Benjamin, because of Mormon's abridgment of the Book of Mosiah, is invaluable. The recorded discourse of King Benjamin, for example, is one of the greatest sermons in the scriptures, and is a practical statement of religious conduct applicable to all times. It is The Book of Mormon equivalent to the Sermon on the Mount.

Verse 13 of the Words of Mormon suggests that the Lamanites had overrun the wicked Nephites who had stayed behind in the Land of Nephi. These Lamanites had come down out of that land to battle the Nephites in the Land of Zarahemla. At that time, the young and vigorous Benjamin fought "with the strength of his own arm" wielding the Sword of Laban that was kept by the Nephite kings throughout their history.

Fortunately, the battle plan and strategy of these Nephites under the leadership of King Benjamin was once again founded in the Lord. In His strength "they did contend against their enemies" until the Lamanites were driven from the "land of their inheritance," which was Zarahemla.

The construction of verses 15-18 suggests that Mormon, anxious because there was so little room left on the Small Plates of Nephi, hastily finished his record in an uncharacteristically awkward style. One cumbersome sentence of no less than 172 words makes up these three verses: "And it came to pass that after there had been false Christs, and their mouths had been shut, and they punished according to their crimes; And after there had been false prophets, and false preachers and teachers among the people, and all these having been punished according to their crimes; and after there having been much contention and many dissensions away unto the Lamanites, behold, it came to pass that king Benjamin, with the assistance of the holy prophets who were among his people - For behold, king Benjamin was a holy man, and he did reign over his people in righteousness; and there were many holy men in the land, and they did speak the word of God with power and with authority; and they did use much sharpness because of the stiffneckedness of the people - Wherefore, with the help of these, king Benjamin, by laboring with all the might of his body and the faculty of his whole soul, and also the prophets, did once more establish peace in the land." (V. 15-18).

These verses could probably be condensed down to the following 16-word sentence, without losing their meaning: "And it came to pass that ... king Benjamin ... did once more establish peace in the land." In effect, Mormon wanted to say that after the Nephites in Zarahemla had dealt with false Christs, prophets, and teachers, and after desertions and defections to the Lamanites by those weak in testimony, with the help of holy men, Benjamin was able to establish peace in the land.

Mormon was an amazing individual who could see beyond the terrible suffering caused by the apostasy of his own people, and who could differentiate behavior from the intrinsic nature of both the Nephites and the Lamanites. He truly believed that his people were "numbered among the people of the first covenant," meaning the magnificent Abrahamic Covenant, that had first been made between the Father of the Faithful and God Himself. (Mormon 7:10). To the very last, perhaps just hours before he was slain by the Lamanites, Mormon wrote: "If it so be that ye believe in Christ, and are baptized, first with water, then with fire and with the Holy Ghost, following the example of our Savior, according to that which he hath commanded us, it shall be well with you in the day of judgment. Amen." (Mormon 7:10).

Mormon's perception was clear and accurate. He could see the autobiographical thread of his people leading backward to Deity, and understood that even the most hardened soul has, within himself, "the acorn of a potential oak, the unsculptured image of a glorified personality." (Truman Madsen, "Eternal Man." p. 17).

"It is a serious thing to live in a society of possible Gods and Goddesses," wrote C.S. Lewis, "to remember that the dullest and most uninteresting person you talk to may one day be a creature which if you saw it now, you would be strongly tempted to worship ... There are no ordinary people. You have never talked to a mere mortal. It is immortals with whom we joke and work, and whom we marry, snub and exploit. Our charity must be a real and costly love ... Next to the blessed sacrament itself, your neighbor is the holiest object presented to your senses. If he is your Christian neighbor, he is holy in almost the same way, for in him also Christ is truly hidden and glorified."

Perhaps this is the hidden meaning in the scripture that enjoins us to "love the Lord thy God with all thy heart, and with all thy soul, and with all thy mind, and with all thy strength. This is the first commandment. And the second is like, namely this, Thou shalt love thy neighbour as thyself. There is none other commandment greater than these." (Mark 12:30-31). Mormon had a great capacity to love his people. The essence of his message on faith, hope, and charity for all is reflected in these lines penned by Edwin Markham: "He drew a circle that shut me out, Heretic, rebel, a thing to flout. But Love and I had the will to win. We drew a circle that took him in."

Mormon felt genuine love for both the Nephites and the Lamanites, in the same sense as the Savior, Who, on the Cross, besought His Father, and prayed: "Father, forgive them; for they know not what they do." (Luke 23:34). He surely would have agreed with the following sentiment, articulated on a smaller scale, but nonetheless relevant: "Wouldn't it be nice if, as we tuck our children into bed after particularly stressful days, we could say something like this. 'I've been watching you, and you are about the most special human being I've ever met. I'm proud to wear your name. I know we had a disagreement today, but that was behavior. It's the person I love. It's behavior I got bothered with, but not you. I love you unconditionally, not based on achievement, but based on you, and your potential. I love you very much.'. (Anonymous). This is charity, the pure love of Christ, and the quality that Mormon personified throughout his writings. The thoughtful student will find its expression throughout Mormon's abridgment of the Large Plates of Nephi, that follows the transitional Words of Mormon, in The Book of Mormon.

Certainly, heaven must be filled with music. As Helen Keller wrote: "I believe that my home there will be beautiful with colour, music, and speech of flowers and faces I love." When all is said and done, and we are reunited at a joyous family reunion, the atmosphere there will be filled with a musical language that enjoys universal expression, recognition, understanding, and appreciation.

Work and Personal Responsibility

"To bring about his eternal
purposes ... the Lord God gave unto
man that he should act for himself."
(2 Nephi 2:15-16).

Our first parents were commanded to work: "In the sweat of thy face," promised God, "shalt thou eat bread." (Genesis 3:19). Israel was likewise charged: "Six days shalt thou labour." (Exodus 20:9). At the time of Christ's mortal ministry, the church received a similar injunction: "If any provide not for his own, and specially for those of his own house, he hath denied the faith." (1 Timothy 5:8). The Latter-day Saints have a long history and tradition of labor: "Work is to be re-enthroned as the ruling principle in the lives of our church membership," declared Heber J. Grant, in the midst of the Great Depression. (C.R., 10/1936).

If we are not hard at work, life can be disastrous. Even if we are on the right road, we're going to get run over if we just sit there. Coming together can be a beginning, and keeping together is progress. But working together is success. "Keep your dish right side up," counseled Brigham Young, "so that when the shower of porridge does come, you can catch your dish full." (D.B.Y. p. 310).

Work is central to the successful implementation of the Plan of Salvation, so much so that we are warned: "The idler shall not have place in the church, except he repent and mend his ways." (D&C 75:29). "He that is idle shall not eat the bread nor wear the garments of the laborer." (D&C 42:42). Honest work is engrained in our nature, and we can even put our spare moments to good use, recognizing them as the gold dust of time.

Idleness can be devastating, because it leads to an erosion of the work ethic and feeds the monster within. Those who waste their time putting forth minimal effort or chasing petty pursuits cannot see that it is not that they have set their goals too high, and have failed to reach them after all they could have done. It is, rather, that they have set them too low, and have reached them far too easily, without the expenditure of honest effort. Homogenizing expectations by lowering the bar doesn't make it easier to make forward progress, it just increases the odds of tripping and falling flat on our faces. An agenda that demeans the value of work corrodes our ability to distinguish between the "cheap thrills" that are so tantalizing and tempting, and the "lofty goals" represented by the work-ethic that is an integral part of God's Plan.

"Aha! Here we have someone paying for the sin of idleness," said Pogo the cartoon philosopher. "The hobnailed boots of indiscretion's marathon dancer tap a rowdy two-step across the terracotta of your consciousness. Reason was cast into the rumble seat of your libidinous juggernaut. Now the piper must be paid!"

"Clean money is pay received for a full day's honest work, reasonable pay for faithful service, fair profit from the sale of goods, commodities, or service, and income received from transactions where all parties profit. Filthy lucre is money obtained through theft and robbery, gambling, sinful operations, bribery, and from exploitation." (Spencer W. Kimball, C.R., 10/1953).

The only man who ever got all his work done by Friday was Robinson Crusoe. The ability to work is a blessing from God. Those who have put their shoulder to the wheel realize that the dictionary is the only place where success comes before work. "I want to bear you my testimony that if you develop the habit of work, " said Ernest L Wilkinson, "it will be the most invigorating, satisfying, even relaxing and greatest blessing of your life. The opportunity to work is God's greatest blessing to mankind, and this means six days of each week." "Let us realize that the privilege to work is a gift, that the power to work is a blessing, and that the love of work is success." (David O. McKay).

If we cannot work to support ourselves, we should first turn to our families for temporal assistance, and then to the church, if necessary, remembering that its Welfare System is designed to sustain life, and not lifestyle. It is designed to get us back on our feet. One of its missions is to empower those with employment challenges. Welfare is at its best when it is the conduit through which its recipients receive the endowment of satisfaction and enjoyment in personal achievement and progress.

Welfare is tied to the Law of Inertia. The best programs are designed to get people moving so that they may maintain forward momentum. In the process, work well done is almost always accompanied by new opportunities to work even harder. In contrast, programs that are designed to help us to glide smoothly and effortlessly through life contribute to our downfall. The blessing of concentrated and sustained effort is that we move to higher planes of achievement. Positive reinforcement ingrains the virtues that accompany the work ethic, and we realize that nothing is really hard labor unless we would rather be doing something else. We move from complete oblivion to knowing how, and then to knowing why, and this can make all the difference. Teach a man to fish, and you have fed him for a lifetime.

We need to prepare ourselves before traveling the road to success, because once we've started the journey, it's almost always going to be uphill. In the process, we should "make no small plans, for they have no magic to stir (our) souls." (Spencer W. Kimball). Providentially, the Lord has provided us with all the elements to create Zion both on earth and in heaven. All we have to do is to get to work and organize these elements into their proper frame and order.

Work without vision is drudgery, while vision without work is dreamery. But work with vision is destiny. The story is told of two men who were resting by the side of the railroad tracks. They had been pounding spikes for a new line, when a train came into view, and slowed down as it passed the work site. As it went by, the President of the line leaned out the window of his personal rail car, waved, and called out. "Hello Jake!." "Hi Paul," Jake responded. As the train disappeared from view, the other worker asked, "Jake. I didn't know you were on a first name basis with the President of the railroad." Jake, replied, "Yes. Twenty-five years ago, we both got our first jobs working for the Union Pacific. At that time, he went to work for the railroad, and I went to work for $1.25 an hour."

We cannot lengthen our stride while sitting down. When President Kimball urged us to new levels of achievement, he knew that our spirituality would be intensified. Christ urged the man in bondage to go the second mile, to double his stride. "The second mile is a gift of spiritual independence that removes the veil of insensitivity to our destiny." (Richard L. Gunn, "Sensitivity and Spirit," p. 197).

Work can prepare us for that destiny. "I will prepare myself, and someday my chance will come," said Abraham Lincoln. He knew that perspiration must precede inspiration, and that "there must be effort before there is excellence." (Spencer W. Kimball).

"Men are that they might have joy," declared Lehi. (2 Nephi 2:25). Work is a key element in that equation, and there is a causal relationship between work and rest. All work and no play makes Jack a dull boy. "Six days is more time than we need to labor," declared Brigham Young. "One third to one fourth of (our) time that is spent to procure a living would be sufficient, if your labor were rightly directed." (D.B.Y. p. 311).

While we are at work, we would do well to remember that to possess the world's goods is not wealth, and is not the real objective of work as it was envisioned by the Plan. "The race," after all, "is not to the swift, nor the battle to the strong, neither riches to men of wisdom." (Ecclesiastes 9:11). One measure of our wealth, the fruits of our labors, is found in our ability to produce conveniences and comforts from the elements. "All the power and dignity that wealth can bestow is a mere shadow, the substance is found in the bone and sinew of the toiling millions. Well-directed labor is the true power that supplies our wants. It gives regal grandeur to potentates, education and supplies to religions and political ministers, and provides the wants of the thousands of millions of earth's sons and daughters." (Brigham Young, D.B.Y. p. 308-309).

But another, far more important measure of wealth is the satisfaction we receive from our efforts to secure for ourselves and our loved ones the blessings of heaven. Our wealth need only be enough to allow us to enjoy health, strength, and power in sufficient quantities that we might be able to share it with others. Do we count among our most prized possessions an endowment of the Spirit? Has our work led us to the Holy Ghost? Is He our constant companion? Does our moral compass point us toward righteousness and truth, are the fruits of our obedience an everlasting dominion, and without compulsory means are the blessings of heaven showered down upon us?

When we are
fully committed,
revelation will bless us
with repetitive moments of
confirmation as we read The
Book of Mormon, when we can
say that through its miracle, our
hearts have been changed by faith
on the name of Jesus Christ, and
and we've been born again.

Worship In Music

"If ye have felt
to sing the song of
redeeming love, I would
ask, can ye feel so now?"
(Alma 5:26).

The purpose of music is to invite the Spirit, to inspire, to motivate, to comfort, to strengthen, and to calm our souls. Music and worship are really inseparably interrelated. Because music is part of a unified whole, the instruments utilized, the way they are played, the volume and tempo, the lyrics if a vocal, the accompaniment, the attire and attitude of musicians, and the atmosphere in which the music is presented significantly influence the message conveyed and the impact on the listener.

Our efforts to touch the face of God are facilitated by the medium of music. Even before the foundations of the earth were laid, there was music when "the morning stars sang together, and all the sons of God shouted for joy." (Job 38:7). 1 Chronicles 16:42 speaks of "trumpets and cymbals ... and musical instruments of God." The Psalms were often accompanied by "the musical instruments of David the man of God." (Nehemiah 12:36). The birth of the Savior was accompanied by music. You can almost hear the melodic strains: "And suddenly there was with the angel a multitude of the heavenly host praising God, and saying Glory to God in the highest, and on earth peace, good will toward men." (Luke 2:13-14). Even in the midst of the Dark Ages, in the 9th and 10th Centuries, medieval monasteries in the Frankish lands of western and central Europe organized, codified, and notated Gregorian chants, and at the beginning of the Renaissance, madrigals set secular texts to music. Unfortunately, that period of time between the fall of Rome and feudalism in the 12th century, before the full flowering of the Renaissance, was largely devoid of music in the traditional sense, with the possible exception of the aforementioned chants and that of troubadours. This underscores the delicate relationship between harmonic music and the Spirit. Boyd K. Packer once said of President Harold Be Lee: "In his 32 years as a General Authority he had learned that the most inspired preaching is always accompanied by beautiful music." ("Ensign," 1/1974).

Between the 12th and the 17th Centuries, minstrels in Western Europe wandered the land entertaining with music that later developed into more formal orchestrations. Gothic cathedrals were designed to accommodate choral singing that in the modern age finds expression in music that inspires millions. On the radio since July 15, 1929, the Mormon Tabernacle Choir is the longest-running broadcast in the world. It helps us to remember the ancient admonition to "sing unto the Lord, all the earth." (1 Chronicles 16:23). We "make a joyful noise...and rejoice, and sing praise." (Psalms 98:4).

In the dark recesses of memory, we "make sweet melody, (and) sing many songs, that (we may) be remembered." (Isaiah 23:16). We follow the example of the Apostle Paul, who wrote: "I will pray with the spirit, and I will pray with... understanding also; I will sing with the spirit, and I will sing with ... understanding also." (1 Corinthians 14:15). The heavens, the earth, and all that are in them join in harmonious strains. Isaiah urged: "Sing, O heavens; and be joyful, O earth; and break forth into singing, O mountains. (Isaiah 49:13)

Joseph Smith encouraged his brethren, exhorting them: "Shall we not go on in so great a cause? Go forward and not backward. Courage, brethren; and on, on to the victory! Let your hearts rejoice, and be exceedingly glad. Let the earth break forth into singing." (D&C 128:22). "Let the sun, moon, and the morning stars sing together, and let all the sons of God shout for joy!" (D&C 128:23).

Lehi "saw the heavens open, and he thought he saw God sitting upon his throne, surrounded with numberless concourses of angels in the attitude of singing and praising their God." (1 Nephi 1:8). King Benjamin longed for his "immortal spirit (to) join the choirs above in singing the praises of a just God." (Mosiah 2:28). In metaphor, Alma expressed our relationship with God. He talked about singing the song of redeeming love. (Alma 5:26). Mormon looked forward to the time when he could "dwell in the presence of God in his kingdom, to sing ceaseless praises with the choirs above, unto the Father, and unto the Son, and unto the Holy Ghost." (Mormon 7:7).

However, there needs to be opposition to fulfil the Plan of the Father, and so wholesome music must have its contrasting genre. No one knows why Satan waited for the electronic age to launch a broadside counterattack against sweet melodies that have for so long strengthened the faith of millions. But clearly, he is now using music in his own twisted way to suit evil purposes. In little more than a generation, he has secularized the sacred. He has suggested that music is somehow enhanced when it is accompanied by indulgence in mind-altering drugs or alcohol. But Acid Rock can be as destructive to the soul as hydrochloric acid can be to the skin. It is delusional and ultimately self-destructive to think that music does not influence our primal instincts. If music does not elevate us to higher planes with melodious strains, it may drag us down under the weight of heavy metal into a cesspool of depravity. Satan also adorns music with scantily clad purveyors of porn and a darkened environment well suited to cloak his evil purposes. His fingerprints come into focus, however, in the glare of stage, strobe, and neon lights.

Lyrics set to music may have a profound influence on the listener, especially when subliminal messages are repetitively drummed into the subconscious. Like the siren song of Greek antiquity, men go mad when they hear the tempting strains. He has many pen names, but it is chilling to discover the true identity of the author of many of the lyrics we hear today. He is a master deceiver, and knows that "this is the one song everyone would like to learn; the song that is irresistible; the song that forces men to leap overboard in squadrons; the song nobody knows because anyone who has heard it is dead." (Margaret Atwood, "Siren Song," 1976).

Of course, the Siren Song refers to "the nymphs who had the power of charming by their song all who heard them, so that mariners were impelled to cast themselves into the sea to destruction. Circe directed Ulysses to stop the ears of his seamen with wax, so that they should not hear the strain; to have himself bound to the mast, and to enjoin his people, whatever he might say or do, by no means to release him till they should have passed the Sirens' island. Ulysses obeyed these directions. As they approached the Sirens' island, the sea was calm, and over the waters came notes of music so ravishing and attractive that Ulysses struggled to get loose and, by cries and signs to his people, begged to be released; but they, obedient to his previous orders, sprang forward and bound him still faster. They held on to their course, and the music grew fainter till it ceased to be heard, when with joy Ulysses gave his companions the signal to unseal their ears; and they relieved him from his bonds." (Homer, "Ulysses").

More subtle influences may compromise the high standard set by faith-promoting music. We live in a vulgar and profane world that is demeaning to the character of those who would call themselves Saints. John Taylor once declared of our own church services: "I think it altogether out of place on such occasions to hear people talk about secular things." (J.D. 22:226). In too many ways, he was saying, we secularize sacred things, and trivialize the celestial. We demean it with careless words or thoughtless musical expressions. .

There are at least 38 different ways the hymns of the church guard against "trivializing the celestial." Each selection in the hymn book is accompanied by a suggestion regarding the emotions with which it should be sung. Each sentiment ennobles the selection with an inspiring quality that invites the spirit in a particular way. These include singing:

Boldly. We sing with boldness when we are confident. The book of Acts records that when the apostles "had prayed, the place was shaken where they were assembled together; and they were all filled with the Holy Ghost, and they spake the word of God with boldness." (Acts 4:31).

Brightly. We sing brightly when we are animated. Isaiah prophesied that the day would come when the Gentiles would come to the Light of Christ and the leaders of government to the brightness of his rising. (Isaiah 60:3).

Calmly. We sing with calmness when we are sure of ourselves. Of the Savior, the Psalmist wrote: "He maketh the storm a calm, so that the waves thereof are still." (Psalms 107:29).

Cheerfully. We sing cheerfully when we do not allow circumstances to dictate our emotions, and when we are at peace even though we are surrounded by turmoil. The Savior instructed His disciples, explaining: "In the world ye shall have tribulation: but be of good cheer; I have overcome the world." (John 16:33).

Confidently. We sing confidently when we have a positive self-image. In "Fiddler on The Roof," wise old Tevya told his daughters: "In Anatevka, God knows who you are, and what he expects you to become." (Joseph Stein). As Proverbs teaches: "The Lord shall be thy confidence." (Proverbs 3:26).

With Contemplation. We pause in our busy lives to ponder the solemnities of eternity, and to "contemplate the word of the Lord." (D&C 124:23).

With Conviction. We sing with conviction when we are sure our course is right. Sometimes we are "convicted by (our) own conscience." (John 8:9). When this happens, we are resolute and sure of our direction as our faith leads us to purposeful repentance, forgiveness, and greater heights of achievement.

With Devotion. We sing with devotion when we have consecrated our hearts, might, mind, and strength to the Lord. All He requires is this: "Thou shalt devote all thy service in Zion; and in this thou shalt have strength." (D&C 24:7).

With Dignity. We sing with dignity because we know we are the children of God. Genesis speaks of "the excellency of dignity." (Genesis 49:3).

Earnestly. We are blessed with the power to be true to our covenants, remembering that the Lord has enjoined us: "Seek ye earnestly the best gifts." (D&C 46:8).

With Emotion. We are overcome with emotion as we realize that God is "ready to pardon, gracious and merciful, slow to anger, and of great kindness." (Nehemiah 9:17).

Energetically. When we are anxious to be about our Father's business, we channel and focus our energy on the tasks at hand. As Alma exhorted his son, so are we encouraged: "Turn to the Lord with all your mind, might, and strength." (Alma 39:13).

With Energy. When we are quickened by the Spirit and when the Spirit gives us voice, we are as Nephi, who exhorted his brethren "with all the energies of (his) soul, and with all the faculty which (he) possessed." (1 Nephi 15:25).

Enthusiastically. We are caught up in eternal burnings when God shows us "His glory and his greatness, and we have heard his voice out of the midst of the fire." . (Deuteronomy 5:24).

Expressively. We sing with expression when we are finely attuned to the whisperings of the Spirit, and respond appropriately. The Savior Himself was the personification of harmony with His Father, "and the express image of his person," when He "sat down on the right hand of the Majesty on high" as a resurrected and perfected being. (Hebrews 1:3).

Exultantly. When we are carried away with the conviction that the Savior will overcome the world we "rejoice and exult in the hope, and even know, according to the promises of the Lord, that (we) are raised to dwell at the right hand of God, in a state of never-ending happiness." (Alma 28:12).

Fervently. When we are zealous in our discipleship, we are as the Apostles of old, who taught a man who "was instructed in the way of the Lord; and being fervent in the spirit, he spake and taught diligently the things of the Lord." (Acts 18:25).

Firmly. When we are quietly confident that we are on a course leading back to our Heavenly Father, we are as the Sons of Helaman, of whom it was written: "Their minds are firm, and they do put their trust in God continually." (Alma 57:27).

Gently. When we are hesitant to disrupt the sweetness of the spirit that we feel, we are as the Psalmist who exclaimed: "Thou hast also given me the shield of thy salvation: and thy right hand hath holden me up, and thy gentleness hath made me great." (Psalms 18:35).

Humbly. We sing with humility when the melody breaks our hearts with contrition. "If my people, which are called by my name, shall humble themselves, and pray, and seek my face, and turn from their wicked ways;" said the Lord, "then will I hear from heaven, and will forgive their sin, and will heal their land." (2 Chronicles 7:14).

Joyfully. When the desire to praise God from the rooftops is unrestrained, we "make a joyful noise unto the Lord," and we "make a loud noise, and rejoice, and sing praise." (Psalms 98:4).

Jubilantly. We sing jubilantly when it dawns upon us that as many as call upon God will be saved by His grace. We are as the Israelites who were instructed: "Then shall ye cause the trumpet of the jubilee to sound...throughout all your land. And ye shall ... proclaim liberty throughout all the land unto all the inhabitants thereof." (Leviticus 25:9-10).

Lightly. The Lord will carry our burdens for us, and "our light affliction, which is but for a moment, worketh for us a far more exceeding and eternal weight of glory." (2 Corinthians 4:17).

Majestically. When we realize that we are sons and daughters of a noble birthright, all else snaps into sharp focus. The Psalmist had this clarity of vision: "All thy works shall praise thee," he wrote, "and thy saints shall bless thee.

They shall speak of the glory of thy kingdom, and talk of thy power; To make known to the sons of men his mighty acts, and the glorious majesty of his kingdom." (Psalms 145:10-12).

Meekly. Our tender feelings reflect the nature of God. Paul spoke of "the meekness and gentleness of Christ." (2 Corinthians 10:1). The Savior Himself said: "Take my yoke upon you, and learn of me; for I am meek and lowly in heart: and ye shall find rest unto your souls." (Matthew 11:29).

Peacefully. As we retreat into the sanctuary of music we find refuge from the cares of the world. When we "publish peace," these "tidings of good … declare unto the people that the Lord reigneth." (Mosiah 27:37).

Prayerfully. Melodious refrains find their way into heaven to reach God's listening ear. "The song of the righteous," He said, "is a prayer unto me." (D&C 25:12).

Reflectively. Our hymns are clothed with unprecedented power as we contemplate our place in the grand scheme, "reflecting upon the great atoning sacrifice that was made by the Son of God, for the redemption of the world." (D&C 138:2).

Resolutely. We share the resolution of the Prophet Joseph to serve God in every circumstance. He declared to his brethren: "I receive you to fellowship, in a determination that is fixed, immovable, and unchangeable, to be your friend and brother through the grace of God in the bonds of love, to walk in all the commandments of God blameless, in thanksgiving, forever and ever." (D&C 88:133).

Smoothly. We sing smoothly when it dawns on us that no wind can blow except to fill our sails, when we are borne up "as on eagles' wings." (D&C 124:18). There are no bumps in our road when we sing about gospel principles. Our music is seamlessly integrated with principled behavior and quietly validates our commitment. As we run life's race, there are no false starts and no dropping of the baton as it is passed on. Symmetry gives us the quiet confidence to endure to the end in righteousness.

Solemnly. Whenever we approach God we are treading on sacred ground. Of the saving principles of the gospel, the Savior told the Saints: "Treasure these things up in your hearts, and let the solemnities of eternity rest upon your minds." (D&C 43:34).

With Spirit. We sing with spirit when we realize that Christ is the way, the truth, the life, and the light, and that without Him, the world would be dreary, tedious, and monotonous. "The Spirit of God burns like a fire within our bosom even as "the latter-day glory begins to come forth. The visions and blessings of old are returning, and angels are coming to visit the earth." (William W. Phelps, Hymn #2, "The Spirit of God").

Tenderly. When we think of the sacrifice of the Savior that was motivated by His love for us, we plead, as did the Psalmist: "Withhold not thou thy tender mercies from me, O Lord; let thy loving kindness and thy truth continually preserve me." (Psalms 40:11).

Thankfully. Every time we remember that He gives us voice, we are as the Israelites of old who "sang together by course in praising and giving thanks unto the Lord because he is good." (Ezra 3:11). David exhorted his people: "Rejoice in the Lord, ye righteous; and give thanks at the remembrance of his holiness." (Psalms 97:12).

Thoughtfully. As "weary travelers (we) find health and safety while (we) contemplate the word of the Lord." (D&C

1245:23). The Lord Himself established Nauvoo House as "a delightful habitation for man, and a resting-place for the weary traveler, that he may contemplate the glory of Zion." (D&C 124:60).

Triumphantly. We recall our sustained efforts, confident that we have fought a good fight, run our race, and have done our best. We remember Moroni's farewell: "I soon go to rest in the paradise of God, until my spirit and body shall again reunite, and I am brought forth triumphant through the air, to meet you before the pleasing bar of the great Jehovah, the Eternal Judge both quick and dead." (Moroni 10:34).

Vigorously. When we realize that the Spirit quickens all life, we are energized to be up and about our Father's business. After Mormon had exhorted his brethren, he was pleased to report that his "words did arouse them somewhat to vigor." (Mormon 2:24).

Worshipfully. When we are truly aware of our surroundings, we realize that we stand in holy places. On Sinai, Moses was told: "Put off thy shoes from off thy feet, for the place whereon thou standest is holy ground." (Exodus 3:5). The Wise Men of the East were inspired to inquire of Herod: "Where is he that is born King of the Jews? For we have seen his star in the east, and are come to worship him." (Matthew 2:2). Our houses of worship provide the opportunity to "stand in holy places, and be not moved." (D&C 45:32).

Heavenly Father and Jesus Christ love music. The Savior revealed how music touched Him, when He said: "My soul delighteth in the song of the heart." (D&C 25:12). Perhaps the inherent power of music is that it permits us to focus on our mutual bonds of experience. The song of the righteous is a prayer because it reaches right in and tugs at our heartstrings, activating resounding harmonies that stir the heavens. It is only natural that such tones should be answered "with a blessing upon (our) heads." (D&C 25:12). Certainly, heaven is filled with music. As Helen Keller wrote: "I believe that my home there will be beautiful with colour, music, and speech of flowers and faces I love." (Midstream). When all is said and done, and we are reunited at a wonderful family reunion, the atmosphere there will be filled with a musical language that enjoys universal expression, recognition, understanding, and appreciation.

Writing on Metal Plates Was a Pain

The prophets in The Book of Mormon recorded how difficult it was to engrave their thoughts upon plates of metal. "We could write but little, because of the awkwardness of our hands .... wherefore, when we write, we behold our weakness, and stumble because of the placing of our words; and I fear lest the Gentiles shall mock at our words." (Ether 12:24-25). "I cannot write but a little of my words, because of the difficulty of engraving our words upon plates." (Jacob 4:1). "And if there be faults, they be the faults of a man." (Mormon 8:17).

Many passages in The Book of Mormon illustrate the difficulty of writing upon plates, and of correcting that which had already been engraven. Mormon for example, realizing that he had not written exactly what he had intended to in his abridged record, added many such clarifications.

It is obvious that the Nephites struggled with the process of engraving on the plates that contained the sacred record. Even in the best of times, the process was tedious. Nephi wrote that he could record "but a few things," and so the prophecies contained in the last eight chapters of 2 Nephi span a time of approximately 14 years. (2 Nephi 31:1). Still, as Nephi had explained earlier in his record: "It mattereth not to me that I am particular to give a full account of all the things of my father, for they cannot be written upon these plates, for I desire the room that I may write of the things of God." (1 Nephi 6:3). In consequence of his recent separation from his Lamanite brethren, it is likely that Nephi was in straitened circumstances that made it difficult to engrave upon the plates. Even in the best of times, the process would have been frustrating for the record keepers.

Jacob recorded: "I cannot write but a little of my words, because of the difficulty of engraving our words upon plates." (Jacob 4:1). A thousand years later, Moroni apologetically recorded. "We could write but little, because of the awkwardness of our hands ... Wherefore, when we write we behold our weakness, and stumble because of the placing of our words; and I fear lest the Gentiles shall mock at our words." (Ether 12:24-25).

Mormon acknowledged his inability to communicate in writing as fluidly as he would have liked, saying in the sacred record: "And if there be faults, they be the faults of a man." (Mormon 8:17). He also composed the Title Page of

The Book of Mormon and there reiterated: "If there are faults they are the mistakes of men; wherefore, condemn not the things of God." How The Book of Mormon is received by the learned and in literary circles, however, is of no concern to the Lord, for "Fools mock, but they shall mourn." Ether 12:26).

Listed below are six dozen (72) passages that illustrate the reality that there were no erasers available to the record-keepers. These and many others give the reader subtle insight into the frailties of The Book of Mormon prophets, throw open the windows to shed sunlight on their humanity, are powerful witnesses to the validity of the record, and address Joseph Smith's testimony that The Book of Mormon was translated by the gift and power of God.

"This is according to the account of Nephi; or in other words, I, Nephi, wrote this record." (1 Nephi Introduction).

"And it came to pass that while my father tarried in the wilderness, he spake unto us, saying: Behold, I have dreamed a dream, or, in other words, I have seen a vision." (1 Nephi 8:2).

"And it came to pass that I beheld that the rod of iron, which my father had seen, was the word of God, which led to the fountain of living waters, or to the tree of life, which waters are a representation of the love of God; and I also beheld that the tree of life was a representation of the love of God." (1 Nephi 11:25).

"Yea, even six hundred years from the time that my father left Jerusalem, a prophet would the Lord God raise up among the Jews – even a messiah, or, in other words, a Savior of the world." (1 Nephi 10:4).

"And that great pit which hath been digged for them by that great and abominable church, which was founded by the devil and his children, that he might lead away the souls of men down to hell – yea that great pit which hath been digged for the destruction of men, shall be filled by those who digged it, unto their utter destruction, saith the Lamb of God; not the destruction of the soul, save it be the casting of it into that hell which hath no end." (1 Nephi 14:3).

"They are written in the book which thou beheld proceeding out of the mouth of the Jew; and at the time they proceeded out of the moth of the Jew, or, at the time the book proceeded out of the mouth of the Jew, the things which were written were plain and pure, and most precious and easy to the understanding of all men." (1 Nephi 14:23).

"And I did rehearse unto them the words of Isaiah, who spake concerning the restoration of the Jews, or of the house of Israel; and after they were restored they should no more be confounded, neither should they be scattered again" (1 Nephi 15:20).

Nephi "did rehearse unto them the words of Isaiah, who spake concerning the restoration of the Jews, or of the house of Israel." (1 Nephi 15:20).

"I do not write anything upon plates save it be that I think it be sacred. And now, if I do err, even did they err of old; not that I would excuse myself because of other men, but because of the weakness which is in me, according to the flesh, I would excuse myself." (1 Nephi 19:6).

"The very God of Israel do men trample under their feet; I say, trample under their feet, but I would speak in other words – they set him at naught, and hearken not to the voice of his counsels." (1 Nephi 19:7).

"Hearken and hear this, O house of Jacob, who are called by the name of Israel, and are come forth out o the waters of Judah, or out of the waters of baptism, who swear by the name of the Lord, and make mention of the God of Israel, yet they swear not in truth nor in righteousness." (1 Nephi 20:1).

"For I know that ye have searched much, many of you, to know of the things to come; wherefore I know that ye know that ye know that our flesh must waste away and die; nevertheless, in our bodies we shall see God." (2 Nephi 9:4).

"I have charity for the Jew; I say Jew, because I mean them from whence I came." (2 Nephi 33:8).

"My beloved brethren, I will unfold this mystery unto you; if I do not by any means, get shaken from my firmness in the Spirit, and stumble because of my over anxiety for you." (Jacob 4:18).

"As in Adam, or by nature, (we) fall, even so the blood of Christ atoneth for (our) sins." (Mosiah 3:16).

"Salvation might come to him that should put his trust in the Lord, and should be diligent in keeping his commandments, and continue in the faith even unto the end of his life, I mean, the lift of the mortal body." (Mosiah 4:6).

"I say unto the poor, ye who have not and yet have sufficient that ye remain from day to day; I mean all you who deny the beggar, because ye have not." (Mosiah 4:24)

"We know of their surety and truth, because of the Spirit of the Lord Omnipotent, which has wrought a mighty change in us, or in our hearts, that we have no more disposition to do evil, but to do good continually." (Mosiah 5:2).

"He was desirous to know concerning the people who went up to dwell in the land of Lehi-Nephi, or in the city of Lehi-Nephi." (Mosiah 7:1).

"And they stood before the king, and were permitted, or rather commanded, that they should answer the questions which he should ask them." (Mosiah 7:8).

"And because he said unto them that Christ was the God, the Father of all things, and said that he should take upon him the image of man, and it should be the image after which man was created in the beginning; or in other words, he said that man was created after the image of God, and that God should come down among the children of men, and take upon him flesh and blood, and go forth upon the face of the earth." (Mosiah 7:27).

"And it came to pass when they had been in prison two days they were again brought before the king, and their bands were loosed; and they stood before the king, and were permitted, or rather commanded, that they should answer the questions which he should ask them." (Mosiah 8:7).

"But a seer can know of things which are past, and also, of things which are to come, and by them shall all things be revealed, or rather, shall secret things be made manifest, and hidden things shall come to light, and things which are not known shall be made known by them, and also, things shall be made know by them which otherwise could not be known." (Mosiah 8:17).

"For these are they whose sins he has borne; these are they for whom he has died, to redeem them from their transgressions. And now, are they not his seed? Yea, and are not the prophets, every one that has opened his mouth to prophesy, that has not fallen into transgression, I mean all the holy prophets ever since the world began? I say unto you that they are his seed." (Mosiah 15:12-13).

"The resurrection of all the prophets, and all those that have believed in their words, or all those that have kept the commandments of God, shall come forth in the first resurrection." (Mosiah 15:22).

"They carried him upon the top of the hill Manti, and there he was caused, or rather did acknowledge, between the heavens and the earth, that what he had taught to the people was contrary to the word of God." (Alma 1:15)

"And thus he cleared the ground, or rather the bank, which was on the west of the river Sidon." (Alma 2:34)

"And this he did that he himself might go forth among his people, or among the people of Nephi." (Alma 4:19)

"Whosoever did belong to the church that did not repent of their wickedness and humble themselves before God - I mean those who were lifted up in the pride of their hearts—the same were rejected, and their names were blotted out." (Alma 6:3).

"He cannot walk in crooked paths; neither doth he vary from that which he hath said; neither hath he a shadow of turning from the right to the left, or from that which is right to that which is wrong." (Alma 7:20).

"I never have known much of the ways of the Lord, and his mysteries and marvelous power. I said I never had known much of these things; but behold, I mistake, for I have seen much of his mysteries and his marvelous power; yea, even in the preservation of the lives of this people." (Alma 10:5)

"Now, when Amulek had finished these words the people began again to be astonished, and also Zeezrom began to tremble. And thus ended the words of Amulek, or this is all that I have written." (Alma 11:46)

"He opened his mouth and began to speak unto him, and to establish the words of Amulek, and to explain things beyond, or to unfold the scriptures beyond that which Amulek had done." (Alma 12:1).

"The Spirit constraineth me that I must not stretch forth mine hand; for behold the Lord receiveth them up unto himself, in glory; and he doth suffer that they may do this thing, or that the people may do this thing unto them, according to the hardness of their hearts, that the judgments which he shall exercise upon them in his wrath may be just; and the blood of the innocent shall stand as a witness against them, yea, and cry mightily against them at the last day." (Alma 14:11).

"And there was no inequality among them; the Lord did pour out his Spirit on all the face of the land to prepare the minds of the children of men, or to prepare their hearts to receive the word which should be taught among them at the time of his coming." (Alma 16:16)

"Now Ammon being the chief among them, or rather he did administer unto them, and he departed from them, after having blessed them according to their several stations, having imparted the word of God unto them, or administered unto them before his departure." (Alma 17:18).

"And as sure as the Lord liveth, so sure as many as believed, or as many as were brought to the knowledge of the truth, through the preaching of Ammon and his brethren, according to the spirit of revelation and of prophecy, and the power of God working miracles in them - yea, I say unto you, as the Lord liveth, as many of the Lamanites as believed in their preaching, and were converted unto the Lord, never did fall away. " (Alma 23:6).

"And thus we see that they buried their weapons of peace, or they buried their weapons of war, for peace." (Alma 24:19).

Note that Mormon does not again make the textual error committed in Alma 24:19: "And they did also bury their weapons of war." (Alma 25:14).

"And now behold, we have come, and been forth amongst them; and we have been patient in our sufferings, and we have suffered every privation; yea, we have traveled from house to house, relying upon the mercies of the world - not upon the mercies of the world alone but upon the mercies of God." (Alma 26:28).

Nor does he make the error in Alma 26:32, when he again uses the phrase: "They have buried their weapons of war." (Alma 26:32).

"God "granteth unto men according to their desire, whether it be unto death or unto life; yea, I know that he allotteth unto men, yea, decreeth unto them decrees which are unalterable, according to their wills, whether they be unto salvation or unto destruction." (Alma 29:4

"Now if a man desired to serve God, it was his privilege; or rather, if he believed in God it was his privilege to serve him." (Alma 30:9).

Therefore, blessed are they who humble themselves without being compelled to be humble; or rather, in other words, blessed is he that believeth in the word of God, and is baptized without stubbornness of heart." (Alma 32:16).

"And now, he imparteth his word by angels unto men, yea, not only men but women also. Now this is not all; little children do have words given unto them many times, which confound the wise and the learned." (Alma 32:23).

"Now, we will compare the word unto a seed. Now, if ye give place, that a seed may be planted in your heart, behold, if it be a true seed, or a good seed, if ye do not cast it out by your unbelief, that ye will resist the Spirit of the Lord, behold, it will begin to swell within your breasts; and when you feel these swelling motions, ye will begin to say within yourselves - it must needs be that this is a good seed, or that the word is good, for it beginneth to enlarge my soul; yea, it beginneth to enlighten my understanding, yea, it beginneth to be delicious to me." (Alma 32:28).

"Now Alma, being grieved for the iniquity of his people, yea for the wars, and the bloodsheds, and the contentions which were among them; and having been to declare the word, or sent to declare the word...his heart was exceedingly sorrowful." (Alma 35:15).

"Yea, I had murdered many of his children, or rather led them away unto destruction." (Alma 36:14).

"And now, my son, this was the ministry unto which ye were called, to declare these glad tidings unto this people, to prepare their minds; or rather that salvation might come unto them." (Alma 39:16).

"Behold, I say unto you, that there is no resurrection - or, I would say, in other words, that this mortal does not put on immortality, this corruption does not put on incorruption - until after the coming of Christ." (Alma 40:2).

"Now, whether the souls and the bodies of those of whom has been spoken shall all be reunited at once, the wicked as well as the righteous, I do not say; let it suffice, that I say that they all come forth; or in other words, their resurrection cometh to pass before the resurrection of those who die after the resurrection of Christ." (Alma 40:19).

"All men that are in a state of nature, or I would say, in a carnal state, are in the gall of bitterness and in the bonds of iniquity." (Alma 41:11)

"According to justice, the plan of redemption could not be brought about, only on conditions of repentance of men in this probationary state, yea, this preparatory state." (Alma 42:13).

"There was now and then a man fell among the Nephites, by their swords and the loss of blood, they being shielded from the more vital parts of the body, or the more vital parts of the body being shielded from the strokes of the Lamanites, by their breastplates, and their armshields, and their head-plates; and thus the Nephites did carry on the work of death among the Lamanites." (Alma 43:38)

Behold, this we know, that he was a righteous man; and the saying went abroad in the land that he was taken up by the Spirit, or buried by the hand of the Lord, even as Moses." (Alma 45:18-19).

"Those who did belong to the church were faithful; yea, all those who were true believers in Christ took upon them, gladly, the name of Christ, or Christians as they were called, because of their belief in Christ who should come." (Alma 46:15).

"And this was their faith, that by so doing God would prosper them in the land, or in other words, if they were faithful in keeping the commandments of God that he would prosper them in the land." (Alma 48:15).

"Now behold, the people who were in the land Bountiful, or rather Moroni, feared that they would hearken to the words of Morianton." (Alma 50:32).

"Thus was the division among them, for the freemen had sworn or covenanted to maintain their rights and the privileges of their religion by a free government." (Alma 51:6).

"And thus they did, and slew all those who had been left to protect the city, yea, all those who would not yield up their weapons of war." (Alma 52:25).

"Teancum, by the orders of Moroni, caused that they should commence laboring in digging a ditch round about the land, or the city, Bountiful." (Alma 53:3).

"And now behold, I have somewhat to say concerning the people of Ammon, who, in the beginning were Lamanites; but by Ammon and his brethren, or rather by the power and word of God, they had been converted unto the Lord." (Alma 53:10).

"Behold, Ammoron, I have written unto you somewhat concerning this war which ye have waged against my people, or rather which thy brother hath waged against them, and which ye are still determined to carry on after his death." (Alma 54:5).

"And now these are the cities of which the Lamanites have obtained possession by the shedding of the blood of so many of our valiant men; the land of Manti, or the city of Manti, and the city of Zeezrom." (Alma 56:13-14).

"And behold, in the end of this book ye shall see that this Gadianton did prove the overthrow, yea almost the entire destruction of the people of Nephi. Behold, I do not mean the end of the book of Helaman, but I mean the end of the book of Nephi, from which I have taken all the account which I have written." (Helaman 2:13-14).

"And in the fifty and first year of the reign of the judges there was peace also, save it were the pride which began to enter into the church - not the church of God, but into the hearts of the people who professed to belong to the church of God." (Helaman 3:33).

"Yield up unto this my people, your cities, your lands, and your possessions, rather than that they should visit you with the sword and that destruction should come upon you. Or in other words, yield yourselves up unto us, and unite with us and become acquainted with our secret works." (3 Nephi 3:6-7).

"The remnant of the seed, who shall be scattered forth upon the face of the earth because of their unbelief, may be brought in, or may be brought to a knowledge of me, their Redeemer." (3 Nephi 16:4).

"And now, behold, my joy is great, even unto fulness, because of you, and also this generation; yea, and even the Father rejoiceth, and also all the holy angels, because of you and this generation; for none of them are lost. Behold, I would that ye should understand; for I mean them who are now alive of this generation; and none of them are lost; and in them I have fulness of joy." (3 Nephi 27:30-31).

"And now behold, as I spake concerning those whom the Lord hath chosen, yea, even three who were caught up into the heavens, that I knew not whether they were cleansed from mortality to immortality – But behold, since I wrote, I have inquired of the Lord, and he hath made it manifest unto me that there must needs be a change wrought upon their bodies, or else it needs be that they must taste of death." (3 Nephi 28:36-37).

"Now there began to be a great curse upon all the land because of the iniquity of the people, in which, if a man should lay his tool or his sword upon his shelf, or upon the place whither he would keep it, behold, upon the morrow, he could not find it." (Ether 14:1).

There is another interesting insight into the awkwardness of working with metal plates. Mormon knew that his abridgment of the Book of Lehi, which ended when King Benjamin was an old man ready to die, would be lost by Sydney Rigdon during the translation process by Joseph Smith. Without it, Book of Mormon readers would not have had access to the account of his life. The Book of Omni, which is a part of the Small Plates of Nephi, deals with King Benjamin in only three of its verses, and what Mormon had written about him in the Book of Mosiah was confined to the last three years of the king's life. The Words of Mormon, tacked on to the end of the Small Plates, serve as a bridge between the Small Plates and Mormon's abridgment. Verses 15 - 18 flow as if Mormon, knowing that there was so little room left on the Small Plates of Nephi, hastily finished the record in uncharacteristically awkward style. Perhaps the straitened circumstances under which he labored also help to account for the fact that one sentence of 172 words makes up these four verses: "And it came to pass that after there had been false Christs, and their mouths had been shut, and they punished according to their crimes; And after there had been false prophets, and false preachers and teachers among the people, and all these having been punished according to their crimes; and after there having been much contention and many dissensions away unto the Lamanites, behold, it came to pass that king Benjamin, with the assistance of the holy prophets who were among his people—For behold, king Benjamin was a holy man, and he did reign over his people in righteousness; and there were many holy men in the land, and they did speak the word of God with power and with authority; and they did use much sharpness because of the stiffneckedness of the people - Wherefore, with the help of these, king Benjamin, by laboring with all the might of his body and the faculty of his whole soul, and also the prophets, did once more establish peace in the land." (Words of Mormon 1:15-18).

God knows us well, and He goes to great lengths to provide for our welfare, as we shoot the rapids of life. It is only the life jacket of revelation that can help us to keep our heads above water as we gasp for air in the turbulence of telestial torrents, as we grapple with the mystery of The Book of Mormon.

Zion

"Awake, and arise from the dust,
O Jerusalem; yea, and put on thy beautiful
garments, O daughters of Zion; and strengthen
thy stakes and enlarge thy borders forever, that thou
mayest no more be confounded, that the covenants
of the Eternal Father which he hath made unto
thee, O house of Israel, may be fulfilled."
(Moroni 10:31).

In the Last Days, said Isaiah, "more are the children of the desolate than the children of the married wife." (Isaiah 54:1). In other words, there shall be a great gathering of Israel from among the Gentile nations, and those who then enter the Fold shall outnumber those who had previously found their way into the church or who were bound by covenant to Christ. Consequently, the Lord commanded Joseph Smith on more than one occasion to "seek to bring forth and establish my Zion." (D&C 6:6, 11:6, 12:6, & 14:6).

To that end, Isaiah had urged: "Enlarge the place of thy tent, and let them stretch forth the curtains of thy habitations; spare not, lengthen thy cords and strengthen thy stakes." (Isaiah 54:2). That is to say, make room for the Children of the Covenant, who will flock to the gospel standard as the gathering of Israel gains momentum. The Lord reaffirmed in the Last Days that "Zion must increase in beauty, and in holiness; her borders must be enlarged; her stakes must be strengthened; yea, verily I say unto you, Zion must arise and put on her beautiful garments" that had been washed clean in the redeeming blood of Christ. (D&C 82:14). Later, He told Joseph Smith that the Saints should remain in Zion "until the day cometh when there is found no more room for them; and then I have other places which I will appoint unto them, and they shall be called stakes, for the curtains or the strength of Zion." (D&C 101:21).

The building of Zion and the establishment of the City of New Jerusalem has been a subject of great interest to members of the church during the years since its organization. But in 1831, the question on the minds of the Saints was: "Where is the city to be located?" The Lord had explained to Joseph Smith in September 1830 only that "no man knoweth where the city of Zion shall be built, but it shall be given hereafter. Behold, I say unto you that it shall be on the borders by the Lamanites." (D&C 28:9).

"Following instructions given in D&C 52 that was recorded on June 7, 1831, Joseph and several elders journeyed to Missouri, preaching as they went. On July 21 of that year, he received D&C 57, in which the Lord explained that Zion would be built in Independence, Jackson County, Missouri." (D&C Class Member Study Guide, p. 11).

This revelation was received in Zion, which is now a suburb of Kansas City, Missouri. "In contemplating the state of the Lamanites and the lack of civilization, refinement, and religion among the people generally, the Prophet (had) exclaimed in yearning prayer: 'When will the wilderness blossom as the rose?'" (Superscript). Four months earlier, he had learned that "before the great day of the Lord shall come, Jacob shall flourish in the wilderness, and the Lamanites shall blossom as the rose." (D&C 49:24). Through his biblical scholarship, he was familiar with the scripture that declared: "The wilderness and the solitary place shall be glad for (Latter Day Israel); and the desert shall rejoice, and blossom as the rose." (Isaiah 35:1).

Four months later, in November 1831, the Lord would reveal: "In the barren deserts there shall come forth pools of living water; and the parched ground shall no longer be a thirsty land." (D&C 133:29). In 1838, at Far West, Missouri, the Lord would promise Joseph: "Therefore, will I not make solitary places to bud and to blossom, and to bring forth in abundance?" (D&C 117:7). He would prosper His people, and Israel would "blossom and bud, and fill the face of the world with the blessings of salvation" through the administration of the Abrahamic Covenant. (Isaiah 27:6).

"When will Zion be built up in her glory?" the Prophet had asked. (Superscript). The Lord told Joseph only that "Zion shall flourish upon the hills and rejoice upon the mountains, and shall be assembled together unto the place which I have appointed." (D&C 49:25). Long ago, the Psalmist asked the same enduring question: "Who shall ascend into the hill of the Lord? Or who shall stand in his holy place?" The self-evident answer: "He that hath clean hands, and a pure heart; who hath not lifted up his soul unto vanity, nor sworn deceitfully. He shall receive the blessing from the Lord, and righteousness from the God of his salvation." (Psalms 24:3-5). Covenant Israel "shall flourish like the palm tree: he shall grow like a cedar in Lebanon. Those that be planted in the house of the Lord shall flourish in the courts of our God." (Psalms 92:12-13). Palms often thrive in what appear to be desert wastes. It is only on closer inspection that oases of underlying currents of life sustaining water are noticed, that bring nourishment to the roots of the thirsty trees.

In September 1831, the Lord assured the young Prophet that "the glory of the Lord shall be upon (Zion), and she shall be an ensign unto the people, and there shall come unto her out of every nation under heaven. And the day shall come when the nations of the earth shall tremble because of her, and shall fear because of her terrible ones." (D&C 64:41-43).

Zion is the world's most tangible reflection of Christ Who is its Standard of Righteousness. He said: "Behold I am the light; I have set an example for you." (3 Nephi 18:16). He is the Light we are to hold up and the Example we are to follow. When He said: "Let your light so shine before this people that they may see your good works and glorify your Father who is in heaven," He meant that He should be reflected in all that we do, so that when others see our good works, their thoughts will naturally turn to Christ. He deserves the credit and His most pious disciples are not worthy to unloose the latches of His shoes. (See Luke 3:16).

The Prophet knew that the House of The Lord could be a homing beacon, and so he wondered: "Where will thy Temple stand, unto which all nations shall come in the last days?" (Superscript). At Fayette, New York, the Lord had promised, "I will give unto you my law; and (in Ohio) you shall be endowed with power from on high." (D&C 38:31). Malachi had also prophesied: "The Lord whom ye seek shall suddenly come to his temple, even the messenger of the covenant." (Malachi 3:1). The prophecy was at least partially fulfilled when the Lord came to the temple at Kirtland, on 4 3, 1836. But from the first days of the Restoration, Joseph Smith knew that if he and the body of Saints were to assist in the establishment of Zion and help to prepare the earth for the Millennial reign of Christ, they would need to be endowed with spiritual and priesthood power found only in the ordinances of the gospel that are administered in the temple.

Mormon's description of Jesus as the Holy Child of God the Father in Moroni 8:3 suggests the intimacy between parents and children, and gives us a glimpse of just how strong is the relationship between our Father and His offspring. Our goal, after all, is to discover the very personal levels of the experiences of the Savior, for when He speaks of "knowing Him," He is referring to a special sense of the word. It is not enough that we know about Him, by reading the gospels, or by listening to others speak of Him. We must know Him through the common bonds and feeling.

Melvin J. Ballard related an experience that might be shared by all those who have received in their hearts the Messenger of the Covenant. He said: "I found myself one evening in the dreams of the night in the sacred building, the temple. After a season of prayer and rejoicing, I was informed that I should have the privilege of entering into one of those rooms, to meet a glorious Personage, and, as I entered the door, I saw, seated on a raised platform, the most glorious Being my eyes have ever beheld or that I ever conceived existed in all the eternal worlds. As I approached to be introduced, he arose and stepped towards me with extended arms and he smiled as he softly spoke my name. If I shall live to be a million years old, I shall never forget that smile. He took me in his arms and kissed me, pressed me to his bosom and blessed me, until the marrow of my bones seemed to melt. When he had finished, I fell at his feet, and as I bathed them with my tears and kisses, I saw the prints of the nails in the feet of the Redeemer of the world. The feeling that I had in the presence of Him who hath all things in his hands, to have his love, his affection and his blessing was such that if I ever can receive that of which I had but a foretaste, I would give all I am, all that I ever hope to be, to feel what I then felt." ("Sermons and Missionary Experiences of Melvin Joseph Ballard," p. 156).

The Lord whom we all seek can be found in His House. This prophecy continues to be fulfilled as temples of the Lord are constructed throughout the earth. Of the Kirtland Temple, Jesus Christ said: "I have accepted this house, and my name shall be here; and I will manifest myself to my people in mercy in this house." (D&C 110:7). This has been true of every temple subsequently built by the church. In the Lord's House, He may be found Who binds us to eternity through the covenants of the priesthood.

Without the temple, civilization is an empty shell and a structure of custom and convenience only. Those who constructed the Tower of Babel did so in order to establish a binding place of heaven and earth where it was hoped that celestial contact could be established. In fact, that profane ziggurat was a vain and corrupt counterfeit of the temple, where alone we can get our bearings on the eternities. The confounding of languages that took place after the destruction of the tower was so that one could not understand another's verbal communication. Its objective was to teach man to rely on the universal language of the Spirit and gain fluency in that supernal means of communication.

In our own day, those who build sanctuaries to be used just one day each week restrict their worship to the time spent while in church. But we cannot draw near to God either spiritually or physically by constructing elaborate edifices for Sunday-only worship. We feel a kinship with God by redefining our nature.

If we resist the character-shaping forces that would lead us to the awakening of our divine potential, or if we "undertake to cover our sins, or to gratify our pride, (or) our vain ambition … behold the heavens withdraw themselves, (and) the Spirit of the Lord is grieved." (D&C 121:37). Speaking of those who are faithful and habitual patrons of the Temple, Hugh Nibley wrote: "Here is a band of mortals who are actually engaged in doing something which has not their own comfort, convenience, or profit as its object. Here, at last, is a phenomenon that commands respect in our day and could safely be put forth among the few valid arguments we now have to induce Deity to spare the human race; thousands of men and women putting themselves out for no ulterior motive. The Temple, as its very name proclaims, is a place where we take our bearings on the universe." ("On The Timely and Timeless," p. xxvii).

When we qualify to enjoy the blessings of the Atonement, we are freed from the bondage created by unresolved sin When we have received the blessing of the temple, our characteristics are simply the result of a spiritual transformation that comes about as we live in obedience to the Celestial Law of the Lord. In this way, a Zion society is created, conceived in Royal Courts on High, fashioned out of our ardor and conviction, and preserved through the ordinances in which we participate in the temple.

In the early days of the Restoration, by and large the converts were extraordinarily devoted to Christ. After entering the Fold, it was often as it had been among the Nephites during the time of the post-resurrection ministry of the Lord, when "many of them saw and heard unspeakable things, which are not lawful to be written. And they taught, and did minister one to another; and they had all things common among them, every man dealing justly, one with another. And it came to pass that they did do all things even as Jesus had commanded them." (3 Nephi 26:18-20).

Without really comprehending what was happening, they were being transformed into a Zion society, "for this is Zion - THE PURE IN HEART." (D&C 97:21). They "were called the church of Christ." (3 Nephi 26:21). What a great example they became for later Saints! As we attempt to embrace the gospel and emulate the Master, we remember His wise counsel: "Ye know the things that ye must do in my church; for the works which ye have seen me do that shall ye also do." (3 Nephi 27:21).

The endowment of spiritual and priesthood power that the Saints would receive in the anticipated temple would be critical to their spiritual welfare. Satan knows the Lord's servants as marked men and women. Therefore, they need a solid foundation of doctrinal understanding, a firm and abiding testimony of the principles of the gospel, of the Plan of Salvation, and of the Savior, a blessing and setting apart by file leaders, the special protection of the ordinances of the Melchizedek Priesthood, the companionship of the Spirit, and the continual prayers of the faithful. Adult members of the church also require the endowment of spiritual power received only in the Lord's House. The ordinances of the temple strengthen them against the influences of the world. "Without the ordinances thereof, and the authority of the priesthood," declared the Savior to Joseph Smith, "the power of godliness is not manifest unto men in the flesh." (D&C 84:21).

Joseph F. Smith wrote of the endowment: "We enter into covenants with the Lord that we will keep ourselves pure and unspotted from the world. We have agreed before God, angels, and witnesses, in sacred places, that we will not commit adultery, will not lie, that we will not steal or bear false witness against our neighbors, or take advantage of the weak, that we will help and sustain our fellow men in the right, and take such a course as will prove most effectual in helping the weak to overcome their weaknesses and bring themselves into subjection to the requirements of heaven. We cannot neglect, slight, or depart from the spirit, meaning, intent and purpose of these covenants and agreements that we have entered into with our Father in Heaven, without shearing ourselves of our glory, strength, right and title to His blessings, and to the gifts and manifestations of His Spirit." ("Improvement Era," 8/ 1906, p. 813.) It would be difficult to more clearly compose a statement explaining the need for establishing a covenant relationship with God. It would be nigh impossible to visualize a more appropriate place in which to do so than the House of The Lord. Therefore, the Lord has given His people a continuing responsibility: "Organize yourselves; prepare every needful thing; and establish a house, even a house of prayer, a house of fasting, a house of faith, a house of learning, a house of glory, a house of order, a house of God." (D&C 88:119).

"For thus saith the Lord God: (Joseph Smith) have I inspired to move the cause of Zion in mighty power for good, and his diligence I know, and his prayers I have heard." (D&C 21:7). Even though conditions in the world would degenerate and peace would be taken from the earth, those in Zion would enjoy the safety and security that only righteousness can guarantee, and there would be such an outpouring of the Spirit that the time would come when the earth would be "full of the knowledge of the Lord, as the waters cover the sea." (Isaiah 11:9).

B.H. Roberts had a great testimony of the prophet, and knew that here was a man who could lead his people to safety and security in Zion. "Having gone word by word and line by line through his writings, and having read everything he could find on his life, he found Joseph Smith to be possessed of a deeper and richer comprehension of (the gathering to Zion) than anyone he had read in the Christian tradition since the apostles." He knew that Joseph Smith was an instrument of the Lord in moving forward its cause. "This conviction never diminished. Joseph Smith told the truth. Joseph Smith was a prism of the Lord Jesus Christ." (Truman Madsen, "Defender of The Faith," p 93).

A primary reason for our consecration of time, talents, and means is to raise holy sanctuaries so that, as the Lord explained: "My covenant people may be gathered in one in that day when I shall come to my temple. And this I do for the salvation of my people." (D&C 42:6). The opportunities for sanctification by the Spirit are never greater than when we enjoy the blessing of the temple. The temple is that most magnificent of earthly constructions, where alone pure knowledge flows as the dews of Carmel. In the Dispensation of The Fulness of Times, the House of the Lord will continue to be a dominant feature of the church and kingdom, and is a tangible confirmation of the fulfillment of prophecy, of the restoration of priesthood keys of authority, and of God's concern and love.

"Subsequently, (the Prophet) received this revelation." (Superscript to Section 57). On January 5, 1831, the Lord had told Joseph Smith: "Thou art called to labor in my vineyard, and to build up my church, and to bring forth Zion." (D&C 39:13). The Saints knew that anciently "the Lord (had) called his people Zion, because they were of one heart and one mind, and dwelt in righteousness." (Moses 7:18). Joseph Smith had learned when studying the Bible that the power or strength of Zion is to "break mountains, to divide the seas, to dry up waters, to turn them out of their course; to put at defiance the armies of nations, to divide the earth, to break every band, to stand in the presence of God." (J.S.T. Genesis 14:30-31). No wonder the Saints sought Zion with such zeal.

Now, the Lord finally revealed: "Missouri ... is the land which I have appointed and consecrated for the gathering of the saints." (V. 1). On September 26, 1830, the Lord told Joseph Smith: "Wherefore the decree hath gone forth from the Father that (the Saints) shall be gathered in unto one place upon the face of this land, to prepare their hearts and be prepared in all things against the day when tribulation and desolation are sent forth upon the wicked." (D&C 29:8). For "the time will come that war will be poured out upon all nations." (D&C 87:2).

To save His people and in fulfillment of prophecy, on 4 3, 1836, in the Kirtland Temple, the Lord directed Moses to restore the keys of the gathering of both Covenant and Blood Israel. One hundred and thirty-nine years later, Spencer W. Kimball declared: "The brighter day has dawned. The gathering is in progress. May the Lord bless us, as we become nursing fathers and mothers unto our (Israelite) brethren and hasten the fulfillment of the great promises made to them." (C.R., 10/1975).

The Lord has not forgotten Israel, although she has repeatedly forsaken Him. "For can a woman forget her sucking child, that she should not have compassion on the son of her womb?" (1 Nephi 21:15). Israel shall yet inherit her former lands in great glory. "For thy waste and thy desolate places, and the land of thy destruction, shall even now be too narrow by reason of the inhabitants; and they that swallowed thee up shall be far away." (1 Nephi 21:19). In 1830, there were fewer than seven thousand Jews living in the Holy Land. In 1980, there were over three million. In 1830, only one in five hundred persons living in the Holy Land was a Jew. In 1980, one in five was a Jew. The prophecies are being fulfilled.

As the end approaches, the Gentile nations of the earth shall assist in the gathering of Israel. "Thus saith the Lord God: Behold, I will lift up mine hand to the Gentiles, and set up my standard to the people; and they shall bring thy sons in their arms, and thy daughters shall be carried upon their shoulders." (Isaiah 49:22). The ensign to which the people would look is the gospel standard. As the Lord told Joseph Smith: "And even so I have sent mine everlasting covenant into the world, to be a light to the world, and to be a standard for my people, and for the Gentiles to seek to it, and to be a messenger before my face to prepare the way before me." (D&C 45:9).

So thoroughly and convincingly will the Lord touch the hearts of the Gentile nations, that He promised Israel through Isaiah that "kings shall be thy nursing fathers, and their queens thy nursing mothers; they shall bow down to thee with their face towards the earth, and lick up the dust of thy feet; and thou shalt know that I am the Lord." (Isaiah 49:23). As we witness the governments of the earth bowing down in humility and assisting the efforts of Israel to gather to the land of her inheritance, we are seeing signs that the Lord is God.

At the same time, those who have persecuted and oppressed Israel shall be punished. "For the mighty God shall deliver his covenant people (and) I will contend with them that contend with thee, and I will save thy children." (J.S.T. Isaiah 49:25). "And I will feed them that oppress thee with their own flesh; and they shall be drunken with their own blood, as with sweet wine; and all flesh shall know that I, the Lord, am thy Saviour and thy Redeemer, the Mighty One of Jacob." (Isaiah 49:26).

For the righteous, though, a way of deliverance has been prepared. "A prophet shall the Lord your God raise up," said Moses. "This prophet of whom Moses spake was the Holy One of Israel." (1 Nephi 22:20-21). Because of His ministry, the righteous will not be confounded. Because they will listen to His counsel, which has been given by revelation to His Prophets, and which is also found in the scriptures, they will not be destroyed. For their own safety, though, they will need to gather in the wards, stakes, and missions of the church. For "the time cometh speedily that the righteous must be led up as calves of the stall." (1 Nephi 22:24).

In fact, the gathering of the Saints to the stakes of Zion is "for a defense, and for a refuge from the storm, and from wrath when it shall be poured out without mixture upon the whole earth." (D&C 115:6). Ezra Taft Benson taught that our stake ecclesiastical units have "at least four purposes. One is to unify and perfect the members who live in those boundaries, by extending to them the church programs, the ordinances, and gospel instruction. (Secondly), the members of stakes are to be models, or standards, of righteousness. (Third), stakes are to be a defense. They do this as stake members unify under their local priesthood officers and consecrate themselves to do their duty and keep their covenants. (Fourth), stakes are a refuge from the storm to be poured out over the earth." ("Ensign," 1/1991, p. 2-5).

The elect are gathered to the church, "even as many as will believe in me," said the Lord, "and hearken unto my voice." (D&C 33:6). It is our mission to preach the gospel throughout the world in fulfillment of the promises of the Abrahamic Covenant, because those through whose veins runs the blood of Israel (the elect) need the foundation covenants. David B. Haight once said that we do not preach the gospel so that people can enjoy better lives. We do it so that they can be saved in the Celestial Kingdom of God.

The Lord said: "No power shall stay my hand." (D&C 38:33). The endowment will empower His missionary army with the spiritual strength to meet any challenge. "Then shall ye, who are a remnant of the house of Jacob, go forth among them; and ye shall be in the midst of them who shall be many; and ye shall be among them as a lion among the beasts of the forest, and as a young lion among the flocks of sheep, who, if he goeth through both treadeth down and teareth in pieces, and none can deliver." (3 Nephi 20:16). Thus, will His missionaries march through Spiritual Babylon in the Last Days, "fair as the moon, clear as the sun, and terrible as an army with banners." (Song of Solomon 6:10). "The nations of the earth shall tremble because of (Zion), and shall fear because of her terrible ones." (D&C 64:43). "And they shall stand afar off and tremble. And all nations shall be afraid because of the terror of the Lord, and the power of his might." (D&C 45:74-75).

In February 1831, Joseph Smith had been instructed that the missionaries should preach the gospel "until the time (should) come when it (would) be revealed ... when the city of the New Jerusalem (should) be prepared." (D&C 42:9). Without modern revelation, we would be in complete ignorance concerning the New Jerusalem. Elsewhere in these revelations, the Lord stated that "Mount Zion ... shall be the city of New Jerusalem." (D&C 84:2). This can be taken literally, or the mountain of the Lord's house can be thought of as both allegorical and figurative, referring to a high place of God, a place of revelation, and certainly to the temple of the Lord. Isaiah made a distinction when he said: "For out of Zion shall go forth the law, and the word of the Lord from Jerusalem." (Isaiah 2:3). "The Lord shall roar out of Zion, and utter his voice from Jerusalem," declared the Prophet Joel. (Joel 3:16). The Lord further clarified the difference between the New and Old Cities of Jerusalem, when He warned: "Let them, therefore, who are among the Gentiles flee unto Zion. And let them who be of Judah flee unto Jerusalem, unto the Mountains of the Lord's house." (D&C 133:12-13).

In vivid terms, the Doctrine & Covenants identifies the New Jerusalem as "a land of peace, a city of refuge, a place of safety for the saints of the Most High God. And the glory of the Lord shall be there, and the terror of the Lord also shall be there, insomuch that the wicked will not come unto it, and it shall be called Zion. And it shall come to pass among the wicked, that every man that will not take his sword against his neighbor must needs flee unto Zion for safety. And there shall be gathered unto it out of every nation under heaven; and it shall be the only people that shall not be at war one with another. And it shall be said among the wicked: Let us not go up to battle against Zion, for the inhabitants of Zion are terrible; wherefore we cannot stand. And it shall come to pass that the righteous shall be gathered out from among all nations, and shall come to Zion, singing with songs of everlasting joy." (D&C 45:65-71).

On February 9, 1831, the Lord had told Joseph Smith: "And ye shall hereafter receive church covenants, such as shall be sufficient to establish you." (D&C 42:67). Later, He said: "A commandment I give unto you, to prepare and organize yourselves by a bond or everlasting covenant that cannot be broken." (D&C 78:11). Because of the ministry of Joseph Smith and others, faith has increased to the point that the Covenant that God made with Abraham has now been re-established all over the world. It has become possible for the fulness of the gospel to be "proclaimed by the weak and the simple unto the ends of the world, and before kings and rulers." (D&C 1:23). The strength of the gospel is its theology, circumscribed by the Abrahamic Covenant, which will bear up under the careful scrutiny of even the most critical minds on earth.

In this revelation, Joseph Smith was told unequivocally: "This is the land of promise, and the place for the city of Zion." (V. 2). That city is the New Jerusalem, and "the kingdom of Zion is in very deed the kingdom of our God and his Christ." (D&C 105:32). The prophet Ether had seen in vision, "the Jerusalem from whence Lehi should come, (and that) after it should be destroyed it should be built up again, a holy city unto the Lord; wherefore, it could not be a new Jerusalem for it had been in a time of old." He also saw that "a New Jerusalem should be built up upon this land" of America. (Ether 13:5-6). Here, the remnant of the house of Joseph would "build up a holy city unto the Lord, like unto the Jerusalem of old." (Ether 13:8).

In this millennial New Jerusalem will reside those "whose garments are white through the blood of the Lamb; and they are they who are numbered among the remnant of the seed of Joseph who were of the house of Israel. And then also cometh the Jerusalem of old; and the inhabitants thereof, blessed are they, for they have (also) been washed in the blood of the Lamb; and they are they who were scattered and gathered in from the four quarters of the earth, and from the north countries, and are partakers of the fulfilling of the covenant which God made with their father, Abraham." (Ether 13:10-11).

As well as a place, Zion is an attitude that focuses our thoughts, words, and deeds on the Law of the Gospel, brotherhood, stewardship, equality, agency, accountability, consecration, charity, and selflessness. "How carefully most men creep into nameless graves," observed Phillips Brooks, "while now and again one or two forget themselves into immortality." Zion requires this higher level of thinking and acting inasmuch as expands our view beyond the limited horizon of our natural sight. Zion requires vision. As Helen Keller observed from her unique perspective:

"Why cannot the soul discard the poor lenses of the body, and peer through the telescope of truth into the infinite reaches of immortality?" ("My Religion," p. 76).

When Joan of Arc was led to the stake, she was given the opportunity to obtain her freedom by denying what she believed. Instead, she said: "I know this now. Every man gives his life for what he believes. Every woman gives her life for what she believes. Sometimes people believe in little or nothing, and yet they give their lives for little or nothing. One life is all we have, and we live it as we believe in living it, and then it is gone. But to surrender what you are and live without belief is more terrible than dying, even more terrible than dying young." (Maxwell Anderson, "Joan of Lorraine," Act 2, Interlude 3). The inhabitants of Zion experience the same burning zeal.

Boyd K Packer said of this dedicated commitment to uncompromising obedience to eternal law: "That which God will never take by force, He will accept when freely given. And he will then return to you freedom that you can hardly dream of; the freedom to feel and to know, the freedom to do and the freedom to be, at least a thousand-fold more than we offer him. Strangely enough, the key to freedom is obedience." ("B.Y.U. Address," 12/1971). The key to a Zion centered mind set is the adjustment of our internal attitudes reflected in the phenomenon of being born again. Once again, we are reminded of the wisdom of Helen Keller, who said that the real tragedy in life is not being born without sight, but living in the shadows without vision. "We are from the Philippines," a young woman said. "It is a beautiful country besieged by nfortunate violence. It is during these challenging times of war that we cling to the gospel and its truth and light. The most glorious addition to our poor country has been the beautiful temple which stands tall and bright in the midst of the city of Manila. It has been a symbol of hope and strength for our growing congregation of Latter-day Saints.

In 1989 the violence became particularly bad. With bombers flying overhead and sharpshooters firing at any moving object, people, young and old, weak and strong, military and civilian began flocking to the grounds of the temple. For four days, we stayed on the temple grounds, and watched as planes dropped bombs all around us. The statue of the Angel Moroni standing tall and bright above the temple was a clear target for any trained fighter pilot. But four days went by and not one bomb touched the beautiful temple, and not one person standing on those temple grounds was injured. It was as if we were surrounded by an army of angels. We felt the protective hand of our Heavenly Father." (Retold by Sister Joanna Hudson, a young missionary).

We are all in the midst of a raging war. Life on earth subjects us to violence, crime, and other dangers everyday. We find ourselves trying to ward off the bombardment of evil, all too often feeling frustrated and helpless. In our schools, at work, and sometimes in our very own homes we face challenges that test our strength to endure. But as Nephi said, we "must press forward with a steadfastness in Christ, having a perfect brightness of hope, and a love of God and of all men." (2 Nephi 31:20). What a great thought! If we remain strong and unfaltering, we can all stand in holy places and be not moved. We can enjoy the safety and security of Zion.

Neal A. Maxwell assured us: "When in situations of stress we wonder if there is any more to give. We can be comforted to know that God, who knows our capacity perfectly, placed us here to succeed. No one was foreordained to fail or to be wicked." ("Ensign," 2/1979). It just isn't in the Plan. We all chose to come to earth to prove ourselves worthy of citizenship with the Saints in the household of faith. We were not placed here by accident. Elder Maxwell went on to say: "When we have been weighed and found wanting, let us remember that we were measured before and were found equal to our tasks. Therefore, let us continue, but with amore determined discipleship. When we feel overwhelmed, let us recall the assurance that God will not press upon us more than we can bear. For the faithful, our finest hours are sometimes during or just following our darkest hours." When Zion is tested, she puts on her strength and shows her true colors.

"The place which is now called Independence is the center place, and a spot for the temple is lying westward, upon a lot which is not far from the courthouse." (V. 3). In the years since the Lord delivered this revelation to Joseph Smith, significant changes have taken place both in the church and in the world. From its temporary headquarters in Salt Lake City, Utah, the gospel is being taken to every nation, kindred, tongue, and people, and prophetic vision is being validated. The stone cut out of the mountain is rolling over the whole earth, and cannot be stopped. (See Daniel 2:34). What a thrill it is for members of the restored church of Jesus Christ to march in the ranks of Christian soldiers who take the battle for truth directly into the camp of the willfully or ignorantly disobedient.

"The land should be purchased by the saints, and also every tract lying westward ... that they may obtain it for an everlasting inheritance." (V. 4-5). In association with His instruction regarding missionary work, the Lord had revealed on June 7, 1831, that "the land of Missouri ... is the land of your inheritance." (D&C 52:42). It seems natural that He would provide this specific instruction to those who were to be fishers of men. After all, the commission of the missionaries is to gather the elect from the world and bring them to Zion. Now, they would be able to include this new revelation regarding the location of Zion as part of their message to those receptive to the truth. The spirit of gathering would become a strong motivator to action.

The inheritance spoken of by the Lord is a great blessing to the Saints, because "we live in a day and in a world full of doubts and confusion, where people do not know what to believe, where tensions are high, where the pace is frantic and progress in terms of righteousness is not a popular goal. Violence and crudity are everyday patterns all around us. What a blessing it is to know there is a haven, a place of rest from the turmoil of the world. The prophets and the Savior have called upon us to (establish Zion), where life has purpose and direction, and where priesthood power is possible." ("Gospel Doctrine Manual," p. 79).

The Lord has told His people: "I hold forth and deign (or condescend) to give unto you greater riches, even a land of promise, a land flowing with milk and honey, upon which there shall be no curse when the Lord cometh. And I will give it unto you for the land of your inheritance, if you seek it with all your hearts." (D&C 38:18-19). When it is transformed to its terrestrial state, the curse on the earth will be lifted. Therefore, Zion must be prepared to receive her King, for at that time only the righteous will remain on the earth. These are they who will have tried the virtue of the word of God in the crucible of adversity.

One reason why all profane government will be destroyed before the Second Coming of the Lord is that its concept of welfare is defined by a detached, disinterested, and ineffectual paternalism, in contrast to the active, meaningful brotherhood that characterizes the inhabitants of Zion. Hugh Nibley spoke of the "Mahan Principle," that he defined as "the great secret of converting life into property." ("Approaching Zion"). There is, we discover in every government action, an economic baseline that ignores the worth of souls. At the present time, the Lord counters this Satanic twisting of the principle of consecration with the Law of Tithing. Beginning in 1838, even though they were in the most straitened circumstances, He declared to the church: "And this shall be the beginning of the tithing of my people." (D&C 119:3). Since its introduction, this Law has remained a foundation principle. Tithing is paid with faith more than it is with currency, and in obedience the Saints are blessed beyond measure. On the other hand, when government has immense powers to siphon off the productivity of its citizens, and when taxpayers contribute involuntarily for the support of programs they cannot morally support, the roots of evil become entrenched. We could learn from the lesson illustrated in The Book of Mormon, when the rulers "were supported in their laziness, and in their idolatry, and in their whoredoms, by the taxes which King Noah had put upon the people; thus did the people labor exceedingly to support iniquity. Yea, and they also became idolatrous because they were deceived by the vain and flattering words of the kings and priests." (Mosiah 11:6-7). In the Zion society envisioned for the Latter-day Saints, the celestial character trait of consecration would be
woven into every fiber of their being.

To His disciples in the Holy Land, the Savior had cautioned: "Take heed that ye do not your alms before men to be seen of them; otherwise ye have no reward of your Father which is in heaven." (Matthew 6:1). Such individuals have not yet been ignited by the flame of faith. They are not yet white-hot sparks struck off the divine anvil of God. Their spirits do not yet generate enough intrinsic energy to power the City of Light.

In Zion, he that would be master is the servant of all. Ralph Waldo Emerson lamented: "Once we had wooden chalices and golden priests. Now we have golden chalices and wooden priests." ("Lectures & Biographical Sketches," p. 229). As Alvin R. Dyer cautioned: "We must not be caught in the bind of building a church and killing the articles of its faith, or permitting form to triumph over spirit. The church and kingdom of God is built by the ardor and conviction of its members. We must be alert to the expansion of its assets at the cost of lost conviction. When buildings or institutions grow bigger and bigger, let us be fearful lest the Spirit will thin out." ("A Foundation for Education").

The Lord has not forgotten His Chosen People. To them, He promised: "This shall be my covenant with you, ye shall have (Zion) for the land of your inheritance, and for the inheritance of your children forever, while the earth shall stand, and ye shall possess it again in eternity," when the earth finally receives its celestial stature, "no more to pass away." (D&C 38:20). When the Son of God comes to receive His Millennial Kingdom, He will come in glory. "Come unto Christ," urged Jacob, "and partake of the goodness of God, that (you) might enter into his rest." (Jacob 1:7). For God's Rest "is the fulness of His glory." (D&C 84:24).

In this sense, Jesus came to the earth in His glory, that is, as a lamb without spot or blemish, worthy at all times throughout His mortal life of the inner peace that is born of righteousness. "The glory of God," after all, "is light and truth." (D&C 93:36). Our progression involves the grand principle that we may be "glorified in truth (until we know) all things." (D&C 93:26). This is the spirit of Zion. It was the possibility of the fulfillment of these promises through a partnership with God that drove the Saints through years of hardship in the hope that they might establish Zion. "Keep all the commandments and covenants by which ye are bound," said the Lord, "and I will cause the heavens to shake for your good, and Satan shall tremble, and Zion shall rejoice upon the hills and flourish." (D&C 35:24). The wicked will be as Belshazzar of old, "whose thoughts troubled him so that the joints of his loins were loosed, and his knees smote one against another." (Daniel 5:6). But those who dwell safely within the boundaries of the Lord's inheritance are promised a safe haven from the insecurity and uncertainty of a worldly lifestyle. Nephi said that those who are of the "kingdom of the devil" are the ones who should fear. They are "all churches which are built up to get gain, and all those who are built up to become popular in the eyes of the world, and those who seek the lusts of the flesh, and the things of the world, and to do all manner of iniquity; yea, in fine, all those who belong to the kingdom of the devil are they who need fear, and tremble, and quake." (1 Nephi 22:23). These institutions that represent the devil's kingdom stand in stark contrast to the government of Heavenly Father.

The Church of Jesus Christ of Latter-day Saints represents itself as the Lord's church on the earth. He owns it, for He organized it and gave Himself for it. It is the sacred depository of His truth and is His instrument for the perfecting of the Saints as well as for the work of the ministry. It is Christ's church in all these respects, but it is an institution that belongs to the Saints. It is their refuge from the confusion and religious doubt of the world, their instructor in principle, doctrine, and righteousness, and their guide in matters of faith and morals. They have a conjoint ownership in it with Jesus Christ, which is recognized in the latter part of the title: The Church of Jesus Christ of Latter-day Saints.

"And now concerning the gathering - Let the bishop and the agent make preparations for those families which have been commanded to come to this land, as soon as possible, and plant them in their inheritance." (V. 15). In March 1831, at Kirtland, Ohio, the Lord had told Joseph Smith that these leaders would "be appointed to purchase the lands, and to make a commencement to lay the foundation of the city; and then shall ye begin to be gathered with your families." (D&C 48:6). "For thou shalt devote all thy service in Zion; and in this thou shalt have strength." (D&C 24:7). When we free ourselves from the bondage of personal agendas, we are guided by a greater sense of our stewardship responsibilities. As King Benjamin declared: "When ye are in the service of your fellow beings," he said, "ye are only in the service of your God." (Mosiah 2:17).

The Creator does not generally intervene personally in our affairs, nor is He typically served directly. The Savior set the pattern when He declared: "Inasmuch as ye have done it unto one of the least of these my brethren, ye have done it unto me." (Matthew 25:40). We all should focus on what C.S. Lewis called "acts of quiet Christianity," those charitable acts of service for which there is no thought of recognition, recompense, or reciprocation.

The Lord has established the pattern for all to follow: "Keep my commandments, and seek to bring forth and establish the cause of Zion." (D&C 11:6). While selfishness results in contention, apostasy, affliction, and persecution, the service of the faithful brings peace, plenty, and unity. Righteous stewards concentrate on the quality of their service, and not on their position or recognition within the church. The only authority the brethren of the priesthood are given is the power to bless the lives of others. God notices and watches over us. But it is usually through the priesthood or those who act under its direction that He meets our needs. "Therefore, it is vital that we serve each other. The abundant life is achieved as we magnify our view of life and expand our view of others and our own possibilities. Thus, the more we follow the teachings of the Master, the more enlarged our perspective becomes. We see many more possibilities for service that we would have seen without this magnification. There is great security in spirituality, and we cannot have spirituality without service." (Spencer W. Kimball, "Ensign," 10/1985). "And Israel shall be saved in mine own due time; and by the keys which I have given shall they be led, and no more be confounded at all." (D&C 35:25). Quoting Isaiah, the Savior declared: "And then shall be brought to pass that which is written:" Awake, awake, put on thy strength, O Zion; put on thy beautiful garments, O Jerusalem, the holy city." (Isaiah 52:1). The Doctrine & Covenants provides the explanation to this scripture: "What is meant by the command in Isaiah, 52nd chapter, 1st verse, which saith: Put on thy strength, O Zion - and what people had Isaiah reference to? He had reference to those whom God should call in the last days, who should hold the power of priesthood to bring again Zion, and the redemption of Israel; and to put on her strength is to put on the authority of the priesthood, which she, Zion, has a right to by lineage; also, to return to that power which she had lost." (D&C 113:7-8).

Brigham Young taught that the power God gives us "is designed to test us and enable us to show to ourselves, our fellows, and all the heavens just how we would act if entrusted with God's power." (Hugh Nibley, "Subduing the Earth," p. 89-90). When we have been unwavering, and have passed our individually tailored tests with high marks, we are made "mighty in word and in deed, in faith and in works." (Helaman 10:5). Under those conditions, we are given the power of God because we can be trusted to do exactly as God would do in similar circumstances.

Joseph Smith clearly taught that the exercise of priesthood power is based solely upon the principles of righteousness. If, in its capacity, we "undertake to cover our sins, or to gratify our pride, our vain ambition, or to exercise control or dominion or compulsion upon the souls of the children of men, in any degree of unrighteousness," its authority is taken from us. (D&C 121:34-37).

"You are, and always will be, independent in that stage of development to which your voluntary decisions and divine powers have led," taught Truman Madsen. "There are limits all along the way to what you can be and do. But you are not a billiard ball. No power in the universe can coerce your complete assent or dissent. This thesis on capacity translates Bergson's metaphor into breath-taking fact: 'The universe is a machine for the making of gods.' ("Eternal Man," p. 18). Zion represents what man has been unable to accomplish for two millennia - the Gathering of Israel and the establishment of a utopian society. Bruce R. McConkie believed that it would specifically be under the direction of the First Presidency of the church of Jesus Christ of Latter-day Saints that this would come to pass. (See "A New Witness for Christ," p. 572).

When the Kirtland Temple was dedicated, the prayer offered by Joseph Smith included a plea that "the children of Judah (might) begin to return" to the lands which God had given to their father Abraham. (D&C 109:63). Soon thereafter, Moses appeared in that temple and committed to Joseph Smith "the keys of the gathering of Israel from the four parts of the earth, and the leading of the ten tribes from the land of the north." (D&C 110:11). Later, by direction of the Prophet, Orson Hyde traveled to the Holy Land and stood on the Mount of Olives, overlooking the Old City of Jerusalem. From that vantage point, he offered a prayer, dedicating that land for the return of the Jews.

With the blessing and power of the priesthood of God vested in the First Presidency and Quorum of The Twelve, Israel shall "loose (herself) from the bands of (her) neck." (Isaiah 52:2). In his explanation of this verse, Joseph Smith said: "We are to understand that the scattered remnants are exhorted to return to the Lord from whence they have fallen; which if they do, the promise of the Lord is that he will speak to them, or give them revelation ... The bands of her neck are the curses of God upon her, or the remnants of Israel in their scattered condition among the Gentiles." (D&C 113:10).

Obedience to the principles of the gospel allows us to wipe the slate clean. As we grow in grace, we enjoy in greater abundance the gifts and power of God by which we may be brought to perfection. Even the Savior "received not of the fulness at first, but continued from grace to grace, until he received a fulness." (D&C 93:12). "And it came to pass that Jesus grew up with his brethren, and waxed strong, and waited upon the Lord for the time of his ministry to come. And he served under his father, and he spake not as other men, neither could he be taught, for he needed not that any man should teach him. And after many years, the hour of his ministry grew nigh." (J.S.T. Matthew 3:22-25). The conditions for receiving the gifts of God in a Zion setting are submission to His will and obedience to His commandments, for we are incapable of perfection through our own efforts. A greater endowment beyond own capabilities is required if we are to take up residence in the Celestial City. Blessed with that endowment, however, we are even now able to enjoy a beautiful spirit in our meetings that are "conducted by the church after the manner of the workings of the Spirit, and by the power of the Holy Ghost; for as the power of the Holy Ghost (leads us) whether to preach, or to exhort, or to pray, or to supplicate, or to sing, even so it (is) done." (Moroni 6:9).

After all, "the great objective of all our work is to build character and build faith in the lives of those whom we serve." (Spencer W. Kimball, C.R., 4/1948). The keys that were restored through the Prophet Joseph Smith allowed his successors to continue the process of sanctification. To put it in terms we can understand, the Lord said: "I am the same which (has) taken the Zion of Enoch into mine own bosom." (D&C 38:4). To be "in the bosom" is a Hebrew idiom derived from the fact that anciently, a man's clothing consisted of flowing robes with a sash, forming a space where precious possessions, and even small children, were carried. The expression implies a very close and favored relationship.

For the early Latter-day Saints, Zion was the City of Light, the Celestial City of God, far removed from the mud and overcast skies, the hardship and persecution, and the sickness and death so familiar to them in their telestial surroundings. Joseph F. Smith said: "If we would carry out that which the Lord revealed, it would only be a matter of a very short time until this people would be in the same condition as were the people of the City of Enoch." (C.R., 4/1921). "And it came to pass (in Enoch's day) that he built a city that was called the city of Holiness, even Zion." (J.S.T. Genesis 7:25). "And Enoch and all his people walked with God, and he dwelt in the midst of Zion; and it came to pass that Zion was not, for God received it up into his own bosom; and from thence went forth the saying, Zion is Fled." (Moses 7:69).

In the summer of 1831, Joseph Smith was immersed in the translation of the Bible. Through his efforts, he gained both doctrinal and historical understanding relating to Zion. This came to him in promptings that motivated him to revise, amend, clarify, and add to that body of literature, particularly to the early chapters of the book of Genesis. He also received many revelations that have been incorporated into The Doctrine & Covenants that shed light on Zion, revealing its nature and characteristics, and making its establishment a realistic opportunity. The Lord's promise was unfolded before the Latter-day Saints as both a challenge and a goal: "And righteousness and truth will I cause to sweep the earth as with a flood, to gather out mine own elect from the four quarters of the earth, unto a place which I shall prepare; an holy city, that my people may gird up their loins, and be looking forth for the time of my coming, for there shall be my tabernacle, and it shall be called Zion, a New Jerusalem. And the Lord said unto Enoch, Then shalt thou and all thy city meet them there; and we will receive them into our bosom; and they shall see us, and we will fall upon their necks, and they shall fall upon our necks, and we will kiss each other; And there shall be mine abode, and it shall be Zion, which shall come forth out of all the creations which I have made; and for the space of a thousand years shall the earth rest." (J.S.T. Genesis 7:70-72).

How satisfying it will be for the Latter-day Saints to "come out of the world, to leave the loneliness and estrangement of a fallen creation and enter the realm of divine experience, to forsake the orphanage of spiritual alienation, and be received into the family and household of the Lord Jesus Christ. They will have left the ranks of the nameless to take upon them the blessed name of Jesus Christ. They are Christians. Through their Master, they will become, in time, joint heirs to all that the Father has." (Robert L. Millet, et. al, "Doctrinal Commentary on The Book of Mormon," 4:202).

The Lord taught us all a valuable lesson when He declared: "I will forgive whom I will forgive, but of you it is required to forgive all men." (D&C 64:10). The Sons of Mosiah knew that their joy and satisfaction in life, meaning their true freedom, and also their eternal salvation, depended on their willingness and capacity to forgive the Lamanites for the perceived injustices that they had committed, that had supposedly harmed their people.

Observations

As we jog along at a measured pace upon the pathway of progress, and we negotiate the twists and turns of mortality while enjoying the aerobic exercise of free will, it is The Book of Mormon that provides us with celestial sign posts to guide us through the telestial traffic jams and conceptual cul-de-sacs that threaten to detour us from the straight and narrow way. The expanding circles of our opportunity, afforded by our obedience to gospel principles, assures each of us that we will have direct exposure to the perfect law of liberty. Thereby, we abandon the tortuous route through Idumea that's taken by those bound for telestial glory. Instead, we follow the unmistakable track that inevitably leads to celestial surety in a heavenly setting.

The poets may have been thinking of Nephites and Lamanites, when they ask: "Why is it that whenever I reach for the sky to climb aboard cloud nine, it evaporates and rains upon my dreams? Is it a matter of science, or simply a matter of fact, that not even a cloud with a silver lining can hold the weight of our dreams without some precipitation? I think I've found the answer to this dilemma. Keep on reaching for the sky, but don't forget your umbrella."
(Susan Stephenson).

The "get even" mentality of retaliation that was practiced by the Lamanites and that today has become popularized in books and films and is reinforced in interpersonal relationships, is contrary to the Savior's teachings. While it may be true that in business, you don't get what you deserve, you get what you negotiate, when the earth has been cleansed in order to receive its paradisiacal glory, a higher standard will prevail. Before that happens, the Saints have a responsibility to prepare the earth for the Millennium, when the lamb and the lion will lie down together in harmony.

The blessing of doctrine that is found in The Book of Mormon is within the reach of all of us, no matter what our cultural, social, political, economic, or religious proclivities may be. The principles that testify of its universal applicability and accessibility are bolstered by the avowal of our Heavenly Father that He is no respecter of persons. (See Acts 10:34).

Because he
knew that Babylon's
image consultants would
confuse conventional wisdom
with the weightier matters of the
law in the tumultuous last days on
earth, Mormon cautioned: "Take heed,
that ye do not judge that which is evil to
be of God, or that which is good and of God
to be of the devil." (Moroni 7:14). In the vast
arena that is the world, there are no shades of
gray for those who have not only received the
Light of Christ, but also the greater power of
the Holy Ghost. For to them it is given "to
judge, that (they) may know good from
evil; and the way to judge is as plain,
that ye may know with a perfect
knowledge, as the daylight
is from the dark night."
(Moroni 7:15).

DSRT
(see Ether 2:3), enjoyed
a ritual prominence within the
Egyptian culture of antiquity, and was
very closely associated with the symbol of
the bee. Deseret now implies industry, as the
church and kingdom overcome everything
opposed to the economy of heaven. Isaiah
foresaw such a society, prophesying
that "they shall build houses, and
inhabit them, and they shall
plant vineyards, and eat
the fruit of them."
(Isaiah 65:21).

Employing the melodic poetry of simile, Isaiah described what life will be like during the Millennium. He painted a portrait of a God-centered society where faithfulness triumphs, and "the earth (is) full of the knowledge of the Lord, as the waters cover the sea." (2 Nephi 21:9). Brigham Young declared: When righteousness dictates the conduct of millennial culture, the earth itself will also be sanctified. With the Spirit of God, "every animal and creeping thing will be filled with peace; the soil of the earth will bring forth its strength, and the fruits thereof will be meat for man. The more purity that exists, the less is the strife; the more kind we are to our animals, the more will peace increase, and the savage nature of the brute creation will vanish away."

In his second inaugural address to a youthful nation, Thomas Jefferson declared: "I shall need the favour of the One in whose hands we are, Who led our forefathers as He did Israel of old, from their native land, and planted them in a country flowing with the necessaries and comforts of life."

When Lehi's sons
returned to Jerusalem to
retrieve the Plates of Brass
that were the written records of
their family, they traced their way
back to their home on the outskirts of
the city and gathered up all the treasures
they had left behind. These they presented to
Laban, to whom they were offered in exchange
for the precious things they really valued. But the
Lord did not allow them to receive the spiritual gift
of the scriptures in exchange for the profane baubles
and ornaments of the world. Ultimately, at the hands
of their unscrupulous cousin, they lost their telestial
trinkets so that the Lord might thereafter prove to
them that He was mightier than man, saw the
end from the beginning, and was firmly
in control of not only their temporal,
but also their spiritual destiny.
Never again would Nephi
doubt that the Lord
would provide.

When the Nephites
became obsessed by blind
obedience and were overzealous
in outward observances, they were
as hypocrites, pretending to be pious,
when, in fact, they were only professors
of religion. All too often, they crept into
nameless graves, while now and then,
as Phillips Brooks suggested, "one
or two of them forgot themselves
into immortality."

"Without faith, we are free to do what we like, and that can be a pleasant feeling at first, because there are no questions of conscience and no constraints except those of custom, convention, and law, and these are flexible enough in most situations. It's only later that the terror will come. We are free, but only in the chaos of an unexplained and an inexplicable world. We are free in a desert from which there is no retreat but inexorably inward toward the hollow core of ourselves." (Morris West). As Jarom cautioned in the 4th verse of his brief record: We need to have faith, (that we might enjoy a) communion with the Holy Spirit."

The prominent feature that is a paralyzing phenomenon of the Last Days is that our society is tormented by an unparalleled polarization of principles contrasted against values, that is accelerating at an alarming rate. On the one hand, is the kingdom of God, while on the other, is a moral and ethical depravity that is nothing less than the cesspool of Satan, whose dominion is typified as a corrupt and idolatrous community. There are, after all, "save two churches only; the one is the church of the Lamb of God, and the other is the church of the devil, wherefore, whoso belongeth not to the church of the Lamb of God belongeth to that great church, which is ... the whore of all the earth." (1 Nephi 14:10).

It shouldn't be hard to follow the path that has been illuminated by principles of the gospel. In the Wilderness of Sinai, the Israelites only needed to look to the Brazen Serpent, the staff of Moses that typified Christ, in order to be saved. "And as many as should look upon that serpent should live, even so as many as should look upon the Son of God, with faith, having a contrite spirit, might live, even unto that life which is eternal." (Helaman 8:13-16).

A multitude of the angelic host that has come down from the throne of God to visit the earth (see Alma 13:22), has included Moroni and John the Baptist, as well as Peter, James and John. As messengers of Jesus Christ, they have restored true doctrine. Because of the ministry of these and other servants, a prophet has been able to confidently declare that "no power on earth or hell can overthrow or defeat that which God has decreed. Every plan of the adversary will fail, for the Lord knows the secret thoughts of men, and sees the future with a vision clear and perfect, even as though it were in the past." (Joseph Fielding Smith, Jr.).

It has always been with the use of the right hand that the faithful have manifested their determination, symbolized righteousness, and have demonstrated the power that comes with obedience to law. The Lord Himself testified that it was He who "laid the foundation of the earth, and (whose) right hand hath spanned the heavens." (1 Nephi 20:13). The right hand is used to ratify the validity of the sacred ordinances of the priesthood, in a symbolic gesture of the power of God that flows to us thru His ordained administrators as they lay their own hands upon our heads to confer blessings, privileges, rights, and responsibilities.

The fate of the wicked is illustrated in a symbolical representation not to be taken literally. Figuratively speaking, a hardening of their hearts is symptomatic of a debilitating illness that, if left untreated, will kill the spirit. Because of its stench, the resultant cesspool of nauseating brimstone will effectively smother a spiritual fire that cannot "dwell in unholy temples." (Alma 7:21).

It was the Liahona that showed the way that the Nephites must follow if they ever hoped to reach the Promised Land. Transliteration from the Hebrew indicates that "Liahona" denotes "God gives light, as does the sun." Notwithstanding that magnetic compasses suggest the way we might go, the Liahona was more than that; it was a spiritual compass that pointed to the way we should go. God has provided each of us with a celestial compass of gospel principles founded on truth to guide us to safe haven before the day of reckoning. It is there for all who have lost their way, to bring them back to the fold of the Shepherd.

The Nephites who had been miraculously liberated from telestial bondage to King Noah saw in a sudden sunburst of spiritual sensitivity that Jesus Christ is the Light of the world. Alma realized that for their faith to prosper, they would need to find new friends in the church, be given the chance to flourish with newfound responsibility, and be nourished by the good word of God. (See Mosiah 23:17).

Shortly before the end of the world, when the Spirit is withdrawn, there will be fires, tempests, and vapors of smoke in foreign lands, and wars, rumors of wars, and earthquakes in sundry places. (See Mormon 8:29-30). For nations will rise up to war with each other, and kingdom against kingdom. (See Matthew 24:6-7). In the end, the consumption that has been decreed by God will make "a full end of all nations." (D&C 87:6).

Enos recalled: "And while I was thus struggling in the spirit, behold, the voice of the Lord came into my mind." (Enos 1:10). When voices come as a surge of pure intelligence that is attended by a burning in the bosom, it is of God. Our search for external warrant is really nothing more than an entrenched desire to receive confirmation regarding intuitions that we have already felt.

Zion and Babylon are contraries that are demonstrated in The Book of Mormon - divided camps lying at opposite ends of the spiritual spectrum. They are, and will forever be, completely at odds with each other. There is little common ground upon which substantive dialogue could ever be introduced, because the solid foundation pillars upon which Zion reposes are philosophically incompatible with the detritus scattered about by the forces of Babylon, that was a repercussion of the War in Heaven. The theology upon which Zion is founded compels its inhabitants to raise their eyes to Heavenly Father for their redemption, while the apologists and the political pundits of Babylon cannot see beyond their own intellect for their salvation, and they can do little more than shrug their shoulders in resignation when they hear the clarion call to amend their behavior and reaffirm their faith.
.

Once again, proper prior parental planning on the part of our Heavenly Father, when He orchestrated the preservation of The Book of Mormon for our day, was designed to prevents poor performance on our part.

Lucifer was characterized by the prophet Isaiah as a son of the morning who had been cast out of heaven for his rebellion (see 2 Nephi 24:12), because he could not abide by the principles that governed the lives of his brothers and sisters, who were nurtured within the warm embrace of their Father. He became Satan, who now rules in Idumea, or the world. The Saints must choose their allegiance, because they cannot hold membership in both the assembly of God and the Great and Abominable Church of the Devil. They cannot hope to live in Zion, while maintaining a summer home in Babylon, any more than they can afford to joy ride through the world, making excuses to stop along the way to partake of its pleasures and sample its tempting treats.

In the last days on God's footstool, we cry "hallelujah!" Before the millennial day, when the signs of the times proclaim that the Second Coming of Jesus Christ is nigh at hand, the faithful will raise their voices to the heavens and "praise our God forever." (See Alma 26:16).

Even when the
Nephites were on the right
road, they got run over if they
just sat there. Work and idleness were
then, and are now, incompatible. There is
a world of difference between the "cheap thrills"
that are so often the focus of attention of the idler,
and the "lofty goals" of the working man. Frequently,
our problem is not that we set our goals too high, and fail
to reach them. It is, instead, that we set them too low, and
we do reach them far too easily. If we mistakenly confuse
our mediocrity for well-deserved success, we will become
conditioned to accept only our marginal effort as the
standard to which we should aspire. Little wonder
that the Lord has said "the idler shall not have
place in the church." (D&C 75:29). God does
not emulate the example of the world by
handing out plastic participation
trophies to everyone who has
merely shown up for
class.

Some have legitimately asked the question:
Why is the phrase "and it came to pass" so frequently
employed by the authors of The Book of Mormon? Mark
Twain wondered this very thing, and famously joked that
if the phrase were omitted from the text, the church could
have instead published "The Pamphlet of Mormon."
("Roughing It." p. 33). As it turns out, however,
the joke is on him. This much-maligned
phrase actually provides powerful
evidence of the authenticity
of the record.

The phrase "and it came to
pass" appears in The Book of Mormon much more
often, page for page, than it does in the Old Testament.
The Book of Mormon contains much more narrative material,
chapter for chapter, than does the Bible, and equally important,
the translators of the King James Version did not always render
"wayehi" as "and it came to pass." Instead, they chose to draw
from a multitude of similar expressions, such as
"and it happened," "and it became,"
or "and it was."

1,449 verses in the Book of
Mormon state a life-preserving truth: "It
came to pass." It did not come to stay! Life
unfolds before our eyes, often in
surprisingly delightful
ways.

The indifferent, unattached, and casual recognition of the Lord Jesus Christ by various Nephites, who were only squatters on the world's stage, disqualified them to receive an inheritance of celestial glory. These Christians of convenience lacked the fire in the belly that characterizes discipleship. Otherwise honorable people, whose faith in the Savior remains uncommitted, will inherit only terrestrial glory as their reward, because they "received not the gospel, neither the testimony of Jesus, neither the prophets, neither the everlasting covenant." (D&C 76:101-102).

Perhaps it will come as a surprise to some, to learn that there still exist doctrines relating to the expansive scope of the Plan of Salvation that simply have not yet been made clear, either in the scriptures, or in the teachings of the prophets. Alma felt that it was always better to keep his opinion to himself, rather than to speculate without a foundation of revelation. It is prudent, he suggested, that one remain silent and be thought a fool, than to speak, and remove all doubt in the matter. When counseling his son Corianton, he underscored this point: "There are many mysteries." he explained, "which are kept, that no one knoweth them, save God himself." (Alma 40:3). He taught that when God withholds understanding from His children, it is always "for a wise purpose," it is never His intention to mislead or to deceive, and we can always be certain that "his paths are straight." (Alma 40:12).

A careful reading of The Book of Mormon begs the questions: Is it the influence of God alone that helps lost souls to bask in the Light of Christ, feel whisperings of the Holy Ghost, change their ways, face their guilt, accept the Atonement, and burst the fetters of sin? Or could it be possible that even the influence of Satan can, in a somewhat convoluted and mysterious way, push us toward the light? Is it not true that opposition in all things is a necessary contrary in our Heavenly Father's curriculum, in the learning laboratory of life?

Mormon emphasized to his son Moroni that when we reach the age of accountability, we must be born again. It isn't a question of our development, or of our maturation, but of generation. One of the most emotional and awe-inspiring events of mortality is birth. It would be difficult to more dramatically conceptualize in poetic metaphor the astonishing process of kindling a divine spark, of igniting our potential, or awakening the sleeping giant of the spirit that lies dormant within the god in embryo, than to say that we must be born again in order to experience eternal life.

The Spirit speaks "of things as they really are, and of things as they really will be," which are manifest in plainness "for the salvation of our souls." (Jacob 4:13). In contrast is the intellectual embroidery that we, at times, prefer to the entire ensemble of the gospel; the frills to the fabric, as it were. Only revelation provided the Nephites, and us, with the absolute anchors that we need. When they gave it a chance, they found that there was more realism in the word of God than there could ever have been in a philosophy of secularism that was doomed from its beginning to be congenitally short-sighted.

Our desire to use The Book of Mormon, as a blueprint for survival in the Last Days fosters an atmosphere of collaboration, cooperation, and conciliation. We are emboldened to share our resources with others so that we might achieve solutions to our problems and find remedies to our trials that could work to our mutual benefit.

We need to begin right now to think about making room in our congregations for the Children of the Covenant, the posterity of Father Lehi, as the gathering of Israel gains momentum. "For Zion must increase in beauty, and in holiness. Her borders must be enlarged. Her stakes must be strengthened. Yea, verily I say unto you .... arise and put on (your) beautiful garments." (D&C 82:14). The Lord our God shall set up the ensign of the church in the Last Days "for the nations." (2 Nephi 21:12). As He told Joseph Smith: "I have sent mine everlasting covenant into the world to be a light to the world, and to be a standard for my people, for the Gentiles to seek to it; to be a messenger before my face." (D&C 45:9).

As it turns out, the Nephites and Lamanites who left the land of Jerusalem and sailed to the promised land were in good company. "In the Hellenistic age, Jews were dispersed over the entire Greek world. As early as 140 B.C., the author of the Sibylline Oracles testified that the whole land and sea were full of Jews. A contemporary of Herod said it would have been hard to find a place in the world where there were no Jews. And Josephus added: "There are no people in the world among whom part of our brethren is not found." Philo spoke of the wide expansion of the Jews over the whole of the earth, and of Jerusalem as the center of the scattered nation." (Abba Eban).

The Nephites and Lamanites
were the offspring of eternal beings,
and deeply rooted within both of these groups
were the seeds of greatness, for they had been endowed
with the potential to completely develop the attributes of their
Father. When they were at their best, they mustered His power by
recommitting themselves to their covenants, and when they did not
allow sin to encroach upon the fortress of their faith, they fought for
the most profound truths and maintained the highest standards. If
occasion required it of them, they were set apart to accomplish these
tasks because theirs was an eternally significant work that was
carried out in a partnership with their Creator. They were set
apart by their convictions, by their enthusiasm, by their
righteousness, and by their faith, and when they
remembered to do so, they prayed that those who
dwelt within the sphere of their influence
would be blessed because of His work
that had been given into
their hands.

Following in
the footsteps of Father Lehi,
his righteous descendants had
the Liahona as a type of Christ to
unerringly guide them. He was
their compass, allowing them
to navigate the desert wastes
of Idumea in the company
of the Spirit, unafraid
of the gathering
darkness.

As late as one hundred and fifty years after the organization of the church, (1980), missionaries were actively proselyting in fewer than half of the nations of the earth. But 36 years later (2016), the missionaries were present in roughly 162 countries in the world. As of that date, the gospel has not been introduced in 57 countries, among them Afghanistan, Algeria, Burma, China, Cuba, Egypt, Greenland, Iraq, Kuwait, Libya, Monaco, Nepal, North Korea, Sudan, United Arab Emirates, and the Vatican City. One gets the idea. Between 1830 and 1970, The Book of Mormon had been translated into 25 languages, but in the next 11 years, there were another 25 language translations. Much work remains to be done, but currently (as of 2016), The Book of Mormon has been translated in its entirety into 94 languages, with selections from the text available in an additional 20 languages.

When the law had been written upon their hearts (see 2 Corinthians 3:2-3), and they truly felt God's forgiveness, the Nephites seized upon every occasion to forgive others, while entreating God to bless their efforts, precisely because it was so contrary to their nature to do so. The opportunity to forgive should never be wasted, because it can awaken within our hearts a spiritual sensitivity that is somehow greater than ourselves. Brigham Young told the Saints that "he who takes offense when no offense was intended is a fool, and he who takes offense when it was intended is usually a fool."

In Nephite society, the meek always reflected poise under provocation and they were sensitive to the needs of others. They were empathic and humble, and they were less concerned with telestial trinkets, but were more focused on celestial certainties. The meek among the Nephites were selfless and harbored no secret agenda. They were repulsed by sin, rejoiced in the truth, were drawn toward the light, and were continually open to that which was good. Meekness may be one of the greatest of all the qualities of God Himself, Who is the possessor of all spiritual gifts. Without it, we are nothing, because our progress in the direction of His Divine Nature cannot sustain its momentum.

The gospel provides the cure for an array of poisonous telestial temptations that, in the garden setting of celestial sureties, are always threatening to choke out their expression. We cannot be saved if we are willing to do nothing more than rally around noble principles. We will be redeemed in the precious blood of the Holy One of Israel when temporal towers fall and Jerusalem has at last triumphed over Babylon, as is so vividly described in Book of Mormon prophecy.

The Hebrew word "seraph" means "burning," and the scriptures speak of "bright, shining seraphs," when describing signs of the coming of the Lord that are complemented by "blood and fire, and vapors of smoke." (D&C 45:41 & 109:79, see Mormon 8:29, where Moroni describes "fires, and tempests, and vapors of smoke in foreign lands," in the Last Days). The metaphors of fire and smoke are employed by the prophets to depict the glory of celestial realms. In the language of Joseph Smith: "God Almighty Himself dwells in eternal fire. Flesh and blood cannot go there, for all corruption is devoured by that fire. God is a consuming fire." Perhaps one day, we'll come to understand how immortality dwells in everlasting burnings. (See Isaiah 33:14).

The shining seraphs encircling God's throne cried one "unto another, and said: Holy, holy, holy is the Lord of Hosts; and the whole earth is full of his glory." (2 Nephi 16:2). In the Hebrew, to repeat something three times makes it superlative, as in "good," "better," and "best." These seraphim were making a statement for all to hear, that there can be nothing more holy than Jesus Christ! He is a lamb without spot or blemish.

The imagery of a white dove has always been associated with peace and with its Author. (See 2 Nephi 31:8). Joseph Smith explained that the "sign of the dove" is an emblem or token of truth and innocence. For those who have been cleansed in the waters of baptism, it will come at the time of their second baptism of fire and the Spirit.

The Book of Mormon inspires us to be our best, to strive to so live that we will remain honest, true, chaste, benevolent, virtuous, and do good to all men. As our faith increases, so will our capacity to see God's influence over every aspect of our lives. We will learn to recognize and accept the suffering that is a part of life, and we will strive to see how adversity is a necessary and beneficial contrary in our experience. When we face trials, we will remember the Savior, Who descended beneath all things, and Who provided us with His example for us to follow. We will be drawn to the light. It will be within our nature to comfortably relate to all that is virtuous, lovely, of good report, or praiseworthy. We will seek after anything that creates an atmosphere that invites the Light of Christ into our lives.

The Book of Mormon helps us to understand that positive energy comes in discrete packages that are dispensed by especially cheerful individual who always have a smile on their face and a spring in their step. These people have dedicated themselves to worthwhile activities that give their lives meaning and purpose. They are committed to self-improvement and engage with others in ways that are mutually supportive. They do not waste time being defensive, but instead welcome constructive criticism. They share their knowledge and ideas with others, and are mentors to those who are on the same path toward self-discovery. They enjoy the journey as much as the destination. They will not allow power or influence to corrupt them or to deter them from focusing their energies on core principles. Even when life throws them a curve, they smile. They realize that happiness is contagious, and as carriers of the condition, they infect others with cheerfulness. They are courteous and thoughtful, and when they speak of others, they do so as if their parrot were the town gossip. They are kind and gentle, especially when interacting with the village idiot. When necessity dictates diplomacy, they celebrate their differences, because they know that we are all children of God, with unique talents and abilities.

Moroni revealed:" Jesus Christ hath shown you unto me, and I know your doing." (Mormon 8:35). "Although The Church of Jesus Christ of Latter-day Saints has earned a prominent part in the great drama of the Last Days, it is not the only force, nor the only means, that the Lord has employed, in order to bring to pass the things of which His prophets, in ancient times, have testified." (B.H. Roberts).

Book of Mormon prophets clearly taught that our physical death would be a necessary part of the merciful Plan of our Father in Heaven. But spiritual death can occur, as well, if we die "as to things pertaining unto righteousness." (Alma 12:16). The first spiritual death occurs when we commit sin after the age of accountability. We can be spiritually born again, however, through the cleansing action of the Holy Ghost, after repentance and our baptism by immersion. But there is also a second spiritual death, or an eternal separation from the presence of God that occurs if we've passed from mortality to immortality without having received the ordinances of the priesthood, and if we thereafter deny the Lord a second time by declining the vicarious work that has been performed in our behalf in the temples of the Lord.

For all of us, the time will come when our dust will return to the earth. (See 2 Nephi 1:14). It will have completed the circle of life back to the Maker and Fashioner of the universe itself. And so, in all our attempts to comprehend the universe, we are just trying to understand ourselves. Every heavy element in our bodies, including the calcium in our bones and the iron in the hemoglobin of our blood, was created by the explosion of a supernova. When we ask, what is the origin of the cosmos, or how does it all come together in such perfect harmony, and what is its destiny, we are really asking life's most basic questions: "Where did we come from, why are we here, and where are we going?"

The Book of Mormon warns
us unmistakably that a pervasive
threat to temporal and spiritual welfare
exists in the genome of every natural man.
It is hidden in an improvised explosive device
called pride, ready to explode and scatter its
lethal contents about in a deadly deluge of
deception. The warning is relevant to all,
but applies in particular to those who
are trying to move beyond a law
of carnal commandments to
embrace a celestial
standard.

To maintain the balance
of spiritual equilibrium, even
righteous Nephites needed daily doses
of study and reflection, just as we do today
as we read The Book of Mormon, so that when they
had spiritual experiences, it could be as if the veil that
was before their eyes were transparent, permitting them to
almost reach out and touch the eternities. Today, as we read
the scriptures, we can feel clear and whole, and at peace with
ourselves and with our environment. We can hold certainty
in our hands; guiding principles can resonate with reality,
allowing us to move forward on the road to our ideals. It
is no wonder that Satan tries to cloud our vision with
the glitz and the glamour of carnal counterfeits that
are nothing but optical and spiritual illusions.
His will-o-the-wisp fantasies can't stand the
heat of the mid-day sun; they'll wither
and die when confronted by the
principles of gospel doctrine
in action.

The Book of Mormon teaches that when the Lord returns, He will come in power, suggesting His personal righteousness. He will come in dominion, as well, in a reference to His authority. He will come in glory, worthy of the inner peace that righteousness brings. He will come in His majesty, which suggests that Jesus Christ is King of all the earth, and that He wields all power and is in control. He will come in might, which means not only of unusual strength, but also that He has power sufficient to the task at hand. (See Alma 5:50).

The challenge for most of us is that we receive too little revelation, and also that we look for it in all the wrong places. In this regard, The Book of Mormon is like a breath of fresh air, especially in light of the prophets' repeated warnings against dalliances with magicians, sorcerers, witches, familiar spirits, astrologers, and exorcists. These cautions are as relevant today as they were in Book of Mormon times. We need to avoid participating in latter-day iterations of divinations, enchantments, and other seances soliciting the intervention of evil spirits. Isaiah mocked those of us who relied on such. He invited "astrologers, stargazers, and monthly prognosticators, to stand and save us from the things that should come upon us. He warned all who would do so, that they would "be as stubble; the fire shall burn them." (Isaiah 47:13-14, see 3 Nephi 25:1).

Prophetic warnings from the pages of The Book of Mormon give us the tools to expose the evil designs of those who have conspired against us in the Last Days. We will not do this "with railing accusation, neither with boasting nor rejoicing," but instead with the measured response one would expect of the Lord's anointed, that is so characteristic of those with the confidence to walk in the light of the Lord. (D&C 50:33).

It is very hard to break bad habits. Today, when he is challenged, Satan gets angry, just as he did with Moses, so long ago. On that occasion, he cried with a loud voice, trembled and shook, but then departed from the great lawgiver, who remained resolute at that pivotal point in his personal progress. Things will be different during the Millennium, however. "Because of the righteousness of his people" who remain on the earth during the thousand years of peace, Satan will be bound, "wherefore, he cannot be loosed for the space of many years; for he hath no power over the hearts of the people, for they dwell in righteousness, and the Holy One of Israel reigneth."
(1 Nephi 22:26).

A classic definition of faith is that it focuses on "things which are hoped for and not seen; wherefore, dispute not because ye see not, for ye receive no witness until after the trial of your faith." (Ether 12:6). We must remember that in matters of faith, it is we, and not the Lord, who are on trial. Out of the sum of our experiences comes the trial of our faith. At the Bar of Justice, which is eminently fair, the evidence will be presented to a fair and impartial Judge. As part of God's perfect Plan, He will allow our previous acceptance or rejection of our faith-based experiences, measured against the backdrop of our subsequent actions, to determine our reward or punishment.

To those who are enslaved by drunkenness and selfish indulgence, ancient prophets have delivered a powerful message. "Wo unto them that rise up early in the morning, that they may follow strong drink, that continue until night, and wine inflame them!" (2 Nephi 15:11). People can be blinded to the pattern of progress that is before their very eyes. "They regard not the work of the Lord, neither consider the operation of his hands." (2 Nephi 15:12). They are captive because of their physical additions; bound with a stupor of thought. Telestial trauma has wiped from their memory any knowledge they might have had of God. "Their honorable men are famished, and their multitude dried up with thirst." (2 Nephi 15:13).

The Book of Mormon prompts us to ask ourselves: What do we want from life? Why do we want it? How can we obtain it? What are our short-term and long-term goals? What are our temporal and spiritual goals? How can we harmonize the two? How can we begin to develop a foundation that is built upon the principles of the Plan? How can we articulate a personal mission statement that will give our lives definition and our decisions meaning, that will imbue every action with a tangible sense of positivity and purpose?

Book of Mormon prophets all taught the same thing, reiterated by The Lord in the Last Days: There can be no latitude in His declaration that He "cannot look upon sin with the least degree of allowance." (D&C 1:31). Hence, there is no alternative to baptism, that typifies the gate through which we must all pass during our journey home to the Celestial Kingdom of God. Faith and repentance lead to that narrow gate, and just beyond its portal lie a remission of our sins, membership in the Church of Christ, and sanctification through receipt of the Holy Ghost. The way is strait and the standard undeviating, with no room for rationalization or compromise. There can be no allowances made for the casual substitution of more relaxed and less stringent entry requirements.

Book of Mormon prophets teach us that, in the spirit world, the paradise of God is the abode of the righteous. The unrepentant go instead to the spirit prison of the unjust to await their day of redemption. (See Alma 40:13). That time will come if they accept the gospel of Jesus Christ and when necessary priesthood ordinances have been vicariously performed for them. Those in the spirit prison who reject the gospel, and thereby deny that salvation comes thru the power of the Atonement of Christ, will have to satisfy Justice by paying for their sins themselves. They will not be redeemed from the Fall until they have personally "paid the uttermost farthing." (Matthew 5:26).

Dare we compare ourselves to the likes of Mormon and Moroni when we read: "Little people, like you and me, if our prayers are sometimes granted beyond all hope and probability, had better not draw hasty conclusions to our own advantage? If we were stronger, we might be less tenderly treated. If we were braver, we might be sent, with far less help, to defend far more desperate posts in the last great battle." (C.S. Lewis).

This is purportedly a Nephite prayer, taken from the sealed portion of the plates: "Dear God, so far today, I've done all right. I haven't gossiped. I haven't been testy, grumpy, nasty, selfish, overindulgent, or lost my temper, and I haven't told lies or cheated others, and I'm very thankful for that, as well. But in a few minutes, I'm going to get out of bed, and from then on, I'm certain I'm going to need a lot more help." (Anonymous).

The power to convey the meaning of gospel principles to others is a gift of the Spirit. It must reside in both the one who delivers the word and the one who is receiving it. This is the magic of gospel instruction. It is a foolproof method for illuminating the good news, because it cannot be mishandled or misrepresented. Without the Spirit, we are as "sounding brass or a tinkling cymbal." (1 Corinthians 13:1), As the Savior warned us: "If ye receive not the Spirit, ye shall not teach." (D&C 42:14). This responsibility is so great, that Jesus Christ admonished Israel, His Nephite disciples, and latter-day Israel thru his prophet Joseph Smith: "Be ye clean that bear the vessels of the Lord." (Isaiah 52:11, 3 Nephi 20:41, & D&C 38:42).

To optimally perform in their roles to the successful conclusion of God's Trilogy: (Where did I come from? Why am I here? and Where am I going?) the Nephites found that they didn't have the luxury during the production of the Second Act to sample the pleasures of Spiritual Babylon, to walk "in (their) own way, after the image of (their) own god, whose image (was) in the likeness of the world, and whose substance (was) that of an idol." (D&C 1:16). Only if the drama were played out within the strictures of the Plan, according to the storyboard that illustrated the principles of the gospel while animating its doctrine, could the anticipated blessings of Zion freely flow. For the Nephites, there was no other way it could work. "Life is all a stage," wrote Shakespeare, but only the script that had been written by God, Who was their Dialogue Coach, would bring out the best in those who participated in the production. They needed to trust in Him and in His approach, which might have been the key element of the inspiration of the most accomplished of the method actors of their day.

The prominent feature of a paralyzing phenomenon in the Last Days is that society is characterized by an unprecedented polarization of principles which is accelerating at an alarming rate. On the one hand is the kingdom of God, while on the other is a moral and ethical depravity that is nothing less than the cesspool of Satan, whose dominion is typified as a corrupt or idolatrous community. There are, after all, "save two churches only," wrote Nephi, "the one is the church of the Lamb of God, and the other is the church of the devil, (1 Nephi 14:10).

The Nephite scriptures teach us that the way that has been illuminated by the principles of the gospel should not be difficult to follow. For the Israelites in the Wilderness of Sinai, it was only necessary to look to the Brazen Serpent, the staff of Moses that typified Christ, in order to be saved. "And as many as should look upon that serpent should live, even so as many as should look upon the Son of God, with faith, having a contrite spirit, might live, even unto that life which is eternal." (Helaman 8:13-16).

When the Nephites exercised prudence, they became adept in following the most politic and profitable course, but their practicality also led them to be circumspect, or cautious. In contrast, when they approached their problems in an attitude of prayerful investigation, their qualities of worldly wisdom and erudition that they had honed so well, lost their value, and when they tried to hide their counsel from the Lord, they quickly found that their private purpose had only diminished the potency of their inquiry. Only after the façade of their artificial veneers had been stripped away, could their spirits become prominently vulnerable to the undeniable whisperings, the urgent promptings, and the unmistakable calls to action that came from the Holy Ghost.

Mormon foresaw our latter-day technological society, as well as its free-fall from faith, with few rules, regulations, or restrictions to temper either moral or ethical depravity. The better angels of our nature respond to righteousness, because the positive energy of foundation principles is immune to the capricious character quirks of those who have compromised their standards in a capitulation to the telestial trauma of secular humanism. Those of weak will cannot deny their noble birthright for very long before it begins to strangle their spontaneity as rapidly evolving children of God. Obedience to our covenants, on the other hand, can bless our lives with a vitality that quickens our spirits in ways that nothing else can. The gospel is a living, breathing entity that interacts with Christ's disciples, who are very much like you!

The Book of Mormon is just the prescription that the Doctor ordered. It will address the religious fever that elevates our testimony temperature enough to get our juices flowing with a visceral appreciation of the doctrine of Christ.

The instinct, insight, intuition, and inspiration that we so desperately seek must always be preceded by perspiration. Where there is no student, there can be no revelation, for "truth comes only to the prepared mind." (Emerson). On one occasion, Joseph Smith asked those who denigrated The Book of Mormon: "Does it remain for a people who never had faith enough to call down one scrap of revelation from heaven, and for all they have now are indebted to the faith of another people who lived hundreds and thousands of years before them, does it remain for them to say how much God has spoken and how much he has not spoken?" (H.C., 11:17-18).

The Book of Mormon invites us to embark upon a journey back through the dim recesses of memory to a place before time itself existed; to the domicile where God created order and stability out of chaos. It was Brigham Young's belief that "all organized existence began then, to " progress either to endless advancement in eternal perfections, or back to dissolution. There is no period in the eternities wherein" His creations "will become stationary," that they are "unable to advance in knowledge, wisdom, power, and glory."

All throughout our primeval
childhood, the nurturing influence
of the Savior helped to settle our minds
relating to the uncertainties that lay before
us. Moreover, we were convinced that He would
not be the author of confusion, as was Lucifer,
a son of the morning (see 2 Nephi 24:12), but
rather of a peace that would hinge, in part,
upon our acceptance of The Book of
Mormon as Another Testament
of Him as our Lord our God
and our Redeemer.

Amulek used the
vivid imagery of the
cross in Alma 34:40-41, to
impress upon the minds of the
poor Zoramites the doctrine of the
Atonement. Its symbolism is found
in the ordinance of the Sacrament, where
the faithful take upon themselves the name
of Christ, and promise to always remember
Him, and keep His commandments. This
sacred rite permits them to enjoy in
greater abundance the godly
qualities of unimpaired
innocence and
virtue.

Familiarity with
Book of Mormon doctrine
encourages us to put our finger
to the pulse of guiding principles and
monitor the status of our obedience. This
enables us to see how the elegant simplicity
of the Plan of our Heavenly Father trumps the
deception, confusion, and complexity of its
convoluted and counterfeit alternatives
that exhibit no detectable sinus
rhythm, at all.

Because
of The Book
of Mormon, when
we find our way back
to our heavenly home, we
may still be clothed in our
tangible trappings but we'll
also discover that we've been
arrayed with the power and
authority of metaphysical
vestments that nurture the
intrinsic light that had
always flickered
from within
us.

One blessing that
comes from reading The
Book of Mormon is that it
provides us with opportunities
to enjoy familiarity with the
Way, the Truth, and the Life,
or, one could say, to have
personal experience with
God, Jesus Christ, and
the Holy Ghost.

We
read The Book
of Mormon that
we might hear the
voice of the Lord that
is unto all, for "there is
none to escape; and there
is no eye that shall not see,
neither ear that shall not hear,
neither heart that shall not be
penetrated." (D&C 1:2).

We are
introduced
thru The Book of
Mormon to the Holy
Ghost, Who is the author
of our acumen, the avatar
of our agency, the architect
of our aptitude, the benefactor of
all of our blessings, the designer of
discipleship, the initiator of insight,
the inventor of intelligence, the patron
of perception, the provider of our praise,
the sponsor of our scholarship, and the
ultimate source of our understanding;
not to mention the craftsman of our
comfort, the guarantor of all gifts,
and the champion of committed
Christians everywhere.

Those who believe in The Book
of Mormon are of one accord, in spite of
varying cultural, social, political, or economic
circumstances. All over the world, its principles
and doctrines are unambiguously understood.
Believers are characterized as brothers and
sisters, whose striking similarities
overshadow any perceived
differences.

As we journey through "this vale of tears" (see Wycliffe's Bible, Psalms 84:6), the real journey to Christ will have only just begun. Having been born again through baptism, we'll "press forward" with complete dedication and with "steadfastness," or with confidence, and a firm determination in Christ, "having a perfect brightness of hope," or perfect faith, and charity, or "a love of God and of all men." When we do this, "feasting upon the word of Christ" by receiving nourishment and strength from the Bible, The Book of Mormon, the Doctrine & Covenants, and the Pearl of Great Price, and if we will then endure to the end in righteousness, we "shall have eternal life," which is the greatest of all the gifts that God can bestow upon us. (2 Nephi 31:20).

By his own personal experience, Alma painfully understood the principles that are related to real conversion (see Alma Chapter 36), as he endured a metamorphosis to which many of us can relate. It pointed him in the direction of humility. He had a conscious and unmistakable recognition of his iniquities, and a deep godly sorrow for his sins. Next came inescapable suffering that stimulated an appeal to the Savior, together with an awakening understanding of the power of the Atonement. Only then, came forgiveness, spiritual enlightenment, and great joy. This encouraged him to commit to a lifestyle that would forever thereafter be characterized by his righteousness.

The Book of Mormon teaches us that "we are created as much from the dust of eternity as we are from the dust of the earth." (Joseph Wirthlin, C.R., 4/2006). In contrast to the coarse, crude, profane, and vulgar materials of the earth, there are at our core, immortal elements that have come to us from our former home. These are untainted, uncontaminated, and undefiled. When God weaves them into the tapestry of our mortal cloth, the injunction that He has given to care for our bodies as if they were temples that glorified Him carries a new meaning whose undertone conveys a sense of immediate urgency.

The Savior recognized that the Nephites were just one branch of the House of Israel. (See 3 Nephi 20:21-22). In fact, Lehi was of the tribe of Manasseh through Joseph, and Ishmael was of Ephraim. (See Alma 10:3). "Now the sons of Jacob were twelve: The sons of Leah; Reuben, Jacob's firstborn, and Simeon, and Levi, and Judah, and Issachar, and Zebulun; the sons of Rachel: Joseph, and Benjamin; And the sons of Bilhah, Rachel's handmaid: Dan and Naphtali; and the sons of Zilpah, Leah's handmaid: Gad and Asher." (Genesis 35:22-26). Leah: Reuben, Simeon, Levi, Judah, Issachar, and Zebulun. Rachel: Joseph (Ephraim and Manasseh / a double portion), and Benjamin, Bilhah (Rachel's maid): Dan and Naphtali, Zilpah (Leah's maid): Gad and Asher. No wonder our desire to be adopted into such a family sometimes seems tentative.

Benjamin taught (Mosiah 2:20-25), that
the perfection of our Heavenly Father renders us
completely helpless to alter the progress or influence
the outcome of any endeavors in which He is engaged.
It was when Moses realizes his utter dependence upon a
Higher Power that he exclaimed: "Now, for this cause I
know that man is nothing, which thing I never had
supposed." (Moses 1:10). It is in that dependance
that we recognize His ordinances as the portal
that opens up to our view possibilities that
would otherwise remain beyond the
reach of our wildest hopes
and dreams.

The Nephite church sometimes
displayed homogeneity, while at other times
it was quite diverse, both of which conditions could
be challenging to members desiring to strengthen their
testimonies. Today, diversity within a church population that
is experiencing world-wide expansion can be equally demanding, but
it can also serve to enrich and strength its members. Zion comes in many
different colors. It speaks Aymara, Dutch, Fijian, French, Mandarin, Russian,
and dozens of other languages. It lives in over 3,500 stakes (2024) in most of
the countries in the world, from Argentina to Zimbabwe. It has over 17 million
members who are red, yellow, brown, black, and white. Zion wears a sarong, a
grass skirt, a blue collar, a tupeno, a kilt, and a business suit. It lives in
igloos, bamboo huts, double-wides, townhomes, cardboard shacks, and
high-rises. Most important of all, it shares a common testimony
that Jesus is the Christ, and that His love, indeed, makes the
world go round. Today, it is more important than ever to
remember that there is no United States of America
in heaven. The great equalizer in the sight of
God is obedience by His children to the
laws and ordinances of the gospel.
In that obedience, all may be
at-one with Christ.

During what
can sometimes be
a long process of the
development of our faith
in The Book of Mormon, it
may become necessary for us to
take a few steps into the darkness
in order to allow the spiritual strong
searchlight of truth to illuminate the
way before us. Only after the trial of
our faith will it be confirmed by the
Spirit that the book is everything
that its authors, and our Lord
and Savior, claim it to be.
(See D&C 17:6).

Every discussion of our faith in the
divine design elements of the Plan of our
Heavenly Father must distinguish it from
its caricatures. Our dialogue requires neither
naiveté, nor gullibility, nor wishful thinking.
It demands our confidence, to be sure, but it is
also more than just optimism. Our faith in
The Book of Mormon, for example, is not only
an exercise in positive thinking, for it is
far more than attitude. Saving faith
can move mountains, or at the very
least, it can illustrate the way to
climb over our obstacles or
walk around them.

It may seem
that the easier way
out is to adopt the ways
of the world. It may be harder
to acknowledge that there exists
with each of us an autobiographical
thread that leads all the way back to
heaven. Sometimes, we forget how The
Book of Mormon has been designed
to transform us, through the Plan
of Salvation, into fine-tuned
and well-oiled machines for
the making of gods.

The Book of
Mormon functions
like a stethoscope with
an astonishing ability to
detect the vital capacity of
our spirit. When our hearts
have broken in contrition,
we are able to quantify the
steady sinus rhythm that
confirms the congruence
that must exist between
our terrestrial world
and the abode of
the gods.

Benjamin clearly taught his people in Zarahemla that when we have been spiritually born of God (see Mosiah 5:7), we are given the invitation to re-write the record of our lives. We can't go back and start a new beginning, but we can begin now to make a new ending. It's the doctrine of Christ that makes it possible for our lives to become fairytales that are waiting to be written by the finger of God.

As we study The Book of Mormon, there comes a familiarity with principles that stands in sharp contrast to society's values that are continually morphed into unrecognizable forms by the shifting sands of cultural expediency. It is our covenants that will shield us from these mutating values, and they will provide a stable moral foundation during our transformation into the full stature of our spirits.

Book of Mormon prophets charted the course leading to repentance. It is a process that winds its way thru the Atonement. It will be difficult to negotiate the path that lies before us, but completing the journey will bring about lasting change. It will require of us great courage, much strength, many tears, unceasing prayers, and untiring efforts. The work is challenging, but its retirement benefits are out of this world.

As soon as we have mustered the courage to tackle The Book of Mormon, we'll be consumed by a divine fire. After all the elements of our moral fiber have been thereby kindled, we will be aflame with faith, and be better prepared to face and to conquer our worst demons.

God's Plan of
Redemption, anchored by
the Atonement that is so clearly
elucidated by prophets of The Book
of Mormon, makes allowances for our
mistakes, that we might learn from them
even as we grasp the horns of sanctuary
and are justified by the Spirit. Our
gospel-oriented homes will then
become the wonderful centers
for the talented and gifted
that were envisioned by
our Father before the
earth fell into
existence.

Book of Mormon
prophets have reassured us with
the cheerful news that forgiveness is a
balm that should be liberally applied to
heal our bruised egos, our bitter feelings,
and our battered birthrights. The Savior's
example also helps us to have bowels that
are moved to compassion for others of
God's children who are struggling
with their own misfortunes, or
who are staggering under
the weight of their own
unresolved sin.

The enticements and seductions of the Devil stand in sharp contrast to the blessings of salvation that follow repentance and forgiveness. (See 2 Nephi Chapter 28). The Atonement of Jesus Christ is the primary weapon in our arsenal that we will need in order to vanquish the father of lies. Our correct understanding of gospel doctrine will go a long way toward re-enthroning the Savior as the God of this earth.

Our faith, together with its conjoined twin of repentance, motivates us to action by jarring us out of collective complacency. When we have decided to make The Book of Mormon a part of our daily lives, we will be endowed with the power to reach out and touch the face of God, as we nurture our spiritual sixth sense that has found an avenue for expression that is within our hearts.

The Book of
Mormon blesses
us with easy fluency
in a celestial language
that is rhythmical, melodious,
soothing to our ears, and calming
to our souls. When we hear the Spirit
quietly whisper: "You're a stranger here,"
we will be comforted by the realization
that it's because we've "wandered
from a more exalted sphere."
(Eliza R. Snow).

We have observed
that many Christians of
convenience will implicitly
sanction the truthfulness of a
precept, principle, or doctrine, but
they often do so without the moral
element of responsibility which we
call faith. Of those to whom much is
given, though, much is expected. The
gift of faith to believe in The Book of
Mormon demands action. So, when
we exercise our agency, even if we've
performed good works, if we do so
without an abiding trust in the
promise of Moroni with which
we have all been blessed, our
works will fall short of
the mark, because
our faith lacks
vitality.

It makes no
difference to our Heavenly Father
whether we are combating the temptations
of the Seven Deadly Sins of lust, gluttony,
greed, sloth, wrath, envy, and pride, or simply the
garden-variety transgressions that we face every
day of our lives. The teachings of the prophets in
The Book of Mormon stipulate that we must go
thru a process of repentance before we can be
admitted into the Church of Jesus Christ
by baptism, receive the gift of the
Holy Ghost, and thereafter
walk in the light of
life.

Our own
journey to the veil
recalls the wisdom of
Winston Churchill, who
said: "There comes for each
of us a special moment when
we are figuratively tapped on the
shoulder and offered a chance to do a
very special thing, unique to ourselves
and fitted to our talents. What a tragedy
if that moment should find us unprepared
or unqualified for that which could have been
our finest hour." Standing before God, angels,
and witnesses at the Judgment Bar, it will be a
fitting conclusion to the hours that have been
spent as eager participants in preparatory
excursions thru Book of Mormon
principles and doctrine.

Thomas Jefferson wrote about "the religion builders" of his day who "had so distorted and deformed the doctrines of Jesus, so muffled them in mysticisms, fancies and falsehoods, and had caricatured them into forms so inconceivable, as to shock reasonable thinkers. Happy in the prospect of a restoration of primitive Christianity, I must leave it to younger persons," he concluded, "to encounter and lop off the false branches which have been grafted into it by the mythologists of the middle and modern ages."

There is no revelation where there is no student, and so as long as we ask the wrong questions relating to The Book of Mormon, we will be at odds with faith. Our rational minds will never be able to bridge the gap that must exist between the profane character of the worldly-wise and the wisdom manifested in God's divine truth.

The account of God's Creation that has survived in the Bible provides precious few details that relate to the Fall of Adam and Eve and to the Atonement of Christ, which is the doctrine that we must understand in order to have the faith to be clean from the blood and sins of our generation, live life in abundance, and become heirs of salvation. Fortunately, these mysteries are explained with stunning clarity in The Book of Mormon.

Every time that we drag ourselves to the mercy seat of the Savior and prostrate ourselves before the altar of faith, gratitude swells in our hearts, and we marvel how The Book of Mormon has lifted our spirits. We examine our lives through the magnifying lens of His Spirit to look for ways to improve. Because of our repentance, the Savior becomes the wind beneath our wings, and within the sphere of His influence, we find ourselves soaring higher than the eagles.

Every time we
encounter the principles
of the Plan during our study
of The Book of Mormon, we find the
sinews of our bodies resonating with
religious recognition as we have our
déjà vu moments. At the end of the
day, everyone who hearkens to
the voice of the Spirit will
eventually come unto
God in this way,
and really
live.

The Book of
Mormon emboldens us
with hope and it blesses us
with the fortitude to be able to
endure. It animates us to seek
after anything that is lovely,
or of good report, or that
is praiseworthy.

It is in
The Book of Mormon
where we learn about the
autobiographical thread that
is intertwined with our sinews,
that winds its way to our Father
in Heaven. The Holy Ghost helps
us to remember the lesson that has
been stitched into our souls: That
we have been placed on the earth
for one reason – that the Plan
might become a machine
for the making of
gods.

There
will come an 'a ha!'
moment for those who are
persevering in their wrestle to
embrace The Book of Mormon,
when the sun shall not go down,
"neither shall the moon withdraw
itself. For the Lord shall be
their everlasting light."
(Isaiah 60:20).

Saving faith has to be more than just an
intellectual acknowledgement of the gospel
principles that are championed in The Book of
Mormon. As a vital contrary, its influence will
extend only as far as our deeds. Therefore, our
works become a necessary companion to our
vital, active confidence that the power of
the Word will have enough inherent
energy to guide us through the
transformation of our lives
into new creatures
in Christ.

The elements of
our Father's Plan that are
clearly defined in The Book of
Mormon speak to our spirits, for
every principle of the gospel carries
within itself a witness that it is true.
Its language is universal and when our
minds have been illuminated by faith, we
will enjoy a familiarity and a practiced
fluency with the revealed word of God
that opens our eyes to vistas of
eternal proportion.

It is in The Book of Mormon where we discover that, among the Nephites, "they who were baptized in the name of Jesus were called the church of Christ." (3 Nephi 26:21).

The depth and breadth of our forgiveness acts as a celestial barometer measuring the way we deal with the high blood pressure of self-inflicted pain and the telestial trauma seemingly exacted by others. Its quality is a cosmic compass, pointing us toward eternal life. It is a stethoscope, measuring the vital capacity of our prideful hearts that must be broken in contrition in order to exhibit the steady sinus rhythm that confirms perfect harmony with the proven principles of perfection. Our forgiveness is a pacemaker that measures out therapeutic doses of doctrinal energy. If we are to have a stable heart rate and avoid the angina of anguish, we must be absolutely and unconditionally forgiving. If we want one day to live comfortably with our Heavenly Father in His kingdom, we must first place the nitroglycerin tablets of tenderness under our tongues to temper the urge to use them as weapons to lash out at others who may have offended us.

We acknowledge
that The Book of Mormon has
become a blueprint for survival in
the Last Days. Ours was to have been
an Age of Enlightenment, but instead it
has become a conceptual free-for-all, with few
rules, regulations, or constraints of any kind.
Righteousness has always responded to the better
angels of our nature because it reflects foundation
principles that are not subject to the vagaries of
men. While they may cope with the trauma
of secular humanism, they cannot live for
long with unrighteousness before it
strangles their spontaneity as
evolving children of
God.

Babylon's image
consultants are prone to
confuse conventional wisdom
with the weightier matters of the
law in the tumultuous last days on
earth. Mormon cautioned: "Take heed,
that ye do not judge that which is evil to
be of God, or that which is good and of God
to be of the devil." (Moroni 7:14). In the vast
arena that is the world, there are no shades of
gray for those who have not only received the
Light of Christ, but also the greater power of
the Holy Ghost. For to them it is given "to
judge, that (they) may know good from
evil; and the way to judge is as plain,
that ye may know with a perfect
knowledge, as the daylight
is from the dark night."
(Moroni 7:15).

The Book of Mormon catalyzes our tenacity to bear our testimonies to the world of what we have been taught by the Spirit, and to certify that it has been as profound for us as it was for the multitude on the Day of Pentecost, when the witness of Peter and the other apostles carried the day as it penetrated the hearts of all who heard them, giving them the desire to ask: "What must we do if we want to inherit eternal life?"

The virtues that we acknowledge as the tender mercies of God (see 1 Nephi 1:20) focus on their ability to touch our hearts and change our nature, to soften us, and to humble us, to make us as pliant clay in the hands of the Master Potter, to mold us as children, and to securely envelop our spirits within the vale of happiness that has been prepared for the Saints.

To the
people among
whom Alma the
Younger ministered,
it may have seemed that
the easier wrong was more
expedient, but that was because
it harmonized with the values of
Babylon. Worldliness surrounded
the Nephites throughout all the land,
and without the stabilizing influence
of the word of God to choose the harder
right, moral equivocation often become
the easier way out, defining bad habit
patterns of behavior that required
the timely intervention of
the Spirit.

Alma showed
his Nephite brethren
how to generate sufficient
faith to burst free of their self-
imposed limitations, teaching how
God has ordained a Plan whereby we
might one day attain His stature and
become all that He now is. But we may do
this only if we've incorporated into our being
and nature His image and likeness. Through
that transformative process, Alma taught that
our corruption will take on incorruption, and
our bodies will become clean and pure,
streaming with intrinsic light.
(See Alma 41:4).

Nephi, the son of Helaman, believed that gaining a testimony of the gospel would require that his people prostrate themselves before the mercy seat of the Lord, that they might more easily feel the sweet influence of the Spirit. He understood that without such a token of contrition, God's "wisdom cannot reveal itself, culture cannot become manifest, strength cannot fight, wealth becomes useless, and intelligence cannot be applied." (Heraclitus, ancient Greek philosopher, from Ephesus).

Alma had taught his grandson Nephi a wonderful truth, that, in the resurrection, we will inherit glorified bodies and we will become re-acquainted with our spirits, never again to be separated by sin. In fact, Alma taught that "the spirit and the body shall be reunited again in its perfect form; both limb and joint shall be restored to its proper frame." (Alma 11:43). Therefore, it makes sense that we would want to keep our bodies as pure and as holy as are our spirits, in order for the gospel to bless our lives, starting right now, as was envisioned by our Father in Heaven when He created His Plan.

Satan, who is the adversary of Book of Mormon principles, manipulates the mutated versions of honor, truth, love, generosity, and virtue to further his agenda. These dreadful distortions of character are made up of bellicose behaviors, recalcitrant rituals, cunning customs, treacherous telestial traditions, hostile habits, duplicitous deviations, insincere institutions, and sneaky social conventions. These fiery contrarian darts have the power to sabotage our noblest efforts to embrace the truth.

Book of Mormon prophet-historians provide unequivocal understanding and unambiguous definitions of eternal truth. These allow us to benefit from the events within which we are swept up, to learn from our interactions with others, to grow within our environment no matter how unique or difficult that process might seem to us, and to protect ourselves with the shield of gospel principles from worldly influences that would otherwise encroach upon the fortress of our spiritual security, symmetry, and sanctuary.

If it were possible to bring together all the written records from our past, we would find that, overwhelmingly, they are "religious in nature; that the primary purpose to which writing has been put thru the ages has been for keeping a remembrance of God's dealing with men." (Hugh Nibley). A striking exception to this rule has been the profusion of the profane propaganda that has poured from the press like an avalanche in the past 200 years. Satan's secular humanists have at last found their forum for falsehood in both the print and electronic media. Little wonder that Jacob warned us that to be learned is good, but only if we hearken to the counsel of God. (See 2 Nephi 9:29).

Consistent with the book of Psalms (149:1), wherein ancient Israel is described as "a congregation of Saints," and on 30 other occasions in the Old Testament, and in at least 73 cases in the New Testament, where the members of the church were characterized as "saints," in The Book of Mormon, both Jacob and Benjamin employed the same term to describe the righteous who believed in the Holy One of Israel. (See 2 Nephi 9:18 & Mosiah 3:19).

Among the Nephites, the outward observances of the Law were as phylacteries. (See 2 Nephi 25:27-30). In The Book of Mormon, we repeatedly see that real justification only comes thru saving faith in the principles and ordinances of the gospel. Really, there are only 2 ways that lie before us. "One leads to an ever lower and lower plane, where are heard cries of despair and the curses of the poor, where manhood shrivels and possessions wear down the bearer; while the other leads to the highlands of the morning, where are heard the glad shouts of humanity, and where honest effort is rewarded with immortality." (John Altgeld).

Those who are stiff-necked have skin so thick and calloused that extraordinary means become necessary to penetrate and touch their spirits. Enos reported: "There was nothing save it was exceeding harshness, preaching, and prophesying of wars, and contentions, and destructions, and continually reminding them of death, and the duration of eternity, and the judgments and the power of God, and all these things, stirring them up continually to keep them in the fear of the Lord. I say there was nothing short of these things, and exceedingly great plainness of speech, would keep them from going down speedily to destruction." (Enos 1:23).

A characteristic of the Last Days is that society has become increasingly polarized. On the one hand we see the kingdom of God, and on the other is the dominion of the devil. Satan's zone of influence is typified as a corrupt or idolatrous community. There are, after all, "save two churches only; the one is the church of the Lamb of God, and the other is the church of the devil, wherefore, whoso belongeth not to the church of the Lamb of God belongeth to that great church, which is the mother of abominations; and she is the whore of all the earth."
(1 Nephi 14:10).

The prophets have blessed us with the eternal truths of the gospel, and they do so in plainness and simplicity, so that all might understand. It is the nature of the apostolic calling to bear witness to all of the world of the divinity of Jesus Christ and teach the path to salvation and exaltation in ways that are easily understood. Since the Bible is today ambiguous, unclear, and even contradictory, it must be the result of errors of both omission and commission that were introduced by uninspired, untutored, and even malicious copyists over the years. (See 1 Nephi 13:28).

For
the Nephites,
the gospel was the
perfect law of liberty,
setting them free to make
good decisions, free to receive
the blessings of the priesthood,
and free to serve others in more
powerful and significant ways.
They were free to enjoy unlimited
opportunity for improvement as
they committed themselves to
the principles of the Plan of
Salvation. They were free
to improve their lives,
beginning in time,
and continuing
in eternity.

Despite
an abundance
of gold and silver
throughout the land,
all the Nephites really
had to show for themselves
was their character, and each
one of them told their own story.
Theirs was a record that couldn't lie
inasmuch as it was stitched within the
sinews of their bodies, as well as upon the
fleshy tables of their hearts. Theirs was a
slide show that will one day be unfolded
before God, angels, and witnesses, who
will innocently ask if they wouldn't
mind providing the narrative.

The
Book of
Mormon uses
faith to fan the
fires of our resolve.
We hope and pray to
have courage to change
the things we can, for the
serenity to accept the things
we cannot, and for God's
wisdom to recognize the
difference between
the two.

The Prophet Alma often
spoke of being "born again." Of the
people in the land of Mormon, he said:
"Behold, (Jesus Christ) changed their hearts;
yea, he awakened them out of a deep sleep, and
they awoke unto God. Behold, they were in the midst
of darkness; nevertheless, their souls were illuminated
by the light of the everlasting word." (Alma 5:7, see Alma
7:14, 22:15, & 36:24). Those who have been born again leave
behind their previous lives, and become quickened to spiritual
things, promising to never again return to their wicked ways.
They change their names and become "saints, a translation of
a Greek word that is also rendered 'holy,' the fundamental
idea being that of consecration or separation for a sacred
purpose; but since what was set apart for God must be
without imperfection, the word came to mean 'free
from blemish,' whether physical or moral. In
the New Testament, the saints are those
who by baptism have entered into
the Christian covenant."
(Bible Dictionary).

"Be not troubled, for when all these things shall come to pass, ye may know that the promises which have been made unto you shall be fulfilled." (D&C 45:34-35). Prior to the Second Coming of Christ it will be as it was in the years before the birth of the Savior, when great signs were given in Zarahemla "to the intent that there should be no cause for unbelief," and also "to the intent that whosoever (would) believe might be saved." (Helaman 14:18-19). For now, the Savior has revealed Himself to all the world thru The Book of Mormon, but ultimately, He will do so "from heaven with power and great glory ... and dwell in righteousness with men on earth a thousand years." (D&C 29:11).

The Book of Mormon speaks "of things as they really are, and of things as they really will be," which are manifest in plainness for the salvation of our souls. (Jacob 4:13). In contrast is the intellectual embroidery that is at times preferred to the whole ensemble of the gospel; the frills to the fabric, as it were. The Book of Mormon gives us the absolute anchors that we so desperately need. If we give it a chance, we will find that there is more realism in the word of God than there could ever be in a secularism that is congenitally short sighted.

The Adversary of all that is good knows every trick, and his strategies among the Nephites and Lamanites were not so very different from those that he employs today. He advocates evil by making drinking and smoking look 'cool,' and by rationalizing cheating, lying, and even stealing. He plays mind games with us to get us to use drugs, and he clothes the latest fashions in fine twined linens. Immorality and swearing are woven into popular music and hit movies. He minimizes the seriousness of sin by telling us "Everyone's doing it." "It doesn't hurt anyone else." "Just once won't hurt." "I can always repent later." "It's not a big deal." And even, "The devil made me do it."

The prophets speak to us from the pages of The Book of Mormon, inviting us to be baptized, that we might enjoy the quiet serenity of the Sabbath day as we never have before. We are introduced to new experiences during our day of worship, service, and rest, that take us far from the tumult of the teeming multitudes and the telestial crowd that too often reflects the lifestyle of the rich and famous.

The wicked Lamanites felt neither love nor loyalty for anything or anyone else but themselves, and enjoyed neither the blessings of unity nor the peace that was the province solely of the righteous. Instead, the father of contention, who is Satan, oversaw their self-destruction and he perversely enjoyed the process. They were punished by their sins, and not so much for them. We think that it is God Who applies punishment, and that He does it externally, the way parents often do, but He does not. We say: "If you don't clean your room, you can't drive the car for a week." God says: "If you don't clean your room, you'll have to live in it for a week." At the end of the day, we will be consigned to endure the consequences of our disobedience to God's law.

When the hearts of the wicked are hardened against the admonitions of The Book of Mormon, and minds are closed to its message of salvation, light is diminished, leaving their faltering spirits vulnerable to the relentlessly aggressive tactics of the Devil. Left alone, they are influenced more by the lies of the Deceiver than by illuminating truth, and they risk being dragged by the heavy weight of his chains of darkness down to the hell of misunderstanding, ignorance, and self-destructive patterns of behavior.

The Cedars of Lebanon that are mentioned in the Bible and Book of Mormon were evergreen, beautiful, aromatic, wide spreading, long lived, and had many uses. (See 2 Nephi 12:13 & 24:8). Members of the church are symbolized by those trees. They will declare that since the destruction of Babylon, no feller, a person who cuts down trees, has come up against them to smite them. In similar manner, it's the righteous who shall "flourish like the palm tree (and) grow like a cedar in Lebanon. Those that (are) planted in the house of the Lord shall flourish in the courts of our God." (Psalms 92:12). Cedars of Lebanon may grow in what appear to be harsh environments. It is only upon closer inspection that the oasis of an underlying current of life-sustaining water may be noticed, that brings nourishment to the roots of the thirsty trees.

"I believe our state after death will be beautiful with colour, music, and speech of flowers and faces I love. (See Moroni 10:34). Without this faith, there would be little meaning in my life. I should be a mere pillar of darkness in the dark. Observers in the full enjoyment of their bodily senses pity me, but it is because they do not see the golden chamber in my life where I dwell delighted; for dark as my path may seem to be, I carry a magic light in my heart. Faith, the spiritual strong searchlight, illuminates the way, and although sinister doubts lurk in the shadow, I walk unafraid towards the Enchanted Wood where the foliage is always green, where joy abides, where nightingales nest and sing, and where life and death are one in the presence of the Lord."
(Helen Keller, "Midstream").

When our foundation has been built
upon the bedrock of the gospel (see 1 Nephi 2:10), we
will be firm and steadfast. As we nurture the habits of
prayer and of repentance, we will begin to love ourselves
and our neighbors. We will experience the joy of service,
insomuch that we will not be easily shaken in our
testimonies (see 1 Nephi 3:29), and we will, in a
coming day, spring up unto eternal life in
royal courts on high, in the Celestial
Kingdom of God.

As we read and
study the thousand-year-
long history of the Nephites
and Lamanites, we realize that
time is an artificial dimension in
which we will never be completely
at ease, for we are eternal beings.
We realize that time is transitory
by definition, and it is only our
perspective that makes it seem
that it is we who move thru
it, when it is really the
other way around.

Sometimes, those who
innocently pursue truth may
still have difficulty finding it. They
don't realize that gaining a testimony of
The Book of Mormon can be like a butterfly.
If we chase after it, we will never catch it. But
if we quietly contemplate the harmony and
the symmetry of the gospel of Jesus Christ,
and we follow the admonition of Moroni
to seek the confirmation of the Spirit,
the joy of the Lord and a peace that
surpasses all understanding
will come and gently rest
on our shoulders.

The Book of
Mormon is an effective
antidote to a telestial poison
affecting those who are caught up in
the trauma of temporal traps, or who have
permitted their faith to become so flawed that
they have been blinded to the impotence of their
false gods. Sooner or later, the virulence of their
infection will catch up to them, and overwhelm
their doctrinal defenses. Without the scriptures
to give them renewed bursts of energy, those
who feel confusion, abandonment, despair,
or disillusionment may succumb to the
poison of the pleasures of the world,
and perish in Babylon.

All
around
the world, the
gospel is shared by
way of a hierarchy that
is based on understanding
at first, and next on acceptance,
then on commitment, and finally
on recommitment. Preaching is similar
to understanding, teaching to acceptance,
expounding to commitment, and exhortation
to re-commitment. Testimony is an expression of
action that follows the internalization of principles.
It is borne with strenuous effort that reflects the price
that has been paid to understand the voice of the Lord
concerning those principles. Testimony is a reflection
of the value placed on direct experience with the spirit,
as it teaches us about those principles. Testimony is
not free, but is purchased at considerable expense.
Testimony releases the power of principles, their
merit and validity, and empowers us to bind
ourselves to those principles by covenants
of action that increase our strength
and endurance, day by day, as
we learn to rely upon the
Lord in all that we
say and do.

The Book of
Mormon grounds us
to practical belief, but
its elements commit us
to an upward thrust.
It confirms that
we are known
to God.

The
Atonement
gives each of us
the opportunity to be
repetitively re-vitalized,
and to be re-introduced to that
magical kingdom where our hopes
and our dreams really do come true,
and we all live happily ever after. When
we wish upon the star of Jesus Christ, it will
make no difference who we are. Anything that
our hearts desire will come to us. If we inject the
energy of our souls into our dreams, no request
we have will be too extreme, and that includes
gaining a testimony of our Savior, of the
mission of the prophet Joseph Smith,
and of the divine authenticity
of The Book of Mormon.

We are not
ashamed to "declare
(God's) doing among the people."
Fearlessly and convincingly, we yoke
ourselves with those "who make mention that
His name is exalted." (2 Nephi 22:4). We link
arms with those who've also made the decision to
"stand as witnesses of God at all times and in
al things, and in all places ... even until
death." (Mosiah 18:9).

Many passages in The Book of Mormon illustrate how difficult it was to write upon plates and to correct or clarify that which had already been engraven. It is obvious that the Nephites struggled with the work of engraving the sacred record. Even under the best of circumstances, the process must have been tedious.

When we have been invited to familiarize ourselves with The Book of Mormon, the responsibility becomes ours. It doesn't belong to anyone else, nor do they have a right to it. If we don't engage our study with our might, mind, and strength, the Spirit will remain silent. Therefore, we must accept the invitation with the intention of carrying out our duty as if our lives depended upon it, as they surely do.

Our Father in Heaven is sensitive to our needs, and He listens to our prayers. In conformity to some spiritual law, we can tap into and draw upon the life force that is the Spirit of God. When we do so, we are, in effect, touching the garment of Jesus.

The Nephites were the happiest when they observed the summons to gather in their sanctuaries to enjoy the companionship of the Spirit, where they would receive not only health in their navels, but also life sustaining marrow in their bones; even as their delighted congregations reverberated with the pleasant sounds of the anticipation of an even more enthralling re-unification in heaven with their Father, Who was their God.

The Book of
Mormon teaches that
the Atonement of Christ
has such power that even if
we've been gravely wounded
by our sins, they will not heal
imperfectly, leaving soul scars.
The Balm of Gilead is a celestial
form of dermabrasion. Through
its application, lacerations that
resulted from telestial trauma
will fade away, leaving no
evidence of spiritual
damage.

It seems that whenever life for the Nephites was going
well, they were fooled into thinking that they could control events
and determine outcomes, when, in fact, most were beyond the vale of
their influence. What they could direct was their creative and adaptive
response to the unpredictable circumstances that were a part of their daily
activities. They would not then be as children who'd been tossed to and fro
as flotsam and jetsam on the sea of life, and who were "carried about with
every wind of doctrine, by the sleight of men, and cunning craftiness."
(Ephesians 4:14). Today, there are those living among us who stand
for nothing but will fall for anything, and who think very little
of cursing the darkness without ever thinking to hold up a
candle. They lack a strong will, but make up for it with
an even more powerful won't. If they bend their knee,
they do so only because they believe that they
are taking a bow.

For those
of us with eyes to see and
ears to hear, The Book of Mormon
is like a breath of fresh air. It throws
open the windows of understanding, that
we might better comprehend the principles of
the gospel that must forever remain as mysteries
to those who have not spiritually prepared themselves
for personal revelation from God. The Lord has assured
us that we "shall know of a surety that these things are
true, for from heaven will (He) declare it unto (us)."
(D&C 5:12). When we seek to understand, and we
ask as Antionah did of Alma: "What does the
scripture mean?" because of our baptism,
we will comprehend the principles
that relate to its doctrine.
(Alma 12:21).

An initial
reading of The Book
of Mormon emancipates us
from self-limiting conditions
that had beforehand blinded us to
a more expansive view of life. It frees
us to pay closer attention to celestial
guideposts and principles. It invites
us to experience more intense and
reflective self-awareness, deeper
and more abiding humility,
reinvigorated confidence,
and incomprehensively
more profound and
enduring faith.

On the fourth day of the creation of the world, God commanded "the greater light to rule the day, and the lesser light to rule the night." (Genesis 1:16). It is intriguing to think of the greater light as the Holy Ghost, and the lesser light as the Light of Christ. The purpose of the lesser light is to lead Heavenly Father's children to His doorstep, where the greater light of the Holy Ghost waits to invite them to enjoy His grace through a portal that the faithful often identify as the teachings in The Book of Mormon and the other Standard Works that describe and define the gospel of Jesus Christ.

Our Father Who dwells in Heaven never envisioned that our testimonies of The Book of Mormon should follow the receipt of signs from above. Our faith precedes the miracle. We must take a few steps into the darkness before the flaming fire of the Spirit will illuminate the way that lies before us. A confirmation by the Holy Ghost will always flow along the pathway that has been created by our faith, even when it passes uncomfortably close to the taunting inhabitants of great and spacious buildings.

The Book of Mormon reestablishes the precise synchronicity that should exist between the daily demands that we all face during mortality and the grand scope of the divine design of our Heavenly Father. It conforms to a majestic clockwork that was calibrated at the creation of the world to coordinate with heaven's time frame.

We read in The Book of Mormon that nearly every time that disobedient Nephites turned their backs on the Law, no matter the magnitude of their temporal preparation, it proved to be of no benefit in avoiding the pitfalls to their progression, with the inevitable consequence that disaster then rained down upon their society. That calamity has been symbolized in the scriptures by the burning of stubble and of chaff that are very quickly engulfed, and then consumed by fire.

The great
day of Judgment
does not lie beyond a
distant horizon, but it is
today. We speak, think, and
act in accordance with telestial,
terrestrial, or celestial laws that
are before us. Just as a barometer
is used to measure the direction
in which the weather is headed,
The Book of Mormon helps us
to be aware of the bearing we
must take if we desire to
reach the shelter and
security of our
home port in
heaven.

The necessity
of the principle of
opposition (see 2 Nephi
2:10-13 & Alma 42:16),
does not give us license to
act recklessly or capitulate in
our behavior to the dark side, in
the mistaken belief that we will be
able to transfer the blame and avoid
responsibility for our comportment.
The Atonement stands at attention
to repair the shattered vestiges of
our lives, and restore us to our
perfect and proper frames, so
that, once again, we will be
as good as new.

No wind can
blow except it fills
our sails to carry each of
us closer to our destination,
in the direction of our destiny
without any delay or interruption,
and without unnecessary cost, loss,
or sacrifice. All that is required of us to
gain a witness of The Book of Mormon is a
contrite spirit. We rely upon the power of our
Redeemer's gentle breeze to nudge our delicate
vessels onward upon the ocean of life, 'though
our intermittent moments of tranquility are
accompanied by the distant reverberations of
thunder. Perhaps what we hear is a seafarer's
shanty. More likely, however, it's the sound
of music from heaven's celestial choir whose
primary purpose is to reinvigorate hearts
that have been broken down through
penitence and in humility.

The day-to-day nuts
and bolts elements of the
Plan are put in perspective by
The Book of Mormon, so that we
might more clearly distinguish
the grey-toned obstacles that lie
in our path. These barriers to our
progression will then stand out
in sharp contrast against the
polychromatic backdrop of
the design that God has
created through the
sacrifice of our
Savior, Jesus
Christ.

Those vacillating souls of anemic will who give up their freedom to choose, in exchange for the flavor of the day or for whatever provocative pleasures their poor choices may provide, will be snared by Satan and bound by strong chains. They recognize, too late, that their misguided loyalties have significantly curtailed their ability to experience the gift of The Book of Mormon and to enjoy the "perfect law of liberty." (James 1:25).

The Book of Mormon clearly describes how we all retain the capacity to develop the nature of God. (See Alma 41:2-6 & 13). After all, we are His children. As any reasonable parent would, He simply asks that we obey household rules. He commands us to repent, to be baptized, and to exercise faith in the power of the Atonement to save us from our sins. He gives us the gift of the Holy Ghost to help us meet these requirements, so that we might have a hope in our Savior, that we might one day gain readmittance to our family compound of glory.

Habitual sin is a quicksand miring the unwary in mind-numbing conformity, a monotonously repetitive predictability, and in an underwhelming convention. (See Alma 41:10 & Mormon 2:13). These are the polar opposites of the imaginative spontaneity and the refreshingly distinctive artistic individuality that are among the blessings that we receive because of our acceptance of the truthfulness of Book of Mormon doctrine.

If the truth were to be told, it's only when we have enrolled in the graduate school of hard knocks, and have pre-paid the required tuition, that we'll obtain the credits that are to be earned by our strict obedience to the daunting curriculum of contrition. We learn to forgive others as Jesus Christ will forgive each of us our trespasses (see 3 Nephi 13:15), through His infinite and eternal Atonement for the sins of the world, from the dawn of time until its glorious end.

Scripture study
can change the course
of the circumstances in
which we find ourselves. First,
we pre-play, and then, we re-play.
Our anticipation of success helps us
to deal with the adversity and setbacks
that will inevitably come to all of us. It is
all a part of God's divine design. But if we
dismissed His guidance and encouragement
that is found in The Book of Mormon, we will
be guilty of turning our faces away from
the habitation of the Lord.

The powerful
symbolism of the Last
Supper has been beautifully
preserved for us in the scriptures.
(See John 13:1-35). In accordance with
revelation, the ordinance of the Sacrament
has been restored. (See Moroni Chapter 4 & 5,
and D&C Section 20). Broken bread represents
the torn flesh of the Savior, and the water
represents His blood that was shed in
His sacrifice and atonement
for our sins.

Embracing
the teachings of The
Book of Mormon will open up
channels of power that release the
resources of the Holy Ghost, so that
our promised blessings may be
fully realized.

During our study of
The Book of Mormon, the Spirit
testifies we are children of God. Of this
truth, there is no question. We know this
intuitively, for "the Spirit itself beareth
witness with our spirit." (Romans
8:16). This may be one of the
reasons we enjoy reading
the scriptures so
much.

"For behold, it is as easy to give heed to the word of Christ, which will point to you a straight course to eternal bliss, as it was for our fathers to give heed to this compass, which would point unto them a straight course to the promised land." (Alma 37: 44). So it is with us. Christ is our ablest Navigator, and when we follow the course that He has charted that leads us to our own "waters of Mormon," (see Mosiah 25:18), we will find that no wind can blow except it fills our sails.

The Book of Mormon serves to orient our sight so that it rests upon the stars, no matter where we may be bobbing about on the ocean of life. Initially, getting a fix on the symbolism of the gospel that will come alive for us with intentional imagery and magical metaphor might seem daunting. However, it won't be long before the messages that have come down to us from the ages will be easily plotted by the Savior's sextant that finds form and substance in that marvelous work and a wonder. (See 2 Nephi 25:17).

All of us are the
children of God who have been
given The Book of Mormon as the
group-sharing component of a work
release program that's been revealed by
Him to see how we would behave when
left to our own devices, after having
received unambiguous instruction
from above relating to what we
should be doing with the time
that we have been allotted
during our search for
truth.

The Book of Mormon
shows us how to reconnect
with our spiritual Birth Parents,
for we are the sons and daughters of
"the living God." (Hosea 1:10). "The Spirit
itself beareth witness with our spirit, that we
are the children of God." (Romans 8:16). As
we ponder the scriptures, we find the answer
to the question that is ever on our minds:
"Have we not all one father?" We are
inspired to ask: "Hath not one
God created us?" (Malachi
2:10).

In The Book of
Mormon, we are shown
to use the tools we will need
to experience God's Rest. As we
wend our way through this vale of
tears, the real journey to Christ has
only just begun. (See Wycliff's Bible,
Psalms 84:6, & Alma 37:45). Within its
pages, we learn how to lay aside all that has
besought us that threatens to destroy us. We
do this that we might embrace the things
of "a better and (a more) enduring
substance." (Hebrews 10:18).

The Book of
Mormon initializes
the Plan of Salvation. Its
ordinances provide us with
an insight into our spiritual
roots that are the outgrowth of
our interconnectivity and our
interdependence with each
other and with God.

Many who have embraced The Book of Mormon will find that it commemorates the reawakening of their immortal spirits. Bathed in its stunning light, they stare in wide-eyed wonder at the beautiful simplicity of the threads that have been woven into a pattern of principles that constitute a vibrant embroidery of simple ordinances that are performed under the guidance of a cadre of tailors who are the apprentices of God.

We receive The Book of Mormon, that the Spirit of the Lord Omnipotent might work "a mighty change in us, or in our hearts, that we have no more disposition to do evil, but to do good continually." (Mosiah 5:2).

Those who will invest in the time to
ponder its teachings will very quickly discover
that The Book of Mormon shows us how to come unto
Christ, Who alone has the power to more evenly distribute
the weight of our temporal baggage, that we might more
comfortably traverse the rocky roads of mortality as
we endure to the end in righteousness, that
we might finally enter in at the strait
and narrow gate of heaven.
(See Helaman 3:28).

We receive The Book of Mormon thru
the infinite goodness of God, so that by
the manifestations of his Spirit we might
have great views of that which is to come.
Rather than multiplying mirrors by
only studying the angles without
increasing the light, the book
has the power to illuminate
our minds through the
inexhaustible power
of the Spirit.

2 Nephi 24:12-14 (and the corresponding verses in Isaiah 14:12) are the only places in the Bible and The Book of Mormon where the name "Lucifer" is used. Commentators believe it is a reference to the King of Babylon, since it comes in the midst of a prophecy about that city, but D&C 76:25-27 cited above confirms that "Lucifer" was the pre-mortal name of Satan, who is the king, or the head, of spiritual Babylon. Dualistic prophecy is at work here. Lucifer was called "a son of the morning" who was "cut down to the ground" because he sought personal power and glory. (2 Nephi 24:12). He gloated: "I will ascend into heaven (and) will exalt my throne above the stars of God; I will sit also upon the mount of the congregation," which is also translated "in the assembly of Gods" or "upon the Mount of Assembly, where the Gods meet" (2 Nephi 24:13). He boasted, "I will ascend above the heights of the clouds; I will be like the Most High." (2 Nephi 24:14). These verses fit neatly into L.D.S. theology that concerns the pre-mortal role of Lucifer at the Grand Council in Heaven, (see Abraham 3:24-26), where God introduced His Plan of Salvation to His assembled spirit children, when the "foundation of the earth" was laid, and "the morning stars sang together, and all the sons of God shouted for joy." (Job 38:7-8).

The Book of Mormon rejuvenates our actions and charges our spiritual batteries, invigorating our vision with infinite perspective, creating pulsing streams of insight, intuition, inspiration, and revelation.

When
we study The
Book of Mormon,
we receive guidance
from the Light of Christ
and the Holy Ghost, and we
are taught the peaceable things
of the kingdom. We matriculate
into a curriculum where we learn
by repetition to understand with
fluency the language of
the Spirit.

It seems
indisputable that
the object and design
of our existence, following
our acceptance of The Book of
Mormon, would be to become the
happiest people who dwell upon the
face of the earth. Our obedience to its
principles will unleash a cornucopia
of the Spirit. We'll quench our thirst
from a well of Living Water, and
devour the nourishing Bread of
Life. Our "cup runneth over."
(Psalms 23:5).

We are
blessed with
the tools we need
to calibrate our lives
so that they conform to
the pattern of our heavenly
home. We have come to earth
from the eternal vantage point
of the abode of the Gods. Thereby,
Heavenly Father caused that our
celestial chronometer be attuned
to a more easily recognizable
temporal scale. At the same
time, he gave us a hint of
heaven by blessing us
with The Book of
Mormon.

When we read The
Book of Mormon, and the
cobwebs are swept from our
minds, we're blessed with the
visitation of the Holy Ghost,
which does nothing short
of filling us with hope
and God's perfect
love.

When we enjoy the Spirit, specific verses from The Book of Mormon are "laid open to our understandings, and the true meaning and intention of their more mysterious passages (is) revealed unto us in a manner which we never could attain to previously, nor ever before had thought of." (J.S.H. 1:74).

Messages that spring from every page of The Book of Mormon exhibit the potential to flow easily and poetically to our minds. Our determination will lead to practiced fluency in the language of the Spirit that is the inevitable result of the inspiration that comes as we approach our study with faith, fasting, and prayer. As our minds are enlightened, we'll be cast off into streams of revelation as we're carried along in the quickening currents of direct experience with the mind and will of God.

Pride is driven
by our selfishness or
self-will, but a spiritual
awakening is encouraged
by a selflessness that leads
us to enlightenment. Pride is
driven by the fear of man, but
a Book of Mormon testimony
is nurtured by our love of our
Father in Heaven. The world's
applause rings loudly in the
ears of the proud, but it is
the accolades of heaven
that warm the hearts
of the faithful.

The arrogant,
boastful, conceited,
haughty, and self-centered
nature of the prideful is easily
trumped by the altruistic, modest,
deferential, and self-effacing
behavior of those whose firm
testimonies of The Book
of Mormon confirm
their faith in the
power of the
Spirit.

Blind
opposition, hostility,
inflexibility, intolerance
enmity, and hatred, are often
the raw and ugly manifestations
of those who would denigrate the merits
of The Book of Mormon, but these are
overwhelmed by the accommodation,
charity, faith, approachability,
hope, and sociability of those
who believe in its divine
authenticity.

Unlike
the faithful,
who approach their
study of The Book of
Mormon in humility,
those who are prideful are
more comfortable with their
own perceptions of truth than
they are with the omniscience of
our Heavenly Father. They pit their
own abilities against His priesthood
power and their own paltry overtures
against His mighty works, and
finally, their stubborn won't
against His beneficient
will.

Those who refuse the invitation of the Spirit to examine the merits of The Book of Mormon frequently have hard hearts and stiff necks, and they are overtly or covertly rebellious. They lack the malleability, pliability, and flexibility of the faithful, that are needed in order to "look to God, and live." (Alma 37:47).

In our anticipation of a spiritual feast as we study The Book of Mormon, the virtue of our labor will be revealed in spectacular simplicity and plainness. The walls of opposition to our purposeful scholarship will crumble and fall away. In our exertion, the Savior will comfort and succor us with the bread of life. As we journey through the harsh and unforgiving environment of Babylon, seeking the Lord while He may be found, oases will spring up in the desert and living water will quench our thirst.

A serious study of The Book of Mormon nurtures our relationship with our Heavenly Father (see Mosiah 4:6 & 3 Nephi 27:7), and with the Holy Ghost (see 3 Nephi 27:20), while, at the same time, its prophets encourage us to accept the Savior as the pre-eminent fashioner of our fortunes. (See 3 Nephi 27:21).

Righteous Nephites quickly learned that for as long as they would remain obedient, their views would become clearer and their enjoyments greater, until they would reach the point where they had overcome evil and had lost their desire to sin. When they had been born again, they left behind their former lives and became quickened to spiritual realities. They covenanted to never again return to their disobedient ways. They changed their names and became as 'saints,' a translation of a Greek word also rendered 'holy,' the fundamental idea being that of consecration, or separation for a sacred purpose. The description came to mean 'free from blemish,' whether physical or moral. In the New Testament, the saints were all those who, by their baptisms, had entered into a covenant with God. (See Bible Dictionary).

If we ignore
the influences of
the Light of Christ and
the Holy Ghost that nurture
our innate yearning to follow our
spiritual promptings to participate
in Book of Mormon study, and allow
ourselves to be preoccupied by trifling
concerns, we sin by omission and risk
settling for a marshland of mediocrity
that can easily degenerate into a
quicksand of sin, from which
there is no easy escape.

Our honesty with
ourselves will test the
mettle of our convictions.
When we've determined to try
the virtue of the word of God in
The Book of Mormon, we've put our
money where our mouth is. But we'll
obtain no proof, and no return on our
investment, until we've acted upon the
basis of trust. Then there will come the
confirmation of the reality as feelings
of self-confidence grow and purposeful
actions replace our tentative overtures.
In essence, we'll need to let go
and let God.

Timid souls
who are cautiously
optimistic and tentatively
faithful will not consciously
intend to ignore the spiritual
promptings that urge them to
put the promise of Moroni to
the test. Their desire simply
fades away like the slow
leak in a bicycle tire,
rather than as a
blowout.

it's only
if we have enrolled
in the graduate school
of hard knocks and have
pre-paid the required tuition
that we'll obtain the credits that
may be earned by obedience to God's
curriculum. In the process, we'll learn
how to show charity to our brothers and
our sisters as a token of our respect for
the demanding performance cost that
is so often tied to their own spiritual
journey that will hopefully lead
to their acceptance of The
Book of Mormon.

If our hearts
have been hardened
against the counsel of the
prophets that could have been
followed by reading The Book of
Mormon, it will be as if our portion of
principles has been further diminished.
Our spiritual defenses against the tactics
of the Devil will crumble, and when we turn
to face our demons and fight our battles, we
may look for help to the right, or to the left,
but to no avail. If we have forgotten how
to look up, we will find ourselves
terrifyingly alone.

Spiritual neglect
always requires that we
take drastic action. The Book
of Mormon is a medical primer
for sinners, and its triage demands
the plastic surgery of repentance and
baptism, followed by the therapy of the
Sacrament, that we may experience a
reversal of our fortunes, and one day
assume the likeness of God in our
character, and His image in
our countenances.

When we
have turned our backs
on the invitation to receive
spiritual nourishment from
The Book of Mormon, and we
remain in a state of alienation
from God by spiritual death due
to our refusal to accept the Savior's
Atonement, our eventual surrender
to inclinations that are carnal,
sensual, and devilish will
be unavoidable.

In lieu
of the Sacrament, and if
we won't regularly repent as
we have been admonished to do
by Book of Mormon prophets,
the Holy Spirit, which has
the capacity to burn as a
fire, must be quenched,
and the Atonement
will lose its power
to save us from
our sins.

The Book
of Mormon blesses
us with an expansion
of eternal opportunities as
we are personally sanctified
thru the receipt of the Holy
Ghost. We learn what it
means to have the
Spirit of God to
be with us.

The fulcrum upon
which the lever that is The
Book of Mormon rests is the
doctrine of the Atonement, with
the principles of faith, repentance,
baptism, forgiveness of sin, and
the receipt of the Holy Ghost
balanced thereon. These
are the polar opposites
of life without
light.

When we
undertake a study of
The Book of Mormon, and
we find ourselves assaulted on
all sides by sounding brass and
tinkling cymbals, if we'll manifest
a prayerful desire to be touched by its
principles, doctrine, and narrative, we
will find within our Savior reserves of
strength to shut out the discordant
cacophony of confusing voices
that are raised by naysayers,
to discover revealed truth,
and to be touched by
the Holy Ghost.

The Book of Mormon
teaches us to suppress the
natural inclinations of the
telestial world that surround
us, continually encroaching
upon our spiritual stability,
and threatening to erode
our faith and testimony
of the principles of
the gospel.

We
approach The
Book of Mormon
that we might come
in the unity of the faith,
and of the knowledge of the
Son of God unto the stature of
the fulness of Christ. As we make
that journey, we retain our distinct
individuality as the spirt born sons
and daughters of God, but we are
unified in every other way.

Captain Moroni was a hero in the
eyes of Mormon, who learned about his
exploits when he abridged the records that
became the Book of Alma. He stands out in the
history of the Nephites as a true friend. Mormon
recorded that he "was a strong and a mighty man.
He was a man of perfect understanding, yea, a man
that did not delight in bloodshed, a man whose soul did
joy in the liberty and the freedom of (his friends) and his
brethren from bondage and slavery. Yea, a man whose heart
did swell with thanksgiving to his God for the many privileges
and blessings which he bestowed upon his (children); a man who
did labor exceedingly for the welfare and safety of his (family).
Yea, and he was a man who was firm in the faith of Christ, and
he had sworn with an oath to defend his (companions), his
rights and his country, and his religion, even to the
loss of his blood." (Alma 48:11:13).

Even though Mormon's abridgment of the Book of Lehi from the Large Plates of Nephi was included with all the other records, he must have sensed that Joseph Smith's manuscript translation up to the Book of Mosiah would be corrupted in some way. Therefore, he went to great pains to insert a brief transitional book on the last leaf of the record comprising the Small Plates of Nephi. In the Words of Mormon, the prophet explained his intention to write an appendage to the Small Plates of Nephi, which he had only recently discovered among all the other plates in the library of the Nephite prophets. "After I had made an abridgment from the (Large) plates of Nephi, down to the reign of this king Benjamin, of whom Amaleki spake, I searched among the records which had been delivered into my hands, and I found these plates, which contained this small account of the prophets, from Jacob down to the reign of this king Benjamin, and also many of the words of Nephi." (V. 3). Mormon also wanted to add a few historical notes, to bring the narrative of the Small Plates of Nephi to the precise point at which the Book of Mosiah began on the Plates of Mormon that had been abridged from the Large Plates.

Those who are zipping along in the fast lane of life can far too easily blow right past Book of Mormon sign posts that might have alerted them, with revelatory thunder, to merge over into the exit lane that leads to heaven's gate. For those who do, there will come a day when the sun shall not go down, "neither shall the moon withdraw itself. For the Lord shall be their everlasting light." (Isaiah 60:20).

The Book
of Mormon
blesses us with
the knowledge that
mortality is only a tiny
fraction of a much larger
reality. It is only when we
suppose it to be the sum and the
substance of our existence is our
perspective faulty. If we cannot
recognize the stability of the divine
center of our faith, and we neglect to
make the expenditure of energy that
is necessary to cultivate its sense of
permanency, everything tends to
collapse into disarray.

The
Spirit throws
open the windows
of our souls and lets in
more light, so that we might
better understand the ideology
driving God's kingdom forward.
These principles and doctrines of The
Book of Mormon are mysteries to those
who have not prepared themselves for the
streams of revelation coming from above.
The Lord has assured us, however, that we
"shall know of a surety that these things
are true, for from heaven will (He)
declare it" unto us. (D&C
5:12).

When we prostrate
ourselves upon the altar of
faith at the feet of the Savior
with sincere questions that have
been on our minds as we consider
The Book of Mormon, we will find
that we are hovering at the edge of
forever. We will leap into a stream
of revelation, to be carried along
in a quickening current that is
nothing less than our personal
experience with God. It is by
the Spirit that we realize
that it is by the stars in
the heavens that we
take our bearings
on eternity.

If we try to define heaven
and earth by subtraction rather
than by addition, we're destined to
fail. The reality of God is infinitely
richer and is more satisfying than any
poor substitute a rational approach might
grudgingly concede could ever exist. The
revelation in The Book of Mormon is a
numerical sum that is far more than
we could ever hope to acknowledge
by counting upon nothing more
substantial than corruptible
lenses provided by our
mortal clay.

Nephi was reluctant to teach his people many things concerning "the manner of the Jews" (2 Nephi 25:5), but at the same time, he reflected: "My soul delighteth in the words of Isaiah, for I came out from Jerusalem, and mine eyes hath beheld the things of the Jews, and I know that the Jews do understand the things of the prophets, and there is none other people that understand the things which were spoken unto the Jews like unto them, save it be that they are taught after the manner of the things of the Jews." (2 Nephi 25:6). Nephi's observation illustrates the significance of Book of Mormon scholarship that focuses on Nephite culture. Without it, it is difficult to understand the manner of prophesying of men like Nephi, Jacob, Enos, Alma, Abinadi, Helaman, Mormon, and Moroni, let alone Isaiah. It can be understood only if one has paid the price to do so. Perspiration must precede inspiration, and there can be no revelation where there is no student.

If we want to open our hearts to the spirit of revelation in The Book of Mormon, we will maintain an unbridled optimism, and will be consumed, as it were, by a divine fire. We will be faithful, or full of faith. When the Pharisees gathered together, Jesus asked them to put revelation to its ultimate test. He simply inquired of them, "What think ye of Christ?" and "Whose son is he?" (Matthew 22:41). Those questions are ever before us, as well.

The more
we read The
Book of Mormon,
the easier it is to craft
with words the sensations
that naturally flow to each
of us as a result of the stirrings
of personal revelation. It becomes
that much easier to generate, and
to sustain, the faith to believe in
the Father, the Son, and the
Holy Ghost.

If we want
to develop the
faith that opens our
hearts to the revelation
of The Book of Mormon, we
need to expend soul-sweat. As
Robert Frost observed: "I shall be
telling this with a sigh somewhere
ages and ages hence: Two roads
diverged in a wood, and I took
the one less traveled by, and
that has made all the
difference."

The
kingdom of God
is growing rapidly in
these Last Days. As it does
so, the Lord wants us to utilize
The Book of Mormon to further our
individual and collective interests.
Even as we recognize and appreciate
our unique qualities, experiences, and
talents, there is a revelatory union that
binds us together in ways that bridge the
cultural chasms that threaten to separate
us into rival factions. We're mystically
united, and the bonds of brotherhood
make us as one.

The Book of Mormon helps
us to receive blessings by binding
us to Jesus Christ thru revelation by
the means of a covenant of action.
Because Heavenly Father always
honors the principle of free will,
our progression will patiently
wait upon our initiative. The
promises of the Spirit of
faith are ever before
us.

When we
isolate ourselves
from sensitivity to our
surroundings, we become
numb to our circumstances,
in the sense that we might very
likely be past feeling. On the other
hand, as our wonder in the revelatory
capacity of The Book of Mormon soars,
we realize how heavily we have borrowed
from the examples of those who have been
our sensible chaperones, our compassionate
critics, our mystical mentors, our spiritual
guides, and our surrogate saviors. These
help our heartstrings to be caressed by
the spirit of revelation with an
other-worldly vibrancy.

The level
of our faith
may be elevated
to something more
dynamic than a simple
mechanical observance of
a multiplicity of ceremonial
rules. The Book of Mormon has
the capacity to introduce us to new
elements and to equations that define
the religions of our day. If we would like
the stability of revelation to prevail, it must
be that opposition exist as the foundation of a
matrix of mayhem, within which the fiery
darts of the adversary will trace an
incendiary trail of disorder.

The
Book of
Mormon is
a conduit of
heavenly energy
that streams forth
from the doorstep of
the Gods. It provides
stability in a world that
has become befuddled by
weights and measures that
have been contaminated by
the evidence tampering of the
adversary. It not only liberates
us from sin, but it also frees us
from incarceration to confusion,
hesitation, skepticism, ignorance,
mistrust, uncertainty, suspicion,
doubt, and worry.

The
Book of
Mormon carries
us in positive and
meaningful ways to
green pastures where we
enjoy the warm embrace of
the Good Shepherd, and where
we are permitted to experience the
intimate touch of His garment,
even if we sometimes feel that
we have been lost in the press
of the crowd within the
sheepfold.

Among the terrifying consequences of the world's fascination with Babylon, and of its adoption of the lifestyle of Beelzebub, is spiritual insensitivity that is born of competition between individuals. Win or lose is the prevailing standard. Zero sum game is the rule of play. While business teaches that we don't get what we deserve; instead we get what we negotiate. In God's revelations, appeasement, concession, mediation, compromise, and arbitration are conspicuously absent. If we are looking for it, we will see in The Book of Mormon His work and glory in action.

After we accept The Book of Mormon and we act upon its promptings, our lives open up in an expansion of eternal opportunities as we obtain a remission of sins, gain membership in the Church, and are personally sanctified by the revelatory experiences that we discover are embedded within our relationship with the Holy Ghost. In a real and tangible sense, the Spirit of God is with us.

in our Book
of Mormon study,
we are unswerving.
We begin to comprehend
the eternities, and we are of
a sound understanding. We
diligently search the scriptures,
that we might recognize the words
of truth. Thru fasting and prayer,
we have the spirit of prophecy, and
we receive revelation; and when we
teach, we do so by virtue of the
power and authority
of God.

The world
is at a loss for
diagnosis, even as we
are sustained by our faith
that the heavens are open, and
that our Heavenly Father, His Son
Jesus Christ, and the Holy Ghost will
provide a virtual war chest of therapies
for our cold, stony, and hard hearts. The
providential guidance that we will receive
from above is manifest in The Book of
Mormon, and is the remedy of choice
for the world's reconciliation with
revealed religion.

The
attention
and adoration
of the world can be a
satanic seduction that
influences us to turn deaf
ears to The Book of Mormon.
If we do so, we leave our coats
of many colors hanging
unappreciated in the
backs of our
closets.

The Book
of Mormon is
of inestimable value.
What can be claimed is
that pennies from heaven are
a revelatory dowry from Deity
designed to foster faith in the
financial stability of God's
treasury and facilitate an
unwavering fidelity to
the Savior of the
world.

The
Book of Mormon
will refreshingly purify
us from caustic influences,
and decontaminate us from
the toxicity that is so prevalent
in the world. It can neutralize
the homogenization process
that occurs when we are
tossed about by the
vagaries of life.

The key
that unlocks the
mystery of The Book of
Mormon rests beyond the
reach of detection by even the
most accurately calibrated and
sophisticated instruments that are
utilized by our terrestrial
scientists.

Elohim is our Father, and His genetic code lies hidden within our DNA sequences. We were born of Him as His spirit children, we have acquired His qualities and characteristics, and we were raised by Him to spiritual maturity, until we could progress no more as long as we remained in our first estate. So, we were added upon, leaving His presence to fulfill our mortal missions. Even now, as "strangers and pilgrims on the earth," we are yet His spirit sons and daughters who enjoy glimmers of His divine nature. (See Hebrews 11:13). The Book of Mormon is a witness that our birthright waits to be made manifest in a supernal display of celestial energy.

When we move from the darkness of benighted thought into the brilliant sunshine and clarity of the light of truth that shines forth from The Book of Mormon, we will find ourselves standing shoulder to shoulder with Alma to "manifest unto the people that (we have) been born of God." (Alma 36:23). We will conquer the self-defeating behaviors and the flawed character traits that we have acquired as a consequence of our mortal condition, and that had aforetime limited our progression. We'll recognize that our salvation consists in finding ourselves "beyond the power of the enemies of our progression, such as dishonesty, greediness, lying, immorality, and other vices." (Joseph Smith).

The virgin birth of the Savior continues
to be the greatest story ever told. The faithful of
every age preserved and passed on the tale, although,
in time, there were many for whom the Bible had become
a magical book, conveying power and knowledge without
the aid of continuing revelation. Moroni envisioned those
living in the Last Days who had "transfigured the holy
word of God," or who had changed the appearance and
substance of the scriptures. (Mormon 8:33). We
are blessed to have the magic of 3 Nephi to
flesh out the meager narratives of the
four more familiar Gospels of
Matthew, Mark, Luke,
and John.

During the
reign of righteous King
Mosiah, most of the Nephites wished
they could live within sight of a church,
while the Sons of Mosiah hoped to serve within
a hundred yards of hell. Sometimes, the Lord will
dispatch His most gifted missionaries to His most
wicked children. He arms them with unwavering
faith, a certain knowledge of gospel principles,
firm and abiding testimonies of the doctrines
of the Kingdom, of His divinity, of God's
Plan, and a blessing and setting-apart
by file leaders, the continual prayers
of the faithful, and an endowment
of spiritual power received
in holy places.

When we read
The Book of Mormon,
we sometimes can hear the
rustling of the robes of angels,
and their voices from the celestial
city as the sound of trumpets speaking
to us, declaring: "Peace on earth, good will
to men." "The heavens declare the glory of God,
and the firmament sheweth his handiwork. (Psalms
19:1). "His voice is heard in the rolling thunder, and His
speech is recorded in the lilac's bloom." (Bruce R. McConkie).
The earth, the sun, the moon, and the stars all "roll upon their
wings in their glory, in the midst of the power of God. All
these things are kingdoms, and any man who hath
seen any or the least of these hath seen God
moving in his majesty and power."
(D&C 84:45-47).

The scriptures teach: "There is
no other name given whereby salvation
cometh; therefore ... take upon you the name
of Christ." (Mosiah 5:8). "Yea, come unto Christ,
and be perfected in him, and deny yourselves of
all ungodliness; and if ye shall deny yourselves
of all ungodliness, and love God with all your
might, mind and strength, then is his grace
sufficient for you, that by his grace ye
may be perfect in Christ."
(Moroni 10:32).

As we read and
study The Book of Mormon,
we join our voices with the angelic
host to proclaim that Christ was born
in Bethlehem. Glory to the newborn
King! "The kingdom of heaven is
at hand; yea, the Son of God
cometh in his glory, in his
might, majesty, power,
and dominion."
(Alma 5:50).

The sacred memory of the birth of the Savior
could have quietly faded away, but as time passed
and events unfolded, there was instead "no greater drama
in human history than the sight of a few Christians, scorned and
oppressed by a succession of emperors, bearing their trials with fierce
tenacity, multiplying quietly, building order while their enemies
generated chaos, fighting the sword with the word, brutality with
hope, and at last defeating the strongest state the world had
ever known. Caesar and Christ had met in the arena, and
Christ had won." (Will Durant). Unfortunately, in the
Last Days, the battle lines are once again being
drawn, and the age-old drama seems to be
repeating itself. It's déjà vu all
over again.

It is in The Book
of Mormon that we visualize
our own passports to perfection. We
are invited to hitch a ride upon the
coat-tails of the Gods, Who will
carry us as upon the wings of
eagles all the way to the
portal of the Celestial
Kingdom.

We read in The Book of Mormon
how Alma had been born again, and had
been set free by the perfect Law of Liberty to reach
his potential. (See Mosiah Chapter 27). As Paul taught
the Romans: "We are buried with him by baptism into death:
that like as Christ was raised up from the dead by the glory of
the Father, even so we also should walk in newness of life."
(Romans 6:3). When he was born again, Alma was as
the acorn of a mighty oak, and was vitalized by
God's nurturing influence to burst forth to
reach the full stature of his spirit.

When we become as
our little ones, "submissive, meek,
humble, patient, (and) full of love," the
enticings of the Holy Spirit will help us to
put off our natural inclination to mischief,
and instead become as saints through
the Atonement of Jesus Christ.
(Mosiah 3:19).

As we read, study, and pray about The
Book of Mormon, we realize that its messages
were meant to amend our nature, so that we might
progress to the point that we reflect the attributes of God
in perfection. Our chaste behavior manifests our love of all
of our Heavenly Father's children. Our righteous stewardship
is but a shadow of His omnipotence. As the Spirit expands the
boundaries of our faith, we quietly scratch the surface of our
comprehension of omniscience. We begin to appreciate the
significance of Christ's mortal ministry, and we
determine to inaugurate our own journey to
Bethlehem, Gethsemane, the Garden
Tomb, and the Silver City.

The lines that are drawn between
"want" and "need" were often blurred by
the Nephites, who focused on telestial trinkets
and temporal trash. Spiritual stagnation made it
hard to recognize the differences between poverty and
wealth. But when they were at their best, they were
more comfortable seeking spiritual gifts rather
than the profane baubles and ornaments
that have always been the obsessive
desire of the world.

"Be still, and know
that I am God," the Savior counseled His
latter-day prophet Joseph. (D&C 101:16). With
that peaceful confirmation came the admonition
to serve Him with all our heart, might, mind, and
strength. (See D&C 4:2, 2 Nephi 25:29, Mosiah 2:11,
Alma 39:13, & Moroni 10:32). All that He asks of us
is that we focus our affections, will-power, reasoning
faculties, and physical efforts on our worship. To help
us do that, God has given us, not only the Greatest
Story Ever Told, but also The Book of Mormon,
and as an added bonus, He has also given
us the Holy Ghost to bear witness of all
that He has done for us.

With the publication and distribution of The Book of Mormon, the swirling clouds of darkness that had for so long enveloped the earth have evaporated before the withering rays of divine truth. The Lord's disciples are not ashamed to use it to "declare his doing among the people." The book makes it easier to "make mention that his name is exalted." (2 Nephi 22:4). It is a portable foundation upon which they may stand "as witnesses of God at all times and in all things, and in all places." (Mosiah 18:9).

With the volatile and incendiary high-octane aviation fuel that is found in The Book of Mormon, the fire of our faith burns nearly as brightly as the new Star that appeared in the night sky over Bethlehem. A gathering of light in the east heralds a bright new day, full of hope and promise. It's a time for us to be streaking across the sky, and up and about our Father's business. If we waste or kill that time, or even if we bide our time, we damage our eternal selves, for "in an hour when ye think not, the summer shall be past, and the harvest ended, and your souls not saved." (D&C 45:2).

Subsequent to the restoration of the gospel and the publication of The Book of Mormon, a war of words and tumult of opinion (see J.S.H. 1:10), that had been initiated by the Reformation has been stilled, and, instead, all is peaceful and all is bright. After all, it was the Savior Jesus Christ who commanded the seas to be still, and they obeyed. And then, in the ensuing calm, "the men marveled, saying, What manner of man is this, that even the winds and the sea obey him!" (Matthew 8:26). Ironically, it was Cicero who observed of the Roman Empire, with a far too narrow perspective, that "he who controls the sea, controls everything." "Soli Deo Gloria."

The Nephites gripped their faith tightly as they hung on for the ride. In the best of times, they let their trust in the Lord cast out their fear. Father Lehi had taught that they'd been driven out of Jerusalem and the land of their forefathers for their own good and for a wise purpose, moving onto the unfamiliar terrain of a land of promise that was fraught with danger, but also with opportunity, and where progress was real and could be measured with a spiritual yardstick.

King Benjamin declared:
"Because of the covenant which you
have made, you shall be called the children
of Christ, his sons, and his daughters; for behold,
this day he hath spiritually begotten you; for you say
that your hearts are changed through faith on his name;
therefore, you are born of him." (Mosiah 5:7). We believe our
Savior, Who has promised that after our sojourn in mortality,
we will "shine forth as the sun in the kingdom of (our) Father."
(Matthew 13:43). Finally, when our faith has been distilled in
the fiery hot crucible of experience into the reduction sauce of
consecration, our every desire will be to glorify God, until
our bodies are "filled with light," in a comprehension of
the solemnities of eternity. (D&C 88:67).

We reflect upon the gifts
of the Spirit and the power of its guidance,
by which we may attain the perfection and stature
of the Savior, so that we may enjoy not only what He
has, but also what He is. If, by the grace of God, we "are
perfect in Christ, and deny not His power, then are (we)
sanctified in Christ by the grace of God, through
the shedding of the blood of Christ ... that
(we) become holy, without spot."
(Moroni 10:33).

Our fallen nature
will change when our lives conform
to the pattern of provident living that was
encouraged by Book of Mormon prophets. Scales
of darkness that had blinded us to the truth will fall
away, the eyes of our spiritual understanding will open,
and our hearts will swell with charity. As Jeremiah promised,
the Savior will become "the Hope of Israel" (See Jeremiah 14:8).
It's an optimistic confidence that there will cease to be contention
throughout all the land, because of the love of God which dwells in
our hearts. It is a wish that envy, strife, tumult, whoredoms, lying,
and murder might cease. When our wish is granted, we'll become
the children of Jesus Christ, and heirs to God's kingdom. We
might well become the happiest people among all those who
have ever been created by His omnipotent hand.
(See 4 Nephi 1:15-17).

In the first century B.C.E. Cicero wrote: "The first law for the historian is
that he shall never dare utter an untruth. The second is that he shall suppress nothing
that is true. Moreover, there shall be no suspicion of partiality or of malice in his writing."
The prophet-historians of The Book of Mormon have been true to this mandate. Although, as
Washington Irving brooded: "It is the rule that history fades into fable; fact becomes clouded
with doubt and controversy; the inscription moulders and columns, arches, and pyramids
are but heaps of sand, and their epitaphs nothing but characters written in the dust,"
yet the accounts of the Nephites and Lamanites stand as shining examples of the
divine model. The Book of Mormon "illuminates reality, vitalizes memory,
provides guidance in daily life, and brings us tidings of antiquity."
It is the "evidence of time, the light of truth, the life of memory,
the directress of life, committed to immortality." (Cicero,
"De Oratore," ii, 36). In its passages, "the centuries
roll back to the ancient age of gold."
(Horace, "Odes," IV, ii, 39).

Heber J. Grant might have been
speaking of those who have accepted the invitation
to try the virtue of the word of God in the Book of Mormon,
when he declared that they "are striving, working, trying to the
best of their ability, to improve day by day. He said "we are in the
line of our duty, if we are seeking to remedy our own defects, if
we are so living that we can ask for light, for knowledge, for
intelligence, and above all, for His Spirit that we may
overcome weakness. Then, I can you, we are in
the straight and narrow path that
leads to life eternal."

In the long run,
it will matter not so much if those who worship
their Creator have identified with the Pharisees or with the
Sadducees, with Buddha, Confucius, Zoroaster, Guru Nanuk,
or even with gods of wood and stone. They may have adhered to the
monotheistic beliefs of Islam or of the Bahá'í, to the pantheistic theology
of Hinduism, Shintoism, or Taoism, with secular humanism or irreligion,
with Catholicism or Eastern Orthodoxy, with evangelicals, fundamentalists,
or Protestants, or with the existential nihilism of the postmodern world. Paul
observed of the Athenians, who were not so very different from us, that they
were inclined to bow down before unknown gods, whom, therefore, they
ignorantly worshipped. What does matter is that, as we undertake
our study of The Book of Mormon, we are preparing ourselves
to stand independently as witnesses of the true and living
God. It was with this in mind that the Apostle Paul bore
testimony to those who had gathered at Mars Hill:
"Him I declare … unto you." (Acts 17:23,
see also 1 Thessalonians 1:9).

Accepting The Book of Mormon as holy
scripture that has accompanied and compliments
the restoration of the gospel may not easy, because, as
Dallin Oaks observed: "Salvation is not a cheap experience."
However, we need the book in our arsenal, as we engage the
forces of Babylon on the field of battle. Because there is
"a great division among the people" regarding how
they accept revelation from God, "the time
has come for a day of choosing."
(D&C 105:35).

Those who only superficially engage in
an examination of The Book of Mormon will
receive very little divine tutorial training as long
as they look in the wrong places for communication
from the heavens. In days past, the prophets repeatedly
warned Israel to avoid dalliances with astrologers, exorcists,
familiar spirits, magicians, sorcerers, witches, and against
participating in any forms of divination and enchantment.
Today, we are familiar with equivalent distractions that have
been repackaged but not repurposed. Their objective remains
unchanged, however. It is to dilute the doctrine of The Book
of Mormon until it has become indistinguishable from the
secular caricatures of God's divine model, and to therby
divert our attention away from the unadulterated
worship of our Lord and Savior Jesus Christ.

A lack of empty parking spaces at the mall defines patterns of subtle self-indulgence, neglect of spiritual responsibility, and even the loss of divine protection, when they accommodate the automobiles of busy shoppers on the Sabbath day. Long ago, Alexis de Tocqueville wrote: "I sought for the greatness and genius of America, but not until I went to her churches and heard her pulpits aflame with righteousness did I understand the secret of her genius and power. America is great because she is good, and if she ever ceases to be good, she will cease to be great." The Book of Mormon is doing no small part in assuring that Zion will flourish. Whether America will retain her genius and power, her goodness and her greatness, remains to be seen.

If we are able to maintain the focus of our faith, the pathway to the summit of our worship will climb steadily to the hill country of Judea. There, we will celebrate the ministry of the Savior, as well as The Book of Mormon that boldly testifies of His divinity. They will tower above us as celestial beacons to the world. They'll invite us to inhabit a Silver City where angels and cherubim may be found singing Hosannas to God's Holy name.

The Book of Mormon is able to answer the questions that have always troubled our spirits, and it empowers us to comprehend with greater clarity the solemnities of eternity. As our understanding expands and as the mysteries of the kingdom are more clearly unfolded thru the discipline of faith, we'll find that we're capable of establishing a more sure footing on the bedrock of unchanging gospel principles.

Despair is the awful feeling that we get in the pit of our stomachs, or the feeling of hopelessness that is the natural result of disobedience. We bring it upon ourselves, since it "cometh because of iniquity." (Moroni 10:22). The laws of God have both blessings and punishment affixed to them. When His laws are obeyed, blessing are given resulting in our happiness. Unfortunate negative consequences naturally flow out of our disobedience, resulting in unhappiness, or misery. The Book of Mormon is our brass ring on the carousel of life. It is our golden ticket, and our winning lottery number, that was free, because it was purchased with the blood of Christ because of His Atonement, redeemable by us for unspeakable joy in the Kingdom of our Father.

The Book of Mormon has the incredible power to facilitate our kinship with those who have been specifically raised up by God from before their births to be the humble understudies to "the Great Jehovah." (Moroni 10:34). "The Lord hath called me from the womb," Isaiah disclosed, "from the bowels of my mother hath he made mention of my name." (Isaiah 49:1). "Once or twice in a thousand years, perhaps only a dozen times since mortal man became of dust a living soul, an event of such transcendent import occurs that neither heaven nor earth is ever thereafter the same. Once or twice in a score of generations, a hand from heaven clasps a hand on earth in perfect fellowship, the divine drama unfolds, and the whole course of mortal events changes." (Bruce R. McConkie). Such have been the circumstances of those who have been called and nurtured to usher in the dispensations of the fulness of times, in support of the ministry of the Son of God.

The Book of Mormon extends an invitation to the children of God to come in from the cold. Those who do so will find a refuge from the wintry winds of confusion and the religious turmoil of the world. They will discover their "instructor in principle, doctrine, and righteousness; their guide in matters of faith and morals." (B.H. Roberts). They "come out of the world, leaving the loneliness and estrangement of a fallen creation to enter a realm of divine experience. They forsake the orphanage of spiritual alienation, to be received into the family and household of the Lord Jesus Christ." (Doctrinal Commentary on The Book of Mormon," 4:202).

Commentary, Compendia, & Observations Index

When we are fully committed, revelation will bless us with repetitive moments of confirmation as we read The Book of Mormon, when we can say that through its miracle, our hearts have been changed by faith on the name of Jesus Christ, and and we've been born again.

Commentary Volume One
Born in The Wilderness

- 1 Nephi
- 2 Nephi
- Jacob
- Enos
- Jarom
- Omni
- Words of Mormon
- Observations
- Author's Note
- Addendum – A Sampling of Scriptures

Commentary Volume Two
Voices From The Dust

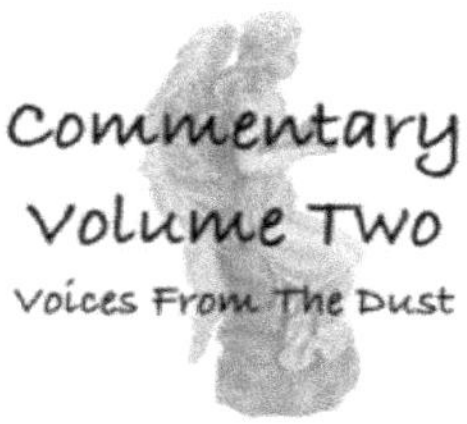

- Mosiah
- Alma
- Observations
- Author's Note
- Addendum – A Sampling of Scriptures

Commentary Volume Three
Journey to Cumorah

- Helaman
- 3 Nephi
- 4 Nephi
- Mormon
- Ether
- Moroni
- Observations
- Author's Note
- Addendum – A Sampling of Scriptures

God knows us well, and He goes to great lengths to provide for our welfare, as we shoot the rapids of life. It is only the life jacket of revelation that can help us to keep our heads above water as we gasp for air in the turbulence of telestial torrents, as we grapple with the mystery of The Book of Mormon.

Compendium
Volume One

- Introduction
- Questions Answered by The Book of Mormon
- Topical Index
- Observations
- A few of my favorite things
- Familiar Scriptures
- Commentary & Compendium Index

Compendium
Volume Two

- Introduction
- Questions Answered by The Book of Mormon
- Topical Index
- Without The Book of Mormon
- Observations
- Introduction to the Isaiah Chapters
- "And it came to pass in The Book of Mormon
- "Ad thus we see" in The Book of Mormon
- "Behold" in The Book of Mormon
- "Wherefore" and "Therefore in The Book of Mormon
- The Appearance of Gold
- The Use of The Name of Christ
- Pragmatism in The Book of Mormon
- Dry Humor in The Book of Mormon
- A Book of Mormon Timeline
- Commentary and Compendium Index

Compendium
Volume Three

- Compendia Index
- Essays That Relate to Teachings in The Book of Mormon
- Observations
- Commentary, Compendium, & Observations Index

Compendium
Volume Four

- Compendia Index
- Essays That Relate to Teachings in The Book of Mormon
- Observations
- Commentary, Compendium, & Observations Index

Compendium
Volume Five

- Compendia Index
- Essays That Relate to Teachings in The Book of Mormon
- Observations
- Commentary, Compendium, & Observations Index

The spirit of revelation accompanies our investigation of The Book of Mormon. Those who undertake such a daunting endeavor view their afflictions, their trials and their tribulations in a new light, and determine to discover how they can work to their benefit.

Compendium
Volume Six

- Compendia Index
- Essays That Relate to Teachings in The Book of Mormon
- Observations
- Commentary, Compendium, & Observations Index

Compendium
Volume Seven

- Compendia Index
- Essays That Relate to Teachings in The Book of Mormon
- Observations
- Commentary, Compendium, & Observation Index

Compendium
Volume Eight

- Introduction
- Hebrew Poetry in The Book of Mormon
- Synonymous Parallelism
- Antithetical Parallelism
- Synthetic Parallelism
- Climactic Parallelism
- Chiasmus
- Book of Mormon Scriptures Illustrating

Observations
Volume One

- 550 Observations

Observations
Volume Two

- 550 Observations

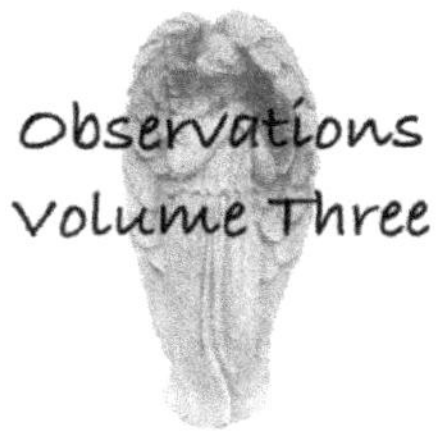

Observations
Volume Three

- 550 Observations

Observations
Volume Four

- 550 Observations

When a society that denies revelation from God is weighed in the balances and is found to be wanting, it can all be traced right back to their spiritual bankruptcy that is on an institutional scale.

Observations Volume 5

- 550 Observations
- Commentary, Compendium, & Observations Index

Observations Volume 6

- 550 Observations
- Commentary, Compendium, & Observations Index

We experience revelatory moments when we encounter truth in The Book of Mormon as our sinews begin to resonate with recognition. Finally, as we hearken to the voice of the Spirit, we will return to our Father Who art in heaven, Who is the Maker and the Fashioner of the universe.

A Book of Mormon Commentary
Volumes One - Three

Compendia
Volumes One - Eight

Observations
Volumes One - Six